ARCHAEOLOGY OF THE BIBLE: BOOK BY BOOK

ARCHAEOLOGY OF THE BIBLE: BOOK BY BOOK

Gaalyah Cornfeld

David Noel Freedman, Consulting Editor

1817

HARPER & ROW, PUBLISHERS

New York, Hagerstown, San Francisco, London

CONTENTS

TRANSLITERATION AND VOCALIZATION OF HEBREW AND SEMITIC WORDS

Consonants:

Aleph   ' a slight breath at the beginning or in the middle of a word, as in *'ashām.*

Ayin   ' a guttural breath at the beginnning or in the middle of a word, as in *ba'al.*

Heth   "ḥ" an initial letter as in *ḥerem*, pronounced like the "ch" in the Scottish *"loch".*

Samekh and Sin are both shown as "s".

Shin   is shown as "š" as in š l š (*shalosh*).

Kaph   is shown as "k" or "kh" as in m l k (*melekh*).

Tsaddhe or Saddhe (Ts or TZ) is shown as "ṣ" as in *ṣemed (Tzemed).*

Vowels:

a   the Hebrew aleph, short "a" as in the English *and.*

â or ā, a long "a" as in the English *father,* or the Hebrew *askārah, shālish.*

o   (short) as in English *dog,* or in Hebrew *ethrog.*

ô   (long) as in English *atone,* or in Hebrew, *adôn, armôn.*

i   (short) as in English *him,* or Hebrew *millah.*

î   (long), as in the French il), the English *keep* or Hebrew *abîr* (abeer) or *saddîn* (saddeen).

e   (short) as in *bed* or, Hebrew, *eben.*

ê   (long) as in *bear* or *cake* or, in Hebrew, *bêth.*

u   (short) as in *bull* or, in Hebrew, *zug* (zoog).

û   (longer) as in *boon* or, Hebrew, *menûhah.*

Vocalization:

Where Hebrew or Semitic words appear in the main text of this book, consonants are usually fully vocalized, e.g. bāmâh. However, in the transliteration of original inscriptions from monuments, seals, etc. only consonants are reproduced (vowel letters were not generally used at the time, or were indicated in only certain cases leaving the vocalization to the Hebrew reader's own sense of what was appropriate), i.e. the consonantal š m š represents shemesh or shamash; 'bd is pronounced 'ebed; lmlk, lamelekh.

INTRODUCTION

The Bible, unlike much religious literature, is not only an anthology of sacred books, containing a series of theological and ethical teachings, but it is the story of the people of Israel who lived in the land of Israel. They had learned to confess their faith by telling their history and by seeing within it the hand of God who rules history. God's own righteous ends in history provided the framework for the biblical understanding of both communal and personal history. This, however, is an interpretation by faith which is not subject to objective testing.

The surviving written records provide us with only glimpses of life in antiquity for the reconstruction of biblical history. Many periods remain obscure due to the silence of the biblical record. To reconstruct the record where it is silent and to illuminate it where it does speak, the modern student has turned to archaeology. The results of excavations may aid him through a study of the material remains and of ancient written sources which lay buried for thousands of years. He can gather from them all the data that throw a direct or indirect light upon the events related in the Bible and upon the background of the ancient Hebrews.

1. ARCHAEOLOGY AND THE BIBLICAL TEXT

The study of archaeology leads the biblical student, nevertheless, to an unavoidable risk. He may find that the biblical events did not occur in the way described, or that many happened in different historical order, thus upsetting the chronological sequence set forth by the writers of the Bible. An example from the Bible concerns the Patriarchs, and their appearance on the stage of history. Was there a gap of more than four centuries between these events and the Israelite invasion of Canaan, as is stated in the books of Genesis and Exodus? Similarly, we may ask whether the Israelite occupation of Canaan took place in a brief but violent campaign as recorded in the book of Joshua. Or, coming to the New Testament, while the resurrection of Christ was an inner certainty to the early Christians, it is something which archaeology cannot illuminate. Nevertheless, the discovery and analysis of the Dead Sea scrolls and Jewish-Christian inscriptions have thrown an altogether new light on the beginnings of Christianity, thereby helping to explain much that is elliptical and foreshortened in the New Testament account of the mission of Jesus and his disciples.

While it is true that for the most part, archaeology has substantiated and illuminated the biblical story, the biblical archaeologist must limit his deductive thinking by rigid scientific discipline. He cannot and does not set out to prove that the "Bible is true" in line with the traditionalist approach of the believer who accepts the biblical text literally, including the short

1

antiquity of life and of man upon the earth; nor does this discipline include the enthusiastic and uncritical approaches expressed — too often in recent years — by popular books on the Bible and archaeology, which follow no set scientific discipline for lack of an understanding of the complex problems involved. The biblical archaeologist can illuminate the historical setting, the cultural background and the events with which the biblical text is concerned. He thus plays a positive role in biblical exposition, but he avoids facile or biased conclusions. He is bound to test his conclusions through a constant examination of material remains, written and unwritten, and by continuing discussion with qualified specialists in the field. The discoveries of the past decades in the Holy Land, and especially in the last few years, in Jerusalem, west and east of the Jordan, and in the south of Israel, call for a reassessment of positions and conclusions in many areas of biblical research. Long-cherished views of scholars have had to be discarded for lack of supporting evidence, while there has been unexpected confirmation of other opinions as a result of these new investigations.

In general we may cite the late E. A. Speiser: "Independent study helps to increase one's respect for the received material beyond the fondest expectations of the confirmed traditionalists" (*Genesis*, Anchor Bible 1, pp. xix-xx). At the same time it should come as no surprise that many scholars have reached revolutionary results through independent analysis of recent archaeological discovery, as will be set forth in the following chapters. Many theories of biblical archaeology which have gained credence, even in the recent past, are now being discarded for lack of acceptable archaeological evidence.

2. THE FIVE BOOKS OF THE PENTATEUCH

The first section of the Bible consists of five books headed by Genesis, and is called the Pentateuch ("five-volume work" in Greek), whereas the traditional Hebrew title is *torāh* meaning "law" but also "instruction, a body of teachings." Despite the title of the works, they are not devoted exclusively to ritual or legal codes. Rather, the book of Genesis, the first part of Exodus, and sections of the other books are characterized by their marvelous stories, to which the Pentateuch owes its universal appeal.

A passage in the book of Deuteronomy (31:9) which related that Moses wrote the *torāh* gave rise to the doctrine of the Mosaic authorship of the whole Pentateuch. Modern scholarship has long since disregarded this dogma. Instead of being entirely the work of Moses, the Pentateuch is a composite work of many hands and periods, including priestly editors and professional scribes. It is the result of a long history of growth, compilation and transmission. Much of its narrative content derives from oral traditions which were subsequently reworked and expanded by revisers of various schools. This accounts for the fact that the five books of the Pentateuch contain so many duplications, inconsistencies, and even contradictions, not to speak of major stylistic differences, the result of the blending of diverse traditions and disparate points of view.

2

Process of Transmission of the Biblical Traditions

More than a century of biblical research has been devoted to the analysis of the process by which the books of the Bible emerged from a welter of traditions, oral and written, and the determination of the main stages of transmission until the present received text. The principal result has been the promulgation of the so-called "Documentary Hypothesis," which is associated with the name of the great German scholar, Julius Wellhausen, because he gave it its classic formulation.

In his literary analysis of the Hexateuch, Wellhausen distinguished four main sources in the Pentateuch. In the simplest form of the theory each of these was regarded as an independent 'document' which had been composed or compiled by a single author or editor. It was understood that various editors had put these sources together with necessary modifications, bridges, and adjustments to produce a connected whole. Working from the same premises and with the same methods, other scholars have found additional basic sources and evidence of more exensive redactional activity in the course of accretion and transmission. The dating of these documents is: J and E (Yahwist and Elohist for their characteristic divine names) before the major prophets of the 8th–7th centuries B.C.; D (Deuteronomist) in the century before the discovery of the document in the Temple in 622 B.C.; and P (Priestly) during or after the Exile (6th century B.C.). Y. Kaufmann and others have defended effectively an earlier date for P, making it roughly contemporary with D. Various scholars have found in the J material two sources, an earlier one J_1 (which O. Eissfeldt identified as L, for Lay Source, running from Genesis 2 to the end of Samuel), and a later one, J_2. The question of the separate status of E has been raised by several scholars and remains unsettled. Though the Documentary hypothesis continues to command general acceptance, there have been serious reactions against it, and, in some cases, an abandonment of the "source-critical" method.

Archaeological discoveries, on the other hand, have had a very important if indirect impact on scholarly analysis and interpretation of the text. The net effect has been to support the general trustworthiness and substantial historicity of the biblical tradition where data are available. In general this means that all strata and parts of the biblical literature deserve a measure of credence, regardless of the date of final edition or publication, and unless direct evidence to the contrary exist. Archaeological information most often sheds light on the background and context of the biblical accounts. When literary materials are available, they offer assistance in the clarification of obscure passages: unusual terms and linguistic features. At times, it is necessary to reassess the biblical tradition when historical evidence supplied by extrabiblical sources is at variance with the record.

Overleaf: Sennacherib receiving the booty from the Israelite inhabitants of Lachish who kneel before him. One of the vast Assyrian reliefs of Kuyunjik

PART I

A. THE BOOK OF GENESIS*

The Book of Genesis consists of the primeval history in chapters 1–11 and the story of the Patriarchs, which takes up the remaining four-fifths of the book, in chapters 12–50.

The first book of the Bible, Genesis, refers to "beginnings." It comes from the Greek *génesis* which means "origin, source." The Greek title is based upon the phrase *bíblos geneseos,* the book of creation, which occurs at Gen 2:4 and elsewhere in Genesis. The book of creation or beginnings may be divided into five sections, each marked by its own "genealogy" and accompanied by a long narrative of events. They are: 1) The beginning of the world (Chs. 1–4); 2) Antediluvian man (Chs. 5–6:4); 3) The Flood Chs. 6:5–9:29); 4) Renewal of man and repopulation on the earth (Chs. 10:1–11:9); 5) The ancestry of Abraham (Chs. 11:10–26).

The first section describes the creation and the principal factors affecting the life of the first human generations. It consists of five-narratives: (a) an account of creation, (b) a second account of creation, (c) the temptation in Eden and the fall, (d) Cain and Abel, and (e) Lamech and his children.

The balance of the book is devoted to the story of the Patriarchs: Abraham and Isaac: Chs. 11:10–25:18; Jacob and Esau: Chs. 25:19–27:46; Jacob and Laban: Chs. 28:1–32:3; Jacob's return to Canaan: Chs. 32:4–36:43; Joseph and his brothers: Chs. 37:1–50:26.

1. PRIMEVAL HISTORY

In accordance with the guiding principles of the biblical tradition, the primeval history has the whole world as its stage, its time span reaching back all the way to Creation. It serves as a prologue and provides a universal setting for the early history of the Hebrews, the particular story with which the rest of the Pentateuch and Bible is concerned.

The account of creation and human prehistory, though couched in the language of biblical religion, did not originate with the Israelites. It contains elements drawn from the polytheistic myths of the Sumerians and Babylonians. This mythology is carefully adapted to the concepts of Israelite monotheism. The similarity in detail only serves to highlight the uniqueness of Israel's single God acting in the world.

a. *Literary Antecedents of the Primeval Sagas*

But while the Hebrew version of primeval times had been adapted to biblical tradition and religion, much of the background material of these early narratives comes from Mesopotamia. This is borne out by the archaeo-

---

* Interested readers would be advised to read with a Bible in hand. Our quotations are taken from the American Revised Standard Version, 1952.

logical discovery of ancient libraries containing collections of mythological texts. The process of remolding old traditions is common in the history of cultures. The same approach was followed by the Hurrians who adopted Mesopotamian traditions and eventually brought them to Canaan (see below: Canaan in the Middle and Late Bronze Ages).

The biblical genealogies before the Flood parallel the antediluvian dynasties of Sumer, the kings of which are credited with enormous lifespans. The names of some of the antediluvian patriarchs reflect Akkadian (Babylonian) characteristics. The stories of Eden and the Tower of Babel are largely Mesopotamian in substance, as are other cycles of the primeval history. Modern research is delving deeper into the complex problems arising out of the early chapters of Genesis and their sagas. It is seeking to determine the extent and manner of the influence of the Mesopotamian and Canaanite epics on the early biblical sagas, as we shall see in the following pages.

b. *The Story of Creation*

Let us begin with the Mesopotamian version of cosmic origins in the *"Enuma eliš,"* the Babylonian Creation Epic, which has much in common with the opening chapters of Genesis. Note the striking correspondence in details and, more significantly, the similar order of events as seen in the following tabulation:

Enuma Eliš	*Genesis*
Divine spirit and cosmic matter are co-existent and coeternal	Divine spirit creates cosmic matter and exists independently of it
Primeval chaos, Tiamat (a mythological figure) enveloped in darkness	The earth a desolate waste, with darkness covering the deep (*tehom*)
Light emanating from the gods	Light created
The creation of the firmament	The creation of the firmament
The creation of dry land	The creation of dry land
The creation of luminaries	The creation of luminaries
The creation of man	The creation of man
The gods rest and celebrate	God rests and sanctifies the seventh day

The Enûma eliš — Babylonian Creation Epic — inscribed on cuneiform tablets, relate the myths of creation from primeval chaos

Babylonian cosmogony and its theory of the origin of man, central to Sumero-Akkadian "science" or "wisdom," was basic to their religion. Such traditions found their way to Israelite scribal schools — either in a direct line from Mesopotamia or indirectly through later Canaanite sources. In their Israelite form these cosmogonic traditions underwent drastic alterations, occasioned by distinctive biblical theological views. Just as the normative religion of the Hebrews diverged from Mesopotamian myths, it expressed a corresponding departure regarding the master of creation. It reflected a monotheistic concept in absolute terms, as opposed to the succession of mythical rival deities in the *Enuma eliš*.

The Mesopotamian 'serpent' monster was no ordinary serpent as implied in Genesis. It is depicted in the mosaic of the Gate of Ishtar in Babylon (6th c. B.C.)

c. *The Story of Eden*

The name of the garden itself is borrowed from the Sumerian (3rd–2nd millennia) *eden,* perhaps indirectly through the Akkadian *edenu,* which meant garden or paradise. Genesis names four rivers which were believed to have converged near the head of the Persian Gulf (present-day southern Iraq) in a rich garden which was the land of the blessed.

The biblical story includes special features such as the tree of life and the tree of knowledge of good and evil in the midst of the Garden, the serpent, a mythical monster rather than an ordinary snake endowed with extraordinary faculties for trouble making, the temptation and fall of the woman, Eve, and the man, Adam, and the subtlety of their relationship and their common bond in guilt, pleasure, and punishment. Such themes of sexual awareness, wisdom, and paradise are known from various ancient sources, as, for example, in a beautiful passage of the Babylonian Gilgamesh Epic (Tablet I, column 4, lines 16ff.) when the legendary hero Gilgamesh meets his rough friend Enkidu. The latter was seduced by the courtesan goddess Ishtar, in a passage noted for its explicit language; he loses his wildness for "he now has wisdom, broader understanding." As Ishtar tells him, "You are wise, Enkidu. You are like a god," and she improvised some clothing for him. The implied quest for immortality in the Hebrew version of the story is paralleled in other ancient literature. The Mesopotamian analogues to this theme are the Tale of Adapa and the Epic of Gilgamesh (Tablet IX), where both attempts end in failure.

A Sumerian king-list enumerated the antideluvian kings of Sumer who reigned a total of 241,200 'years' based on an unknown calendrical system

d. *From Eden to Flood*

There are two genealogies of the line of Adam in chapters 4 and 5, one through Cain to Lamech and his musically and mechanically minded children Jubal and Tubal-cain, the other through Seth to Lamech and his son, Noah, the hero of the Flood story. These are paralleled by Sumerian genealogical lists which bridged the gap between Creation and Flood. The most striking, common features are the sharp diluvian divide and the abnormal life-spans attributed to the principal figures. The number of Hebrew prehistoric patriarchs is eight in ch. 4, while the number in ch. 5 is ten; in the Babylonian documents the number varies between nine and ten. The years in the Hebrew list (ch. 5) run into the hundreds (totaling 1656), while those of the reigns in the Babylonian list run from 18,600 to nearly 65,000 'years'. The source and significance of these extraordinary numbers remain a puzzle of chronology in both the Mesopotamian and Israelite traditions.

e. *The Flood Story*

The biblical account of the Flood Story in Genesis 6:1–9:17 goes back to Mesopotamian cuneiform sources which contain a number of versions of the flood story. The most ancient is from the Sumerians, the story of Ziusudra, but it is incomplete. The most extensive and best known prototype is found in Tablet XI of the Gilgamesh Epic, which also has most in common with the biblical story. In the Mesopotamian epic, Gilgamesh seeks the last survivor of the flood to learn from him the secret of survival and immortality. After many adventures, Gilgamesh finally meets Utnapishtim, the Babylonian hero of the flood. He tells Gilgamesh that he owed his life to Ea, the god of wisdom, who warned him of the coming deluge in a dream and granted him immortality. In both stories the hero leads a remnant in building an ark, riding out the flood, discovering dry land by sending out a series of birds, and giving thanksgiving offerings when the flood had fully abated. But while the Babylonian flood is the result of the spiteful actions of the gods, the Bible presents it as an indictment of mankind for its sinfulness. The Flood Story may ultimately derive from memories of a giant cataclysm actually experienced in recent geological times. Evidence of such an event has been uncovered by Lees and Falcon in a survey of Lower Mesopotamia. Waters from the Persian Gulf submerged a large coastland area owing to a sudden rise of the sea level some thousands of years ago in one of the pluvial periods. Heavy rainfall accompanied by

Right:
A series of clay tablets inscribed with the Babylonian account of the flood and the Gilgamesh Epic (Nineveh, 7th c. B.C.)

Below:
Presumed figure of the Mesopotamian hero and King Gilgamesh of Sumer (ca, 2700 B.C.) from Khorsabad, dating to the 8th c. B.C.

undersea eruptions may well have left an indelible impression on the survivors.

In S. Loewenstein's opinion, the Flood Story, originally a Mesopotamian epic, was first recited as a Hebrew epic about the hero Noah and later turned into prose. It reached the Hebrew medium through Canaanite literature rather than as a Mesopotamian import. The evidence supporting this view is a pottery fragment of the Mesopotamian epic of Gilgamesh found in a Canaanite stratum of Megiddo dating to the El Amarna period (15th century B.C.) and a fragment of the Flood Story found in Ugarit (northern Canaanite kingdom).

Clay fragment of the Babylonian Epic of Gilgamesh found at Megiddo, dating to the 14th c. B.C.

f. *The Table of Nations*

The biblical list of nations (ch. 10), which provides a schematic arrangement of the major cultural divisions of mankind, specifying ancient nations and their great cities, contemporary with early Israel, derives from Mesopotamian sources reflecting the world situation toward the end of the 12th century B.C. According to E. A. Speiser, the figure behind the hero Nimrod, famed for his prodigious deeds, is not the Babylonian god, Ninurta, but the Assyrian emperor, Tukulti-Ninurta I, who reigned from 1234 to 1200 B.C. He was known for his military achievements, in particular, the conquest of Babylon, as well as his building projects at home. The genealogical lists, which actually reflect political and economic filiation, as well as cultural affinities, prominently feature the early *Aramean* groups. These groups emerged from the wilderness toward the close of the 2nd millennium, gained a foothold in the region of North Syria between the Assyro-Babylonians in the East and the Canaanites in the West, and gradually expanded their territory and their authority in that area.

The four registers of the restored stela of Ur-Nammu (ca. 2060–1955 B.C.) suggest that the subject was the building of a *ziggurat* (temple-tower). The king is seen carrying a basket and building instrument as a token of his devotion to the rising shrine

g. *The Tower of Babel*

The story in ch. 11 has the most explicit connection with Mesopotamian sources of any of the materials in Genesis 1–11. The Israelite author, however, used them to explain the scattering of human beings on earth and the multiplicity of languages, suggesting that there was increasing tension between God and man over the proper limits of the latter's activity. While the ultimate source of the biblical story is doubtlessly the great temple-tower of Babylon, the tradition has been mediated in literary form and the biblical writer was apparently influenced by the account of the building of Babylon and its temple, Esagila, given in lines 60–62 of the *Enuma eliš* epic. Standard practice with respect to religious architecture in Mesopotamia included the year-long preparation of sacred bricks, which preceded the solemn placement of the first brick. The Akkadian text reads: "The first year they molded its bricks. And when the second year arrived they raised the head of Esagila toward Apsu (the boundless expanse of sweet waters above the heavens)." Moreover, the Sumerian name Esagila means "the structure with upraised head" while the Akkadian rendering for "they raised its (Esagila's) head" is a play on the same word. It appears that the biblical phrase "with its top (literally "head") in the sky" harks back to the Mesopotamian versions, as does the biblical expression "Let us make bricks," a reference to the building customs of Babylon. The Hebrews used this material to criticize man's folly and presumption in challenging the supremacy of God.

It is interesting to note that both W. G. Lambert and B. Mazar place this story around 1100 B.C. Lambert dates the Mesopotamian sources to this period, while Mazar, who believes that the bulk of the materials in Genesis belongs to the same era rather than the Middle Bronze age, suggests that the Mesopotamian literary traditions reached Israel, not only through the medium of Canaanite culture, but more directly through the movements of caravaneers and merchants from East to West.

2. THE KENITE METALWORKERS OF THE SOUTHERN ARABAH

A startling stray reference in Gen. 4:22 emerges out of context of the Mesopotamian image of the 'beginnings' of mankind when out of the blue, as it were, it identifies the Kenites as the traditional 'first' metalworkers. This has led to considerable scholarly theorizing in the past, but recent discoveries in the valley of Timnah, north of Elath, prove that the reference in question is actually grounded in the history of the land of the Bible, i.e. the biblical Late Bronze and not in the enigmatic traditions of the early chapters of Genesis.

The Kenites, apparently a clan of the Midianite settlers in the southern Arabah, made their appearance in the Timnah valley in the 14th–12th centuries B.C. (see Exodus: A Midianite Sanctuary at Timnah) and they

Egyptian smelters and artificers weighing and recording gold, blowing through tubes to heat the metal for casting, and (above) fashioning the molded objects

Smelting furnace of the Kenites at Timnah, south of Canaan, showing the melting bowl and, before it, the tapping pit of copper ore between the flanking stones (14th c. B.C.)

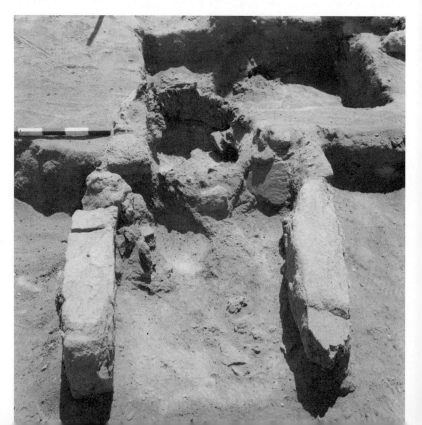

bore close ties of kinship with the Israelites during various stages of their settlement in Transjordan and Southern Canaan (see: Joshua–Judges).

Direct evidence of bronze and iron working methods in the Late Bronze are provided by excavations in the Timnah valley. Its vertical white sandstone walls were attacked with stone hammers and the copper nodules picked out of the heaps of shattered sandstone. By this method, about 20 kgs of nodules could be 'mined' by one man in a day's work, enough to produce 2–4 kgs. of copper. 'Dressing' or winnowing of copper or iron took place in the saucer-shaped hollows on the slopes next to the actual mining works where many grinding implements were found. The winnowing operation could have utilized the strong north wind prevailing on the open horizontal surface or, alternatively, the local inhabitants mined the ore and women and children grinded it and sorted the ore from the gangue. The ore was then carried to smelting sites.

3. ABRAHAM'S GENEALOGY AND THE ḤARAN ANCESTRY

The end of ch. 11 resumes the genealogical record that was interrupted at the end of ch. 5 to accommodate the stories in chs. 6–10. The two genealogical segments once may have been part of a single document, which incorporated the very old tradition of the Aramean ancestry of Abraham into the larger framework of the primeval history of Genesis. The final genealogy of Abraham also serves as a bridge to the central narrative of the Patriarchs. Thus the name Naḥor, attributed to both the grandfather and brother of Abraham, is identical with that of the city, *Naḥur*, which is known from the Mari tablets of the 18th century B.C. It was in the region of Ḥaran, situated west of the Balikh river, a tributary of the Euphrates. Another place name in the area was Serug, which was the name of Abraham's great-grandfather. This interchange between personal and place names is a common phenomenon in the ancient Near East; in this case it reflects the close cultural contacts between Abraham's family and the region and supports the tradition that this was their homeland for a long period of time.

The mention of Ur of the Chaldeans brings up a complex problem. Ur was an ancient and renowned Sumerian center, as demonstrated by thousands of cuneiform records, but was never connected with the Chaldean branch of the Aramean peoples. They were late arrivals in western Mesopotamia, their appearance dating to the 12th century B.C. (cf. The Table of Nations, above). In the Bible they are identified with the group that ultimately took over the Babylonian kingdom with Nabopolassar and Nebuchadnezzar as kings of that dynasty (625–562 B.C.; cf. II Kings 25, Jeremiah, Ezekiel). While the "Chaldean" references in Gen. 11:28, 31 and 15:7 remain an anachronism, the mention of Ur by itself may have some historical basis. Behind the settlement in Ḥaran, which is supported both by tradition and the evidence of the names, there may have been an earlier sojourn in Ur, but beyond the mere mention of the place the Bible is silent, and we have nothing to add. The historic homeland of the patriarchs was the

11

Fragment of carved war scene
from Ebla (Tell Mardikh)
dating to the end of the Early
Bronze III (ca. 2400 B.C.)

region of Ḥaran. While this cannot be disputed — though it has not been attested by archaeology — the main question which remains in abeyance is the true hisorical and archaeologically valid background of the story of the Hebrew patriarchs.

Let us preface the study of the patriarchal period with a review of the Canaanite background before the appearance of the Hebrews.

4. THE RICH EARLY CANAANITE ARCHIVES OF EBLA

The excavations at Ebla (Tell Mardikh) 30 miles south of Aleppo, Syria, conducted by Drs. P. Matthiae and G. Pettinato, uncovered more than 15,000 inscribed cuneiform clay tablets dating to the latter part of the third millennium (Early Bronze IV). They were written in Sumerian and Canaanite (the ancestor of Hebrew). They contain references to the Canaanite cities of Hazor, Megiddo, Gaza and 'urusalima' (Jerusalem) and include also stories recounting the creation of the world and a great flood corresponding to the biblical accounts of the world's beginnings.

Most of the documents are economic texts recording the receipt and shipment of goods to distant centers. Other tablets are literary, legal, diplomatic, historical and geographic in content. They show that Ebla was the capital and cultural center of an early great Canaanite kingdom which shared in the civilization of the Near East. Myths known from ancient Mesopotamia circulated throughout the kingdom and the laws of Ebla corresponded in many ways to those known in Mesopotamia from somewhat later sources.

Wooden feminine figure from
the palace of Ebla (Early
Bronze IV)

Thus, long before the time of ancestors of the patriarchs, Syria and Palestine shared in the mythic and cultural traditions of Western-Semitic Sumer and Akkad. Wherever the remote ancestors of the Israelites may have lived or wandered, they might have had access to and been in contact with the traditions behind the *early* stories of Genesis.

5. CHRONOLOGICAL TABLE OF THE MIDDLE AND LATE BRONZE AGES IN CANAAN

Date	Archaeological Period	Historical Period	
2200 to 2000 B.C.	Middle Bronze Age I	Middle Canaanite	
2000 to 1800 B.C.	Middle Bronze IIA	Urban Expansion in Canaan	
1800 to 1630 B.C.	Middle Bronze IIB	Middle Canaanite	Hyksos Period from 1720
1630 to 1550 B.C.	Middle Bronze IIC (The Transition period to the Late Bronze)	Middle Canaanite	Hyksos Period to 1575
1550 to 1400 B.C.	Late Bronze I	Late Canaanite	Egyptian Rule in Canaan
1400 to 1300 B.C.	Late Bronze IIA		El Amarna Period and the Ḥabiru
1300 to 1200 B.C.	Late Bronze IIB	Early Hebrews	
1200 to 1150 B.C.	Iron Age IA	Israelite Settlement in Canaan	Israelite I
1150 to 1100 B.C.	Iron Age IB		

B. CANAAN IN THE MIDDLE AND LATE BRONZE AGES

1. THE HYKSOS AND THE '400 YEAR STELE'

The period from the end of the 18th century to the middle of the 16th century (equivalent to the later part of MB IIB and all of MB IIC) was marked by the invasion of Egypt by Asiatic peoples called the Hyksos and the establishment of an empire including that country, Canaan, and Syria. In the list of kings and other notables are numerous Semitic names; some of these are similar to patriarchal names, like *ya'qob-har*. For a long time, some association between the patriarchal groups and the Hyksos has been taken for granted, and this view has been supported by reference to two chronological items preserved in the Bible. The first states that "Hebron was built seven years before Zoan (Tanis) in Egypt" (Num 13:22) and is usually connected with the Hyksos conquest of Egypt and founding of that city around 1700 B.C. The other text states that the Israelite sojourn in the district of Tanis lasted for 430 years (Exod 12:40). This figure has been linked with the Hyksos era of Tanis, symbolized by the '400 year stele' erected shortly before the accession of Rameses I around 1320 B.C., and commemorating the rule of the god Seth over Egypt. Seth in shown at the top of the stele wearing an Asiatic garment and headdress, which in other Egyptian representations are associated with Ba'al, the chief Canaanite deity. The stele reads: "Year 400, fourth month of the third season, day 4, of the king of Upper and Lower Egypt; Seth, the Great of Strength..." If the ascendancy of the god Seth in Asiatic garb is related to the domination by

Bichrome pottery vessel of the Late Canaanite period (1500–1200 B.C. from Tell Nagila)

Jericho, the oldest city in Palestine, already lay in ruins in the Middle Bronze Age, before the days of Joshua (see Part III)

Ground plan of the Middle Bronze temple-fort of Shechem

After the expulsion of the Hyksos, Shechem expanded. An outer wall was built of huge boulders, thus meriting the term 'Cyclopean'. A new gate complex was erected in the northwest section (see below (D, 8). This marks the transition to the Late Bronze Age

these foreign kings, this stele places the beginning of their rule around 1720 B.C. In any case, the 400 year anniversary marks the date of the refounding of Tanis by Rameses I. By adopting Seth, the pharaohs of the 19th Dynasty established themselves as the official successors of the Hyksos rulers, whose ancient capital was Tanis. The Hyksos were expelled by native Egyptian chieftains who established the 18th Dynasty and inaugurated a new era in Egypt, the New Kingdom (see photo in Exodus, 2).

2. THE HURRIANS

The widespread movement of peoples in the Near East during Middle Bronze IIB abated somewhat and the political situation in the northern tier was stabilized with the emergence of the major kingdoms of the Hittites in Asia Minor and of the Mitannians in northern Mesopotamia in the middle of the 16th century B.C. The principal groups in the latter were Hurrians and Indo-Iranians. As a result of these developments, Syria and Palestine came under the influence of these new groups and were infiltrated by representatives of all of them. They gained ascendancy over the native population, constituting an aristocracy governing from strongly fortified cities. They were known as *marianu* and typically fought from chariots in contrast with the lower classes who served as foot-soldiers. Each city-state constituted a feudal fiefdom ruled by a prince or kinglet with the help of the nobility and warrior class. At the bottom of the pyramid were the native groups, the urban landless poor and the serfs or semi-slaves of the rural areas permanently attached to the landed estates. This period, Middle Bronze IIC, marks the transition to the Late Bronze Age.

3. MATERIAL AND SOCIAL CHANGE

The principal architectural change in this period was the construction of massive city walls, and, unlike earlier structures of the Middle Bronze age, these were made from squared and carved stones laid out in regular courses, topped by bricks. The wall was completed by a well-fortified gate suited to the passage of chariots. Striking examples are the massive cyclopean wall at Shechem and the glacis of Tell Beit-Mirsim modelled on fortifications in eastern Anatolia. This type of construction eventually became standard throughout the coastal plain and in the hill country of Canaan.

Another important innovation of the period was the construction of fortified temples, termed "temple-forts" by B. Mazar. The best example is the rectangular two-story building in the walled city of Shechem. It had a long hall inside the thick outer walls with an entrance in the front. The statue of the deity was placed at the end of the hall facing the entrance. This temple was contemporary with a Canaanite temple at Megiddo. Both lasted through the Late Bronze Age II, and then were destroyed in the 12th century B.C. The contemporary stratum of Megiddo (VII A) marks the last wealthy and fortified Canaanite city. In its treasury a hoard of about 200 carved ivories was found, representing Canaanite art at its best. Another temple of the same period is the 14th century sanctuary of Hazor found by Y. Yadin. It consisted of a porch with two pillars, a hall and then the Holy of Holies, with a rectangular niche in the rear wall. Many elements, such as the tripartite division and the two pillars in the porch, have counterparts in the Temple of Solomon (cf. Kings). It was destroyed by Joshua in the second half of the 13th century B.C.

Thutmose IV (early 15th c.) rides over wounded Canaanites and their chariotry on a battlefield

4. THE PEOPLE OF CANAAN

An indication of the social stratification of Canaan may be found in a double list of prisoners captured by Pharaoh Amenhotep II of the 18th Dynasty in his second campaign into Canaan in 1443 B.C.:

First List	*Second List*
550 Marianu (chariot-riding knights)	127 governors of Retenu (the Egyptian name for Canaan)
240 wives of the above	179 brothers of the above
640 Canaanites	3600 'Apiru
232 sons of governors	15,200 Shosu (nomads)
323 daughters of governors	36,300 Huru or native Canaanites
	15,070 Nuhašše, natives of north
270 concubines of all foreign provinces	Syria
	30,652, their wives

The Canaanites in these lists were middle class natives, not serfs. The 'Apiru (or Ḫabiru; see discussion below) were a social group outside the official classification and lacked definite status. The Shosu were wandering Semitic clans who are known to have crossed into eastern areas of Egypt in periods of drought and famine. This situation, which conforms in many ways to the biblical portrayal of Canaan in the book of Genesis, persisted until the Israelite occupation of the land.

Canaanite man and woman painted on a jar (Middle Bronze). Note a resemblance to the Early Bronze Ebla carving shown above

5. THE PROBLEM OF THE ḪABIRU

Gen 14:13 calls Abraham a Hebrew, *'ibri*. In biblical scholarship there has been extensive investigation into the possible connection between the biblical *'ibrim* (Hebrews) and the landless *'apiru* or *ḫabiru* mentioned in documents from Mesopotamia, northern Syria, and Egypt from the 19th century onward. There has been particular interest in the Amarna tablets which describe the *'apiru* activity in Canaan immediately preceding the biblical period.

These tablets were discovered in A.D. 1887 near Tell el-Amarna, the site of the capital and royal residence of Pharoah Amenophis IV (Akhenaten), and his father Amenophis III. They come from the royal archives, which contained approximately 150 letters written by the vassal kings of Canaan and western Asia to the Egyptian pharaoh.

In the Late Bronze I period (Late Canaanite), Canaan was under nominal

One of the Tell el Amarna tablets (15th–14th c. B.C.) which mention the 'apiru (ḥabiru) involved in disorders in Canaan before the Israelite invasions

Statue of Idrimi, a king of northern Syria, relating his seven years of exile among the 'apiru of Canaan (ca. 1500)

Egyptian rule, with city-kings paying tribute to their overlords and providing wheat and other agricultural products. The gradual disintegration of Egyptian rule was revealed in the tablets which were written in Akkadian, the international language of the period. In them we see a confused political situation and a period of transition in Canaan. There are plots, counterplots, and conflicting accusations, but they vividly project the conditions of life and the social structure of the local population in the Late Bronze Age (15th–14th centuries B.C.).

The 'apiru were not an ethnic group, nor did they come from a single geographic location. Rather they were a loosely defined, constantly shifting social class of people. This view is supported by a number of observations: a) References to them are scattered throughout a millennium in lower and upper Mesopotamia, Asia Minor, Syria-Palestine, and Egypt; b) Their names do not come from a single language but reflect the languages of the regions where they are met, whether Akkadian, Hurrian, or others; c) When the homeland of individual 'apiru is identified, they may be natives, or from neighboring or distant countries; there is no uniform pattern. In short, they are not necessarily members of the local population; they cannot be identified with any single social class of the population, and often are described as outcasts or residents without status or citizenship rights; they do not have common occupations in the community where they dwell. The common denominator seems to be that they are associated with various ethnic groups, as dependents, mercenaries, or hangers-on.

A possible link between the Amarna letters and the Bible may be found in the traditions concerning the fate of Shechem and the early history of Jerusalem (see Part III). Nevertheless, there can be no direct identification of the Amarna 'apiru (ḥabiru) with the biblical 'ibrim; the intervening century or two alone would rule it out. Furthermore, the origin of the Hebrews does not accord with the description of the cuneiform 'apiru who consist of a variety of wandering and landless groups, not clearly identifiable with any of the settled peoples among whom they lived.

Conclusions

Need one wonder that the anonymous Israelite historian described Canaan before the Israelite conquest as a land of many diverse peoples, seven according to tradition, even more in fact. They possessed a superior material culture, at least to anything the Israelites had. In the words of the man who spied the land in the days of Moses: "The people who dwell in the land are strong, and the cities are fortified and very large" (Num 13:28).

This is the land Abraham came to know when he travelled west in pursuit of his destiny, as may be determined on the basis of archaeological discoveries, both written and unwritten materials.

The traditional picture presented by the biblical writers finds substantial support in the available data, although in the light of scholarly investigation and evaluation, some adjustments in detail have proved to be necessary. It is remarkable how much of the tradition has withstood the test of time and scientific accuracy.

C. THE STORY OF THE PATRIARCHS

1. THE SECOND SECTION OF GENESIS

In dealing with the historical narrative, beginning with the second part of Genesis and continuing through the Pentateuch and on into the books of Joshua, Judges, and Samuel, we have adopted the viewpoint of Professor B. Mazar, eminent biblical scholar and archaeologist, who believes that in its present form the narrative is a unified product of the early monarchy, and that it all bears the marks of that age.

To quote his words which are of the utmost importance in understanding the position:

"Though it is undoubtedly true that the Israelites retained vague memories of the common origin and destiny of the tribes in the remote past, and traditions about the names and genealogies of their forefathers, of their origin in Mesopotamia and their connections with the "sons" of Naḥor, of their migration to Canaan, and of their descent to Egypt, a penetrating analysis of the accounts recorded in Genesis does not permit us to consider them as a faithful representation of the actual history of the Patriarchs and their exploits. Nor can we consider them to be ancient sources from which we may reconstruct, to any significant extent, the stages of the Israelite emergence against the background of general history, dwelling on the processes and developments relating to the lives of the Patriarchs over the generations, till the time of the formation of the "amphictyony" of the twelve tribes of Israel.

In my view, it is much more within reason that the way of life and the ethnic and socio-political picture reflected in the patriarchal accounts correspond to the end of the period of the Judges and the beginning of the monarchy. That is to say: the 'life-setting' (Sitz im Leben) of these accounts, part of which are certainly based on folk-legends from the time of the Israelite occupation of Canaan, derives principally from a time that preceded by only a generation or two that very period during which the great historiographic work was given its original written form. This hypothesis is supported by certain data which can be interpreted only against the background of their historic period" (*Canaan and Israel*, Hebrew ed. p. 136).

What this means for our study is that while the Israelite traditions concerning their ancestral heroes correctly identified them with the pre-Mosaic, pre-Israelite past, the stories as they have been preserved for us reflect, both in substance and in local color and detail, the events and circumstances of a much more immediate past, namely the period of early settlement, the Judges, which itself borders and blends with the contemporary situation. Certain memories of a more distant past have survived, and they can be illuminated by archaeological data of the Middle Bronze Age, chiefly from Mesopotamia, but the large bulk of recorded tradition belongs to a much later date, thus making the historical, social, and cultural traditions of Genesis 12–50 contemporary with those of the later books. Therefore we will draw on the archaeological riches of the early Iron Age to shed light on and

17

to fill gaps in the biblical record, whether in Genesis or in Judges, books which, chronologically, belong together rather than apart.

No one would deny that in their present form the narratives from Genesis to Samuel are the literary product of the monarchic period. It should be recognized as well that any such narrative will combine traditional elements of great antiquity with others of lesser antiquity and some items that are close to, if not at, the time of the final author or chronicler. The question is where to draw the lines and how to be fair in dealing with the traditional material, editorial revisions, and complete rewriting. While all scholars recognize these points in principle, in practice they emphasize one factor more than another, or even to the exclusion of others. We would like to strike a balance, on the one hand conceding that there are many anachronisms in Genesis, too many to dismiss as accidental or incidental, and on the other hand there are too many oddities and peculiarities which must reflect very distant times and places to rule out the survival of old materials or insist that it is mostly contemporary with the monarchy which produced the narrative.

When compared with Joshua–Judges, and certainly Samuel, Genesis stands in sharp contrast even after conceding all the similarities. When compared with Middle Bronze Age documents and artifacts, Genesis is also quite different, though there are familiar echoes here and there. Admittedly, there are too many Philistines, Arameans, and camels, not to speak of other major and minor points, for anyone to be comfortable with traditional views which relegate the Patriarchs to a background of the Middle Bronze Age.

2. CHAPTERS 12–50 OF GENESIS: THE PATRIARCHAL TRADITIONS AND THE FORMATIVE STAGES OF EARLY ISRAEL

The first three verses of ch. 12 describe Abraham's call and commission, and the beginning of the continuous story which is the main concern of the Bible, in contrast with the earlier prehistory which provides a setting and serves as a backdrop for the all-important narrative. It opens with the story of Abraham and his family, then extends to his descendants and their descendants, and finally to the nation of which he was the ancestor. The narrative is not merely the story of individuals, of families or a people, but the saga of a new religion and a new society, and its quest for identity and existence. Amazing though its impact was on world civilization, it is our responsibility to examine the historical aspects of the narrative and relate them to available archaeological or epigraphic evidence. Let us preface the study of the patriarchal period with a review of the Canaanite background, before the appearance of the Hebrews.

The historical narrative, as distinct from the prehistory, begins with startling suddenness in Genesis 12. Nothing stated in the preceding chapters prepares us for the sudden appearance of Abraham and his descendants, the *'Ibrîm*, on the historical stage of Canaan in the Middle Bronze Age. This is the period to which many biblical scholars are inclined to assign Abraham and the other patriarchs in accordance with traditional chronology which specifies a period of more than five centuries between Abraham and the Exodus from Egypt. The difficulties will be discussed below.

Let us first remark that archaeology, despite great strides in understanding the Canaanite background of the Middle and Late Bronze Ages, has revealed no historical trace of the Hebrews to corroborate the patriarchal narratives *as a whole*. The reader must remember that archaeology cannot prove specific biblical stories to be literally true; it can only judge the accuracy of the backgrounds and customs found in the Bible. It is in this sense that archaeology bears on Genesis. It allows us to ask: When could this have happened and what is its historical background?

Above:
Seven-cup offering vessel from a Late Canaanite sanctuary at Beth-Shemesh

Below:
Fragment of a ritual clay jar (early Israelite period)

3. ABRAHAM AND THE PATRIARCHAL NARRATIVES

Leading scholars, notably W. F. Albright, Nelson Glueck, and G. Ernest Wright, have set a date for Abraham in the Middle Bronze Age or in the first part of the second millennium B.C. In this view Abraham lived in the Negeb (south), contemporary with the oldest settlements there. A closer examination of the biblical text in light of archaeological discoveries of the past decade tends to discount such theories. The Canaan of the patriarchal traditions proves to be significantly different from the Middle Bronze Age Canaan of the archaeologist. Abraham's Canaan is not a land of semi-nomads, but an area dotted with city-kingdoms, with a highly developed culture and building activity. He is the chief of a clan of herdsmen, warriors, and farmers, who lived in areas bordering on established cities such as Hebron, Jerusalem, or Shechem, even Gerar and Beersheba (the latter did not exist in the Middle Bronze Age).

The respect of Israeli scholars for the received text and their independence of the Documentary Theory (see Introduction) is not influenced by any orthodox interpretation but rather by a critical reassessment of the text in the light of archaeological and epigraphic findings. Their guide in dating the historical period of the persons and events of the Bible is primarily the *sitz im leben* or "life-setting" of the events in question. They contend that the patriarchal stories can best be understood in the setting of social and political conditions prevailing in Canaan when it had already been invaded by various groups. These invasions are hinted at by the traditions in Genesis 14 with Abraham as a charismatic chieftain, in chapters 20–21 when the ancestors of the Israelites were mingling with other occupants of the country, and by chapter 34 dealing with the Hebrew occupation of Shechem by Simeon and Levi, sons of Jacob, the ancestral names of early Hebrew clans.

Let us first examine these examples to see what bearing archaeology has on their historical content.

a. *Abraham, the Charismatic Hebrew Chieftain in Canaan*

The Abraham of chapter 14 is depicted in a far more realistic fashion than the familiar unworldly patriarch of faith and kindly words and deeds. He is a prosperous and powerful chieftain settled in southern Canaan, who

19

can mobilize a sizable troop among his retainers, and put foreign invaders to rout. This is a far cry from his image in the rest of Genesis, but, nevertheless, it is being substantiated by new discoveries. The narrative has all the ingredients of historicity. The first part deals with the expedition of Chedorlaomer, king of Elam and his allies, which contains elements familiar from ancient epics. W. F. Albright suggested the identification of Chedorlaomer with the Elamite Kutir-Nakhunte I, as the exploits of this monarch were widely reported in Akkadian annals and were retold often in later generations, when it was localized in Canaan. It was a common device of the ancients to incorporate epic themes into historical accounts, or even into royal annals.

The setting of this story is international, the approach impersonal, and the phraseology may be ascribed to a non-Israelite source. This is supported by the fact that Abraham is referred to as an *'ibri*, Hebrew, in v. 13. Elsewhere, the description of *'ibri* is applied to Israelites by, or for the benefit of, foreigners. They did not use it among themselves. If the non-Israelite origin of this passage is correct, it would tend to establish the "historicity" of Abraham, for an outside source would hardly make a charismatic figure of a foreign legendary hero. Commenting on this, E. A. Speiser states: "If Abraham was cited in a historical or quasi-historical narrative that was written not by Israelites but by outsiders, it necessarily follows that Abraham was not a nebulous figure but a real person who was attested in contemporary sources. Short of a non-Israelite text mentioning an Abram, son of Terah, or an Isaac, son of Abram, this is as close as we can as yet come to a direct epigraphic witness of the patriarch" (*Genesis,* Anchor Bible, p. 108). A parallel problem is the life-setting of Abraham.

b. Abraham and Melchizedek

The second part of the story relates the encounter between Abraham and Melchizedek, king and priest of Salem. The encounter has now been located by B. Mazar at 'En-rogel, the lower spring southeast of Salem (Jerusalem before the Israelite occupation) at the intersection of valleys leading to it from the south (*The Mountain of the Lord, Excavating in Jerusalem,* p. 156, 1975).

B. Mazar attributes this chapter to the early days of the monarchy in view of its two-fold purpose:

(1) To substantiate the Israelite right of possession over the land on both sides of the Jordan, from El-paran, which apparently is none other than Elath, all the way to the region lying south of Damascus, on the basis of the father of the nation having acquired it by virtue of his victory over external enemies.

(2) To mention Abraham's relationship to Melchizedek, king of Salem, and a priest of 'El-'Elyon, who had blessed the father of the nation and received from him a "a tenth of everything." The words of the poet in Psalm 110 may well testify that with the conquest of Jerusalem by David the genealogical tradition which had linked the rulers of the city of Melchizedek — and with it the right of possession over the city — was transferred to the House of David.

4. ABRAHAM'S COVENANT AND THE HISTORICAL '400 YEAR' STELE

The same tendencies of the Davidic United Monarchy which we saw in Genesis 14 continue in chapter 15. We read in vv. 18–19: "To your descendants I give this land, from the river of Egypt to the great river, the river Euphrates, the land of the Kenites, the Kenizzites..." The borders outlined here circumscribe a territory which extends from western Mesopotamia to the Wadi el-Arish in the northern Sinai. There is a close correlation between these boundaries and those of the kingdom of David and Solomon, and the exact form of the promise in Genesis 15 seems to have been shaped by those who saw its fullfilment in the tenth century B.C. It was not until David that the Kenites and Kenizzites were incorporated into Judah and ceased to be separate ethnic entities. It was only in this period that Israelite dominion extended beyond Damascus, close to the Euphrates.

This chapter poses another interesting problem with its '400 year prediction' (15:13), which has been a foundation of biblical chronology for over two millennia. Taken literally, this would place the activity of the Patriarchs in the Middle Bronze Age, around 1700 B.C. There is a problem, however, in that it is agreed by many scholars today that this chronological item corresponds to and stems from an Egyptian source. It represents the 400-year anniversary of the rule of the god Seth over Lower Egypt, celebrated by the Egyptians and commemorated by the Tanis (Zoan) stele (see Part II; Exodus). There is the statement in Num 13:22 to the effect that "Hebron was built seven years before Zoan in Egypt." The coincidence between the figures, together with the Hebron-Zoan reference, does suggest that the Tanis area and its 400-year anniversary are somewhere at the root of the 400-year tradition of the sojourn in Egypt (see above B, 1).

5. WHAT PERIOD ARE THE PATRIARCHAL NARRATIVES ROOTED IN?

With this reservation in mind, we must review pertinent episodes in Genesis to determine whether the patriarchal narratives are rooted in the period dating four or five centuries before the era of the settlement in Israel (13th–12th centuries B.C.), or whether the episodes may be dated in the days when Israelites and Canaanites were co-existing in Canaan during the formative stage of the tribal federation. If the latter view is correct, this would be the time when the Philistines were already in the country (Genesis 20–21 and below: The Presumed Anachronisms in Genesis) around the 12th century B.C. The early Hebrews were already mingling with the other occupants of the land (exemplified in Genesis 14, 23 and 34), buying and possessing property, and settling in various parts of Canaan before the disintegration of the top-heavy and oppressive feudal system of the Canaanites. In the narrative about a deed between Abraham and the sons of Heth (23), the legal details are indebted to later patterns than those of the Middle Bronze. Hence the historical reliability of the narrative can

21

Canaanite house at Gibeon. Its roof beams had rested over the row of stone pillars seen in the center

be reassessed by attributing it to its proper historical setting, at the end of the second millennium.

This later dating is supported, in particular, by the poetic passages inserted in the patriarchal accounts, such as the Testament of Jacob (Genesis 49), which stresses Judah's ascendancy over the other Israelite tribes, Isaac's blessing of Jacob and Esau (Genesis 27), and Noah's curse on Canaan (Gen 9:25–27). All of these are attempts to justify Israelite hegemony in Canaan and neighboring areas. B. Mazar has concluded: "That notion corresponds precisely to the national and religious spirit which surged within the Israelite people during the period of the United Kingdom (David and Solomon) and the extension of its borders far beyond the limits of the Israelite settlement. It is reasonable to assume that the traditions of Genesis were given their original written form during the time when the Davidic empire was being established, and that the additions and supplements of later biblical writers were only intended to help bridge the time gap for contemporary readers." When it was first written down, "the authors of Genesis had recourse not only to the national traditions then current, but also to various literary works, including Mesopotamian and Canaanite mythological and epic works. Some of them were imbedded in Genesis... in the spirit of Israelite monotheism" (*Canaan and Israel*, p. 134).

D. BIBLICAL TRADITIONS AND CUSTOMS, AND ANCIENT NEAR EAST PARALLELS

1. SARAH GIVES HAGAR TO ABRAHAM

The tale recorded in Gen 16:1–16 has long been compared to practices in Hurrian texts from the city of Nuzi in eastern Mesopotamia. One of them records the marriage of a certain Shennima to Giliminu. Their agreement provides that if Giliminu fails to bear children, she shall secure for Shennima a slave from the Lullu country as a concubine; in that case Giliminu shall have authority over the offspring. In assigning Hagar to Abraham to produce offspring, Sarah acted in conformity with Hurrian laws, the apparent source of many patriarchal practices.

Clay figurine found in Jerusalem (7th c. B.C.)

2. THE TERAPHIM OR HOUSEHOLD DEITIES

The significance of the household deities which Rachel stole from the house of Laban is now well known (Gen 31:19–55). They were figurines, at least sometimes in human form, which could be used for purposes of divination. More significant for this passage is the fact that possession of the teraphim could signify legal title to a given estate, particularly in the case of daughters, sons-in-law, and adopted sons. It was not just concern for piety, but threatened loss of real property that motivated Laban to pursue his daughters and the missing figurines.

Below:
The ubiquitous figurines in the *Dea Nutrix* attitude abound in Palestinian excavations. They bear a close relationship to the *teraphim*

Left:
Woman's interest in birth as expressed in an 8th c. Cypriot clay statuette. The woman in the middle 'sits on the knees' of her companion while she is being attended by a midwife

3. ARE NUZI PARALLELS RELEVANT TO GENESIS?

These examples represent only a few of the many insights into ancient practices gained from the discovery of cuneiform documents from Mari, Nuzi, Alalakh, Boghazköi, and other centers of Near Eastern civilization. While these parallels are useful in explaining archaic biblical customs, they come from such diverse periods and places that they are less useful in pinning down a date for the biblical narratives. There are customs of people living east of the Tigris (Nuzi in the 15th century B.C.): a variety of documents from the Canaanite kingdom of Ugarit in northern Syria from the 14th-13th centuries; royal archives from the upper Euphrates (Mari) from the 18th century; treaties of the Hittite kingdom from the 13th, or correspondence of the Egyptian empire at Tell el-Amarna from the 14th century. Roland de Vaux points out the limitations of using these parallels in speaking of the customs of Nuzi: "If they are limited to this region and to this period, they cannot be used to enlighten the history of the patriarchs who were never east of the Tigris; if they are not limited to this region and this period they cannot be used to date the patriarchs." Moreover, while Hurrians had settled in Canaan, they did not become an important ethnic group there.

The Near East in the Middle Bronze Age; note the place of Ebla.

This leaves the question: "When did the Hebrews become familiar with these Near Eastern traditions? Surely not when they were slaves in Egypt or when they were unorganized tribesmen struggling for existence in a hostile land. This acquisition of international 'wisdom' traditions is more appropriate to the period of the early monarchy or later, after Israel had become like the other nations.

4. TRADITIONAL SACRED SITES

A major theme of the book of Genesis is the association of the patriarchs with sacred sites, with special emphasis on the erection of altars and the offering of sacrifices by them. It may be assumed that these accounts would date to a period when memories of events from the period of settlement of the tribes in the land were still fresh and when the traditions about their ancestors and their ties to sacred sites were still current.

In fact, most of the sacred sites associated with the fathers of the nation are located within the core of the original Israelite settlement, i.e. in the Negeb, Judah, Mount Ephraim (Samaria) and Gilead, east of the Jordan. The biblical tradition identifies them with the major tribal shrines and cultic celebrations during the period of the Judges (12th–11th centuries B.C.) and the beginning of the monarchy.

A related motif of the patriarchal traditions is the erection of *massebôt*, "pillars," at sacred sites near terebinth trees. Hebron is especially noteworthy in this connection: the terebinth of *Mamre* and the burial field and cave of Machpelah are central to the Abrahamic traditions. These associations with the patriarchs made Hebron an ideal candidate as the first royal capital of Judah. The link between the founder of the new dynasty, David, and the ancient heroes, would have enhanced the claims to legitimacy and prestige of the former, and would have received appropriate emphasis if not specific literary formulation in contemporary documents.

A conical Phoenician *Bethyl* found at Paphos, Cyprus bears a close analogy to the biblical *Beth-el* (sanctuary) and its sacred pillars (masseboth)

Right:
A row of ten masseboth (sacred standing pillars) enshrined the Middle Bronze high-place of Gezer.

Left:
Several masseboth face the Midianite shrine of Timnah (which replaced the Egyptian temple). This high place may bear a certain relationship with the obscure origins of Mosaic ritual

5. THE PRESUMED ANACHRONISMS IN GENESIS

Beersheba, where Abraham dug his well in amity with the 'Philistines' (see below), became a center of worship early in the days of the Israelite settlement, but not before. The accounts of the patriarchs binding themselves to the inhabitants of the cities by treaties and protective arrangement seem to reflect a phase of co-existence with the native Canaanites, before the latter were overcome militarily, integrated politically, and absorbed commercially during the period of the Judges. At Beersheba, a Hebrew sacrificial altar was found dating to the early days of the kingdom (see Part V, B). Here again a site which is prominent in the traditions of Genesis plays a central role in the period of the monarchy.

Until recent years biblical commentators have regarded references to the Philistines and the Arameans, whose appearance on the local scene dates to the 12th century B.C., as anachronisms. There is a growing tendency, however, to re-evaluate their historicity in the patriarchal narratives.

a. *Abraham, Isaac, and the Philistine Kingdom of Gerar*

We have seen above that Abraham's social and economic position was not of a nomad or bedouin in the Beersheba wilderness during the first half of the Middle Bronze Age, but rather that power in the Negeb was divided among several city-kingdoms similar to those existing elsewhere in Canaan during the Late Bronze Age. We know that there was no large settlement between Gerar and Beersheba during the Middle Bronze Age. The close contacts maintained with Egypt in patriarchal times do not harmonize with what is known of the Middle Bronze Age, which is the only period in Palestinian history when no contacts worth mentioning are known to exist. The scant evidence of Middle Bronze settlements in the Negeb or the Sinai as tradeposts or way-stations on the caravan routes does not correspond with the description of settlement in the patriarchal period.

The progress of excavations at Tell Beersheba since 1975 has shed new light on biblical Beersheba prior to the monarchial period, before it had become a walled city (identified with stratum V of the dig). A fort dating to early Iron Age I has been uncovered below the ancient gate area, built apparently in the early days of the monarchy (10th century B.C.) The fort was protected by a casemate wall some 150 feet long, flanked by towers at the corners. It guarded the ancient well and the adjacent buildings dotting the tell, including some thin walls built on bedrock over the brow of the hill. Y Aharoni deduces the great importance of Beersheba during early Iron I as a center of Israelite settlement in the days of Samuel: he had sent his two sons there to "judge" or govern the town (1 Sam 8:1–2).

The fort and settlement are related to a chain of smaller forts extending over the Negeb as far south as Kadesh-Barnea. The latter are connected with early settlements and roads dating to the early part of the 11th century B.C. The question which arises is who erected them? It is clear from recent surveys and excavations that they co-existed with the earliest Iron Age occupation in an unwalled town at Beersheba. The latter's early fort already lay in ruins before the erection of the entire city wall in monarchial times (tenth century B.C.; stratum V) which covered it, as well as the adjacent dwellings.

b. *The 'Well of Abraham'*

A deep well, already cleared up to a depth of 130 feet from the top of the tell and situated outside the city wall, is linked with the three phases of settlement during early Iron I, which corresponds to the early strata (2 and 3) of settlement in neighboring Tell Meshash dating to the 11th century B.C. The unbroken pottery found in the area near the Beersheba well

Left:
The deep well excavated outside the Israelite gate of Beersheba dates to an earlier period, before the city was fortified, presumably in the days of Abraham. This represents one of the rare archaeological links with the story of the Patriarchs (Gen. 21:25; 26:25)

Above:
Stone altar found outside the gate entrance. The most intriguing problem raised by the excavation of Beersheba is that of its ancient cult and ritual hinted at in the patriarchal stories of Gen 21; 26; 46. The later large altar of sacrifices found within the well-planned city constructed in the days of the United Kingdom, is described in Part VI: Amos

Left, below:
The earlier phase of Beersheba is represented by an unfortified settlement; but in one of its phases (Stratum VII of the excavation) a fortress about 165 feet wide overlooked the well.
V – Section of solid wall.
VI – Late 11th century house.
VII – 11th century fortress

belongs to the transition period between the Late Bronze and the Iron Age. This new evidence leads to the following conclusions:

(a) This important well, dug so painstakingly from the top of the tell and close to the holy place of Beersheba, was invested with great importance in biblical tradition (Gen 21:33; 26:23–24, 33–34, etc.). Y Aharoni, B. Mazar, and other leading scholars believe it is probably the well associated with Abraham (Gen 21:31) but not an Abraham of the Middle Bronze age. Potsherds of the 12th to 11th c. B.C., found in the deepest layer (Stratum VI), indicate that the mound was settled in the period of Judges, although it was apparently unwalled at that time. The well is adjacent to, but outside the wall.

(b) From early times there was a massive horned altar at the holy place. After its destruction, it was the site of a non-Israelite sanctuary which stood there until Hellenistic times. The stones of the Israelite altar had been removed and reused elsewhere on the tell. Nevertheless, the excavators were able to locate most of the pieces and to restore the original altar, which is the pride of the archaeological expedition, and a witness to early Israelite cultic practice at Beersheba.

(c) The new data are of great historical importance, and if the proposed interpretation is correct, they tend to reinforce the theory advanced by B. Mazar and others that the patriarchal traditions connected with Beersheba relate to the historical period of Israelite settlement (Early Iron Age) and not to the traditional era of the patriarchs (Middle Bronze Age).

6. THE PHILISTINES OF GENESIS

The Genesis accounts of the relations between Abraham, Isaac, and Abimelech, king of Gerar, are consistent with the conditions existing between the Israelite tribesmen of Judea and their sub-groups in the Negeb and the Philistine kingdoms during the last quarter of the 11th century. The background of Genesis is essentially the same as that of the books of Samuel. If Abraham belongs to the Late Bronze Age, there is no reason to consider the reference to the Philistines as a serious anachronism. The text may be more accurate than most modern scholars are willing to concede.

The political and social conditions existing in Canaan after the 13th century invasions of the Sea Peoples (a group which included the Philistines), were similar to those facing David and his mercenaries when they lived in the western Negeb as vassals to Achish, the Philistine king of Gath. Archaeological surveys in that area have turned up artifacts that are characteristically Philistine, dating to the second half of the 12th and beginning of the 11th centuries B.C.

7. ABRAHAM, ISAAC, AND THE HISTORICAL ARAMEANS

The Aramean people are known in the stories about Abraham, Isaac and Jacob as natives of Aram, Ḥaran, and Naḥor, where the patriarchal families mingled with Arameans such as Laban and his clan (Gen 20:20–34;

24; 29; 31). Though many scholars have argued vigorously for the existence of "proto-Arameans" before the 12th century B.C., there is no convincing evidence to support that position. Cuneiform sources indicate that Tiglath-pileser I (1116–1078 B.C.) was the first Assyrian king to fight the Ahlame-Arameans, semi-nomads of the steppes between the middle Euphrates and eastern Syria. They gained a foothold in western Mesopotamia in the course of the 11th century at locations mentioned in Genesis. This may explain the historical importance of the genealogical lists of Aram as the younger branch in a federation of tribes of Nahor (Gen 22:21). It also clarifies the important status accorded in biblical tradition to the figure of Laban, the Aramean whose center was at Haran.

A brotherly pact between two parties. Middle Bronze engraving from Ugarit

We know that the Arameans abosorbed the Hurrian culture in western Mesopotamia. They eventually spread south to the area of Damascus and into Transjordan or Gilead, where their territory impinged on that claimed by Jacob's clan. Gen 31 explains that the name Gilead is derived from Hebrew *gal 'ed* (*yegar šahādûtha'* in Aramaic), a mound of stones in a sacred high place which defined the boundaries between the two peoples. This reflects the state of affairs before the long wars between David and the more warlike Arameans of his day.

The Genesis stories accurately reflect the presence of the Arameans in the Near East during the second half of the 11th century. This observation helps solve a geographical problem in the biblical account. We are told (Gen 31:23) that Laban pursued Jacob and his livestock for seven days from Haran to Gilead; this is an impossible feat unless we take into consideration the fact that Aramean territory lay much closer to Gilead than Haran proper. The encounter of Jacob and Laban is concluded by the erection of a pillar or *massebâh* consecrated to the respective deities of the contracting parties in compliance with treaty pratices through the ancient Near East.

8. CONDITIONS AT THE END OF THE SECOND MILLENNIUM

Transport, raiding, and warfare in the southern and eastern steppes were greatly facilitated by the domestication of the camel. This did not happen until the end of the second millennium. Until that time, transportation of people and goods was carried out by ass caravans. Their territorial range was limited by their greater need of water. The frequent mention of camels in the patriarchal narratives would have to be regarded as anachronistic, if we dated them in the Middle Bronze Age. This is not the case, however, if we place them in the 12th century B.C. or even later, when the camel was domesticated in Palestine.

a. *Jacob-Israel and Esau-Edom*

In Gen 36, which includes Edomite genealogies and stories, Essau-Seir is the ancestor of the Edomites just as Jacob-Israel is the eponymous ancestor of the Israelites. The prominence given to Esau in the patriarchal tradition suggests that during the formative stage of Israel, Edom played a very pro- 29 minent role. Though they are linked with the Horites in Gen 37:20–39, the Edomites were not Hurrians (see above), who appear in the Bible as uncircumcised people dwelling in Shechem. The biblical glimpses of the Edomites, including the tantalizing lists of political leaders in chapter 36, may be illuminated and fleshed out as archaeology pursues this elusive people in its historical settlements since the late 14th or early 13th c. B.C.

b. *The Capture of Shechem*

The account of the rape of Dinah (Gen 34) and the capture of Shechem by her brothers, Simeon and Levi, presents the events as personalized history. This account may be rooted in traditions of certain ethnic relationships of the early days of the settlement of the Israelites in Canaan. The slender evidence it presents rests on a historical foundation. In Gen 34:2 Hamor, chief of Shechem, is called a Hivite, but the Septuagint translation identifies him as Horite. We know that Shechem was inhabited at that time by Hurrian elements, because: a) the Shechemites were still uncircumcised, whereas the Semitic Canaanites would have been circumcised; b) the Amarna letters despatched to Egypt from Shechem show that Hurrians were active in central Palestine from about 1400 onward.

A new city wall and eastern gateway were built in Shechem in the Late Bronze age, consisting of two towers, each 23 × 42 feet, containing guard rooms. See the picture of Shechem's cyclopean wall, above

There is also an obscure reference to the capture of Shechem in Gen 48:22; here, in what may be the oldest tradition of all, the antagonists are Jacob and the Amorites. A final story concerning Shechem in the period of Judges is found in chapter 9 of that book. It tells of the breaking of a treaty between the Israelites and the Shechemites and the destruction of the city by Abimelech (see below, Part III).

c. *The Story of Judah and Tamar*

Judah, we are informed, had left his kin and moved to Adullam, in the Canaanite lowlands to the west (cf. Genesis 38). There he marries a Canaanite woman and has three sons by her. The significance of the story goes far beyond a mere narrative about one of the eponymous ancestors of the nation. It reflects a current tradition related realistically with the early settlement of the tribe of Judah, its relations of peaceful coexistence with the Canaanites in the coastal plain, how it branched out into clans, and how they expanded.

Let us mention one archaeological detail out of many, namely the seal-and-cord chosen by Tamar to confirm her testimony and guarantee the identity of the person by whom she was pregnant. The seal-and-cord were not chosen for their intrinsic value but for purposes of personal identification to be produced at the critical moment in the narrative. The seal mentioned here was of the well-known cylinder variety, found everywhere in the Near East, but especially in Mesopotamia. Numerous specimens have turned up in Palestinian excavations. These seals were often perforated vertically for threading with a cord, so that the seal-and-cord were worn around the neck as a unit. The seal served as the legal surrogate for the person wearing it. Its impression on a tablet signalized the owner's acknowledgment of full responsibility with respect to the contents, and is the equivalent of a modern document duly signed and sworn.

9. THE STORY OF JOSEPH

Genesis 37–48 are devoted to the story of Joseph. Its sustained human drama is unsurpassed in the whole Pentateuch. Despite its rich characterization, the novella lacks historical references which would help to pin down its date. It serves to close the patriarchal period, and offers a rationale of the descent of the Hebrews to Egypt. It also provides a link to the eventual Exodus from Egypt. There are numerous problems, however, which make its dating uncertain, though there are numerous details which derive from and are consistent with the traditions of the ancient Near East. The motif of an adulteress (Gen 39) turning on a young man who spurned her was well known to the Egyptians from "The Tale of the Two Brothers." Joseph's tunic of many colors in 37:3 should properly be translated as an "ornamental tunic." Cuneiform records refer to a *kutinnu pišannu* (cf. Hebrew *kutonet passim*) as a ceremonial robe which could be draped around statues of divinities and had appliqué ornaments sewn onto it.

It was appropriate that Joseph was given the Pharaoh's signet ring in Gen 41:42, for in Egypt the vizier was known as the "Sealbearer of the King of Lower Egypt." The gift of the gold chain is another authentic touch; it sanctioned a vizier's control over regulation of the food supply.

In Gen 44:5 we read of Joseph's cup which he used for divination. There is ample evidence of this sort of divination whereby oil or water was poured into a bowl and interpretations and forecasts given on the basis of the liquids inside.

The land of Goshen (Gen 45:10) is identified with the region of the   31

Wadi Tumilat (cf. Part II: Exodus). "The region of Rameses" as it is called by the Egyptians in Gen 47:11, is synonymous with it. It is often argued that the use of the name "Rameses" is an anachronism in Genesis since the royal name became popular only in the 19th dynasty, i.e. not before the end of the 14th century. This is one more reason to date the contents of the book of Genesis much later than the traditional patriarchal period in the Middle Bronze Age, and much closer to the presumed date of its composition in the Iron Age.

10. THE TESTAMENT OF JACOB (Gen 49), ONE OF THE EARLIEST BIBLICAL WRITINGS

The poem is Genesis 49 is composed of short sayings about each of the twelve sons of Jacob. This format invites comparison between this poem and Deuteronomy 33 which contains the same form, as well as Judges 5, where most of the tribes are listed and praised or censured for their participation in the Israelite war against Sisera and the kings of Canaan. Due to careful linguistic analysis there is now a consensus that these poems are among the earliest pieces of writing in the Bible. In their present form they are authentic products of the premonarchic age of Israel, and being poems with a fixed structure, they are less likely than prose passages to have been changed by subsequent editors.

It is likely that the comment on Simeon and Levi in Gen 49:5–7: "Simeon and Levi are brothers; weapons of violence are their swords" relate an episode of the settlement of Shechem (see Part III: Conquest of Canaan). Another verse that deserves comment is 49:13: "Zebulun... shall become a haven for ships." The coastline of Canaan from south to north (Sidon) was dotted with small natural inlets serving as harbors where ships could take shelter at night, as they did not travel in the dark. This accounts for the closeness of these harbors to each other.

PART II

EXODUS; LEVITICUS; NUMBERS; DEUTERONOMY

A. EXODUS

Following Genesis, the book of Exodus pursues the traditions from the days after the clan of Jacob had settled in Egypt and after the death of Joseph. It is the history of the departure of Israel from Egypt. The second half of the book gives an account of the encampment at Sinai under Moses' leadership, the establishment of the covenant bond with God, and the worship in a tabernacle.

Its contents may be grouped as follows:

Chapter 1:1–7	An introductory statement linking Genesis and Exodus
Chapters 1:7–2:22	Oppression of Israel; early life of Moses and flight into the desert
Chapters 2:23–13:22	The call of Moses; interviews with Pharaoh; the ten plagues; the Exodus from Egypt
Chapters 14:1–18:27	Crossing the Reed Sea and the wilderness journey to Mount Sinai
Chapters 19:1–20:26	The revelation of Yahweh to the people at Mount Sinai; the Decalogue
Chapters 21:1–24:18	The Book of the Covenant and the ratification or renewal of the covenant
Chapters 25:1–31:18 35:1–40:38	The priesthood; the building of the sanctuary and its furnishings
Chapters 32:1–34:35	The story of the worship of the golden calf and the subsequent events. The last chapter is a renewal of the covenant and the cultic Decalogue.

Exodus is one of the most familiar books of the Hebrew Bible, for the events of this book are central to Israelite history. We only need to list the central traditions of the book to see its importance for biblical thought:

The vision and call of Moses at Horeb: Exod 3:1–4:17

The plagues: Exod 7–11

The institution and law of the Passover: Exod 12:1–13:10

The Song of Moses: Exod 15:1–21. This is very early poetry.

The Decalogue and the Book of the Covenant: Exod 20:1–23:33; 24:7.

> The Ten Commandments are followed by the Book of the Covenant, the first and oldest statement of the law of the Pentateuch.

The worship of the golden calf: Exod 32

The critical reader of the Bible should be aware that the introductory 33

Asiatic slaves at work under taskmasters "making bricks to renew the workshop at Karnak" (1450 B.C. tomb at Thebes)

statement (Exod 1:1–7) linking the settlement of the descendants of Jacob with the amorphous peoples of the Oppression and Exodus is a secondary addition in the view of most scholars. The traditions behind Genesis and those of Exodus arose from different groups who banded together in Canaan to become Israel and only later were joined to make a single history of Israel.

1. EGYPTIAN DATA ON ISRAEL IN EGYPT

There is still no direct evidence from Egyptian sources on the vital story of the Bondage and Exodus, or of Moses, his encounters with Pharaoh, and the plagues. Few episodes in Israel's history have aroused as many conflicting views among scholars in interpreting the biblical tradition and its background.

Egyptian sources tell us that various wanderers from the east, including families of herdsmen, would enter Egypt and settle in the pasture lands of the Egyptian Nile Delta and its eastern approaches. The Egyptian papyrus, Anastasi VI, tells of the permission that was granted to clans of Shosu from Edom to cross over to the pools of Per-atum (see below) to get water for themselves and their animals. This is the earliest Egyptian reference to Edom, and it refers to the arrival of semi-nomadic Semitic clans which were then settling in the hill regions of southern Transjordan. Papyri from the border fortress of Merneptah at Teku describe the careful watch kept on the passage of nomadic clans through the network of forts along the desert border, the biblical "Wall (shur) of Egypt." These nomads were often subjected to land taxes and to the corvée (forced labor) by their Egyptian rulers.

The "400 year stele" erected by Rameses II at Tanis (Zoan) commemorated the founding of the city in the Land of Goshen

2. THE LAND OF GOSHEN

The clans of Israel were concentrated in the "land of Goshen," the southern extension of the "region of Rameses" (see discussion on Gen 47:11), where Rameses I had rebuilt Tanis (Zoan) and erected there the "400-year stele" (see above, Part I, C, 4: Abraham and the "400 Year Stele"). Tanis

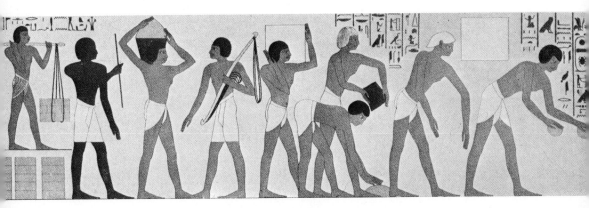

was renamed Per-Rameses, the house of Rameses. The land of Goshen extended from Zoan-Tanis to the store-city of Pithom and to the depression of the Wadi Tumilat east of the Delta. At the end of the last century E. Naville had already identified the great mound of Tell el-Mashkuteh as Pithom, which Rameses II had built up and resettled as a border fortress in eastern Egypt. Several stelae and a temple were discovered there, consecrated to the god Atum, adding credence to its identification as Pithom (*Per-Atum* = House of Atum). Other inscriptions found there recently suggest the identification of the tell with Teku, probably biblical Succoth, the Israelites' first station after their flight from Per-Rameses. Some scholars believe that the city was known by both names, Per-Atum and Teku.

3. THE DATE OF EXODUS AND CONQUEST

Most scholars are agreed on dating the Israelite Conquest of Canaan, west of the Jordan, around the middle of the 13th century B.C. Support for this chronology comes from the following data: a) The naming of "Rameses" as one of the cities built by the Israelites in Goshen (Exod 1:11) at the beginning of the reign of Rameses II and its identification with Per-Rameses; b) the Merneptah stele erected by Rameses' son Merneptah (1236–1223 B.C.) on one of his expeditions to Canaan, which mentions Israel as one of the peoples which he defeated in Canaan ca. 1230; c) the settlement of southern Transjordan in the 13th century. N. Glueck's archaeological surveys have shown that there was little settled occupation of the area in previous centuries. Therefore, Edom, Moab, and Ammon, mentioned in the narratives of the Conquest, could not have been in existence at an earlier time. These data, taken together, place the Exodus early in the reign of Rameses II (1304–1237), the two invasions of Transjordan either late in the 14th or early in the 13th century (see Numbers), and the major entrance into Canaan no later than 1230 B.C.

The historicity of the Exodus is undeniable, though it is not possible to establish from any outside source the name of the disparate elements or "mixed multitude" (12:38), nor the size of the groups that gathered eventually at Kadesh-Barnea before the invasion of Transjordan. But we do 35

Egyptian landowner supervising the produce — fruit, wine, fish — gathered by slaves

have contemporary documents which establish the historical background of the period of bondage and escape. In the reigns of Rameses and Merneptah, Asiatics, including Ḥabiru, were employed in various types of work for the king; some became officials but most served in forced labor in the fields (mostly in fruit plantations or as vintners), in mines, and in the construction of public buildings. This is in line with the biblical reference to the building of Pithom and Rameses, the royal city of the 19th Dynasty, at Qantir, 13 miles south of Tanis. The building of these cities was necessitated by the new Egyptian policy which shifted the main center of government to the north and near the travel lanes which led to Canaan.

4. THE BIBLICAL CHRONOLOGY

Some scholars do not believe that Rameses II was the Pharaoh of the Exodus because his dates conflict with the biblical chronology in 1 Kgs 6:1, which counts 480 years from the Exodus to the founding of Solomon's temple in 965 B.C. This traditional reckoning places the Exodus in the mid-15th century or at the time of Thutmose III. This chronology is suspect, however, because it is based on the calculations of a later source. According to traditions stemming from a priestly source, the writer figured that there were 12 generations of priests from Aaron to Azariah of the House of Zadok, the first chief priest to officiate at the Temple, and that each generation was 40 years long. Thus he arrived at 480 years from the Exodus to the founding of the Temple. The artificial nature of this calculation militates against its use in reconstructing history. But, if we take 25–27 years for an average generation and count 12 generations, although this also may be an artificial figure, we arrive approximately at the beginning of the 13th century.

There is also scepticism about the total number of 600,000 heads of families given in the biblical tradition (Num 1:46; 26:51). The consensus

Egyptian relief at Thebes representing Rameses II attacking fortified Dapur held by the Hittites in Syria

is that it must have been a much smaller group that eluded the Egyptian army and crossed the wilderness. There have been several attempts at explaining the large figures given in Numbers. According to G. E. Mendenhall, following a suggestion by Flinders Petrie, the Hebrew word *'eleph* refers to the village or other population unit which provides troops from among its able-bodied men, and is not the number 1000 here. He arrives at a total figure of about 6,000 men as the maximum martial strength of the Israelite army during the period of the Judges. Albright believed that the figure reflected the total population of the United Kingdom in the time of David and his ill-fated census. There are other possibilities but Mendenhall appears to be on the right track in recognizing the census roll as a military list. Hence, Num 1 refers to 600 small units.

5. A HISTORICAL CHAIN REACTION

While the biblical chronology is problematic here, it is possible that this central event took place as a result of the violent wars Rameses conducted against the Amurru of Central Syria and his failure at Kadesh on the Orontes in 1286 B.C., which initiated a chain reaction. The decline of Egyptian power in Canaan allowed the recapture of Syria by the Hittites and their advance to the areas of Damascus and northern Transjordan. This in turn gave rise to a series of rebellions of the city-kingdoms throughout Canaan against the Egyptian overlords. The Hittite advance into Syria may be related to the biblical report of the rise of the Amorites in Transjordan and the founding of the kingdom of Heshbon in Num 21:26. Rather than resulting in a clear-cut victory, the struggle between the Egyptians and the Hittites for Canaan sapped the energy of both great powers, leaving both too weak to completely dominate the land. The power vacuum promoted the resurgence of local kings and of nomadic tribes from Seir (Edom) to Egypt's eastern border. This accounts for

37

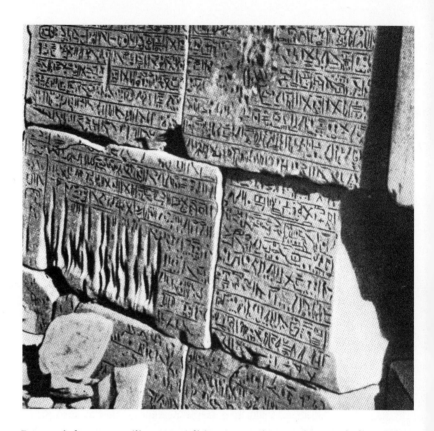

Rameses' frequent military expeditions to various regions including Edom
and Moab. Egyptian sources mention violent encounters in the lands of
the Shosu bedouins and adjacent mountains of Seir, as well as the destruction
of their settlements. An inscription found at Luxor tells of the capture of
many fortified cities including Boterat in Moab, lying on the King's Highway east of the Jordan. Rameses left no stone unturned to regain control
and ensure communications along this major trade route. Forts were built
at strategic points along the way and the Egyptians began exploiting the
copper mines at the south of the Arabah in the Negeb, as we learn from
the discovery of the remains of an Egyptian temple near Timnah.

6. THE JOURNEY THROUGH THE WILDERNESS

The route of the Exodus and Wanderings remains a difficult and tantalizing problem. The location of the many encampments, and especially
of Mount Sinai, seems to be beyond precise determination. Only the geog-
raphy of the beginning can be established with some degree of certainty
as it is connected with names also known from Egyptian sources and located
east of the Delta. The Israelites journeyed from Rameses to Succoth (Exod
12:37), identified with *t-k-w* of Egyptian texts and modern Tell el-Mashkuteh. It was a border fortress on the Wadi Tumilat west of the Bitter
Lakes, presently along the course of the Suez Canal. From there they
travelled through Etam on the edge of the desert to Pi-hahiroth between

Migdol and the Mediterranean Sea, in front of Ba'al-zephon (Exod 14:2).
Migdol is an Egyptian fortress northeast of Sile (modern Tell el-Heir) near
Qantara, mentioned by Seti I and later Egyptian sources. Ba'al-zephon
was a temple for mariners (Zeus-Casius of the Greeks) located on the
narrow arm of land that embraces the Sabkhat-Bardawil lagoon (the ancient
Gulf of Serbonis) and separates this lagoon from the Mediterranean (see
map).

It was at Pi-hahiroth that the Egyptians overtook the fleeing Israelites
who were saved miraculously at the Reed Sea as described in the Song

The narrow arm of land that
embraces the Sabkhat-
Bardawil lagoon (Gulf of
Serbonitis) or the 'Reed Sea',
is regarded as the northern
route which the Israelites
followed in their Exodus.
Remains of an Iron Age I
settlement were discovered
at Casius

of the Sea (Exod 15:1–18:21). The familiar rendering, the "Red" Sea, derives from a mistranslation of the Hebrew, and originally Egyptian, word *suph* which means "reed." It probably refers to papyrus marshes near Rameses. Unfortunately, there is not enough data to say more than that the Reed Sea was a shallow body of water, perhaps east of the Delta; perhaps it was the Gulf of Serbonis (the lagoon of Sabkhat Bardawil) which separated Migdol from Ba'al-zephon (see map).

Another reference to this stage of the journey comes from Exod 13:17–18: "God did not lead them by way of the land of the Philistines, although that was near ...lest the people repent when they see war..., but God led the people round by the way of the wilderness toward the Reed(!) Sea." Because scholarly opinion holds that the Philistines did not precede the Israelites into the land, this reference must be an anachronism. The Philistines or "Sea Peoples" settled on the coast of southern Palestine in the 12th century B.C. The coastal route, also called the 'Way to the Land of the Philistines', would have been convenient, but it was precluded because it was guarded by a network of Egyptian forts.

7. THE NORTHERN AND SOUTHERN ROUTES

The route of Israel's journey through the wilderness is still open to question. The choice between the "northern" and "southern" theories rests primarily on the location of Mt. Sinai which is problematic. According to the "northern" theory, Sinai should be close to Kadesh-Barnea (see Exod 15:22), the well-watered oasis which held a central place in the wilderness period, possibly Jebel Hilal, 30 miles to the west. The incident of the quails in Num 11:31–32 is consistent with a route along the Mediterranean coast where swarms of migrating birds drop exhausted after their flight across the sea. On the other hand, there are traditions which locate Sinai at a greater distance from Kadesh (Num 33:16–36; Deut 1:2) and support a southern route. This hypothesis rests on early Christian traditions which locate Sinai at Jebel Mûsa, Mt. Moses, in the south of the Sinai Peninsula. It is here that Justinian I dedicated a monastery to St. Catherine of Alexandria in A.D. 527 to protect the hermits who lived in the Sinai wilderness since the 5th century. Supporters of this theory point out that Jebel Mûsa, 7,497 feet high, is a more likely candidate for the awe inspiring theophany than is Jebel Hilal at 2,927 feet. If this identification is correct, however, it would imply that the Israelites made a long, difficult, and topographically unnecessary detour in the rough and waterless part of the peninsula. A third hypothesis would place Mt. Sinai in or near Midian on the eastern, Asiatic side of the Gulf of Aqaba. The episode of the burning bush in Exodus 3 implies such a location, and other evidence tends to support it. The lack of a clear, continuous tradition about the location or even name of the mountain suggests that there may have been more than one such experience and that several traditions have been blended imperfectly.

Whatever the route, the Israelites ended at Kadesh-Barnea, an important cross-roads on the highways leading from Egypt. This was the central assembly point for forty years and the largest oasis in the Sinai wilderness. Only a few of the way stations can now be identified and those very hesitantly. At any rate they stem from several sources, some of which are very ancient, and were joined together only later. We should remember that only small numbers of people with cattle and scant food and water can move in the wilderness, especially in the southern part of the Sinai Peninsula.

8. MOSES

The debate over the historicity of Moses, just as the quest for the historical Jesus, has led nowhere. Archaeology is unable to confirm the existence of a single individual, so we must rely on the biblical accounts. It is clear that certain legendary motifs have been added to the story, particularly in the narrative of Moses' birth and abandonment to the river. A similar legend was told of Sargon of Akkad and numerous other ancient heroes who were certainly historical figures.

It seems an inescapable conclusion that a certain personality, who completely dominates the traditions of the Exodus, initiated and directed the revolutionary events which bound Yahweh with a nation, Israel, through the covenant. It was the heroic achievement of Moses to have rallied an amorphous agglomerate of slaves and outcasts and imbued them with the faith to adhere to a single god, Yahweh.

One must also consider certain realistic details in the life of Moses, such as his marriage to Zipporah, daughter of the priest of Midian. The early date of the tradition is unquestionable; by the time of the Judges the Midianites had become bitter enemies of Israel. A later description of Moses would not have included the marriage of the great lawgiver to an enemy. Even more, how could any tradition allow Moses to be guided by a Midianite priest unless it were early and authentic?

9. THE SANCTUARY AND ARK

The sources which describe the desert sanctuary (Exod 26; 36–40) go into great detail about the construction of the tabernacle, how it was set up, and what its furnishings were. This idealized description in its present form is a late priestly tradition. It has proved impossible to sort out all the data so as to produce a sequential picture of the stages of tradition, but broad lines can be determined. The original tabernacle was a portable tent of simple manufacture. The last, improved model doubtless served David in Jerusalem before the Temple was built, and the present description is most likely to reflect the latter rather than the former phase. The *mishkan* (Dwelling) was a collapsible temple made of wooden frames of the desert acacia wood. They were put together making a rectangular building $30 \times 10 \times 10$ cubits ($175 \times 52.7 \times 52.7$ inches), which opened on the eastern side. It was covered with bands of fine woven material, sewn together to make two big pieces fastened with hooks and clips. They were embroidered with   41 figures of cherubim. Goat skins covered the material "like a tent over the Dwelling." Lastly, skins of rams, dyed red, covered the whole frame, and were in turn covered by very light leather hides. A curtain covered the entry and an ornate veil was drawn across the innermost ten cubits and marked the division between the Holy Place and the Holy of Holies. The only object in the latter was the Ark of the Testimony (Exod 26:33; 40:21), while the Holy Place contained only the lampstand and the table of shewbread. An altar, with the basin for washing, stood outside the entrance of the Dwelling (Exod 40:30). An open court around the Dwelling (100×50 cubits) was formed by a barrier of bronze posts and silver curtain rods from which linen fell to the ground. It was suggested on the basis of a bas-relief from Palymra (as illustrated here) that the Dwelling was a tent like their own dwelling places during their wanderings in the Sinai.

10. A MIDIANITE SANCTUARY AT TIMNAH

Recent excavations have been conducted by Y. Aharoni and B. Rothenberg at the Egyptian copper mining center in the Timnah valley, some 18–20 miles north of Elath. Egyptian pharaohs from the days of Seti I to Rameses III, and later, Rameses IV and V (14th to 12th centuries B.C.) had maintained there large-scale primitive copper smelting facilities. They were manned by the indigenous Amelekites of the southern Negeb, as well as the Midianites and Kenites of the Arabah and Midian. The Kenites, it will be remembered, possessed metallurgical traditions going back to pre-biblical times as recorded in Gen 4:22. The Egyptians had also erected at Timnah a sanctuary to the goddess Hathor, "The Lady of the Turquoise," who was also worshiped at the mines of Serabit-el-Khadem in Sinai, also mined by Semitic workers. This temple was destroyed, then rebuilt between the 14th and 12th century B.C. The actual maintenance of Egyptian mining enterprises is further attested by the Papyrus Harris I, dating to the reign of Rameses III. Thousands of artifacts in clay or metal, of both local, probably Midianite, and of Egyptian provenance, attest to the expansion and vitality of the Midianite culture, stemming from sedentary and semi-sedentary centers southeast of Elath and extending to the threshold of Arabia in the northern Hedjaz. They represent a witness to the history of the days roughly corresponding to the periods of Exodus and the wanderings of disparate Hebrew clans in the semi-arid areas south of Canaan and Transjordan. They bespeak some cultural and social interrelations between the Midianites and Kenites on the one hand, and the early Hebrews. They serve to authenticate the tradition of the relationship between Jethro, the Midianite priest, who was father-in-law and adviser of Moses.

Toward the end of the 12th century, the temple the Egyptians had rebuilt was destroyed, apparently by earthquake. Shortly thereafter all evidence of the former cult was displaced by the Midianites who kept up the exploitation of the mines. The excavations show that the shrine was roofed

Left:
The final Midiante phase of the former Egyptian Hathor temple at Timnah, seen from the east. It is situated beneath the rock overhang of the cliffs popularly known as 'Solomon's Pillars'. A row of masseboth (standing pillars) is seen at the edge of the court of the sanctuary (center of picture)

Above:
The Midianite copper serpent with a gilded head found in the holy of holies of the sanctuary. It is suggestive of a metal serpent fashioned by Moses (see Numbers 2:9)

Left:
Crushing and ore-grinding tools of the Timnah mining camp

Below:
The portable tent-shrine carved on a bas relief of the Temple of Bel in Palmyra (eastern Syria) is suggestive of the 'Dwelling' in the desert

The Midianite offering bench built against the wall with, in the foreground, one of the stone-lined post-holes for the tented sanctuary

with a tent, presumably as a desert sanctuary, and its holy of holies contained a copper snake with a gilded head as a votive object. The other radical change in the character of the shrine was the erection of a row of *massebôt* or stelae facing the inner sanctuary, and an offering bench built against the sanctuary wall. The votive snake was found in the inner holiest spot of the sanctuary and numerous other copper votive artifacts and decorated pottery attributed to the Midianite phase of the cult in the sanctuary.

These discoveries strongly confirm the interrelationships between early Israel and the Midianites-Kenites (cf. Exodus 18:12–17). The votive snake of the desert sanctuary of Timnah may furnish an actual background to the tradition of the serpent Nehushtan of Num 21:9. The excavations may

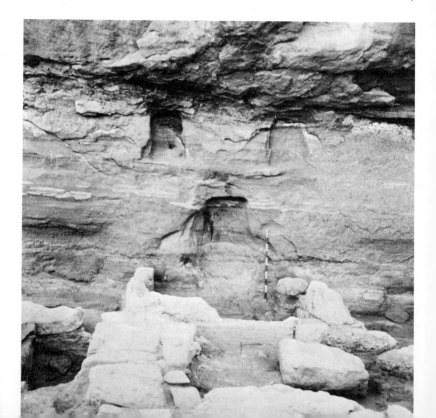

The 'Holy of Holies' of the Midianite sanctuary with three niches in the background, beneath the rock overhang

cast some light on the nature of Moses' tent-sanctuary and lend support to those scholars who have proposed that the cult of the invisible El or Yahweh of the Exodus period, who tented among his people and whose proper dwelling was a tent, may have been of Midianite-Kenite origin. Regardless of the theological implications raised by the discoveries, it is clear that they provide a cultural and historico-geographical background of facts and data related to the obscure phases of the wilderness narratives.

11. THE ARK OF THE COVENANT

The Ark of the Covenant contained the two stone tablets on which the ten words of the Law were inscribed. God had given them to Moses (Exod 31:18) and he put them inside the Ark (25:16; 40:20; cf. Deut 10:1–5). The Ark, as described in Exod 25:10–12 and 37:1–9, was a chest made of acacia wood, about four feet long by two and a half feet wide, and two and a half feet high. It was covered by gold plates and had rings attached, through which poles were inserted for carrying. A plate of gold, the size of the Ark, called the *kappôreth*, was laid over the Ark. Two cherubim stood at each end of the *kappôreth* overshadowing it with their wings. Like the description of the Dwelling, the traditions of the Ark were influenced by the memory of Solomon's temple, where the Ark stood in the Holy of Holies, overshadowed by the cherubim (1 Kgs 8:6). It is also likely that the objects and arrangements in the Temple were influenced by the prior practice in the Tabernacle. Nevertheless, the passage in Num 10:33–36, which describes the Ark on its travels preserves a much older tradition and evokes the spirit of the earlier age when the Ark symbolized the immediate presence of the deity and accompanied him and the people into battle.

It is difficult to say how the Israelites envisioned God mounted on the Ark. The most likely picture has him seated above it on a throne formed by the cherubim (for such a cherubim throne see photo). The Ark itself would serve as his footstool. In an early Psalm he is described as mounting a cherub, but this is figurative language reflecting the imagery associated with the Canaanite storm god. Many scholars believe that the *Kappôreth* over the Ark was a later tradition and became a substitute for the Ark in the post-Exilic period after the destruction of the Temple by the Babylonians. Thus the *kappôreth* filled the role formerly ascribed to the Ark as the sign of the divine presence (Lev 16:2, 13).

12. THE PASSOVER PASCAL SACRIFICE

One custom, the pascal sacrifice, ordained in the Book of the Covenant (Exod 23:18) and in the cultic Decalogue (34:25), has been maintained throughout the long history of Israel. The descriptions in Exod 12:27, Num 9:2, and Deut 16:6 speak more vividly than archaeological discovery. This sacrifice is still celebrated by a sect of Samaritan Jews according to the biblical tradition on the night of the 14–15th day of Nisan (the first month

Canaanite and Phoenician carvings of the 13th–10th c. B.C. describe the king as seated on his throne; its side consists of a lion-headed winged sphinx or 'cherub'. The king's feet rest on a footstool

Left:
Lambs slaughtered by the Samaritan sectary Jews on their Passover feast celebrated on Mount Gerizim above Shechem

Right:
The slaughtered lambs are roasted in fire pits then consumed by the whole community to commemorate the Exodus from Egypt

of the ancient calendar) and is accompanied by the eating of matzot (unleavened bread) for seven days.

The sacrifice was first offered by the Israelites on the night of their flight from Egypt so that the avenging angel would bypass their homes. The killing and roasting of the yearling lamb was done by every Israelite in his home, not in a sanctuary, and anyone could partake. The meat had to be eaten during the night, with any leftovers being burnt. The sacrificial blood was then smeared on the doorpost to mark each Israelite home and prevent their first-born from dying. The festival commemorates and heralds the historical continuity and common fate of the people, and it bespeaks the experience shared between those who partake in the eating of the sacrificial meat and the Israelites who were saved from Egyptian bondage.

13. THE SAMARITAN SACRIFICIAL RITUAL

The celebration and feeling of communion with the historic event is celebrated by Jews in drastically modified form on the Seder night. But the ancient customs are practiced to this day by the tiny Samaritan community in Shechem and Holon, who observe Judaism according to the literal ordinances of the Pentateuch (Torah) and disregard Rabbinic or later norms of Judaism. Pascal lambs are slaughtered and skinned before nightfall, accompanied by hymns and prayers conducted by their High Priest. The lambs are skinned and roasted whole in deep pits lit by brush fire and consumed by every member of the community; the extraordinary ceremony continues until late in the night.

46

14. ANCIENT CULT AND THE SOURCES OF THE BOOK OF EXODUS

Certain scholars, following the lead of J. Pedersen, regard the unit Exod 1–15 as a kind of Passover *haggadah* or book of ritual. On this view it was the celebration of the Passover that produced the narrative, which in effect explains the purpose and rationale of the celebration. The rest of the book then consists of descriptive notes and other helpful information relating to the central theme: deliverance from bondage in Egypt and the appropriate ways in which to worship God and praise him for his mighty deeds. While the methods are drastic and the conclusions are extreme, there is merit in the view that cultic celebration was central to Israelite faith and life, that the observance and reenactment of the sacral event made each participant also a sharer in the original experience. Unlike other religions, the central events in Israelite ritual were historical, therefore unique and unrepeatable. The tradition therefore could not be created by the cult, but rather was influenced and shaped by aspects of it. Because of the historical nature of the religion, the cult was dependent upon the tradition and not the other way around. We would deny that the celebration of the Passover was the only historical event; on the contrary, the event itself and the memory of it, however adapted and altered in transmission, was the factual basis on which celebration and observance were built. They were a reenactment, not merely of previous celebrations, but of the event.

a. The Oldest Materials in Exodus

A great deal of attention has been paid over the last 100 years to the historical background of the three or four collections of laws in Exodus. On the basis of this research, W. F. Albright concluded that the Decalogue (Exod 20:2–17), containing the oldest laws in the Pentateuch, parts of the Book of the Covenant (20:23–23:33), and possibly Exodus 24 can be traced back to the 12th–11th centuries B.C. Probably the earliest piece of writing in the book, however, is the Song of Miriam (15:1–21) whose 12th century date has been established by the linguistic studies of Albright and his students. While the law codes reflect social conditions and legal traditions of the days of the tribal confederation (Judges, Samuel), the Song of Miriam probably does not postdate the events it describes by very much and, along with Judges 5, is the oldest Israelite poetry in the Bible.

b. The Character of Civic and Cultic Legislation of the Pentateuch

In his classic form-critical studies of the legislation of the Pentateuch, A. Alt distinguished between case law which was typical of all communities in the Near East and "apodictic" law which he regarded as unique to Israel. This type of law has the familiar form of the short imperative injunctions of the Ten Commandments, which are found in slightly altered form in Deut 5:6–21. Other laws couched in similar form may be found in Exod 22:18, 23:19, Deut 14:21, and elsewhere. This form is rare in the ancient Near East, although there is a comparable pattern in the treaties between

47

the Hittite emperors and vassal kings in the second half of the second millennium B.C.: "You shall keep the land which I give you, and shall not covet any territory of the land of the Hatti." This is also true of Assyrian vassal treaties of the first millennium (which are very different in other respects), which indicates a common pattern of thought about the relationship between the suzerain and his vassals. The Israelites adapted the pattern from the diplomatic to the religious sphere, as they regarded the covenant as a treaty between Yahweh, the god-king, and Israel his vassal people, in which protection by the suzerain and obedience by the vassal are principal ingredients.

The group of "casuistic" (case) laws in the Bible reflects the principles of justice in ancient Israel. They begin with a conditional sentence which introduces a hypothetical case and then prescribe a certain action to settle the case. They served an exemplary purpose and offered guidelines for those who were entrusted with responsibility and authority in such matters. This is the common form of legislation in the Near East, dating back to the third millennium, and is well illustrated in Hammurabi's Law Code. Ancient law codes were not like their modern counterparts, which are deliberately set up as comprehensive codes in the form of statutory law, but rather were compilations of typical or representative cases intended to edify the faithful, admonish the faithless, and provide counsel for the local judiciary.

Mid-section of the stele of Hammurabi inscribed with his Law Code (282 laws). Discovered at Susa, 18th c. B.C. Some of its laws bear similarities with the codes of the Pentateuch

B. HISTORICAL BACKGROUNDS IN THE BOOKS OF LEVITICUS, NUMBERS, AND DEUTERONOMY

We have dealt thus far with the Patriarchs, the Bondage, the Exodus, and their historical backgrounds in so far as they are illuminated by extra-biblical sources. As the reader is aware, little can be said of Moses in this sense. Though he was no less historical than Rameses II, archaeology is silent in the case of Moses for he left no material witness behind. We must say the same of much of the rest of the other three books of the Pentateuch, in so far is they relate civil and cultic legislation and only sporadically contain historical narrative.

The reader of the Pentateuch must be constantly aware that the narratives and formulations of laws and customs of pre-monarchial times, as we have them, were modernized in succeeding periods. This is particularly the case for the period of the United Monarchy, when the royal courts and priestly schools in the Temple promoted the writing of historical annals and the formulation of legal and religious data. They probably revised some details of older traditions, in part to make them relevant to their audience, and added other pertinent details which reflected the thinking of their own times. Contrary to the assumption of older biblical scholarship, however, the use of a tradition by a later writer does not make the tradition itself late or inaccurate. Current research tends to show that the writers belonging to the priestly circles (see Introduction, 2) were both conscientious and careful in transmitting older tradition, and, given the limitations of the era, were reasonably accurate.

1. BIBLICAL AND CANAANITE EPICS

Biblical scholars have been rewarded greatly in their search for material from early Israel by the studies of the form and language of early Hebrew poetry. These studies have been enormously advanced by the discoveries at Ras Shamra, ancient Ugarit, in northern Syria. Among the few thousand tablets found there, there are several Canaanite mythological epics and shorter hymns in a dialect very close to biblical Hebrew; they all date to the latter half of the second millennium (14th–13th centuries B.C.). This poetry shows that early Hebrew poets shared poetic style and diction with their Canaanite predecessors (see Part XII: Psalms). Because these tablets can be dated archaeologically to the period immediately preceding the biblical period, they have aided in dating and understanding the early Hebrew poetry. By careful study of linguistic and poetic features, W. F. Albright concluded that the Song of the Sea in Exodus 15 was the earliest preserved Hebrew poem of any length, and that the Song of Deborah (Judges 5) is only slightly later from a stylistic point of view. The similarities with Canaanite poetry may be seen, for example, in Exod 15:17, which reads: "Thou wilt bring them in and plant them on the mount that is your possession, the place, O Lord, which thou hast made for thy abode." In the Baal epic from Ugarit, 49 we find: "in the midst of my mount..., in the holy place, in the mount of my inheritance" referring to Mount Safon, Baal's holy mountain, which has been identified as Mount Casius in Lebanon. There are many other close resemblances in vocabulary and style between Canaanite and Hebrew poems, though there are also marked differences, especially in terms of religious outlook and sense of history. Other old poetry in the Pentateuch includes Genesis 49 (see above) and its companion Deuteronomy 33 and the Oracles of Balaam, consisting of the poetic passages in Numbers 23 and 24.

2. DATING THE PENTATEUCHAL LEGISLATION

In the Pentateuch we have a considerable body of legislation, carefully collected and arranged in later centuries. These laws and regulations are often recorded in more than one form, showing that there has been a long and complex history of transmission from the original. They have been preserved in documents of different ages, which in turn have been edited and revised in the process of consolidation. Ultimately the communal and institutional background of Israelite law is to be found in the twelve tribe system of the period of Judges. In the eyes of the Israelites, law is based on and rooted in the covenant. Case law (see Exodus) reflects the impact of the covenant on the life of Israelite society, which was powerfully influenced by the basic set of obligations to God spelled out in the covenant.

The Letters of Ugarit, a dynamic north Canaanite kingdom in Syria, had developed an important literature consisting of epic songs praising the deeds of gods and heroes. There is much in common, as we shall see, both in language (akin to Hebrew) and in content, between these epics and biblical literature (see Psalms; Job)

C. LEVITICUS

Leviticus has the least amount of narrative of any of the books of the Pentateuch. It is limited to Aaron's priesthood (chs. 8–9), the punishment of Nadab and Abihu (10:1–7), the ritual error of Eleazar and Ithamar (10:16–20), and the stoning of a blasphemer (24:10–14, 23). The rest of the book deals predominantly with cultic matters, especially the Levitical priesthood, from which it derives its name. It is part of the Priestly corpus, which stretches from Exodus 25 to Numbers 10. Leviticus may be divided as follows:

Woman bathing. Clay figurine

1:1–7:38	Laws of sacrifice; burnt offerings, cereal offering, peace offering, sin offering, and supplementary material.
8:1–10:20	The consecration of the priests. This section follows Exodus 40, the completion of the sanctuary.
11:1–15:33	The laws of purification
16:1–34	The Day of Atonement
17:1–26:46	The Holiness Code
27:1–34	Instruction concerning oaths and tithes

Left:
Bath (Lev 15:12 on purifying earthen vessels)

Below:
Pan used for frying. Found at Lachish (Lev 6:14 on the laws of the cereal offering before the altar)

1. RITUAL PURITY (LEVITICUS 11–15)

The ideas underlying this section go back to pre-Mosaic times. An unclean object was not simply dangerous in itself, but because it was repulsive to or prohibited by God, it endangered his continuing protection of the group which did not exclude the unclean. It was an important task of the priesthood "to distinguish between the holy and the common, and between the unclean and clear" (Lev 10:10). Behind these laws of cleanness stands early hygienic experience, coupled with broad and somewhat naive generalizations, ancient superstitions, simple prejudice, and deliberate avoidance of religious practices of the Canaanites which were abhorrent to Israelite religion. Uncleanness was both a physical, i.e. ritual, and a moral attribute, and in both senses it was considered contagious.

The abominable rite of child sacrifice to the Phoenician god Molekh is illustrated in this stela from Carthage, describing a priest holding a child

a. *The Laws of the Holiness Code* (*Leviticus* 17–26)

These laws pertain to the life of the community as well as to public worship and the festal year. The code gets its name from the injunction in 19:1: "You shall be holy, because I, the Lord your God, am holy," which is repeated several times in this section.

b. *Idols*

One of the basic biblical ordinances prohibits the manufacture and worship of idols (cf. the Decalogue: Exod 20:3–5; Deut 5:8–10). A different form of the injunction appears in Lev 19:4: "Do not turn to idols or make for yourselves molten gods." This reference doubtless includes images of all kinds, not only the large statues located in pagan sanctuaries, but also the numerous figurines, whether metal or clay, which were pressed from a single mold, leaving the back as a flat background. These plaques, with representations of the chief Cannanite goddesses, including Asherah, Astarte, and Anat, were associated with the fertility cult. Among the thousands of figurines, as well as molds, found in excavations in the Holy land, a characteristic type features a goddess with her hands resting against her sides. She is depicted with full breasts in the stance of the nursing mother goddess (*dea nutrix*). Plaques in the form of a woman in labor, her hands clasped over her abdomen, may have been intended as an inducement to fertility or as a charm to ease labor pains. These anthropomorphic figures may be likened to the *teraphim* (household deities) in the story of Rachel (Gen 31:34). There were small male idols as well, though they are comparatively rare in excavations.

The vast quantity and ubiquity of these figurines illustrate the persistence and success of pagan forms of worship in Israel. For the bulk of the people, some form of syncretism, combining faith in Yahweh, the God of Mosaic tradition, with an acknowledgment of the fertility figures, seems to have been prevalent through the centuries of the First Temple. The vehemence of the attack on such practices reflects how widespread they were and how difficult it proved to be to eradicate such blatant violations of the covenant code.

c. *The Sacrifice of Children*

The practice of human sacrifice has been demonstrated in the excavations of the Phoenician colony at Carthage and attributed to both the Carthaginians and the Phoenicians by numerous classical authors. The abolition of this barbarous sacrifie (Lev 18:21) took place as a result of the reform of King Josiah (637–609 B.C.; cf. 2 Kings 23:10). The ban refers to the sacrifice of children to the Phoenician god Molekh, observed in the days of King Manasseh (698–642 B.C.) in the Valley of Hinnom on the southern edge of Jerusalem. The place was named Tophet or the "place of burning."

2. ARCHAEOLOGY AND THE LEVITICAL CITIES

The rule laid down in Lev 25:32–34 (cf. Num 35:1–8) that 48 Levitical cities be established throughout the conquered land, has raised serious problems as to when they existed and what their function was. It is agreed upon by scholars that these priestly passages are of later date, but that these problems could be solved only through a study of the excavations in the various towns listed as Levitical cities. A parallel list of the 48 cities appears in Joshua 21 and 1 Chronicles 6. Gezer, for example, was a Canaanite center which was annexed only in the time of Solomon. Other Levitical cities such as Gibbethon, Elteke, and Gath-rimmon were also annexed at that time. Others had been destroyed by Pharaoh Shishak or by Aramean invaders after Solomon's time and were repopulated some centuries later. The excavations at Beth-shemesh and Tell Beit Mirsim (Debir) show them to have been walled cities with typical casemate wall construction, containing royal stores and serving as administrative centers; e.g., strata IIa and B3 at Tell Beit Mirsim.

B. Mazar concludes, therefore, that the establishment of this network of cities, which served the state by fulfilling secular, cultural, and administrative responsibilities, dates primarily to the time of Kings David and Solomon. The appropriation of state lands for the establishment of such centers goes back to the days of Egyptian rule in Canaan, when the pharaohs appropriated land and devoted it to their gods. Papyrus Harris (first half of the 12th century B.C., in the days of Rameses III) mentions estates of the god Amun which include fortified Canaanite towns, containing stores for goods which the people paid in taxes. Each city had a temple and a team of priests who were in charge of both the religious ritual and secular administration.

Female figurines in "Dea Nutrix" attitudes were common household possessions among Canaanites and Hebrews who mingled for centuries before the former were assimilated

Left:
General view of the Canaanite sanctuary of Beth-Shemesh.

Right:
A storehouse north of the settlement with utensils *in situ*

D. NUMBERS.

The miscellaneous material that makes up the book is presented within the general framework of a record of the wanderings in the wilderness, beginning in the spring of the second year after the Exodus and ending in the events that followed the death of Aaron, the priest and brother of Moses, in the 40th year after the Exodus (Num 33:38). The concluding passages contain edicts issued to Israelites in the Plains of Moab east of the Jordan.

Geographically and chronologically, the book's material falls into five main sections:

Numbers 1:1–10:10	This section purports to deal with the departure from Sinai but actually contains supplements and appendices to the Priestly Code in Leviticus. At the heart of it is the census list (chs. 1–4). A second list appears in ch. 26.
Numbers 10:11–21:35	The wanderings in the wilderness from Mount Sinai to Kadesh-Barnea, a period of about 40 years.
Numbers 22:1–24:25	Balaam blesses Israel.
Numbers 25:1–33:49	The encampments and journeys in the wilderness and the Plains of Moab, including the recurrent themes of the danger and rejection of idolatry (see: The Conquest of Transjordan).
Numbers 33:50–36:13	Miscellaneous laws; Levitical cities and female inheritance.

To be properly appreciated, the book's bewildering contents must be read for what they are, a miscellany of itineraries, lists, laws, and traditions which later editors preserved as part of the heritage of a past too distant to be distinct, but too vital to be forgotten. As we shall see, much of this material retains valuable information concerning the "setting in life" of certain historical events culminating in the conquest of Transjordan.

Netting quail on the northern shore of Sinai; after their flight over the sea, the birds fall exhausted into the nets

1. THE ASCETIC NAZIRITES

The law in Num 6:1–19 codifies a very ancient custom and adapts it to the Levitical (late priestly) ritual. To signify his special status as one dedicated to the service of God from birth, the Nazirite is separated from the world and its ways, adopts the ascetic vows of abstaining from all intoxicating drinks and leaving his hair unshaven. Nazirite vows could also be taken for briefer periods and specific occasions. There are historical reminiscences of actual Nazirites in the stories of Samson (Judges 13–16) and Samuel (1 Samuel 1).

Recent excavations conducted on Mount Scopus have uncovered an ornate tomb of a Nazirite dating to the last century B.C., or the first century A.D. This discovery shows that, by the end of the Old Testament period, a Nazirite was not necessarily a poor man who renounced worldly possessions. Nevertheless the tradition of pious poverty is preserved in early Christian writings; for example, James, brother of Jesus, was a pious Nazirite. The term must not be confused with "Nazarean," Hebrew *notsri*, meaning a citizen of Nazareth, and also the Hebrew term for "Christian."

2. THE RED HEIFER

One of the most difficult references in the Priestly source is the ritual of the ashes of the Red Heifer (Num 19:2–10) which are used to prepare 'the water of impurity, for the removal of sin" (v. 9). The rite originally was pagan and involved magical elements in putting evil spirits to flight: e.g., the use of red as a protective color, and the sevenfold sprinkling of blood with its vital powers.

This ritual maintained its importance in the days of the Second Temple and is often mentioned in the Mishna and Talmud in connection with the ritual on the eve of the Day of Atonement, when the red heifer was taken out of the Temple courts and slain on the Mount of Olives, then burned with cedarwood, hyssop and scarlet stuff. B. Mazar, in his excavations near the Temple Mount, investigated the whereabouts of the special path which led from the high Temple courts to the steep valley of Kidron and then up to the Mount of Olives. He noted, however, "that the purification rite of the Red Heifer was performed only five times throughout the whole period of the Second Temple, though the reason for their rarity is unknown. It is not likely that a permanent pathway had been constructed for these occasional rites; a temporary pathway was doubtless prepared for each occasion, and in the nature of the case, no evidence of it has survived" (B. Mazar, *The Mountain of the Lord*, p. 151).

3. ISRAEL AND MIDIAN

The Midianites, who later became enemies of Israel, played a vital role in Israel's earliest history. According to the tradition Yahweh first revealed himself to Moses in the land of Midian (Exodus 3), Moses was married to a Midianite woman (Exod 2:21–22), and Israel's legal system was initiated with the help of Jethro, the Midianite priest (Exod 18:13–27). According to Num 10:29–32, Moses requested the guidance of Hobab to lead Israel through the wilderness. This tradition had the ring of authenticity, for the Israelites were state slaves in Egypt, not seasoned veterans established in their own land like the Midianites. The latter were also involved in the earliest traditions of the priesthood and ritual known to Israel and were intermarried with clansmen of Judah and Simeon from the days of wandering onward. W. F. Albright has pointed out that the Midianites and the Kenites, who stemmed from Midian, and the ancestors of the Israelites belonged to the

Crushing enclosure for copper ore at ancient Timnah mining camp

Crushing and ore-grinding tools, Timnah

same or related groups. B. Mazar believes that the Midianites had established a sanctuary at Arad at the time the Israelites were settling in Canaan and that it was maintained later by the Israelites, reflecting a close relationship between the two groups. This is where the tenth century Judean sanctuary and altar were discovered (see III: An Early Israelite Sanctuary at Arad; cf. II. Exodus: A Midianite Sanctuary at Timnah). A writhing serpent made of copper, five inches long, was found among hundreds of votive objects which had been brought to the Timnah sanctuary. This serpent is reminiscent of the account of a plague of poisonous snakes in Num 21:9. The ancient narrative would seem to imply that the copper snake which Moses erected on a pole had curative and cultic power, similar to that found in neighboring cultures.

4. WHERE DID THE MIDIANITES COME FROM?

Midianite decorated pottery, such as that discovered in the metallurgical district of Timnah, had previously been found in smelting camps of the western Arabah valley and on the island of Fara'un (or Coral Island) in the northern part of the Red Sea, as well as in sites of the eastern Arabah and Edom, which N. Glueck dated to the 13th–12th centuries and called 'Edomite' ware. There is good archaeological evidence for its origin in north-western Arabia, in the area traditionally known as Midian and some 100 miles south of Elath-Aqaba. A survey of Midian (1970) describes the site of a kiln at Quarrayah where the Midianite wheel-made decorated pottery had been produced, according to P. Parr. The Timnah pottery which originated in Midian provides the first absolute dates for the ancient Late Bronze sedentary and semi-sedentary sites of Midian, the seat of a Midianite civilization which expanded further north and which inseminated early Israel. (See Exodus: A, 10; A Midianite Sanctuary at Timnah.)

5. THE SONG OF THE WELL

An interesting fragment from a poem, probably Moabite, appears in Num 21:17–18, though it is attributed to Israel:

Spring up, O well — Sing to it ! —
Well which the princes dug,
which the leaders of the people hollowed out,
with their staff and their sticks.

This song, although we have only the opening lines, is among the oldest poetry in the Hebrew Bible, along with the Oracles of Balaam in chs. 23–24. Its setting and meaning are clarified by an understanding of the nature of the soil in the wilderness. In low-lying areas of Transjordan and in the valleys of the Negeb, one comes suddenly upon damp land in very dry surroundings, at times marked by clumps of vegetation. Such a place is known to the Arabs as a *temileh*. The earth can be dug easily and water is found at a shallow depth. This is the kind of well dug by the ancients "with their sticks."

Ceramic receptacle found in the Deir 'Allah sanctuary inscribed with name of the Egyptian queen Tausert (1205–1194 B.C.)

6. THE BALAAM STORY

The narratives concerning Balaam (Numbers 22–24) contain four poems (23:7–10, 18–24; 24:3–9, 15–24) which were the basis of one of W. A. Albright's pioneering studies in early Hebrew poetry. Balaam was a seer from Pethor, south of Carchemish near the Euphrates, who was invited by the king of Moab to cast a curse on Israel, but found that he was able only to bless it. Albright explains the historical background as follows: The people of Moab and Midian invited the famous diviner to curse Israel, but he declined their offer and advised the Moabites and Midianites instead to make a covenant with Israel. They agreed to make the pact which embodied matters relating to intermarriage and to syncretic religious observances which both the Israelites and their pagan neighbors could observe in amity. But some unyielding Israelites refused to compromise, regarding it is a prostitution of the sacred traditions and as blatant paganism; the plan miscarried and refused in hostility between Israel and Midian.

7. THE DEIR 'ALLAH INSCRIPTIONS

J. Hoftijzer reports (1975) an astounding discovery of a dozen or so inscribed plaster panels which fell off the walls of a ruined Late Bronze temple at Deir 'Allah (biblical Succoth) near the Jordan river, in central Transjordan. Two or three of these short inscriptions, written in so-called

One of the clay panels of Deir 'Allah sanctuary inscribed in an obscure script (end of 13th, or early 12th c. B.C.)

cursive Aramaic script in black and red ink, and couched in poetic style, purport — according to this Dutch scholar — to give an independent narrative of the prophecies of Balaam, his visions and experiences. The panels themselves date to the 8th–7th century B.C. and the temple was destroyed by earthquake and fire. Hoftijzer believes that the figure of Balaam, named *seer of the gods* in the panels, enjoyed for a considerable time a prominent position in some specific religious tradition in Transjordan. Moreover, this is the first instance of a non-biblical prophecy, inscribed in plaster, located in Transjordan. It will be noted that Balaam in the biblical text, clearly belongs to an ancient tradition from Transjordan and that the inscriptions discovered, in which he is presumed to play a central role, came from a Transjordanian sacred site. The biblical tradition relates that this non-Israelite prophet had been summoned to the locality by the king of Moab. The panels are currently being deciphered and analyzed by Israeli scholars. Much more is to be learned from this discovery, and further elucidation may be expected as a result.

8. THE LAND OF SHUTU AND ARCHAEOLOGY

There is reference in the fourth oracle (24:17) to the "sons of Sheth," who appear in poetic parallelism with Moab; these apparently are the tribe of *Shutu,* known from Egyptian sources, which list three of its rulers. It is probable, according to Y. Aharoni and B. Mazar, that the land of Shutu is the ancient name for Gilead and the land of the Cushites, who appear along with Midian in Hab 3:7. Evidently these passages preserve the names of the ancient population in these regions. Evidence from archaeology indicates

58

that Gilead, southern Transjordan and the Negeb did not have extensive settled populations in the later centuries of the Middle Bronze and Late Bronze Ages. This area must have been also the homeland of nomadic tribes, such as *Sheth* (Shutu) and *Cush*, who have left few traces easily identifiable after 3000 years (cf. XI: Habakkuk).

The picture of a caravan of Semites arriving in Egypt, perhaps via the King's Highway, is preserved in a wall painting from the early 19th century B.C. Egyptian tomb painting at Beni-Hasan. It depicts 37 'Ammu Asiatics from the land of Shutu (apparently Gilead in Transjordan) who are delivering black eye paint to Egypt. Their leader is named Ibsha and he bears the Egyptian title "ruler of a foreign country."

But archaeology reveals, on the other hand, that somewhat later Egyptian sources from the days of Rameses II (early 13th century) describe strenuous campaigns which he led in the lands of the *Shosu* (Sheth) including Mount Seir (later Edom) and the destruction of many settlements. A contemporary Egyptian inscription from Luqsor relates the capture of several walled cities, including Boterāt along the King's Highway in southern Moab.

The stele of Balua is a remnant of sedentary occupation in Moab in the 13th c. B.C.

9. THE STELE OF BALU'A

The stele featuring three figures, discovered south of the Arnon river along the ancient highway, is another Moabite remnant of sedentary occupation dating from the 13th century. Its mysterious inscription has not yet been deciphered, but that is also the case of other Transjordan inscriptions before the Canaanite-Hebrew alphabet prevailed. Finally, a temple of the late Canaanite period (13th century) discovered by J. B. Hennessy at *Amman*, provides the first evidence of an amplitude of pottery, local and imported, of that period, in the highlands crossed by the King's Highway. The existence of fortified cities there does not argue for the absence of sedentary settlements during the period, but neither does it provide definite evidence of the establishment of the kingdoms of Moab, Ammon or Edom as early as the thirteenth century B.C. The biblical tradition seems to imply this as will become evident below.

Israelites, under the leadership of first Moses, and then Joshua, effected the Conquest in stages and by various routes as suggested by different biblical traditions, namely Numbers 13; 14:44–45; 20:14ff.; 21:4–27; 33; 34:1–12. The time span, however, was not limited to a single generation, or just over 40 years, as required by the biblical chronology. At different

From their base at Kadesh Barnea, the Israelites invaded Transjordan by two different routes: First, in the late 14th or early 13th century B.C., by the Way of the Arabah and King's Highway, through territories later occupied by the kingdom of Edom, Moab and Ammon. A second invasion in the 13th century followed the roundabout route which controlled the Negeb via Elath and finally ended in eastern Transjordan. A former attempt to reach Canaan directly had failed. The land of Canaan was invaded later by groups of Israelite tribes. The final stage is described in the map below.

times, Israelites marched out of the oasis of Kadesh-Barnea on the northern border of Sinai; but the course of conquest was far more complex than is indicated in the summary statements. It lasted from the fourteenth to the middle of the twelfth century B.C., as becomes evident from recent research.

Two Routes from Kadesh-Barnea to the Jordan

A plausible reconstruction of the sequence of events follows:

a. Two traditions in Numbers preserve memories of journeys eastward and attempts to penetrate the less populated areas of Transjordan. One from chapter 33 lists a series of stations and settlements on the "Way of the Arabah" and the King's Highway, from Kadesh-Barnea to the "plains of Moab." They crossed the areas of Edom and Moab and faced the Jordan on the east before these kingdoms, not to speak of the Ammonites, were organized by peoples culturally and linguistically related to the Israelites, and before they could offer any opposition. This movement may have occurred in the late 14th or early 13th century B.C. when the Israelites settled down in their camp at Abel-Shittim in the plains of Moab, after fighting the Midianites. In any case, the southern and sparsely populated portions of Transjordan which were outside Egypt's sphere of control served as the first objective for entry and conquest. Numbers 33:37–49 reflects the earliest traditions of various tribes which invaded Transjordan. (See map.)

b. The second invasion (Numbers 20:14ff.; Judges 11:17–18) occurred in mid-thirteenth century. When the Israelites encountered the opposition of the kings of Edom and Moab, who did not let them proceed along the King's Highway, they went up by way of a roundabout desert route (Numbers 21:4), which led south to Elath, then wound around the whole Negeb and continued through the wilderness east of Transjordan. The journey came to a halt away from the Jordan, between the kingdom of

Canaan remained within Egypt's sphere of control in the 14th century as evidenced by Sethos I's punitive campaigns described in the reliefs from Karnak. In the upper register the king is walking behind his chariot, carries prisoners under his arms and leads rows of bound captives from Canaan. The lower register shows him returning to Egypt with captive *Shosu* nomads while he is met by officials at the border fortress of Sileh

A limestone figure of a king of Moab, or deity found in Amman; Probably 10–9th c. B.C.

The seal of Adoni Nur the Ammonite

Moab and the new Ammonite state. There they were confronted by the forces of Sihon, the Amorite (Canaanite) king of Heshbon (21:21ff.), one of the few cities in Transjordan, and had to fight to make their way to the Jordan River. Sihon had extended his territory as far south as the Plains of Moab before the arrival of the Israelites, but the latter were victorious, and settled in the fertile areas of Gilead prior to their invasion of Canaan west of the Jordan. The tribe of Gad came in the first wave of Israelites, as attested in the Moabite Stone, a royal inscription of a later king of Moab, Mesha (ca. 850 B.C.): "The men of Gad had always dwelt in the land of Ataroth" as far as the river Jabbok. Another participant in the early invasion was Asher, full brother of Gad in the genealogies of Genesis. The biblical tradition goes on to relate the conquest of the land of Og, king of Bashan and his sixty fortified cities (Deuteronomy 3:5). The Amarna tablets (see Genesis, B, 5) refer to the presence of the 'Apiru in this area; while the equation of 'Apiru with Hebrew is not universally accepted, there may be some connection between the biblical traditions and the Amarna records concerning the earlier penetration of the 'Apiru into the territory. The different routes mentioned in the biblical stories and the archaeological evidence support the view that the Israelite Conquest was not carried out at one time, but over a period of time in several waves. These were later blended into the single narrative now preserved in the Bible.

The establishment of well-organized kingdoms in Edom and Moab during the thirteenth century and in Ammon somewhat later is abundantly attested by archaeology. The excavations in the copper mining settlements in the southern Arabah (north of Elath) show a peak of activity between the thirteenth and twelfth centuries B.C.; the high level of material culture they had reached by then is exemplified by a special type of decorated "Edomite" pottery. This illuminates the biblical traditions of the "border of Edom" in Numbers 20:14ff. and Deuteronomy 2:4ff. It also serves to explain Solomon's great interest in the area three centuries later, and his continuing efforts to exploit the possibilities of the Negeb and the Arabah and stimulate trade with other wealthy population centers of the Arabian peninsula such as Sheba.

The Battle of Arad

c. An attempt to invade directly into the hill country of Judah from Kadesh-Barnea was made early in the thirteenth century B.C. but it failed to penetrate the chain of fortified Canaanite cities in the Negeb. The Israelites were driven back by the king of Arad at nearby Hormah (Tell el-Meshash). Excavations at both of these towns have yielded no evidence of Israelite occupation for the next century and a half.

11. STAGES OF THE CONQUEST

We have come to realize from the assessments of the previous chapters that the traditional biblical picture of the wanderings of the pastoral patriarchal clan in Canaan, followed by centuries of bondage in Egypt, does not gibe with the irrefutable historical and archaeological data of the Middle and Late Bronze Ages in Canaan or Egypt. Moreover, no extra-biblical references mention the existence of the Israelites in Egypt, Sinai or Canaan if we except the references to 'Apiru (Ḥabiru) who are not considered the biblical ancestors of the Hebrews in the 15th or 14th centuries. But the Israelites were moving into Transjordan and Canaan and settling there since the early 13th century B.C., as indicated in Numbers, then in the books of Joshua-Judges, but in different stages and at different times, unlike the consolidated biblical accounts. Moreover, the persistent and dynamic settlement of Israelites in Israel in the 13th and 12th centuries was no isolated phenomenon. It followed considerable 'Apiru agitation against the Egyptian and Canaanite feudal kings, and it is related to a great wave of Aramean tribes exerting pressure on all the lands, from settlements in western Mesopotamia and northern Syria, and expanding into these areas to the Jordan. The Edomites, Moabites and Ammonites settled east of the Jordan in about the same period. The Israelite tribal migrations were activated by these broad moves, by the weakening of Egyptian power both in Goshen and Canaan, and finally by the concurrent invasion of the Sea Peoples (Philistines) into the coastland and western lowlands of Canaan (see below: Part III). All of this hastened the process of settlement and occupation. In any case, the process was not the concerted plan of the whole federation of tribes under one chief, Joshua, but the achievement of isolated tribes or groups of Israelite tribes throughout a long period of time, as may be gathered in Judges (Part III).

E. DEUTERONOMY

The book of Deuteronomy, as we have it, is almost entirely from the hand of the Deuteronomist, the D source (see Introduction: The Documentary Hypothesis), whose editing is dated apparently to the end of the monarchial period. Much of the material which the Deuteronomist incorporated, however, derives from Exodus and the older traditions which reflect the premonarchial period. What distinguishes this book from the rest of the Pentateuch is not so much its content but rather its style. Unlike the Covenant Code where laws are succinctly stated in either "apodictic" or "casuistic" form (cf. Exodus: The Character of Civic and Cultic Legislation), in Deuteronomy these laws are expanded with sermons or exhortations. These sermons are composed in long, complex sentences, often containing parenthetical remarks.

The book may be divided into four sections, as follows:

Deuteronomy 1:1–11:32	Introductory speeches which review the wanderings in the desert, the conquest of Transjordan, the meaning of the Law, and then a preview of the Conquest of the country west of the Jordan. These discourses underscore the fundamental principles upon which the Law and the Covenant are based and call on the people to remain faithful to Yahweh and his Law.
Deut 12:1–26:15	The Deuteronomic Code. This section lists some 70 laws pertaining to every aspect of the life of Israel in the promised land.
Deut 27:1–30:20	Closing speeches. At the heart of this section are blessings and curses; a blessing for those who are obedient to God and his Covenant, a curse upon those who were unfaithful.
Deut 31:1–34:12	The conclusion to the Pentateuch, including the appointment of Joshua, the "Song of Moses" (ch. 32), the "Blessing of Moses" (ch. 33). The last chapter relates the death of Moses.

1. THE DEUTERONOMIC CODE

It has long been recognized that almost half of the laws of the Covenant Code (Exodus 21–23) reappear in Deuteronomy though in modified form. It has been suggested that the new code of a later date was intended to replace the older laws, taking into account the social, political, and religious development which had taken place between the early centuries of settlement and the seventh century B.C. However this hypothesis does not establish an adequate principle of selectivity which governed the Deuteronomist's treatment of the older source. No explanation is given as to why the greater part of the covenant code was not incorporated into the book of Deuteronomy. It is possible that the Deuteronomist regarded those provisions as obsolete or no longer pertinent to existing conditions. Lacking this material, the Deuteronomic Code would have been an inadequate substitute for the earlier legislation. It is probably better to see both as being rooted in the same ancient traditions.

M. Weinfeld, a leading authority on Deuteronomy, points out that its fundamental distinction is not so much in the legislation it embodies, but in its characteristic homiletic style. One of the points of departure from the earlier legislation is the Deuteronomist's passion for social justice. This is particularly clear in its emphasis on the release of debtors and slaves. This quality is commonly attributed to the influence of the prophets. M. Weinfeld and S. Sandmel have found another source of this humanism in the "wisdom" circles which produced Proverbs and Job (see Part XIII). Thus the Deuteronomist's work blends law, wisdom, and prophetic concern.

2. THE ALTAR OF SACRIFICE AND THE BAMAH

One of the most important innovations in Deuteronomy is the centralization of sacrifice ordained in the opening chapter of the Deuteronomic Code (Deuteronomy 12). This law reflects the religious reforms of King Josiah (see Kings), which sought to neutralize the influence Canaanite religion had upon the people. The requirement runs counter to earlier Israelite practice, as the author recognized (v. 8), and is clearly established by archaeology.

Altars were the focal point of both high places, bāmoth, and temples. The bāmāh was essentially a Canaanite site of worship, but was acceptable also in earlier Israelite religion. They were usually open areas, with sacred trees and stone pillars, massebôth, associated with the altar, as well as buildings for the use of priests and the storage of garments and other equipment. These high places were often linked with sites of importance from the patriarchal period. The altars recently excavated at Arad and Beersheba in the Southern Kingdom probably belong to this category. Altars also were erected in conjunction with royal sanctuaries, such as those of Jeroboam of Northern Israel at Dan and Bethel.

The simplest altars were made of heaped earth or stones; a large, flat rock, often with natural or carved depressions at the top, could serve as an altar. These stones were not to be hewn, as the use of iron could defile the stone. More elaborate altars, despite the prohibition of steps in Exod 20:26 (cf. Lev 6:10), were built in tiers, though most were simply large cubes, such as the bronze altar of Solomon's Temple (I Chr 4:1), which measured 20 cubits long, 20 cubits wide, and 10 cubits high. Other altars were made of hewn stone and provided with horns, as is the case with the numerous smaller incense altars which have turned up in excavations and chiefly the large altar discovered at Beersheba (cf. VI, Amos: The Altar and Sanctuary of Beersheba).

3. MAGIC AND WITCHCRAFT

Suggestive "Abomination" theme of Canaanite witchcraft (see Deut 7:26)

Although magic and witchcraft were practiced throughout the ancient world, in Israel they were forbidden by a law attributed to Moses (Deut 18:10–14). While archaeological traces of the practice of witchcraft have been found in abundance in excavations in other Near Eastern countries, there is also evidence of certain superstitious practices which prevailed among the Israelites. This included vessels impressed with snakes, fertility figurines to help in pregnancy or childbirth, and amulets and charms worn by women and children. The use of amulets was widespread and apparently persistent, although they were condemned by kings, lawmakers, priests, and prophets, as they involved trust in gods other than Yahweh. An amulet against night demons has been unearthed, dating to the period of the monarchy. Archaeology has also uncovered other Canaanite fertility symbols which were used in Israel. Several Hathor-Ashtoreth figurines came from Israelite Gezer and nearly 200 of these objects were found in eighth century levels at Samaria. Indeed, almost every major excavation in Israel has produced numerous hand-size plaques, depicting the nude fertility goddess, dating from the Bronze and Iron Ages as late as the sixth century B.C.

One of the items in the list of women's finery in Isa 3:18–23 is an amulet or humming shell (*lāḥāš*) which may have been connected with snake-charming. Snake-deities are known to have been widely worshiped by the Canaanites and many vessels engraved or impressed with snakes have been discovered in excavations of levels dating to the Canaanite and Israelite periods. Bronze serpents were found in the Canaanite levels at Hazor, Megiddo, Gezer, and Shechem, and serpent-symbols have turned up in significant numbers in the Iron Age levels at Gezer, Beth-shean, Megiddo, and Tell en-Nasbeh. We have referred above to the tradition of Num 21:9 about Moses and the bronze serpent.

A "pazuzu" demon common to Mesopotamian witchcraft

PART III

A. THE BOOKS OF JOSHUA — JUDGES

The book of Deuetronomy ends with the death of Moses, and the scribes and theologians responsible for the final ordering of the Hebrew Bible felt that this distinctive event marked the end of an era. They thus ended the Torah at that point. Working from the evidence of composition, we can safely say that this judgment was not a literary or historical one. Joshua, the sixth book of the Bible, is inseparable from the Pentateuch in outlook. On the one hand, its story line is directly connected to that of Numbers, chiefly ch. 33 which describes the first stage of the conquest of Transjordan (see II; Conquest of Transjordan), while, on the other, its world view is one with Deuteronomy's (cf. Deut 29:8 and Josh 1:8). More generally, the Pentateuch points forward to the promised possession of Canaan and Joshua's book depicts the fulfilment of the promise. The editors of Joshua were motivated by the idea expressed repeatedly in Deuteronomy: God's presence in history is a palpable one.

As we shall often have occasion to remark, the historical matter in the Bible is not offered as a straightforward, mechanical record of the facts, but rather as an interpretation of them. Difficulties with the story of the Conquest in Joshua do not arise because the Biblical tradition is obscurantist. Quite the contrary — they exist because the tradition was constantly seeking to understand and thus reinterpret itself. The narrative of Joshua may leave something to be desired as objective history-writing; nonetheless, it contains important factual data and its intrinsic value can hardly be questioned.

1. THE STORY OF THE BOOK OF JOSHUA

The book of Joshua is the epic story of its chief character's leadership of Israel. It begins with his divine call and ends with his death; the story of the conquest is thus tightly bound up with the fabric of Joshua's life.

According to tradition, Joshua crossed the river Jordan and captured the town of Jericho after the miraculous destruction of its walls (chs. 2–6). Recent excavations at Jericho have shown that the town was not occupied in Joshua's time. A close reading of the biblical text will reveal that the story itself is somewhat garbled. These two facts suggest at the outset that the Conquest as presented in Joshua is a literary reinterpretation of events the complexity of which later Israelites were unable to grasp fully. From Jericho, Joshua went on to capture Ai, thereby gaining a foothold in the central highlands (chs. 7–8). Joshua then, the text relates, moved into Judah (chs. 9–10) and Galilee (ch. 11), establishing Israelite enclaves throughout Canaan within the first generation after Moses, under his own leadership. Thus far chapters 6 through 12; in chapters 13 through 22, the conquered territory is divided among the Israelite tribes.

The book ends with the solemn convocations at Shechem where the Ark of the Covenant is established in the sanctuary, and with Joshua's farewell addresses (chs. 23–24).

2. AN UNCOMPLETED CONQUEST

Two significant sections in the book provide evidence which tend to correct, on the eve of Joshua's demise, the former picture of a sweeping conquest under him, covering the whole land from Dan to Beersheba. One is the first verse of chapter 13 specifying that "there remains yet very much land to be possessed. This is the land that yet remains..." either in Canaanite or Philistine possession. Furthermore, the opening chapter of Judges lumps together as a unit the various districts still unconquered by Joshua but which should be conquered and then divided among the tribes. In fact these territories are considered as already allotted piece by piece in Joshua 15–19. These contradictory statements cannot be regarded as deliberately falsified as they resulted from the ancient historiographer's outlook on the destiny of the promised land, nor should our remarks be regarded as an attempt to discuss the book of Joshua as fictitious. Many stages of the Conquest are described realistically: the details of battle strategy and execution reveal an intimate and detailed knowledge of the area and times. It may be deduced, therefore, that the Israelite historiographer handed to posterity a *consolidated* biblical tradition. This still preserved early information, but then in the course of time it was associated with other data, and finally consolidated into a new affirmation which constitutes the traditional view that colored the historiography of the Bible. This, and the discoveries of archaeology, added to epigraphic finds, obliges the historian to examine anew the biblical text and rethink its sequence, in order to disentangle the factual elements, i.e. to determine which statements and data are part of an earlier tradition and which are a later tradition. A classic example: The conquest of Hebron and Debir, originally by Caleb and Kenaz (Josh 15:15; Judg 1:12–15), was associated later with Judah (Judg 1:10–11), then finally with Joshua leading all Israel (Josh 10:36–39).

At this juncture, it must be pointed out, first, that the contents of Joshua must be read in conjunction with the book of Judges which corrects sweeping idealizations and consolidations of fact. Traditions centered around Joshua were recorded in the book after his name, while traditions relating to the tribes were gathered in the book of Judges. Secondly, the two books, considering them combined historical background material, are really illumined by archaeological data and ancient non-biblical epigraphic documents. What then was the sequence of events?

3. THE BOOK OF JUDGES

The first two chapters of the book of Judges list those territories conquered after Joshua's death as well as those which proved resistant to Israelite penetration. The bulk of the book (chapters 3 through 16) describes the exploits of local leaders who defended certain parts of the country against incursions of Israel's neighbors. The various wars described, except for the Song of Deborah (chs 4–5), are local affairs limited to particular geographical regions, usually associated with only one tribal territory. These traditions culminate in the great Samson cycle.

Major and Minor Judges: The framework of the book of Judges is later than its contents and seems to accord equal significance to all the judges. In fact, the actual traditions about the mighty deeds of the minor judges, Shamgar, Jair, Tola', Ibzan, Elon and Abdon have not been preserved; it is only stated that they judged the people at a certain locality or, alternately, their wealth receives emphasis (Judg 10:4; 12:9, 14). Even the major judges, Othniel, Ehud, Deborah, Gideon, Jephthah and Samson vary greatly in importance.

Canaanite chariot-riding knights *(marianu)* and foot soldiers. 13th c. ivory carving from Megiddo

Sea people invading Canaan by land

B. THE BIBLICAL TRADITION AND ACTUAL HISTORY OF THE CONQUEST IN THE THIRTEENTH CENTURY B.C.

The invasion of Canaan after the death of Moses, as related in the book of Joshua, began at Gilgal, the first Israelite camp and sanctuary west of the Jordan, and was followed by the capture of Jericho and Ai. Thereafter the book gives the picture of a rapid systematic conquest of the whole of western Palestine (Canaan). It is widely recognized that the Joshua narrative greatly oversimplifies matters and telescopes both time and circumstances to make it appear that all Israel under the single leadership of Joshua achieved the conquest of Canaan in a single generation (40 years). At the same time the basic tradition of violent conflict and many details have been confirmed by archaeological discovery. It is possible to recognize the data and reorder the sequence of events on the basis of careful attention to the biblical text and the archaeological evidence.

The stories of the capture of Jericho and Ai contain many legendary features, especially the sudden collapse of the walls of the former, when considered from a rigorous historical point of view. The capture of the two cities during this period has not been confirmed archaeologically. Jericho had lain in ruins more than a century before the arrival of the Israelites, while the case with Ai is much worse. That city had been destroyed and abandoned in the Early Bronze age a thousand years before Joshua. Many scholars believe that the tradition of Joshua 8:1–29 may relate to a small, unfortified village established at *et-Tell* on the acropolis of the Early Bronze city during Iron Age I (ca. 1200 B.C.) and that this site was biblical Ai. The men of Ai may have been the first inhabitants of the Iron Age village. However, Bethel appears to be one of the first Canaanite cities to be conquered in the mountains of Ephraim. It was destroyed toward the end of the thirteenth century (Judges 1:22–26) as confirmed by archaeological excavation at the site.

Abject humiliation of a defeated chief and his followers brought before the ruler amid celebration and music. Ivory carving

1. THE CONQUEST

The complete picture of the gradual conquest and settlement of Canaan — the principal penetration took place in the early part of the thirteenth

An Israelite Iron Age house in the new village built over ancient Ai, with benches constructed along the walls

The Lachish high-place or *bāmâh*, dating to the 13th century and consisting of the altar platform and benches for offerings

century — emerges from a process of combination and reconstruction of events described in the books of Joshua and Judges. Although in the present arrangement the narratives in the two books are sequential, actually they overlap, and together they describe the same general circumstances from different points of view. Thus the account of the conquests of Joshua, which were limited in extent, is only part of the picture, and must be supplemented by the stories of the incursions of the clans of Caleb, Kenaz, and Judah (Joshua 15:13–14; Judges 1:12–15), as well as other events in the saga of the settlement of the land. In the process of transmission and compilation major traditions relating to the Conquest were consolidated around a nucleus of authentic data concerning Joshua, resulting in the basic account of unitary invasion and overwhelming victory under his aegis in the book of Joshua. Other accounts including the exploits of the separate tribes and individual leaders were collected in the book of Judges, to be regarded as supplemental, and subsequent to the main account. These fragmentary accounts of tribal activities in the early period of settlement, found in the opening chapter of Judges, nevertheless have high historical value and require the most careful

71

Ivory carving of a Canaanite woman; from the Megiddo treasury

Clay statuette of a Canaanite

consideration in any reconstruction of the actual course of events. Certainly they convey a more realistic picture of what happened than the conventionalized military sweep portrayed in the book of Joshua. Archaeological excavations provide another mass of information bearing on the history of this period, sometimes confirming, sometimes challenging the tradition, sometimes shedding light on the circumstances and clarifying puzzling situations, sometimes raising new questions and posing problems to which new answers must be given.

On the basis of the extensive evidence for this period unearthed at numerous sites during the past decades, both scholarly analysis and synthesis have progressed to the point of providing a plausible and satisfying reconstruction of the sequence of events and the dates or at least the chronological range of their occurrence. Consideration of some of the more significant artifacts and the pertinent information on the date of the Conquest to be derived from them follows:

One of the most important of these consists of a clay bowl found in the destruction debris of the last Late Bronze city of Lachish. It bore an Egyptian inscription, which included a date, the fourth year of an unnamed pharaoh. On the basis of typological and stratigraphic considerations, the bowl and the inscription must be dated in the later part of the thirteenth century; hence the most likely attribution is to the reign of Merneptah (ca. 1234–1224 B.C.), who is known to have conducted a military campaign in Palestine or at least to have made the claim. This pinpoints the destruction of Lachish after 1231, perhaps a generation after the main Israelite invasion in the mid-thirteenth century. Excavations carried out at Lachish, Tell Beit Mirsim (Debir), and Tell el-Hesi (Eglon), have demonstrated that these cities suffered a total destruction during the same period, at the end of the Late Bronze age.

2. THE MERNEPTAH STELE

Another vital source of information is the stele erected by Merneptah (XIXth Egyptian Dynasty) at Karnak in his fifth year, ca. 1230 B.C. He boasts of many victories in the general area, specifically citing Israel whom he claims he "laid waste, his seed is not." This is the first time the name Israel appears outside the Bible; here it is the designation of a people, though precisely what its composition or its structure was cannot be determined. Moreover, it provides us with a demarcation between the first and second waves of Israelite penetration in the thirteenth century. By then the Joseph tribes (see below) had moved into the area taking some territory by force, but also establishing peaceful relations with key cities of that region, such as Shechem, Tirzah, and Tappuah. The two peoples intermingled and shared in cultural and military alliances, even entering into formal treaties. We may find here an explanation of the fact that such cities as Shechem were not the target of Israelite attack at the time of the Conquest. Such a powerful concentration of forces in Canaan may have represented a threat to Egyptian suzerainty and prompted Merneptah to punish both the rebellious Canaanite cities and Israelite enclaves. This was presumably Egypt's last serious attempt to reclaim or capture lost territory in Asia; Merneptah's punitive raid probably stalled, for a time, the progess of the Joseph tribes in gaining control of their territory.

3. WAVES OF CONQUEST

a. *The House of Joseph*

The House of Joseph, including the tribes of Ephraim, Manasseh and Benjamin had penetrated the hill country in central Canaan by the thirteenth century B.C., and settled there permanently. This was followed several years later by the battle over Gibeon in the Benjamin area, between the Israelite tribes led by Joshua and a league of five Canaanite cities of the hill country, among them Lachish and Eglon, led by the king of Jerusalem. The flight of the Canaanites over the steep ascent of Beth Horon was recalled in a vivid figure preserved in an ancient corpus of Israelite poetry, the lost "Book of Jashar"; a brief extract from the victory ode is quoted in Joshua 10:12–13. This remarkable episode and the extraordinary role ascribed to Joshua probably constitutes the nucleus of the tradition about his leadership, around whom the historiographers of Israel then wove the whole story of conquest. Jerusalem itself fell after a short time into the hands of the Jebusites who held it for about two centuries until the time of David.

The Merneptah (1236–1223) B.C. stele from Thebes which contains in line 27 the only mention of the name *Israel* in all Egyptian records

b. *Judah and Allied Southern Tribes*

The House of Joseph did not reap the fruits of this first victory over the Canaanite league. It was Judah and the other Leah tribes allied with it which gained the benefit. They apparently belonged to the later group which entered Canaan about the middle of the thirteenth century, as described in Judges 1:1–20. Moving down from the north, they captured Jerusalem, then relinquished it and gained a foothold in the hill country of Judah. The tribe of Simeon moved south and occupied Beersheba and Canaanite Hormah (Tell el-Meshash). At approximately the same time, the southern clans of Caleb and Kenaz settled in the region of Hebron and Debir, while the Kenite clans moved north to occupy the area of Arad where they established a sanctuary (cf. Arad below).

c. As Egyptian power waned toward the end of the thirteenth century, the southern Israelite tribes expanded into the *Shephelah*, i.e. the foothills

Canaanite charioteers in battle

Battling over a fortified city in Canaan. Egyptian relief from Medinet Habu

and the broad coastal plains, and defeated the Canaanite kings of Gezer, Lachish, and Makkedah (Joshua 15; follow the arrows on the left of the map).

d. Finally the other Leah tribes, along with Issachar, Zebulun and Asher, which had moved from Transjordan during the first and second waves of invasions (see above), separated from the main body and settled in various parts of Galilee and on the border of the remaining Canaanite cities of the northern coast (henceforth known as Phoenicia in accordance with Greek usage). Archaeological evidence shows that the Israelites established themselves in the forested hill country and flourished from the beginning of the Iron Age (ca. 1200 B.C.). Lacking chariotry, field weapons, and siege engines, however, they were not yet ready to pit their strength against the prosperous fortified Canaanite city kingdoms around Hazor.

e. *The Conquest of Galilee*

There are separate biblical accounts of two crucial campaigns in Galilee which resulted in the end of Canaanite power. One is found in Judges 4–5, which consists of a prose narrative (chapter 4) and the well-known Song of Deborah (chapter 5), which celebrate the victory of Deborah and Barak over the Canaanite forces led by Sisera in the plain of Jezreel. The other is in Joshua 11 and describes the battle of Meron and the destruction of Hazor, the chief city of the region. Though the sources assume a lapse of time between the two campaigns, Joshua preceding Deborah by several generations, B. Mazar believes that they represent two stages in the same war; on the basis of the biblical and archaeological data, it is possible to reconstruct the episodes and set them in the proper historical framework. The bulk of the Israelite tribes, including the powerful Joseph group, joined with Naphtali, Zebulun and Issachar, who had settled in Galilee and were hard pressed by the Canaanites, against a coalition of Canaanite kings. Confident in their

Conquests and Battles

Areas of Continuous Settlement

Canaanite Cities, Unconquered

MEDITERRANEAN

Tyre
Abel-Beth-Maacah
Dan
DAN
Beth-Anath
Merom
Kedesh
Achzib
Beth-Shemesh
ASHER
Hazor
Gath
Acco
Ramah
Kinnereth
Aphek
NAPHTALI
Adamah
GESHUR
Achshaph
Aphek
Ashtarot
Hannathon
ZEBULON
Kedesh
Carmel
Shimron
ISSACHAR
Dor
Jokne'am
Jarmuth
HAVOT YAIR
Kamon
Megiddo
Beth-Shean
Ham
Aron
Ta'anach
Ramoth-Gilead
Gath
Ible'am
Rehob
Phahel
Hepher
Bezek
Jabesh-Gilead
Abel-Meholah
Tirzah
Mahanaim
Penuel
AMMON
Adam
Aphek
EPHRAIM
GAD
Japha
Zeredah
Betonim
Lod
Timnath-Serah
Rabbath-Ammon
Ja'azer
Jabneel
Bethel
Ai
Jericho
Beth-Horon
Mizpah
Abel-Shittim
Gezer
Aijalon
Be'eroth
Beth-Horon
Heshbon
ASHDOD
Zor'ah
Jerusalem
Beth-Hoglah
Beth-ha-
Ekron
Beth-Shemesh
Jeshimoth
Bethlehem
Medeba
Ashkelon
Adullam
GAD
Libnah
JUDAH
Ataroth
Jahaza
Gaza
Eglon
Hebron
Kiriathaim
Dibbon
Debir
Ziph
Aro'er
Gerar
Carmel
Eshtemoa
DEAD SEA
Raphia
Beersheba
Arad
Sharuhen
SIMEON
Hormah
MOAB
Aro'er
Kir-Moab
Zoar
EDOM
PHILISTIA

superiority in equipment (chariotry) and numbers, the Canaanites boldly advanced in the plain. At the foot of Mount Tabor, however, sudden rains produced a flash flood in the Kishon river, swamping the ironwheeled chariots, whereupon the Israelites attacked and defeated the immobilized Canaanite army. It is possible that those who escaped from this debacle attempted to regroup around Hazor, but were pursued by the Israelites at Meron (Joshua 11:1–13) which is identified with Marun-er-Ras in northern Galilee. The remnant of the Canaanite forces was destroyed there, leaving the city of Hazor open to assault; stripped of defenders it fell into the hands of the Israelite army.

The excavations of Hazor, the largest city in Canaan, demonstrate beyond question that it was destroyed around the end of the thirteenth century B.C. A new population, presumably Israelites who had lived in modest villages in Galilee, settled over the vast ruins, as indicated by the distinctive types of pottery. Moreover, the fall of Hazor serves as a chronological marker for the northern military campaigns, indicating that they took place during the interregnum between the XIXth and XXth Egyptian dynasties (roughly 1200 B.C.). The decline of Egyptian power had opened the way for the decisive wars between Israel and Canaan.

4. GRADUAL PROCESS OF SETTLEMENT DURING THE DAYS OF JUDGES

In the course of the twelfth century, in the period of the "Judges" (charismatic leaders of various tribes), the number and size of Israelite

The basalt *maṣṣeboth* or standing pillars found in the 13th century temple of Hatzor. One was engraved with a pair of hands upraised in a gesture of prayer toward a disc, probably symbolizing the moon-god. The statuette of a seated god and an offering bowl are seen on the left settlements increased steadily, although the people lived in constant danger of invasion from without, and dissension and subversion from within. The biblical historian, appalled by the endless succession of near disasters, organized the traditional materials into a fixed moralizing pattern: When the Israelites were faithful to their God and obedient to his will, they were secure and prospered. When they rebelled against their Lord and quarreled among themselves, then they fell prey to foreign invaders like the Moabites or Midianites, or finally to the Philistines, or to local tyrants like Abimelech. In their distress and suffering, God took pity on them and raised up a deliverer, one of the Judges, who rescued them from their plight. Then for a while they enjoyed success and security, until they reneged on their obligations to God and the cycle of misfortune would begin again.

The Sanctuary of Ba'al Berith

History can survey developments of Judg 8–10 in terms of war and shifting boundaries, with an occasional glance at the details and circumstances which produced the changes. One especially significant sequence concerns the great charismatic judge, Gideon, who saved Israel at a moment of dire peril, but was succeeded by a son, Abimelech, who brought ruin upon himself and near disaster to his people. He attempted to rule over all Israel after establishing a power base in Shechem. With his family connections and the memory of his father's great deeds, he was able to put together an alliance of Shechemites and Israelites centered around the sanctuary of Ba'al-Berith, Lord of the Covenant. The remains of this temple-fort, called Beth-millo and built in the last phase of the Middle Bronze age, were un-

The *beth-millo* or platform of the temple of *Ba'al-berith* (Lord of the Covenant) at Shechem with the great broken slab maṣṣebah reerected in the forecourt. Two sockets for maṣṣeboth in the background (see arrows) marked the entrance to the most sacred area where rituals were held.

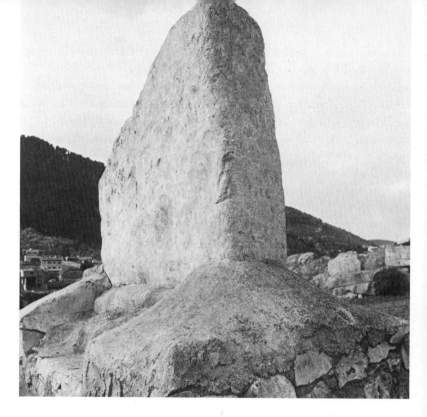

Detail of the great slab *maṣṣebah*. The splendid stele is associated with the 'great stone', the witness of the solemn convocation in Joshua 24:25–27

covered over the acropolis of Shechem. The great temple, 108×92 feet in size, had massive walls eighteen feet thick and contained a large beaten-earth altar; its entrance was flanked by a pair of *massebôth* (sacred pillars). The city gates were originally of the triple type, consisting of parallel pairs of massive stone blocks. The temple had been reconstructed before the Israelite Conquest on a somewhat smaller scale; a huge *massebâh* stood in front of the entrance. Shechem at this period (14th century) is mentioned in the Amarna letters (see Genesis), when the ambitious Labayu ruled the district as an ally of the 'Apiru and a rebel against Egypt.

Shechem was destroyed after the Amarna Age, perhaps around 1300 B.C. Convincing evidence has been assembled by L. Toombs, one of the excavators of the site, to demonstrate this point. Whether this destruction can be associated with the traditions in Genesis 34 and 48:22 or should be attributed to a pharaoh of the XIXth Dynasty (Seti I or Rameses II), or some other invader, remains an open question. But there is no reason to doubt that from that time there were Israelites in or around the city. In any case these data provide the background of the story of Abimelech who was "made king by the terebinth [or oak] of the pillar at Shechem" (Judges 9:6), a sacred tree near the *massebôth,* after being supplied with money from the sanctuary of Ba'al Berith. Later, the Shechemites rebelled against Abimelech, who took revenge on them by razing the walls of the city. Many of the specific structures and places in the story have been identified by the excavators: the *Beth-millo* with the ancient temple built on a platform (*millo*; Judges 9:20) associated with the terebinth of the pillar; the city gate with the fourteenth century east gate (Judges 9:35, 40, 44). The filling of pits beneath the temple with charcoal and early twelfth century pottery supplies evidence of Abimelech's devastation of Shechem.

Finally, critical reading of the passages outlining the borders of the tribal territories in the book of Joshua (15–19) offer help in understanding the nature and gradual process of the Israelite occupation. The tribes settled first in the vicinity of the Canaanite cities; it was only at a later stage that the Canaanite centers fell into their hands. This is evident from the excavations at Bethel and the remains of Tappuaḥ.

5. WERE THE TRIBAL TERRITORIES DIVIDED UP IN JOSHUA'S TIME ?

Chapters 13 through 22 of Joshua detail the division and distribution of the whole land of Israel. While on the surface the scheme is a simple one, the text shows signs of editorial working, reflecting a long complex history of development. This will also become apparent from the contradictions between the books of Joshua and Judges. The basis for the description is the administrative system which was in effect in the late period of Judges and early part of the Monarchy. This is most obvious from the fact that some of the land mentioned in the second part of the book was conquered not by Joshua, but only by later Israelites.

A more accurate picture of Israel's land distribution and tenure at this time can be constructed from a critical evaluation of the text; rudiments of it are given in the map of Israelite settlement (Part III). Tribes and clans gradually established themselves in the shaded areas in the heartland of the country. Only after the long and often irregular process of preliminary settlement could firm territorial claims be made and ratified; the latter process generally required a strong central administration. It is only natural that the territorial boundaries of monarchic Israel of later centuries be projected back into Joshua's time, since those limits were the ultimate outcome of the exploits attributed to him, temporary fluctuations notwithstanding.

The more advanced stage of settlement, also accompanied by much insecurity, brings to an end one period of conquest and settlement and ushers in the traditional biblical *period of the Judges*. Actually, the periods of Joshua and Judges intertwine, as has been observed. In general the Hebrew tribal society infiltrated and broke down the Canaanite feudal system during the period of Joshua-Judges.

6. THE UNCONQUERED REGIONS

Two documents, on the other hand, are preserved, which define the unconquered regions of historic Canaan:

a. The list of some 19 unconquered cities in Judges I. They faithfully represent the historical situation during the later period of the Judges, namely the presence of several cities which separated Judah (and Jerusalem, then Jebus) from the central part of Israel; a few cities on the coast, and those in the corridor (Megiddo, Beth-shean) which separated central and 79 northern Israel. These cities appear in Judges 1, but for reasons explained above they are defined in the biblical tradition of Joshua 15–19 as cities ordained for tribal inheritance (though the inheritance fell due closer to the time of the writing of the tradition, probably by an annalist of the court of David or Solomon.)

b. The "land that yet remains" (Josh 13:1 and Judg 3:3; see map), These areas were occupied in the south by the Philistines and in the north of Israel by the "Sidonians" (Phoenicians) and Arameans. All of them remained outside the limits of Israelite conquest, though a different outlook, reflected in later biblical traditions handed down in Numbers 34, regarded them as part of the land Yahweh promised Moses.

7. THE NEW PICTURE OF SETTLEMENT IN THE NEGEB

A new perspective of the settlement of the southern tribes, Judah, Simeon and the allied Kenites (Midianites) in the eastern Negeb emerges from the excavations conducted by Y. Aharoni at Arad, Meshash and Beersheba, as explained in the accompanying illustrations.

An Early Israelite Temple at Arad

One of the outstanding contributions was the discovery of an ancient temple at Arad in southern Israel. It stood on the grounds of an Israelite citadel, and was the first Israelite sanctuary to be uncovered in an excavation. It is oriented westward and its layout and contents recall, in many respects, Solomon's Temple in Jerusalem. It shows an even more striking resemblance to the biblical description of the Tabernacle in the desert (see Exodus-Deuteronomy), and consists of a main hall from which three steps lead up to the *debir* (Holy of Holies) at whose entrance were found two incense altars. A small *bamāh* (high-place) and a *massebāh* (stone stele) stood in the center of the Holy of Holies. In the outer courtyard stood an altar for burnt offerings, which was a square of five cubes approximately seven feet on each side, conforming to the measurements of the Tabernacle in Exod 27:1 and built of earth and unhewn field stones (Exod 20:24–25). Other features of the sanctuary also bore a close resemblance to the biblical description of Solomon's sanctuary. But the early history of this high-place and temple is even more intriguing because Arad had been settled before the days of the monarchy by a Kenite clan akin to the Midianites and descended from Hobab the priest, Moses' father-in-law (Judg 1:16; see: Exodus: A Midianite Sanctuary at Timnah). The Kenites built a high-place and altar on the highest point overlooking the plateau of Arad. In the days of Solomon (10th century B.C.) or shortly afterwards, a temple was built in this strategic center (Greater Arad), over the early Kenite high-place, as shown in our pictures of the Holy of Holies and altar. Several high-places had existed in Israel before and during the days of the Judean Monarchy, but this one may have been destroyed by King Hezekiah (eighth century B.C.), or more likely by Josiah who concentrated the religious ritual in Jerusalem in the seventh century B.C., as described in II Kings 22.

The significant rich trove of ostracons found there will be described under
I, II, Kings.

8. OTHER DEVELOPMENTS IN THE PALESTINIAN WORLD

The changes that are associated with the central portions of southern
Canaan at the end of the Late Bronze Age reflect historical processes which
left no feature of the whole Canaanite sphere unaltered. The kingdoms of
Moab, Ammon and Edom arose at the same time Israel did. The military
federation organized around the Philistine Pentapolis can hardly be later,
and may well be earlier (see I Samuel). The technological developments
of the Early Iron Age are better known. The development of slaked lime-
plaster cisterns revitalized many of the area's potential centers of settlement
that had been dormant since its massive deforestation earlier in the Bronze
Age. We will discuss some of these changes and related features in the
pages that follow.

Archaeological research has proved that the Israelites did not bring a
uniform tradition of material culture with them, and they borrowed in
the main from previous inhabitants, partly in building construction, mostly
in weapons, in art objects and especially in pottery. The Canaanite product
was an excellent model to imitate. In the beginning, the imitation produced
more primitive vessels in the same style. But unique vessels soon developed

Model of the Arad sanctuary

in a clearly definable style found among the Israelite tribes. In fact, the adoption of Canaanite culture coupled with rapid crystallization of independent forms is a familiar theme through all phases of Israelite tribal life.

a. *The Early Israelite House*

It has become evident from very recent excavations that the Israelite type of tripartite house as a homogeneous structure appeared for the first time in the period of the Judges (12th–11th centuries B.C.). It is generally built with an inner open court surrounded by rooms, as shown in our illustration. Early examples were found at Tel Far'ah south of Beersheba and at Tell Meshash, in a 12th century settlement on virgin soil. It was believed at first that this type of house was of Late Canaanite or Philistine origin, but there is evidence to show that it may be an independent Israelite tradition which was realized in constructions even before the days of the monarchy.

b. *Introduction of Slaked Lime-Plastered Cisterns*

Plastered and whitewashed water cisterns have been found in Canaanite Late Bronze strata in various excavations, including the deep water cistern of Hazor in stratum XIV. The device was not original to the Israelites, as it shows up in Canaanite cities which proved very inventive in assuring emergency water supplies. The Israelites took to it very quickly, as illustrated, and it helped them to found small independent settlements, widely dispersed and unrestricted by the limited number of local springs and wells. The narrow confines and heavy concentration of their zones of occupation, first on the periphery of the Canaanites, then in their midst, left their impression in the special development of their society. As seen above, they first imitated, then improved on their neighbors, both culturally and materially (see II Samuel and I Kings).

"Four-room houses" of the early Israelite settlement at Tell Meshash

PART IV

THE BOOKS OF I AND II SAMUEL

A. SAMUEL

The Bible presents Samuel as a man who filled many different roles. According to Albright these should be considered as differences in emphasis and no longer appear as hopeless contradictions but as contributions to a more complete historical picture.

At birth, Samuel was pledged to service at the temple at Shiloh by his mother, Hanna. As a *nazir*, he was devoted to an ascetic life and performed Levitical duties at the sanctuary. This may explain why 1 Chr 6:28 lists Samuel among the families of the Levites, rather than the more historical genealogy in 1 Sam 1:1 which identifies Samuel as a Ephraimite.

We are told that Samuel became recognized throughout Israel as a prophet early in his career (1 Sam 2:20). As such he becomes the prototype of the prophets, particularly of the northern kingdom, who announce Yahweh's election, favor, or displeasure with Israel's kings. In addition, Samuel is depicted as a local seer who could be consulted on small matters for a sum of money. There is the interesting footnote in 1 Sam 9:9 which states that "the one who is now called a prophet was formerly called a seer."

1. THE CONTENTS, IN HISTORICAL PERSPECTIVE

Although divided into two, the Hebrew scribes regarded the two books as one, without interruption.

1 Samuel	*Parallels in 1 Chronicles**
Samuel's childhood and relationship to the Shiloh priesthood (Chapters 1–3). The loss of the Ark, its wanderings, and return (4:1–7:2), which is continued in 2 Samuel 6.	
Samuel as judge and prophet (3–17)	
The accession of Saul (8–14:9)	1 Chr 8:33, 40, 12:2
Conflict with Samuel (15:10–35)	
David's anointment (16:1–13)	
Beginning of David's adventures (17–20)	1 Chronicles 12
David as outlaw; Saul's defeat and death (21–31)	1 Chronicles 12

---

* The books of Chronicles contain passages of annalistic and factual material of the most reliable type, parallel to 1 and 2 Samuel, as indicated in the list of contents. This is also true of Chronicles and Kings; 1 Chronicles 1–8, however, is noteworthy mainly for its genealogical lists.

Iron sword discovered in Philistia

2 Samuel
Second account of Saul's death and his elegy (Chapter 1)

2: THE INVASION OF THE SEA PEOPLES

The first half of the twelfth century witnessed two related developments of great importance for the history of the Israelite settlement. One was the invasion of the land by the Sea Peoples who came from the north and west, from Asia Minor and the eastern Mediterranean, the islands like Cyprus and Crete and the Aegean. These people spoke Indo-European languages and belonged to that culture, in contrast with the local inhabitants who spoke northwestern Semitic dialects. The other was the concomitant decline of Egyptian power in Canaan and the virtual abandonment of the territory which had been held actually and nominally for centuries.

The literary sources (both biblical and non-biblical) convey a picture of the Philistines as a vigorous, talented segment of the Sea Peoples, who left not only their name but a permanent influence on the land which they invaded and settled: Canaan which became Palestine. The Bible states that they came from Crete, and this is doubtless true of some of them; others seem to have come from the mainland. They belonged to the wave of "Sea Peoples," who, like the horsemen in Europe millennia later, came by sea and land to ravage and ransack the coastal regions of the eastern Mediterranean around 1200 B.C. They migrated from the Aegean Islands and Asia Minor under pressure from the Dorians who invaded the Greek mainland, a development which in turn is related to the events celebrated in Homer's epic of the Trojan war.

In contrast to the Israelite invasion which began a little earlier and was much more modest in size and impact, the Sea Peoples carried out an extensive campaign of destruction and conquest. Apparently they gave the *coup de grace* to the great Hittite empire and very nearly overturned the Egyptian state as well. At the same time, Mycenean power disintegrated on the Greek mainland. Some of the Sea Peoples, taking advantage of the decline of the empires, had already invaded Palestine and Syria in the late thirteenth century. According to Egyptian documents, they attacked the Syrian and Egyptian coasts at the beginning of the reign of Rameses III

Opposite page:
The great naval battle between Rameses III and the Sea Peoples (which included the Philistines). Four Egyptian boats (right, equipped with oars and sails) engage five Philistine boats (distinguished by a bird's head on both prow and stern). The Philistines are tall, shaven and wearing feathered head-dresses and breastplate or shirt. They fought with round shields. Reliefs in the temple of Rameses III at Medinet Habu

(1196–1164 B.C.). Rameses III defeated them in Syria and repelled them finally from the Egyptian mainland, but only after fierce attacks on sea and land had threatened the survival of the kingdom. Nevertheless, an inscription of Rameses III from Beth-shean indicated that he re-established the Egyptian base there and rebuilt the temples. In fact, he settled some of the Sea Peoples as garrison troops in parts of Canaan, thus enlisting those aggressive warriors in his service as a mercenary border guard to prevent further invasions. Anthropoid coffins, containing the bodies of Philistines, have been found at Beth-shean, Tell-Far'ah and elsewhere in Palestine. The Sea Peoples consisted of five groups: *p-r-š-t* (Philistines), *t-ḳ-r* (Sikel), *s̀-ḳ-r-s*, *d-n-n* and *w-š-š*.

Rameses' victory and subsequent control over parts of Canaan did not deter the Philistines from occupying the southern coastal region, with Gaza, the former Egyptian provincial capital, as one of their major cities. An Egyptian source indicated that Dor (south of present-day Haifa) was occupied by the *t-ḳ-r*. The story of the Egyptian priest, Wen-Amun, illuminates the situation in Canaan at the beginning of the eleventh century. He had been sent to Byblos to acquire cedar trees to construct a sacred barque for the god Amun. By that time there was no trace of Egyptian authority or influence and while some memories of earlier contacts persisted along the Phoenician coast, Wen-Amun was confronted with a measure of contempt and the demand for cash on the line. His first stop was the Dor harbor where he

A warrior of the Sea Peoples wielding his battle axe

was robbed and elicited neither support nor sympathy from the chief of the *t-k-r*. As he pursued his journey, probably to Tyre, he seized a boat belonging to the *t-k-r*, thus recouping part of his loss. While eleven ships pursued him, he eluded them and sailed for Cyprus.

Philistine authority during the eleventh century extended as far as the valley of Jezreel, while their influence and presence were everywhere in the land. They controlled the coastal towns of Ashkelon, Ashdod and Jaffa (present-day Tel-Aviv) and imposed their rule upon the local populace. They were also busily engaged in sea trade. They were organized into a confederation comprising five cities, each ruled by a *seren* (tyrant in Greek). They set about extending their territory and in due course they became the dominant political force in Palestine. A few generations previously the Israelites had settled in Canaan, mainly in the hill country. With the collapse of the Canaanite military forces and city-states, the Israelites were left to bear the chief brunt of the Philistine drive for hegemony. With their monopoly of iron tools and weapons and their effective military organization, the Philistines proved more than a match for the Israelites and reduced them to the status of vassals (as reflected in the Samson stories, Judges 13–16, especially Judges 15:11). In this period the Philistines flourished as a political and cultural force, extended their control over the whole coastal plain of Palestine, and thereby threatened the political and economic future of Israel. They were the first to introduce the use of iron into the country, a new element which would ultimately revolutionize the way of life of the whole of civilization. They had brought it from the Hittite hinterland and maintained a monopoly of the product until the days of King Saul (I Samuel 13:19–22). Philistine soldiers carried iron weapons and their farmers used iron tools. The description of their well-armed champion, Goliath, seems to sum up this military superiority (I Samuel 17:4–7).

Right:
Core of the Philistine temple uncovered at Tell-Qasileh with the altar and bases of three *maṣṣeboth* (standing pillars)

Above:
Philistine pottery coffin found at Beth-shean where the invaders were eventually garrisoned by the Egyptians

Philistine incense jar showing man holding two pillars; found in the temple

Tell Qasileh

The excavation of Tell Qasileh on the northern bank of the Yarkon river has uncovered a small harbor founded by the Philistines, as indicated by the lowest levels of occupation (XI–XII) of the twelfth century B.C. The findings show evidence of agricultural and industrial activities: granaries, baking ovens, oil and wine presses, a smelting furnace and dyeing utensils. There are also remains of fortifications from the same period. The city served later as one of King Solomon's harbors (see below). The most remarkable discovery was a Philistine temple from the twelfth century with a courtyard surrounding it. The altar of sacrifices and the steps leading to it appear in the center surrounded by numerous ritual vessels and cult objects. It would be hard to separate the architecture of this sanctuary from the temple of Dagan at Gaza described in Judges 16:29. Two main pillars, whose bases were discovered in the excavations, seem just far enough apart to require the full extension of muscular athletic arms such as Samson's to reach around them and pull them down.

The excavation of Gerar (Tell Šera), the biblical city of the Negeb where Abraham had settled. The structure on the right is the Israelite 'four room' house. The older Canaanite complex is on the slope to the left

3. THEIR CITIES AND CULTURAL ATTRIBUTES

a. *Ashkelon*

We read in the famous elegy of David over Saul and Jonathan: "Tell it not in Gath, publish it not in the streets of Ashkelon" (2 Sam 1:20). This actually refers to the bazaars of that famed city which possessed the only safe harbor in southern Palestine and was a great trading center. Its importance as a center of crafts and arts is indicated by the temple of Ptah, the god of the city; we also find his name among the famous ivory carvings discovered in the royal treasure of Canaanite Megiddo of the 13th–12th centuries B.C. This Egyptian deity was identified with the god Chusor, or

87

Figure of a female deity
whose lower part merges with
a throne

Part of a Philistine clay
beer-jug from Ashdod

the older "Kotar wa-Ḥasis," the craftsman god of the Canaanite pantheon. The culture of greater Canaan had inseminated the Philistines.

b. *Gath*

The constant process of action and reaction between the Israelites and Philistines seems to have effected changes in the political structures on both sides. According to B. Mazar, Gath was raised in this period to supremacy over the Philistine cities, and its ruler, Achish, was king of the whole pentapolis. During the period David served as a vassal of the king of Gath (1 Sam 27:5–6), exercising rule over a fiefdom of his own in the Ziklag region. It is identified with Tell esh-Sheri'ah, a prominent mound east of Gerar.

c. *Ashdod*

Excavations of Ashdod show continuous Canaanite occupation since the 17th century B.C. It was destroyed by the Sea Peoples at the end of the Late Bronze Age, and later occupied by the Philistines. It became one of the principal cities of the pentapolis. The Philistine levels revealed a rich material culture including a number of interesting objects: the figure of a female deity whose lower part merges with a throne, a musician's stand, and many offering tables which attest to the local religious practices.

d. *Jaffa (ancient Joppa, modern Tel Aviv)*

The period of Israelite settlement began with the fourth level (second half of the 13th century B.C.) of the excavations of ancient Joppa. Remains of the Israelite fortress were uncovered; at the threshold was a bronze bar that supported the corner of the left gate. The Philistines attacked the city and destroyed it, leaving characteristic signs of their presence there. This prevented the Israelites from using this seaport or the one further north at the mouth of the Yarkon river, where boats took shelter in the wintertime when the sea was stormy. The reference in Josh 19:45 to the Yarkon river as the border of the tribe of Dan which "ran over against Joppa" is now dated by most scholars to the Davidic period when Israelite expansion was at its peak. In other words, Jaffa remained outside the boundary of Israelite settlement for most of the classical period. A link between Jaffa and the Greek world may be reflected in the so-called "Andromeda rocks" off the old harbor, which are associated in tradition with the legend of Perseus and the well-known princess of that name.

4. THE CANAANITE COASTLAND AND HINTERLAND

The territory north of Philistia and northwest of Israel is generally called Phoenicia, the Greek equivalent of Canaan. It was actually the northern part of Canaan and the last retreat of the Canaanites from the pressure of Israelite and Philistine expansion. It first achieved a distinctive identity in the Early Iron Age, although it had always been an important trading center. The great coastal city of the second millennium, Byblos, reappears in this period, but it is dwarfed by the great city-states, Tyre and Sidon. The greatest concentration of the Phoenicians outside Palestine was in North Africa; their language is called Punic, which is simply a Latin form of Phoenician. The great city of Carthage (Phoenician: *qart hadašt* = "new city") is well known from Roman tradition and records. Other major Phoenician colonies are known from Cyprus, Sicily, Sardinia, and Spain.

The first Assyrian empire under Tiglath-pileser I held the tribes of Syria in check, but, following his death in 1078 B.C., the hold of Mesopotamia on western Syria practically ceased. This stimulated the Canaanites north of Mount Carmel, known as the *Phoenicians*, to establish their own autonomy in Tyre, Sidon, and Byblos; it also allowed the Sea Peoples to plant themselves more firmly.

The Phoenician contribution to Israelite civilization best known from the Bible is architectural: Hiram of Tyre seems to have supplied Solomon with everything but the land for his temple. A greater contribution, the alphabet, is discussed below.

The north Canaanite hinterland in the Early Iron Age was apportioned among small kingdoms compounded of Arameans and Hittites. The latter had moved south from Anatolia as a result of the collapse of the Hittite empire and brought with them a knowledge of statecraft which they were able to adapt to their new home. These petty states appear frequently in the stories of David's imperial expansion, but their history is not otherwise well known.

Figurine of a Canaanite goddess cast in a mold (Nahariya)

5. EVIDENCE OF THE MARCH OF PROGRESS

The time was ripe for the expansion of sea trade along the coasts and the sea lanes established by the preclassic Greek Mycenean civilization. The decline of Egyptian sea power had left a vacuum which was rapidly filled by both the Phoenicians and the Sea Peoples who opted for peaceful trade after their violent migrations of the preceding century. Philistine influence penetrated to inland Israel as we gather from pottery finds in the towns of western Judah and Tell Beit Mirsim and Beth-shemesh.

Excavations have been conducted at many of the sites central to the books of Samuel, and the results have cleared up important points of detail in the role of Samuel in the successful transition from the federation to the monarchy. Further light has been shed on this process by discoveries of two other sources of information: a) the discoveries among the Dead Sea Scrolls of early recension of fragments of the book of Samuel, found in Cave IV at Qumran and in the Ezra Synagogue in Cairo, and b) the Aramean treaty inscriptions at Sefiré (see 1, 2 Kings).

B. EVOLUTION OF THE ALPHABET

A proto-Canaanite inscription BŠLŠT painted on a pottery bowl from Lachish (13th c. B.C.)

The origins of the various arts and crafts figure prominently in the traditions of many peoples, and the book of Genesis comments briefly on the children of Lamech who devised agricultural tools and musical instruments (Genesis 4). But nothing is said about the invention of the alphabet, surely one of the most remarkable achievements of the human race. The oldest alphabetic writing extant in a Semitic language is to be found on a few inscriptions from the land of Canaan; they date from the 17th or 16th century B.C. Confirmation that this handful of characters actually belong to an alphabetic system was provided from an unlikely source, the turquoise mines of Serabit el-Khadem in the western Sinai. In 1948 W. F. Albright restudied the inscriptions in a West Semitic dialect which had been uncovered in a series of expeditions to the site. He concluded that Sir Flinders Petrie had been correct in attributing them to the period of the New Kingdom, in the 15th century B.C. or earlier. The earlier date has now been fixed firmly by evidence of different kinds, and the Sinai inscriptions provide us with enough material to recover and reconstruct this oldest known Canaanite alphabet. Apparently it was the Semitic workmen there who were responsible for developing the first alphabetic script. Using modified forms of Egyptian signs, but interpreting and applying them to a West Semitic dialect, these men devised an extremely simple and extraordinarily effective system for transcribing the sounds of their language.

The two controlling principles were *acrophony and consonantism*. According to the first, each letter originally was a pictograph representing some common object, though in time they all became highly conventionalized. The sound of the letter was the same as the initial sound of the word which described the pictograph; e.g. the letter *b* was originally a drawing of a house, which is called *bayt/bêt* in West Semitic; the initial sound of that word is *b* which is the value of the symbol. According to the second principle, only consonants were represented in the alphabet, not vowels. Since all syllables in proto-Semitic begin with consonants, the necessity for representing them is obvious. Vowels are another matter, especially if the vowel is regarded as originally attached to the consonant, as is the case in syllabic writing. The full separation apparently took place in two stages, with consonants being identified first and only in later stages of the alphabet, the vowels. In the past decades numerous inscriptions in the proto-Canaanite alphabet have been found in Palestine and gradually all the letters have been identified and, with few exceptions, their true pictographic values have been established. By the early stages of the Iron Age, the Phoenicians had taken a final important step in normalizing their alphabet into 22 consonants and gave it to the world as the most efficient means of written communication.

By the end of the Late Bronze Age, the Canaanites had devised at least two alphabetic systems. One of these, the linear, was the ancestor of the Phoenician, Hebrew, Aramaic, Greek and Roman alphabets; the other, written with cuneiform wedges, did not survive into the Iron Age.

Palaeo-Sinaitic inscription (15–13th c. B.C.)

The alphabet was developed by the Canaanites in the course of the Middle and Late Bronze ages, and the early years of the Iron Age. It was adopted, with suitable modification, by all of their neighbors, beginning in all likelihood in the 11th century. Since Hebrew in its northern (Israelite) dialect is almost identical with Phoenician, we can hardly talk of borrowing; we would say they shared a common language and a common alphabet. In the case of other dialects and languages there can be no doubt that Phoenicia was the center of radiation.

1. SIGNIFICANCE

The following description of the significance of the alphabet, by Cross, rightly focusses on the shift away from syllabic writing (in which each sign designates a syllable, and in its simplest form one consonant and one vowel) to a kind of pseudo-syllabary in which the sign designates one consonant and any vowel.

"This act of abstraction and simplification, absent from all previous syllable systems, created the alphabet: The step taken was unique. Once the alphabetic principle was discovered, it spread rapidly throughout the ancient world. The revolution may be compared with the invention of writing itself. High civilization was the creature of writing. The invention of the alphabet principle put literacy in the reach of everyman, permitting the democratization of high culture" (F. M. Cross, Israel Explor. Soc. 10; 1972).

The importance of the alphabet in the economic and social development of Israel can hardly be understated since it was the medium by which the biblical traditions were reduced to permanent form.

2. EXPANSION OF ALPHABETIC WRITING

Great strides were made in the use of Canaanite consonantal writing during the period of the Pax Philistea: namely the standarization of the 22-consonant alphabet and of writing from right to left. The trade relations between Philistia, Phoenicia, and Israel were an important factor in the rapid spread of this cultural medium.

The alphabet was carried to the early Greeks by Phoenician traders. Phoenician inscriptions from numerous Mediterranean sites testify to the extent of the Phoenician trading empire. They also enrich our evidence for the development of the alphabet adopted and adapted to earliest Greek counterparts from the tenth century onward.

3. TRANSITION TO TRULY HISTORICAL WRITING

The books of Samuel cover a major transitional period in Israelite history, the rise of the monarchy out of the tribal federation. As 1 Samuel opens, Israel consists of a loose organization of tribes struggling to maintain its existence; at the end of 2 Samuel, Israel is a national power, possessing all the benefits and drawbacks of central authority, and commercial culture.

These changes affected every aspect of Israelite life and religion and gave rise to traditions that remain central to Judaism to this day.

One of the changes that accompanied the rise of the monarchy, illustrated in the books of Samuel, is the transition to truly historical writing in the modern sense. It is instructive to compare the treatment of the figures of Samuel and David. The picture of Samuel is drawn from several traditions which sometimes conflict and sometimes complement each other. On the other hand, the career and personality of David are presented in a single coherent narrative that begins in 1 Samuel and stretches to the beginning of Kings. The author of this narrative not only tells us the major events of David's life but also explains why and how they happened. They are told with such intimacy that we feel that we are reading an eye-witness report.

1	2	3	4	5	6	7	8	9	10
ʾ	alef					א	A	alpha	A
b	beth					ב	B	beta	B
g	ghimel	?				ג	Γ	gamma	G
d	daleth					ד	Δ	delta	D
h	he					ה	E	epsilon	E
w	waw	?				ו	Φ	phi	V
z	zain					ז	Z	zeta	Z
ḥ	heth	?				ח	H	eta	H
ṭ	teth	?				ט	Θ	theta	
j	yod	?				י	I	iota	I
k	kaf					כ	K	cappa	K
l	lamed					ל	Λ	lamda	L
m	mem					מ	M	mi	M
n	nun					נ	N	ni	N
s	samekh	?				ס	Ξ	csi	
ʿ	ayin					ע	O	omicron	O
p	pe					פ	Π	pi	P
ṣ	sade					צ			
q	qof					ק			Q
r	resh					ר	P	ro	R
ś	sin					שׂ			
š	shin					שׁ	Σ	sigma	S
t	tau					ת	T	tau	T

Table showing the progress of the alphabet, from the Palaeo-Sinaitic to the Phoenician and Hebrew and, eventually to the Greek and Latin:
1. Phonetic sound.
2. Hebrew name.
3. Palaeo-Sinaitic.
4. Canaanite script, 12th c. B.C.
5. Phoenician, 9th c.
6. Hebrew cursive 8th c.
7. Modern Hebrew.
8. Greek alphabet.
9. Greek name.
10. Latin alphabet

C. THE RISE OF THE MONARCHY

The most important aspect of Samuel's career was his decisive role in the introduction of monarchy into Israel. Under the threat of growing Philistine power, it became obvious to many in Israel that the voluntary confederation of tribes was no longer able to cope with the organized military power of the Philistines.

1. THE PRICE OF MONARCHIAL GOVERNMENT

In describing these important events, Hebrew historiographers, who were unwilling to tamper with old traditions, accepted different versions even if they were contradictory. For instance, two opposed opinions — one welcoming the establishment of the monarchy, the other critical of royal practices — produced two conflicting accounts of Saul's accession; in the narratives in 1 Sam 9:1–10:16 only the positive aspects of kingship are mentioned, while 1 Sam 10:17–27 presents only the drawbacks of the monarchy. Samuel's warnings and arguments came under four heads, which reflected contemporary conditions:

a) subjecting the people to service in the army; b) appropriation of the peoples' property by the king; c) the *corveé* tax, paid by physical labor on public projects, and d) subjecting the people to slavery, which actually took place under Solomon to support his great enterprises (see Chapter V: Character of Kingship).

By convening the people to elect a *nagid*, Samuel bridged the gap between a charismatic and monarchial government, the prevailing pattern in the ancient Near East.

2. THE SANCTUARY OF SHILOH

About the middle of the 11th century B.C., the Philistines defeated the Israelites at the battle of Ebenezer (1 Samuel 4) and removed the Ark from the central sanctuary of Shiloh. Excavations indicate that they also overran and destroyed towns in Judah and Ephraim (central Palestine), including Shiloh, Tell Beit Mirsim (Debir), and Beth-zur and achieved hegemony over most of Palestine for more than a century.

Excavations have revealed that the city of Shiloh enjoyed an era of prosperity in the period of the Judges when it was fortified. It perished in a violent conflagration, presumably set by the Philistines, which is alluded to by Jeremiah and the author of Psalm 78 (see v. 60). It was revived only a few centuries later.

3. END OF THE TRIBAL FEDERATION

The constant Philistine menace was the great challenge that forced the Israelites to face up to the problem of their survival as a distinctive religious

Seal of "Jaazaniah servant of the king" found at Mizpah (2 Kings 25:23). The fighting cock was the high official's crest.

community and a cohesive national entity. This marks the end of the federated tribal society during the period of the Judges and the beginning of a united monarchy under King Saul, which established Israel as the dominant force in the country, which would be designated the "land of Israel."

Samuel, the last of the charismatic judges, first won a victory over the Philistines at Mizpah in the land of Ephraim (Tell en-Nasbeh). Its main period of occupation is the Iron Age. The excavators uncovered the main part of the city, which contained many four-room houses typical of the period, some of which were unusually large and built with pillars to support roofs. On top of the tenth century casemate wall, there is the outstanding wall and gate built by King Rehoboam in the ninth century. Hebrew seals and seal impressions were among the most abundant finds, one bearing the inscription "Jaazaniah servant of the king," dating to the seventh century B.C.

The biblical sources do not mention any of the cultural attributes of the Philistines, except to point out that they had enjoyed a monopoly of iron tools and weapons which they used as a means to subjugate the Israelites. As a result of this imposition, a popular resistance movement developed. Though its primary motive seems to be the removal of economic restrictions, it aimed ultimately at the expulsion of non-Israelites from the land and the unification of the tribes. This Israelite guerilla warfare was facilitated by the distances separating the Philistine garrisons and the difficulty in maintaining safe communications in the hill country where the Israelites lived in large numbers.

4. KING SAUL. THE MODEST CAPITAL: GIBEAH OF BENJAMIN

The city was founded in the early days of the Israelite settlement and then destroyed before Saul's time as a result of the fierce war waged by the other tribes against Benjamin because of the crime against the Levite's concubine (Judges 9–10).

Saul's citadel of Gibeah was in the form of a courtyard surrounded by a casemate wall (containing inner rooms) and strengthened by four towers as shown in the diagram

Excavations have uncovered a rectangular citadel; its wall was made of undressed blocks, and there was a square tower in the excavated corner. It was apparently built by Saul, and served as his modest royal residence. It was subsequently named after him, Gibeah of Saul (1 Sam 11:4; 15:34), after Saul's defeat at Gilboa. Later, it was rebuilt by David (2 Sam 23:39). It was rebuilt for a third time in the later days of the monarchy, when it was surrounded by a feeble casemate fortification.

The struggle between the Philistines and Israel continued throughout Saul's reign in the lowlands of the Shephelah, but until the final battle he was able to achieve a stalemate and the enemy was kept out of the heartland and the hill country. In the end the Philistines attacked Saul from their bases (Megiddo, Beth-shean) along the *via maris* in the Plain of Jezreel and inflicted on Israel a crushing defeat at Mount Gilboa. Saul and his sons were impaled over the gates of Beth-shean. After Saul's defeat at Mount Gilboa, the balance shifted in favor of the Philistines. Though they had crushed Saul and had helped to drive a wedge between Saul and David, their tactics failed in the end. The crisis in Israel proved to be temporary thanks to the emergence of David as a national hero.

Part of the underground conduit or ṣinnor leading to the Giḥon spring held by the Jebusites. Its damage by David led to the capture of Jerusalem (2 Sam 5:9)

D. DAVID

As indicated above, the domination of the Philistines over Israel was a temporary phenomenon. In the end Israel was victorious, and it was David, the brilliant military leader and charismatic political figure who turned the tide.

1. THE CAPTURE OF JERUSALEM

Unlike the siege of Jericho, where we have an elaborate description of the battle and no supporting archaeological evidence, the capture of Jerusalem by David is described in a single verse in 2 Sam 5, but there is corroborative material data. Archaeologists have found part of a city wall built by the Jebusites in the Middle Bronze Age (ca. 1800) to protect the Gihon spring lying in the Kidron valley, as well as a system of shafts and tunnels to reach the underground source of water. According to the traditional interpretation of 2 Sam 5:9, David's men were told "to go up the water shaft to attack..." That would mean crawling up an almost perpendicular shaft to suprise the inhabitants of the city. While possible, it seems unlikely and B. Mazar has proposed a different analysis of the passage and reconstruction of the event. In Hebrew the verse reads *wayyiga' bassinnor* which means that "they struck (and damaged) the horizontal conduit" which brought the water from the source to the mouth of the spring shaft. According to the parallel account in 1 Chr 11:4–9, which doesn"t mention the shaft, Joab was the first to go up

Salient of the Jebusite wall of Zion (Jerusalem) ca. 1800 B.C. , made of rough boulders, which was protected by another wall, seen on the right against the city, possibly storming the wall at the lower end of the eastern fortification, close to the Kidron valley. A strategy combining an attack on the wall at one point and the disruption of the city's water supply at another offers a more logical solution to the problem of the capture of the city (B. Mazar, *The Mountain of the Lord*, p. 168).

2. THE PUZZLE OF THE MILLO TERRACES

The verse "and David built the city about from the Millo inward" (2 Sam 5:9) has challenged comprehension, chiefly because the word *millo* was erroneously identified with a specific location in Jerusalem. Recent excavations have shown that the Millo consisted of supporting walls and stone terraces built in gradients, erected over the steep slopes of the southeastern hill of Zion, where the oldest city was established in pre-Israelite times. The houses of the town were then built upon these terraces, and in Solomon's time, the city began to expand westward, over the top of the hill. From that time on, great care was taken to keep the terraces in good repair to protect against erosion from rain water and to allow further expansion on the hillside.

3. DAVID'S EMPIRE

David consolidated the nation established by Saul; he united the tribes, along with several alien client groups, and conquered neighboring countries under a stable system of government. Under his extraordinary leadership, Israel became for a time a major international force in the Near East. As a

The Canaanite or Jebusite wall made of large boulders (below) protected the underground Gihon spring, the main source of water of early Jerusalem. The wall above it is Israelite result of his victories over the Philistines, Moabites, Edomites, Ammonites, and Arameans, he extended the boundaries of Israel as far as central Syria in the northwest and the approaches of the Euphrates in the northeast; the entire coast from Mount Carmel to south of Joppa became Israelite and the Philistines were reduced to paying tribute.

4. THE CHIEFS OF DAVID'S MIGHTY MEN

At the core of David's military organization were the 37 leaders of his standing army, described as "the chiefs of David's mighty men who gave him strong support in his kingdom" (1 Chr 11:10). They were recruited by him during his career as a vassal chieftain and remained personally loyal to him through his life. They were at the head of his troops when he was anointed king, first at Hebron and later in Jerusalem. These men served as the king's bodyguard and also as battalion leaders, commanding infantrymen and auxiliaries, much as did the *maryannu,* the chariot-riding knights of the Canaanite city-kingdoms of an earlier age. The most important sources on the subject are the two colorful lists in 2 Sam 23:8–39 and 1 Chr 11:10–47, which identify the men and add details.

5. THE MUSICAL GUILDS

Biblical tradition is consistent in acknowledging David as the father of Israelite music. His career began as a lute player in Saul's court. The memory of his contribution to the development of Israel's musical institutions was so powerful in later generations that practically everything in the way of liturgal music (including the Psalms) was attributed to him, much as all the laws were traced to Moses. However exaggerated these views may be, there can be little doubt that he was chiefly responsible for their establishment in Israel, and that the musical guilds date back to the time of David in connection with the Temple services. We know from older sources that there was a rich tradition of Canaanite sacred music, which was taken over and adapted in Israel. The names of the guilds recorded in Chronicles reflect the older pagan background: e.g. Asaph, Heman, Ethan or Jeduthun; elsewhere we read of Heman, Khalkol, and Darda "the sons of Maḥol," i.e. members of the orchestral guild (see Psalms). The creation of musical instruments is attributed to the gods or Titans (semi-divine beings) in Near Eastern and Mediterranean mythology and in the Bible to the descendants of Cain, the eponymous ancestor of smiths, metal-workers and instrument-makers. The secrets of instrument-making and playing were guarded by the guilds and passed from generation to generation of those who were set aside for this service to the Temple and to the royal palace. There are many striking representations of musicians in finds from excavations (as for example, the remarkable incense altar from Ashdod, or the older ivories from Megiddo). In the list of prisoners captured by Sennacherib after the siege of Jerusalem in 701 B.C., musicians of the royal court namely male and female singers, were mentioned prominently.

Left:
A musician playing the harp
surrounded by friendly
animals. Decoration on an
11th c. B.C. Megiddo vase

Center:
Iron plough from Tell bet
Mirsim (2 Sam 12)

Right:
Iron pitchfork (10th c. B.C.)

6. THE PAX DAVIDICA

Archaeological evidence reveals that there was a population explosion in Judah during and after the tenth century B.C. when the peace and prosperity David brought made it possible to build many new towns. This expansion was facilitated by two technological advances: the slaked lime cistern and the iron plow tip. The new cisterns allowed people to settle farther from water sources and the plow tip greatly increased the yield from the soil. The same phenomenon took place in Europe, after the Dark Ages, when the introduction of the large plowshare revolutionized agriculture. This was followed by the tremendous commercial and industrial expansion under Solomon, which accounts for the rapid growth of Jerusalem in his days.

7. JERUSALEM

Jerusalem thus became the new center of the traditional league of twelve tribes; its sacral character was emphasized by the transfer of the Ark of the Covenant there and the erection first of a shrine and then of the Temple in the city. The United Monarchy saw itself as heir to the ancient league which embraced both north and south Palestine, and devoted its efforts to centralizing both political power and religious authority at the same place: the holy city of God, Jerusalem. In time the traditions and terminology associated with Yahweh's desert mountain sanctuary, Sinai, were appropriated for the temple in Mount Zion, as the political traditions of the tribal league were assigned to the king and the royal entourage. God's covenant of promise to Abraham was applied to the royal home and the royal city, and both were held to be inviolate and inviolable, eternally protected by the Deity. The Temple of Mount Zion, the holy city Jerusalem and the Dynasty of David were indissolubly linked in royal theology and hymnody, and in the minds of both prophets and people, leaving a permanent legacy in the religious traditions of both Judaism and Christianity; messianism was derived from the historical reality of David and Jerusalem, and projected into the eschatological future was the hope of a restoration of a glorious past.

The United Kingdom
created by David comprised
Palestine on both sides of the
Jordan and the various vassal
states bordering it on all sides

THE UNITED KINGDOM

PART V

A. THE BOOKS OF 1 AND 2 KINGS AND CHRONICLES

Originally the two books of Kings were one, as in the case of Samuel. They are a chronological continuation of the latter and are about the same length. Their historical narratives cover a period of about four centuries, from the tenth to the sixth B.C. and are paralleled roughly by 1 Chronicles 29 to 2 Chronicles 35 as shown in the table below. The history of the monarchy in these books may be divided into three main parts:

1. 1 Kings 1–11 covers the United Monarchy. The first two chapters complete the history of David's reign which is the main theme of 2 Samuel 9–20, and then describe the accession of Solomon. Chapters 3–11 present a dazzling picture of Solomon's rule over the United Kingdom of Israel, the climax of 1 Kings.
2. 1 Kings 12 – 2 Kings 17 deals with the schism of the United Kingdom and then gives parallel accounts of the separate kingdoms of Judah and Israel (Samaria) up to the destruction of the latter.
3. 2 Kings 18–25 continues the history of the kingdom of Judah, after the fall of the Northern Kingdom, up to the destruction of Jerusalem in 586 B.C. and the exile of the Judeans.

THE CONTENTS IN HISTORICAL PERSPECTIVE

Dates: It is important to recall that the first certain date in biblical history — the battle of Qarqar between the Assyrians and a coalition of western kingdoms in 853 B.C. — was established through archaeological findings. This has resulted in a more reliable and precise chronology of this period than has hitherto been available.

The United Kingdom

Date B.C.	Kings	The Event	Chronicles
970–968	1 Kgs 1–2	The last days of David and the accession of Solomon to the throne	1 Chr 29:20–30
968–965		Co-regency of David and Solomon	
965	1 Kings 3	The beginning of Solomon's sole reign	2 Chronicles 1
	1 Kings 4	Extracts from the royal annals, a new and vital element of Israelite literature	
	1 Kings 4–5	Solomon's ambitious building activities	2 Chronicles 2–4

Date B.C.	Kings	The Event	Chronicles
	1 Kgs 8:1–9:9	The account of the dedication of the Temple	2 Chronicles 5–7
965–928	1 Kgs 9:10–10:29	Miscellaneous data on the reign, especially concerning Solomon's economic activity	2 Chronicles 8–9
	1 Kings 11	His marriages to foreign princesses; the decline of his rule	

The Divided Kingdom

Date B.C.	Kings	The Event	Chronicles
928	1 Kgs 12:1–24	The Schism	2 Chronicles 10
	1 Kgs 12:25–14:20	Jeroboam, first ruler of the Northern Kingdom	2 Chronicles 11–12
	1 Kgs 14:21–15:24	Rehoboam, Abijah, and Asa, Kings of Judah	2 Chronicles 13–16
	1 Kgs 15:25–28	Shishak's campaign	2 Chr 12:1–12
907–882	1 Kgs 15:25–16:28	Nadab to Omri (Northern Kingdom)	
871–851	1 Kgs 16:29–22:40	King Ahab of Israel and the prophet Elijah story cycle. The battle of Qarqar (853 B.C.)	
867	1 Kgs 22:41–50	Jehoshaphat of Judah	2 Chronicles 17–20
851	1 Kgs 22:51– 2 Kgs 1:18	Ahaziah, the sixth king of Israel	
	2 Kgs 2:1–25	Completion of the Elijah stories; prophet Elisha's succession	
850 851–843	2 Kgs 3:1–8:29	The Elisha cycle; the reigns of Jehoram of Israel; Kings Jehoram and Ahaziah of Judah	2 Chronicles 21–22
842	2 Kgs 9:1–10:36	Jehu of Israel	
	2 Kings 11–12	Queen Athaliah and King Joash in Judah	2 Chronicles 22–24
814–800	2 Kings 14	Jehoahaz and Jehoash of Israel	2 Chronicles 25
799–785	2 Kings 14	Amaziah, eighth king of Judah; Jeroboam II of Israel	2 Chronicles 25
786	2 Kgs 15:1–31	Uzziah, ninth king of Judah; chaos in the Northern Kingdom	2 Chronicles 26
758–742	2 Kgs 15:32–16:20	Jotham and Ahaz, tenth and eleventh kings of Judah	2 Chronicles 27–28
722/1	2 Kings 17	The destruction of the Northern Kingdom	2 Chronicles 28

Date B.C.	Kings	The Event	Chronicles
727–698	2 Kings 18–20	Hezekiah's reign; Assyrian King Sennacherib besieges Jerusalem; Hezekiah and the prophet Isaiah	2 Chronicles 29–32
697–640	2 Kings 21	Manasseh; his apostasy; Amon	2 Chronicles 33
640	2 Kgs 22:1–23, 30a	Josiah, the 15th king, and religious reformer	2 Chronicles 34–35
609–597	2 Kgs 23:30b– 25:7	The last kings of Judah; from Jehoahaz, the 16th, until Zedekiah, the 19th; the last days of Jerusalem	2 Chronicles 36
586	2 Kgs 25:8–30	Destruction of the state of Judah and the Exile. The last verses (22–30) recount the murder of Gedaliah and the release of King Jehoiachin in Babylon, after the death of the Babylonian King Nebuchadnezzar.	2 Chr 36:22–23, which is not parallel to 2 Kings (cf. Ezra 1:1–3) but mentions the decree of Cyrus which heralded the Restoration of the Commonwealth (see Part XIV)

Foundation Rock and presumed site of the Holy of Holies. The scars and markings reflect the vicissitudes of the site over four millennia. It stands now below the Islamic Dome of the Rock

B. SOLOMON

1. WHAT DID SOLOMON'S TEMPLE LOOK LIKE?

The Temple was oriented east-to-west, with its vestibule facing the rising sun. Solomon constructed the Temple of large rectangular stones and beams of valuable cedar and cypress wood brought from the forests of Lebanon and northern Syria. No traces of Solomon's Temple have been found on top of the Temple Mount. Any possible surviving remains of it, or of the palaces built nearby (the House of the Forest of Lebanon and the Porch of Justice), would lie buried beneath the Moslem sanctuary, Haram esh-Sherif, built in the seventh century A.D., which is forbidden ground for archaeology. The most reliable archaeological evidence regarding the plan of this temple derives from a comparative study of contemporary sanctuaries at Tell Ta'inat on the Syrian coast, at Samal in northwestern Syria, and at Ḥamath in central Syria. The temple at Ta'inat is of special interest because of its close resemblance to the larger Jerusalem Temple. It is oblong

Ground plan of the palace (a) and the small shrine (b) of Tai'nat which is strikingly similar in plan to Solomon's tripartite sanctuary: 1. the entrance hall; 2. the main hall, and 3. the *debîr* (Holy of Holies)

Plan of Solomon's temple showing two pillars facing the entrance, the three divisions of the sanctuary and the outer chambers (yaṣia) flanking it on three sides

1.

and divided into three parts; cf. the tripartite division of the Jerusalem
Temple into the 'ûlam (entrance hall), the hêḳāl (main hall), and the
inner debîr or Holy of Holies. An earlier prototype is the Late Bronze
temple (16th–13th centuries B.C.) found at Hazor in Galilee or even Ebla
(Tell Mardikh, of Early Bronze IV) near Aleppo (see Genesis A, 4). Similar
elements appear in Canaanite temples at Shechem, Megiddo, Beth-shean, and
finally the Israelite high place at Arad (see Part III). Apparently all that is
left of the Jerusalem Temple is the foundation rock on which the debîr rested,
which is now the heart of the Moslem sanctuary of the Dome of the Rock.

According to 1 Kgs 6:31, olive wood doors separated the hêḳāl and the
debîr. The whole temple was built on a platform and was 165 feet (100
cubits) long, 82 feet wide and 82 feet high. These measurements include
the width of the wall and the storehouse, the yāzî'â, a three-storied structure
with numerous chambers which was built around the sanctuary on three
sides.

2. THE FURNISHINGS OF THE TEMPLE

The sanctuary furniture and ritual objects were patterned after contemporary Phoenician equipment; most of the master craftsmen and skilled
artisans also came from Phoenicia. The cherubim, whose wings screened
the Ark of the Covenant (see Part II, A, 11), were winged sphinx-like
creatures common to the mythological art and iconography of the ancient
Near East. Numerous examples occur among the ivories of Megiddo and
Samaria (see below), as well as in pottery incense altars from Ta'anach and
Megiddo.

The menorah, a candelabrum with seven branches, is known only from
the period of the Second Temple; older antecedents in the form of lamps
with seven spouts have been found.

A stand to wheel around large vessels in a sanctuary

Through archaeology we have an idea what the base and bronze lavers of the Temple looked like. There are parallels in the Megiddo open-work stand and a carriage base from Larnaka, Cyprus, whose large wheels are reminiscent of the base in the Bible.

The massive free-standing bronze pillars, Jachin and Boaz, flanked the outer entrance. They were elaborately decorated and crowned with bronze capitals. Similar columns have been discovered in Israel, and Phoenician temples are reported to have had them. Such pillars were outstanding achievements of bronze metalwork as they had to be cast in special molds. Sennacherib of Assyria boasts of such a feat some 250 years later.

The Temple was in the center of a court surrounded by a thick wall. In the court stood the great Altar of Sacrifices built of untrimmed stone, which was the focus of the daily sacrificial ritual. There was also the immense "sea" of bronze which was supported by 12 cast oxen. Its exact appearance remains a mystery; the nearest parallel may be the two huge cauldrons in an Assyrian relief depicting the temple at Musasir in Iraq (last quarter of the eighth century B.C.), or the large cauldron from Amatheus although it is male of stone, not bronze.

3. SOLOMON'S FORTIFICATIONS

It was also during Solomon's reign that new methods and styles in the building of fortifications were introduced: the extensive use of the casemate ramparts consisting of a thick outer wall and a series of blind rooms, filled with packed earth and rubble; at times they were sealed by a parallel inner wall. The blind rooms served as storage-chambers on occasion. In this way, the rampart was widened and strenthened, as is evident from the excavations at Megiddo, Hazor, Gezer, Tell Beit Mirsim, Beth-shemesh, Tell Qasileh, all dating from Solomon's time. The first ramparts on the eastern flank of the City of David also were built in this period. This casemate wall was not abandoned after Solomon's time but continued in use as an inner defensive wall (see below: Ahab).

The terse biblical statement (1 Kgs 9:15) that Solomon built Megiddo has been extensively amplified by archaeological excavation. They show that his plan covered three essential features of the ancient city: the fortified buildings, the gates, and the water supply. The Solomonic city gates at Megiddo, Hazor, and Gezer consist of two square towers and three pairs of buttresses with narrow passageways and chambers which served as guard-rooms or armories (illustration). The approach to the gate was at an angle, running along the city wall. Any enemy chariots approaching along the wall were thus exposed to the defenders on the wall when attacking the gate.

4. HYDRAULIC SYSTEMS AND TUNNELS

Solomon's underground hydraulic works, later enlarged by King Ahab, were found at Megiddo, Hazor, and Gezer. The one at Megiddo consisted

Casemate wall (with inner rooms) built by Solomon at Hatzor. Seen in the foreground and left

Eastern side and upper level of Solomon's Gate of Megiddo. The entrance rests over a lower and older section (foreground)

Reconstructed site of the 8th c. self-contained water system of Hatzor. It consisted of a shaft reaching 126 feet to the underground water table where it met a 67 feet horizontal tunnel lying outside the walls of the city, but beyond the enemy's reach

Above:
Underground water pool,
Hatzor

Right:
Reconstructed model of
Israelite Megiddo. The
governor's residence is in
the background; the stables
are to the left and the gate in
the foreground. The lower
section to the right shows the
older Canaanite city

of a vertical shaft lined with a masonry retaining wall. At its lower end, the vertical shaft became a steep passage which passed under the city wall and continued as a long tunnel with an arched ceiling. The tunnel ended at a cave and spring which lay outside the wall. The people could make their way unobserved to the cave, which was camouflaged. Inside the cave lay the burned skeleton of a guard who seems to have died when the cave was seized in a surprise attack and set afire. The Hazor tunnel was dug inside the city to reach the underground water level. Its shaft was 100 feet deep and the tunnel descended some 50 feet deeper, ending apparently in a pool. The Gezer tunnel, a shaft 27 feet deep with a sloping tunnel 132 feet long led to a perennial spring at a depth of about 100 feet. It belonged to an older Canaanite type, probably of the Late Bronze Age.

5. A NEW TYPE OF ARCHITECTURE

The appearance of beautifully hewn and dressed stones in public buildings in the days of Solomon was a marked improvement over earlier building; it imitates the technique of stone-cutting practiced in Phoenician cities. The

Below:
Reconstruction of citadel gate
at Hatzor (Ahab's reign,
9th c. B.C.)

Right:
Proto-Aeolic capital from the
days of the Monarchy,
Jerusalem

external surface of the hewn stones is dressed with narrow borders, varying in width, on two or four sides, while the center of the ashlar block protrudes in a roughly rounded boss. Such stones were used in the foundations and lower courses, while those above ground were smoothed without protruding bosses. They were laid in header-stretcher fashion, successive courses alternating in orientation. Buildings constructed this way were provided with deep foundation trenches dug in bedrock to a depth of about 10 feet.

Hewn stone pilasters stood as engaged columns at regular intervals along the walls and in the corners. They were usually crowned by capitals of a proto-Aeolian type (illustration). These architectural methods were used in Israel until the Exile.

6. REMAINS OF SOLOMON'S CITIES

Among the cities specifically mentioned as having been built or rebuilt by Solomon, several major sites, including Megiddo, Gezer, Hazor, and Lachish, have been excavated extensively. Some of their fortifications, monumental gates, public buildings, and stores have been preserved; one such building is the small palace of Baana ben Ahilud, the governor of Megiddo appointed by Solomon. It was his duty to provide food for the royal household one month each year; the large palace (see model) was reserved for special ceremonies and royal visits.

7. SOLOMON'S INTERNATIONAL TRADE

Solomon took advantage of Israel's geographic location between Egypt, Syria, and southern Arabia to play an active role in international commerce, along with his Tyrian (Phoenician) allies. Important finds in Sardinia, Spain, and North Africa dating to the late 11th and early tenth centuries

Vassals bringing tribute to the king. Assyrian bronze engraving depicting the surrender of Tyre (9th c.)

109

Above:
Chariot and Syrian horse

Right:
Merchant ship in Solomon's fleet, *Tarshish* type; 13th c. B.C.

Below:
Unloading logs from the boats to the wharf

Right:
Phoenician boats transporting logs in tow or aboard along the shores of the Mediterranean; 8th c. Assyrian relief.

B.C. have shown conclusively that the Phoenicians spread westward through the Mediterranean world as traders and colonists, after David had destroyed the Philistine confederacy and its maritime power around 1000 B.C. This trans-Mediterranean shipping was led by the Sidonians and Tyrians, employing larger and stronger seagoing vessels than had previously been known. More ambitious ship designs could be realized by efficient use of the great cedars and firs of Lebanon and Cilicia (Asia Minor) and technological improvements such as bands and spikes in naval construction. This expansion attained its height in the ninth century and had passed its zenith by the middle of the eighth century when Greeks entered the seafaring competition in earnest.

Solomon's ships, built with Tyrian help in the port of *Ezion-geber*, near

Elath, took part in independent or joint expeditions to Ophir. The location of Ophir is still debated (South Arabia? East Africa? or India?) but we have evidence that it was a source of gold in an ostracon found at Tell Qasileh on which was written "Gold from Ophir to Beth-horon — 30 shekels." The Israelites went as far as Tarshish (probably in Spain), from which they brought precious metals, ivory, and other exotic products. The word *tarshish* apparently meant "metal refinery" in Phoenician and became the name of the sites where the Phoenicians established such installations, as in Sardinia and Spain.

Clay figurine from Shikmona;
Israelite period

The manner in which bulkier cargos, such as timber, were carried to David and Solomon (2 Sam 5:11; 1 Kgs 5:1; 1 Chr 14:1) is depicted in Assyrian reliefs. They show small river-boats manned by Phoenicians carrying logs stretched out on their upper deck, or tied to their sterns and trailing behind in the water. These cargo vessels moved down the coast from Cicilia or Lebanon by day and took shelter by night in the small coves and inlets of the eastern Mediterranean. The boats were unloaded at the mouth of the Yarkon river or Tell Quasileh (modern Tel Aviv) and the timber transported by ox-carts to Jerusalem for the great building operations of David and Solomon: the Temple, the royal palaces, and the elaborate homes of the nobility.

According to an obscure passage in the Bible, Solomon's merchants purchased horses from Ku'e (Asia Minor) and chariots from Egypt, and bartered them to the Hittite kings in Syria (1 Kgs 9:26–27; 2 Chr 8:17–18). David, and to a greater extent Solomon, created chariot squadrons for their army, and Solomon built special cities for his chariots. The famous stables found at Megiddo are, however, to be attributed to Ahab.

a. The Myth of Solomon's Mines

Solomon's copper mining activity cannot be identified with the popular "Solomon's mines" near Elath which are of Egyptian origin. There is no evidence of any copper mining or smelting in the Arabah valley between the 12th and 2nd centuries B.C. The credit given to Solomon belongs to Egyptians and Midianites a few centuries earlier (see: Exodus, A Midianite Sanctuary at Timnah). These negative results concerning mining are corroborated by the passages in 1 Chr 18:8 and 22:3 which indicate that David secured his metal from Syria. Furthermore, Solomon imported iron from the western Mediterranean in his boats of Tarshish. His fame in developing the Arabah emerged from his international seafaring enterprises based at the port of Ezion-geber, or Tell el-Kheleifeh, near modern Elath. Excavation there has revealed a small fortified center for warehousing, industry, and sea trade.

b. Shikmona

Another interesting aspect of Solomon's maritime expansion was revealed by recent discovery of a harbor city at Shikmona, south of Haifa, with the remains of four-roomed houses, oil presses, and a variety of artifacts dating from the tenth century. The place had previously been settled by Canaanites,

South Arabian (Sabean) scene
of a queen and attendants.
Late Iron age

but was taken over by David or Solomon as they consolidated their control of the country.

c. *Solomon and Arabia*

A Sabean kingdom was already established in Yemen (South Arabia) by the time of Solomon. Sedentary civilization and the use of writing (derived from the Old Canaanite alphabet) has been traced back at least to the tenth century, while camels had been domesticated in Arabia before the 11th century. Therefore, there is good reason to accept the biblical tradition that caravan trade between northern and central Syria, including Canaan, and southern Arabia began not later than the mid-tenth century B.C. The chief purpose of the Queen of Sheba's famous visit to the court of Solomon was probably to conclude a trade treaty, involving the exchange of the exotic spices of South Arabia for the agricultural produce of Israel, and more complex dealings for the manufactured products of third countries like Phoenicia.

8. THE CHARACTER OF KINGSHIP — PALESTINE AND PHOENICIA

Biblical tradition defines clearly the two functions of kingship in Israel: the king was chief executive, administrator and judge and also the commander-in-chief of the army and director of the nation's foreign policy. It was in the second role that David consolidated the tribes into a nation and built a standing army capable of defending it. The importance of royal justice was universally recognized in the ancient Near East. It is well illustrated in the inscription of Yehimilk, king of Byblos, a contemporary of Solomon. It says at one point: "May Ba'lshamem and the Lord of Byblos and the Assembly of the Holy Gods of Byblos prolong the days and years of Yehimilk in Byblos for (he is) a righteous and an upright king before the Holy Gods of Byblos!"

The Yehimilk inscription

In most countries the authority and power of the king were regarded as absolute and beyond challenge, though in practice his position rested on the support of the army, priesthood, and aristocracy. In Israel the authority of the king was delimited by divine law. His role and power were carefully defined by a tripartite covenant involving the priesthood, the king, and the people represented by the elders and army officers. The distinctive principle governing the Israelite monarchy was that all persons, including the king, were subject to the rule of law, namely the law revealed by God.

9. THE CLASSIC ERA OF BIBLICAL WRITING

It is commonly agreed that Solomon was a great patron of literature and the arts, and it is not accidental that his name was closely associated with the writing of songs and proverbs. The authorship of Proverbs, Song of Songs, and Ecclesiastes was attributed to him according to popular tradition, which was perpetuated in Scriptures in the same manner that David's name was attached to many Psalms, even if these books gradually crystallized into their present form later (as described below in the respective chapters).

There is no doubt that royal secretaries and royal records proliferated in the days of Solomon and David; royal archives are often referred to in the books of Kings and Chronicles in such terms as "And the rest of the acts of King *NN* and all that he did are inscribed in the records of the royal chronicles of Israel and Judah." The term *sofer*, "scribe" or "secretary" had the same broad range of meaning in those days as it does today. Thus it may refer to the person who actually writes at someone's dictation, or copies a text, like an office secretary. Or it may refer to a high official in the government, like cabinet members in the United States: Secretary of State, Treasury, Defense, etc. So the "scribe" in the royal establishment of Israel had cabinet rank, was educated, skilled in writing and widely read: such was "Jonathan, David's uncle, ... a counsellor, being a man of understanding and a scribe" (1 Chr 27:32). Similar examples may be found in 1 Chr 2:55 and 4:9–10.

Israel's chroniclers had a literate audience which read and appreciated their writings and it was the duty of the Levites scattered throughout the land to teach the people ritual, ethics, and letters. This literary and cultural level was not peculiar to Israel. The Phoenicians were equally literate, both peoples speaking and writing closely related Canaanite dialects. Scribal guilds were an institution in Canaan long before the Hebrew conquest. As was the case in much of the ancient Near East, its members served not only in the royal courts but in every town where they recorded official documents and served as public secretaries.

Overleaf:
The Northern Kingdom of Israel and Southern Kingdom of Judah after the division of David's and Solomon's United Kingdom

King Sam'al of northern Syria and his scribe, a high official. (9th c. from Sinjirli)

C. THE DIVISION INTO TWO KINGDOMS

The empire left by Solomon fell apart as a result of the opposition of the northern tribes to the heavy taxation and forced labor imposed by the king. Rather than speaking of the dissolution of a single nation, it may be more accurate to see the period of the United Monarchy as an interlude when two separate political entities were welded together by the personal power of David. We have observed that in the Song of Deborah (see Judges) only the ten northern tribes are mentioned, implying that the southern tribes are isolated from them and constitute a separate group. Later, the numerous references to "the men of Judah and of Israel" in the stories of the time of Saul suggest that this distinction was already recognized before the time of David. It will be noted that on Saul's death, the existence of separate states, north and south, was taken for granted when Ishbaal was made king of Israel and David king of Judah. In sum, even a centralized government was unable to overcome deep-seated differences and unify the separate groups permanently. This schism left two weak kingdoms, Israel (the Northern Kingdom) and Judah, which were soon attacked by Shishak, the Egyptian pharaoh, as recorded in an inscription in the Amon Temple at Karnak. It provides a long list of places in both Judah and Israel which were overrun by Shishak's army and details of his raid not mentioned in the Bible.

Fragment of an Egyptian stele marked *Shishak*, the pharaoh who invaded Palestine in Rehoboam's time

1. JEROBOAM, REHOBOAM, AND SHISHAK

Immediately after Shishak's campaign (the last quarter of the tenth century) radical changes were made in the construction of defensive walls to increase their strength. Solid walls, made of stone or a stone foundation with a brick superstructure took the place of the casemate wall. This "offset and inset" (slight salients and recesses) wall was further protected by superstructures. An outstanding example of the new type of work is seen in Megiddo's 11-foot thick wall. Rehoboam, king of Judah, undertook to build 15 such fortresses at Judah's most strategic points to guarantee the security of his kingdom and encourage its economic growth. There were large and flourishing cities, dating to the period following Jeroboam and Rehoboam,

Seal of "Shema servant of Jeroboam" (the second); 8th c. Jasper, from Megiddo

Reconstruction of the stables of Megiddo; built by King Ahab

Opposite page
First row left:
Monumental flight of steps
leading to the High Place or
bāmâh of Dan, an open air
sanctuary
Right:
Characteristic Israelite
masonry of the sanctuary,
showing alternate 'headers'
and 'stretchers' in the wall
Second row, left:
The horned altar discovered at
Dan, measuring 16 × 16
inches and 14 in. high
Right:
Bench at the right of
the entrance to the main
gate, where the elders sat for
judgment
Third row, right:
The ashlar stone structure to
the right of the threshold of
the gate and the paved street
leading into the city
Left: Detail

at Megiddo and Hazor as well as at Samaria (see below). The famous
stables at Megiddo (illustration) also belong to this period.

2. THE SANCTUARY AND MONUMENTS OF TELL DAN

Jeroboam, first ruler of the Northern Kingdom, erected "golden calves"
at the sanctuaries of Dan and Bethel after the schism of the United Kingdom
(1 Kgs 12:16 ff.). He meant both to rival Jerusalem as a cultic center and
to establish parallel sanctuaries at both ends of his kingdom. The discovery
of the high place at Arad (see Part IV), also founded during Solomon's
days or shortly thereafter, indicates that kings established small royal sanctuaries (*miqdaš melek*) in old cities on their borders to demonstrate their
sovereignty in the region. In this way we can explain the presence of sanctuaries not only at Dan, Bethel, and Arad, but also at Beersheba on the
edge of the desert which separated Israel from Egypt (see below: Amos).

Judging by the change in pottery types after the destruction of Dan
(Laish) in the middle of the 11th century B.C., it was then settled by
Israelites who migrated from the region near present-day Tel Aviv.

The excavations conducted by A. Biran since 1968 uncovered a large
structure from the Israelite period on the northwestern part of the tell
(Area T). Its fine masonry, laid in headers and stretchers, resembles the
monumental Israelite constructions found in Samaria and Megiddo. In fact
it is a *bāmâh* or high place, that is, an open air sanctuary. An almost square
structure, roughly 60x62 feet, was discovered in the center. Its thick outer
walls were made of dressed limestone except the northern side which was
built up of large basalt blocks. The area enclosed by the walls was filled
with basalt stones, forming a wide, flat platform.

On the southers edge of the *bāmâh*, facing the town, a massive set of
steps, 27 feet wide, was uncovered, built directly against the outer wall of
the *bāmâh*. This stairway is built partially over earlier masonry. Pottery collected there dates to the ninth century. The first stage of the Israelite *bāmâh*,
measuring 20x61 feet, probably comes from the reign of Jeroboam I (1 Kgs
12:31). A second stage of the high place, with a still wider monumental
stairway, is attributed to Ahab (1 Kgs 20:34; 22:39)

a. *The City Gate*

After several seasons of excavation, a complete outer and inner gate
complex, with a stone-paved square, a road, and a massive city wall emerged.
The inner gate is built of lage basalt blocks; it is about 97 feet long and had
a width of 50 feet. It consisted of two towers and four guardrooms. The
paved street leads westwards into the city, then turns toward the top of the
mound.

A great deal of attention was paid to an unusual structure and bench
at the entrance to the gate. It is located along the outer wall of the northeastern tower. This is, according to biblical tradition, where the elders used
to "sit at the gate" (Ps 69:12) to deliberate and settle cases (cf. Ruth 4).
The remarkable structure located near the bench is built of ashlars and

originally had small columns with decorated capitals at each of its four corners (two of which were found *in situ*). The structure as a whole may have served as a throne or judgment seat, such as the one at the entrance of Samaria where the kings of Israel and Judah met on occasion (1 Kgs 22:10).

Why then was the stone structure and the bench outside the inner city gate, facing the outer wall and gate? There is sufficient archaeological evidence to infer that a massive wall enclosed this plaza. It is an example of "the square at the gate of the city" mentioned in the Bible (Judg 19:15–17; 2 Chr 32:6). The gate complex was built at the end of the tenth century, probably by Jeroboam I (1 Kgs 11:28).

b. *Standing Stones (maṣṣebôth)*

The *maṣṣebôth* were large stones or groups of them which were used for cultic purposes, usually found in Israel at sites associated with high places (e.g. 1 Kgs 14:23; 2 Kgs 17:10) and temples. They stood on a pedestal at the entrance to the "tower temple" of Shechem (see Judges). An elaborate group of ten of these stones, up to ten feet in height, were found at Middle Bronze Age levels of Gezer, lined up in three rows, with an altar standing in the center. The temple at Hazor (13th century B.C.) also had ten basalt *maṣṣebôth*, although they are much smaller. One was engraved with a pair of hands upraised gesturing toward the moon. Five stones stood near a temple at Timnah, center of the copper works near Elath. A *maṣṣebâh* has also been found at the center of the high place of Arad (ninth century).

The massebah or standing pillar set up in the Holy of Holies of the sanctuary of Arad

In the days of the United Monarchy these sacred stones were condemned because of the association with idol worship and particularly the Baal cult (1 Kgs 14:23; 2 Kgs 3:2; 17:10; 18:4) Their extensive use in Canaanite and Israelite rural worship stigmatized them and made them unfit for the religion of Yahweh.

Royal ashlar masonry at
Samaria, capital of the
Northern Kingdom

3. THE DYNASTIES OF OMRI AND JEHU (882–745 B.C.) IN ISRAEL

The Northern Kingdom regained much of its earlier strength with the advent of the dynasty of Omri in 882 B.C. By then Israel had to face the ever-growing aggression of the Arameans of Damascus, who had displaced Israel's authority over Transjordan in the days of King Baasha (907–882 B.C.). Omri, like David, abandoned the old provincial capital and moved to a new site, Samaria, which was free from any older tribal associations, making it a strictly royal city, the possession of the Omride dynasty. This remained the capital of the kingdom until its capture by the Assyrians in 722 B.C.

Excavations there had produced extensive evidence of the achievements of the northern kings during the ninth-eighth centuries and illustrated the material and cultural progress resulting from diplomatic alliance with the Phoenicians as in the days of Solomon. By then Tyre had become the mightiest sea power in the Mediterranean and its colonies had spread as far as Spain and Africa. A vivid detailed picture of Phoenician trade with Israel is given by the prophet Ezekiel (Ezekiel 27).

Proto-Aeolian capitals and
pilasters at Samaria

a. *Samaria's Remains*

Samaria was founded in 880 B.C. by Omri and enlarged by his son, Ahab. The former built his acropolis at the top of the hill, enclosing it by a wall of fine ashlar masonry and later enlarging it with a casemate wall. The lower town was protected by a massive wall of ashlar stones which surrounded the acropolis. On the acropolis two walls were found. The "inner wall," as it is called by the excavators, was five feet thick and encircled the summit of the hill, circumscribing an area of 194x106 yards. Its stones were laid in header (perpendicular to the direction of the wall)

Ivory carvings from the palace at Samaria. Mid 9th c. B.C.

33.2565

and stretcher (parallel to the direction of the wall) formation. Several buildings were discovered within the walled area, among them the remains of the Israelite palace, with its central court; the outside measurements are 89x79 feet. An "outer wall" was found to the north of the acropolis, apparently built by Omri. Ahab strengthened the defenses by adding a broad casemate wall about 33 feet wide, thus expanding the fortified area. The gateway seems to have been in the southwestern corner. On the eastern side of the acropolis proto-Aeolian capitals were found, suggesting that this was the main entrance to the inner area. In the west, between the "inner wall" and the casemate wall there was a storehouse measuring 59x92 feet, labelled the "House of the Ostraca" because of the inscribed potsherds found there. In the northwestern corner a pool measuring 23x16½ feet was unearthed and remains of the city gate were discovered on the eastern side of the summit.

Six phases of pottery and six corresponding periods of building, between 876 and 722 B.C., were decisive in dating the remains: Layer 1 (Omri); Layer 2 (Ahab); Layer 3 (Jehu and his successor); Layer 4 (Jeroboam II); Layers 5–6 (alterations and repairs). A layer of ashes over these levels is attributed to the Assyrian conquest and destruction. Furthermore, the lower strata of Layer 1 prove that there was already a small settlement on the hill of Samaria when Omri bought it from Shemer.

Two groups of small finds at this site deserve special attention. The first is the plaques found in the palace, mainly ivories of Phoenician and native workmanship in a style that is a symbiosis of Mesopotamian and Egyptian motifs. The palace was Ahab's "ivory house" (1 Kgs 22:39), which the king had built for Jezebel, his highly sophisticated Phoenician consort. The ivories of Samaria, incidentally, supply a visual parallel to the ornaments of the Temple. The finds at Samaria also substantiate the biblical account of Phoenician influence at the court of Ahab and Jezebel. Even such a small detail as the horns of the altar (1 Kgs 2:28) has now been confirmed by archaeological discoveries at Megiddo, Dan and Beersheba. The prophetic strictures against idolatry can be better appreciated against the background of the numerous Astarte figurines found in the excavations at Samaria.

b. *The Samaria Ostraca*

In the western part of the acropolis were the royal storehouses in which 63 ostraca (inscribed pottery sherds) were found. They record the dispatch of wine and oil, giving the date, the place of origin, the recipient and the commodity, followed by numerals. For example, inscription number 1 reads:

> In the tenth year, to Shemaryahu, one jar of old wine
>
> | | | | | |
> |---|---|---|---|---|
> | Pega (son of) Elisha | 2 | | Ba'ala (son of) Elisha | 2 |
> | Uzza (son of) Kabesh | 1 | | Yedayahu | 1 |
> | Eliba | 1 | | | |

The written sources from the days of the Divided Monarchy, including the Samaria ostraca, the Siloam inscription, the Lachish letters, and those from Arad and Beersheba, and many other isolated finds, provide interesting sidelights on the political, religious, and military history of the period.

c. *The Abundance of Archaeological Finds*

There are indeed few periods in the history of the northern and southern kingdoms when the archaeological finds — written and silent — so accurately reflect the political events and the internal affairs as known to us from the literary sources. And the particular character of these finds fill in our knowledge for those regions which the biblical literary sources deal with very casually, such as districts in the north and the neighboring states in Transjordan. The wealth of finds is true of the abundancy of seal impressions (see below 9, d), the weights and measures, as well as the contemporary types of pottery which we illustrate in the margins of our pages.

4. ISRAEL VERSUS ASSYRIA AND ARAM

The Northern Kingdom's expansion continued under Ahab (871–851 B.C.); Jehu (842–815) was forced to pay tribute to Assyria, but held his own among the neighboring nations and even gained a significant victory over the Arameans (816) besides quelling rebellions in Moab and Edom (see below). Toward the end of the ninth century, the Arameans under Hazael overran both Israel and Judah, which were reduced to a state of helplessness. But their fortunes revived at the beginning of the eighth century. The Kingdom of Israel reached a third peak in the days of Jeroboam II (785—749 B.C.), while Judah prospered under the rule of Uzziah (Azariah: 797–739). In the latter part of the eighth century Israel's influence shrank and its position became increasingly precarious, owing to the growing power of Assyria (which at least liberated Israel from the onslaughts of

Aram). The death of Jeroboam II and his son Zechariah (748 B.C.) brought an end to the dynasty of Jehu. Between 748 and 722 B.C. five kings ruled over a much smaller Israel. It suffered a serious setback under the blows of Tiglath-Pileser III, who invaded in 733–732 B.C. Hazor was destroyed and rebuilt as an Assyrian town. When Sargon II invaded Palestine again, Samaria fell (722 B.C.), its inhabitants were deported, and the Kingdom of Israel came to an end.

a. *Shalmaneser III and the Battle of Qarqar*

In his campaign against the massed armies of the Arameans and Israel in 853 B.C., Shalmaneser enumerated on bronze tablets from Tell Balawat eleven countries which marshalled some 70,000 troops, 3,940 chariots (of which 2,000 were Ahab's and came partly from the famous stables at Megiddo which housed about 500 horses, and 1,000 camels from Arabia. We have noted that the first fixed date in biblical history, 853 B.C., was established through archaeological finds in Assyria. Thus, archaeology has helped to pinpoint events and to supply a wider view of the biblical past, discovering phenomena in ancient Israel not preserved in its literature.

ASSYRIAN EMPIRE

in the latter part of the 8th c.BCE.

(names rendered in Assyrian; see article).

The battle of Qarqar proved inconclusive. Shalmaneser, however, invaded Palestine again 12 years later, this time winning a clear-cut victory over the "House of Omri" as the Northern Kingdom was known in Assyria, and exacting heavy tribute from Jehu of Israel and the king of Tyre. Though the Bible is silent on this, Shalmaneser III, in the "black obelisk" from Nimrud (now in the British Museum) described ^{m}*ia-ú-a mār* ^{m}*hu-um-ri*, Jehu of the house of Omri, bowing down to the ground in submission (illustration). This is the only extant representation of a king of Israel, but it is doubtless typical rather than specific. We owe a debt to the Assyrians for the fact that they were the only ancient people who left us faithful graphic descriptions of Israelite dress and weapons in their environment, from the time of Shalmaneser to that of Sennacherib (see below). Nothing comparable has survived in Israel itself.

During the Omride period, Aramean-Israelite hostility was resolved by treaty (1 Kgs 20:34) which granted the Arameans special economic privileges in Samaria. In return Israelites were given the right to open bazaars in Damascus.

b. *The United Aramean Power: Damascus*

The unification of Aram and the rise of Damascus was mainly the work of Ben-hadad II. The new capital became the center of a large kingdom with an effective civil and military administration controlling all major lines of communication in western Asia. The Aramaic language spread as the international language of business and administration throughout the area, its script and language being closely related to biblical Hebrew. At the battle of Qarqar, Aram and Israel were unified because of Shalmaneser's threat. When that danger abated, the alliance collapsed and Ben-hadad inflicted a decisive defeat on the combined forces of Israel and Judah at Ramoth-gilead east of the Jordan (852 B.C.; 1 Kgs 22:1–35), in which Ahab lost his life. Ben-hadad's successor, Hazael, invaded both Judah and Israel. The representation of a king, "our lord Hazael" is found on an ivory plaque from Arslan Tash.

c. *The Mesha Stone*

Mesha, king of Moab, took advantage of Ahab's wars with the Arameans in order to rebel against Israel, whose rule extended into Transjordan. He set out to recover the independence of his ancient kingdom; then he rebuilt and fortified it. The stele, in a typically boastful recital, credits victory to his military strategy. The Bible attributes the Israelite withdrawal to the horror and abomination felt when Mesha "took his eldest son... and offered him for a burnt offering upon the wall. And then came great wrath upon Israel and they withdrew" (2 Kgs 3:27). The stele itself was discovered at Dibon in Transjordan in 1868. It was offered for sale to the French archaeologist Clermont-Ganneau who refused to pay the price asked by the Arabs. They later broke it into pieces in order to get a better price by selling it piecemeal. Some of the larger fragments finally found their way to the Louvre in Paris where they were pieced together; thanks to an impression taken previously, many of the missing portions could be restored. When deciphered, the stele confirmed the historical biblical record in the main though it gave a variant account of the events. The 34 lines of the remarkable inscription are in Moabite, a dialect akin to biblical Hebrew. For a century this was a unique royal inscription from a Palestinian king of the period of the first Temple, but a few others have been reported found recently in Transjordan.

5. THE EARLY PROPHETS: ELIJAH AND ELISHA

Elijah and Elisha, in addition to Samuel's school of wandering ecstatic prophets, belong to the early or formative phase of Israelite prophecy, which is distinct in character and spirit from the prophecy of the eighth century (see Part VI: The Classic Prophets). These prophets of the early phase had much in common with the diviners or seers (Samuel: 1 Sam 9:9; Balaam: Numbers 22–24) found elsewhere in Near Eastern antiquity, although a detailed comparison shows that there are many differences as well. Cuneiform tablets from Mari, texts from Egypt and Byblos illustrate how holy men divine while in states of frenzy. An idea that runs through both biblical and extra-biblical prophecy is that the prophet is the messenger of the god. For example, a sacrificial text from Byblos refers to a prophet with the following words: "Bring up the god! Bring up the messenger who is carrying him! It is Amon who has sent him."

Prophets during the early period are often mentioned in a context which suggests the existence of recognized groups specializing in invocations. So it is in the days of Elijah and Elisha (1 Kgs 20:35 ff.; 22:6, 10; 2 Kgs 2:3, 5; 4:1; 6:1). There is frequent mention of companies of prophets of the Lord, including groups located at Jericho, Bethel, and Carmel. The scene described in 1 Kgs 18:20 ff. is typical of the activity of Elijah, the oracle of Carmel. As the contest between the prophets of Baal and the prophet of Yahweh reached its peak, sacrifices were offered at the top of the mountain, at a site now known as Muḥraka or "burning place" (the site of the Carmelite Monastery of St. Elijah). B. Mazar is of the opinion that the Baal against whom Elijah contended was Baal Shamîn (or Baal Shamêm), the Lord of Heaven, a deity of cosmic significance among the Canaanites. Other scholars hold that it is Tyrian Baal, also known as Melkart, the god of the underworld. Sanctuaries to Baal Shamêm were situated mostly on the tops of mountains, notably Mount Carmel, as well as peaks which dominated Phoenician settlements in the Lebanon, at Carthage in Africa, and Karatepe in northern Syria. Many scholars identify the deity with Zeus Olympios in the Hellenistic period. In fact, Baal Shamîn is identified in the book of Daniel with the dominant deity of the Hellenistic Syrians who ruled Palestine in the second century B.C. on the eve of the Hasmonean revolt (cf. the books of Daniel and Maccabees). A temple to Baal Shamêm was also discovered in the Nabatean religious center of Seia in the Hauran (northwest Transjordan).

Another characteristic of the earlier prophets was the transmission of their art from generation to generation. Elijah trained Elisha and named him as his successor (2 Kings 2, a truly dramatic narrative). Elijah and Elisha worked a variety of similar miracles. In the eighth century, however, divination and miracles played a much less important role in the activity of the prophets (see Part VI: The Classic Prophets).

Left:
A prince, or the god Melkart, out hunting as depicted on a Phoenician silver bowl. This brings to mind the taunts of Elijah addressed to the priests of Baal "Cry aloud, for he is a god... or he is hunting, or he is on a journey.."

Right:
In his stele, Mesha, king of Moab tells of his wars with the kings of Israel (2 Kings 3). The inscription is in the Moabite dialect close to biblical Hebrew (ca. 850 B.C.)

6. JEHOSHAPHAT — THE ALTAR AND CITY OF BEERSHEBA AND THE CITIES OF THE NEGEB

Several excavations and archaeological surveys have thrown light on the outstanding achievements of Jehoshaphat (867–851 B.C.). A contemporary of Ahab, he was one of Judah's best and most enterprising kings. He attempted to renew the commercial shipping from Ezion-geber but failed

125

Map of ancient towns of southern Judah and the Negeb

because a great storm wrecked his fleet. By then, Beersheba, founded in the 12th–11th centuries B.C., had become the most prosperous city of the Negeb as demonstrated by the extensive excavations conducted by Y. Aharoni, which uncovered the large altar of sacrifices that had stood in the sanctuary of Beersheba, well known from biblical traditions (see Part VI: Amos).

Many new settlements established in this period have been discovered in the northern Negeb, east of Beersheba. For example, Tell Gharreh, located between Beersheba and Arad, was surrounded by a casemate wall. Tell Meshash dated to the same time, with its numerous four-room houses, characteristic of Israelite architecture of the period. Various other settlements were founded in the northern part of the Judean wilderness, "the fortresses and store cities" built by Jehoshaphat (2 Chr 17:12). This has been confirmed by excavations of the "City of Salt" where the Essene community would be established several centuries later.

7. THE NEGEB FORTRESSES

From the tenth century onward, fortresses were built in the Negeb in the course of the southward expansion of the Judean kingdom. More than 20 have been located, but only a few excavated. Their outer defense is usually a casemate wall with rooms lining it and a courtyard in the center. Some of them, dating from the eighth-seventh centuries B.C., are rectangular (130x160 feet) with projecting towers, as at Kadesh-Barnea, Khirbet Ghazza, and Arad. An earlier type (probably tenth century) consists of irregularly shaped buildings without towers, similar in size to the later ones. A third type, dating to the tenth century, was also a fort without towers, some 70 feet square, found on the roads to Kadesh-Barnea and in the southern arid areas of the Negeb.

At Arad, six levels of fortresses were found covering a period from the tenth to the early sixth century B.C., each one built on the ruins of the preceding one. The walls wre built of well-cut and bossed ashlar masonry. The wall of the earliest fortress was of the casemate type; that of the suc-

Model of the citadel of Arad in the Negeb (end of the 8th c. B.C.)

ceeding five levels was solid and strengthened by a beaten earth glacis and an outer wall; it was also strengthened by rooms built against the inside of the wall. The change in wall types were made to strengthen the defenses against improved methods of assault, and more powerful siege engines. An Israelite high place was discovered on the northwestern side of the citadel and dated to the tenth or ninth century B.C.

An inscription on a fragment of stone was found in the northeastern Sinai at Kuntillat Ajrud, dating to the days of Jehoshaphat. It is dedicated to Obadia, son of "Adnah the commander."

8. THE ADMINISTRATIVE DIVISION OF JUDAH

Relationships between Israel and Judah had stabilized in the ninth century B.C. as the House of David finally accepted the separate existence of Israel. Jehoshaphat reorganized the administrative structure of Judah in the 12-district pattern (2 Chr 17:2). Most scholars agree that this is the source of the Judean town-list incorporated in Josh 15:21–62 by a later historiographer of the book of Joshua, though it is based on an earlier plan devised by David or Solomon.

Another of the great kings of Judah, Uzziah (786–758 B.C.), a contemporary of Jeroboam II, helped to enlarge Judah's domain over large areas of the Negeb, including parts of Philistia and Edom, with the idea of protecting and expanding the caravan trade. As stated, large forts surrounded by casemate walls and defended by eight towers were erected at main highway junctions and on the borders. The same king carried out vast building projects and strengthened the fortifications of Jerusalem. Both he and his son, Jotham, increased the size of the Judean military forces. An ossuary, inscribed in Aramaic and purporting to contain the bones of Uzziah, was discovered not in the royal necropolis, but in the ancient cemetery at the foot of the Mount of Olives. It will be recalled that Uzziah had to resign the kingship because of his leprosy, and this fact may help to explain the curious disposition of his bones.

Inscribed tablet from Arad in the Negeb specifically identifying the sanctuary as the 'house of Yahweh'

Above:
Seal of *Yehozerah ben Hilkiyahu servant of King Hezekiah*

Right:
The twelve regions of the United Kingdom and Judah (later divided into twelve districts)

Below:
Top of a tomb comprising a square shaft which gave access to the burial chamber. The latter had a square opening in the ceiling, the 'nephesh' or memorial. The round hole was made by people who came accidentally on the tomb, or by grave robbers. Discovered west of the Temple Mount excavations, Jerusalem

THE XII REGIONS OF THE UNITED KINGDOM. AND JUDAH

9. THE LAST TWO CENTURIES OF JUDAH

The Judean monarchy had to struggle continually for survival in the face of Assyrian, and later, Babylonian imperialism as well as periodic attempts by Egypt to sway the small Palestinian states from their allegiance to these northern empires.

The campaigns of Sennacherib, well known from Assyrian annals, are referred to in 2 Kgs 18:13–35, 2 Chr 32:9, 21, and Isaiah 36 and 37. During Hezekiah's reign Judah suffered a devastating invasion by Sennacherib and lost dozens of cities and villages to the Assyrian army. At the end only Jerusalem and its environs were left, and they were under siege (701 B.C.). Through the payment of a huge tribute, the city was saved and the Assyrians lifted their siege. The Assyrians immortalized the siege and capture of Lachish, one of the fortresses guarding the approaches to Jerusalem, in a series of great wall reliefs, now collected in the British Museum. Archaeologists have discovered the broad wall Hezekiah built around the new Upper City quarters of Jerusalem, to protect the extension of the city on the west side. A section of the wall has been uncovered in the Jewish

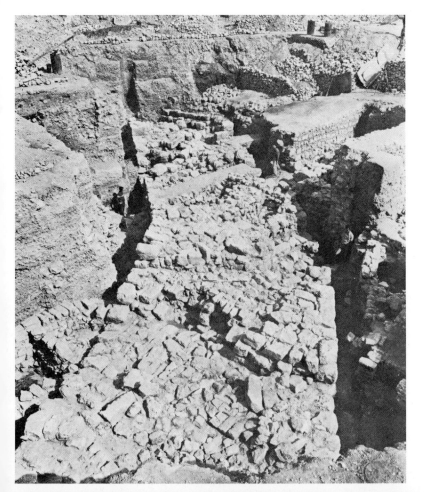

A section of the 'broad wall' built by King Hezekiah at the end of the 8th c. (2 Ch 32:5) uncovered in the Western Hill (Upper City, or Mishneh) and over 20 feet wide

Lower left: An inscribed sherd found in the Ophel (most ancient part of Jerusalem) bearing names such as *Yehezkiyahu, Abijahu, Zephanyahu, from the Valley of Jehosaphat*

Lower right: Epitaph of the secondary burial of King Uzziah, carved apparently in Second Temple times and found on the Mount of Olives, far from the royal necropolis as he died of leprosy (2 Ch 26:23)

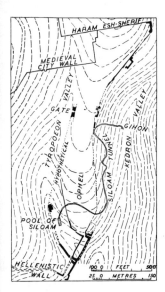

King Hezekiah had a long and somewhat winding tunnel dug under the lower Ophel. This brought the water of the Gihon spring directly to the Siloam pool situated within the city walls. It was covered and made immune to Assyrian onslaught

Quarter of the Old City, revealing a broad rampart 23 feet thick and built of large unhewn stones, fitted together without mortar. The remains consist of two to seven courses of stone reaching a height of about ten feet along a length of 128 feet. This represents only the foundations of the wall laid on bedrock; it served to reinforce and extend the original boundary of the city of David and Solomon (see below: Recent Discoveries in Jerusalem).

a. *Hezekiah's Tunnel and the Siloam Inscription*

Hezekiah's greatest engineering achievement was a tunnel that has survived intact to this day. He decided to provide the city with a new reservoir of drinking water within the city walls and safe from Sennacherib's onslaught. He had a tunnel 1,750 feet long dug in the rock to bring water from the Gihon spring to the Siloam pool. The dramatic story is told in 2 Kgs 20:20 and 2 Chr 32:30 ff., spelling out the accomplishment in detail. The feat is also commemorated in a Hebrew inscription carved in the side of the tunnel near its exit to the pool. It related how the tunnelers, working with picks, had started at opposite ends and finally met, completing their task.

b. *Recent Discoveries in Jerusalem*

Large quantities of pottery and other artifacts dating to the Monarchy were discovered in the excavations of the Ophel (the most ancient part of Jerusalem) and at the foot of the Temple Mount. Remnants of Israelite houses and a cave complex were uncovered by Kathleen Kenyon in the trench she dug below the upper Hasmonean wall and fortress (see Part IX, A). An intresting epigraphic item is the Ophel ostracon found in 1924, dating to the end of the Monarchy and bearing familiar names such as

In 1976, the excavations at the Temple Mount uncovered the terraced area known as *Beth-Millo* dating to the days of the Judean Monarchy, seen in the foreground, with remains of Herodian structures at a higher level

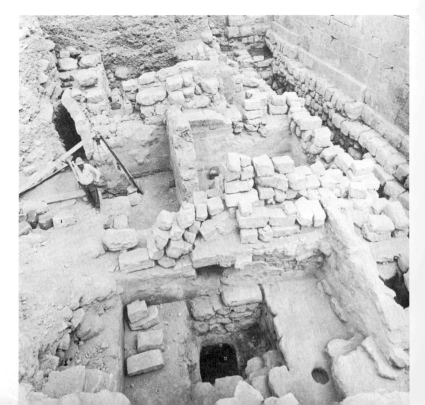

Hezkiyah and Abiyahu (illustration). Numerous historical structures have also been discovered by B. Mazar since 1976 in the upper Ophel.

c. Tombs

A sizable cemetery of the eighth century B.C. has been discovered by Mazar on the slope of the valley facing the Western Wall of the Temple Mount. The tombs were carved in the rock, each comprising a square shaft or flight of stairs which gave access to a large burial chamber. The latter had a square opening in the ceiling, apparently the *nephesh* (memorial) which was covered with stone slabs or a gabled structure. This cemetery was used by the upper class population of Jerusalem. Due to the expansion of the city toward the upper (Western) hill, the cemetery was abandoned in the days of Manasseh (mid-seventh century B.C.). Another group of rock-cut tombs had been discovered previously and was attributed to the House of David by R. Weill, but the "royal" theory still lacks verification. One of the tombs had a shaft leading to a vaulted tunnel 54.4 feet long and 13.2 feet high, which ended at a stone bench in which a niche was carved, probably to hold a coffin. Numerous rock-cut tombs on the eastern side of the city have been discovered in recent years.

In 1927 J. W. Crowfoot uncovered masonry blocks which stood on cliffs overhanging the valley. He assumed that it was the Valley Gate of the lower city, but before this theory could be checked the land was built over by Arabs of the village.

The biblical tradition makes mention of the "King's Garden" located at the bottom of the valley near the Siloam Pool; it is irrigated by an overflow of that pool. The gardens are still there and flourish for the same

The Hezekiah tunnel near its outflow to the Pool of Siloam

Ancient Israelite tombs situated in the Ophel (the core of the Davidic city) truncated as a result of quarrying in Roman times reason, a living verification and reminder of the ancient tradition (B. Mazar, *The Mountain of the Lord*).

d. *Royal Seal Impressions*

Hundreds of royal seal impressions have been found on various Judean tells in recent years. In the center of a typical impression there is a symbol, either a four-winged scarab or a double-winged sundisk, accompanied by the inscription *lmlk* "of the king," while below it is written either a place name: Hebron, Socoh, or Ziph, or *mmšt*. Y Aharoni has proved conclusively that the four-winged seal impressions were inaugurated by Hezekiah before Sennacherib's campaign, while the double-winged symbol was adopted during the first half of the seventh century and was abandoned before the reign of Josiah (640 B.C.). The use of these seals corresponds to the reorganization and consolidation of Judah into four administrative centers for, among other purposes, the collection of taxes in the face of the impending war with

Gate excavated west of the Ophel

Assyria. This explains the use of the name of the three Judean cities and *mmšt*, probably an abbreviation of "the state." The taxes, paid in agricultural produce, were collected in the four royal store cities. The figures in the seal impressions are based on foreign originals. Such pagan motifs on Judean seals disappeared after Hezekiah's time, a consequence of Josiah's religious reforms.

Jar-handle bearing a seal impression with the word *Lamelekh* (Belonging) to the king/*Socoh*

10. JOSIAH'S REFORM AND THE DESTRUCTION OF JERUSALEM

Judah had a final period of political and religious resurgence during the reign of Josiah (640–609 B.C.) as Assyrian power disintegrated at the end of the seventh century B.C. The young king cast off the foreign yoke, expanding Judean authority over all Palestine. Simultaneously he removed the foreign cults associated with Assyrian influence and instituted a ritual purification throughout the land (2 Kings 22–23; 2 Chronicles 34). The biblical tradition associated the reform with a dramatic discovery, made in some dark recess of the Temple chambers, of a scroll of the Book of the Covenant or part of the Book of the Law we call Deuteronomy. This was impromptu archaeology with far-reaching consequences. Though Josiah's reforms preceded the destruction of the state by the Babylonians in 586 B.C. by only 36 years, they had a lasting effect in focusing worship and ritual on the Temple Mount.

Concomitant with the centralization of the cult, worship at the many high places (e.g. Dan, Bethel, Arad, and Beersheba) was terminated by order of Josiah. The priests of the Judean high places "from Geba to Beersheba" (2 Kgs 23:8) were transferred to Jerusalem. The elimination of the high places of the northern kingdom was far more drastic than in the south. The sanctuaries of Dan and Bethel were defiled by burning human bones on their altars, while the territory was annexed into the framework of the enlarged kingdom. The high places of Beersheba (see below: Amos) and Arad may already have been suppressed by Hezekiah who is quoted as "saying to Judah and Jerusalem 'You shall worship before this altar in Jerusalem'" (2 Kgs 12:22).

The wars of this period (2 Kings 24–25) and the events leading up to them are also reflected in extra-biblical sources. The royal annals and the reliefs of Sennacherib of the siege of Lachish (2 Chr 32:4; Isa 36:2) present textual and visual evidence of his campaign against Hezekiah. The defenses of Lachish represented in the Assyrian reliefs are identical to those uncovered in the excavation of the city. The famous Babylonian Chronicle contains a record of the events of the last years of the Judean kingdom including an account of the capture of Jerusalem in 597 B.C. by Nebuchadnezzar. Other Babylonian inscriptions and an Aramaic letter from the king of Ashkelon contribute further details.

Another piece of evidence of the time is an ostracon found at *Mesād Hashavyahu*, a small fort near Yavneh-Yam on the coast. It is a letter of a wronged peasant to the officer of the fort, and it shows how the social laws of the Bible are reflected in contemporary life during the reign of Josiah.

Winged scroll of *Ziph* on a jar handle bearing a *Lamelekh* seal impression. The latter were presumably stamped by royal officials as a guarantee of the capacity of the store-jars so stamped

Right:
Assyrian cuneiform tablet of Esarhaddon binding his Median vassals by treaty (as suggested by the decoration) and compelling them to support the succession he imposed on Media

Left:
Hebrew ostracon from Masad Hashavyahu relating a peasant's complaint against royal officers

Y. Aharoni excavated a royal fortress and palace at *Ramat Rahel*, south of Jerusalem, which he dated to the last years of the realm. This is the only palace of a Judean king found in archaeological excavations. The walls were constructed of ashlar blocks like those at Ahab's palace at Samaria. The palace was decorated with proto-Aeolic capitals, and had impressive window casements. Among other finds was a painted potsherd depicting the king, possibly Jehoiakim, seated on a throne (or chariot).

A section of the Black Obelisk of Shalmaneser (9th c. B.C.) depicting the dress of caravaneers from Israel and Syria

11. ISRAELITE CLOTHING

Carved ivory inlays found in excavations at Megiddo (13th–11th centuries B.C.) and Assyrian murals of the seventh century give us a fairly good idea of dress-styles and their evolution in biblical times.

Richer clothing of the period is illustrated by the woman who wears a cloak (simlah) and long veil, and the priest in his long tasseled robe (From a Phoenician stele of the 10th c. B.C.)

From the earliest times, the basic undergarment was the kiltlike loincloth worn next to the skin, called the *'ezôr* (2 Kgs 1:8; Isa 20:2; Jer 13:1 ff.) Many Egyptian paintings show such a garment wrapped around the loins and tied with a belt or girdle (*hagorah*). For religious functions, a shirt or apron was tied around the body (1 Sam 2:18; 2 Sam 6:14). The Hebrew term is transliterated as "ephod," which refers also to an elaborate priestly garment (Exod 28:6–12). The next most common outer garment was the tunic, the *ketonet* or *chiton*. This garment was made by simple folding of a rectangle of cloth in half and sewing up the sides, leaving openings for the head and arms. This could be worn open or closed, with or without sleeves, depending on individual needs. The most frequent term for a top garment, possibly worn over the tunic, is the *me'il* (1 Sam 2:19; 28:14; 1 Chr 15:27), which in many English versions is wrongly translated as "coat" (as in the case of Joseph). Apparently it was worn also by people of high rank; such a costume is pictured on the borderstone of a Babylonian king (ca. 1100 B.C.).

Most people in the ancient Near East wore a shawl or cloak made of wool or linen draped around the body over the tunic. Biblical terms for this garment, variously translated, are the cloak-*simlāh* (Deut 21:13; Ruth 3:3) or *salmāh* (Mic 2:8; 1 Kgs 11:30). The *sa'ip*, a long veil (Gen 24:65; 38:14), a woman's upper garment, is illustrated in a fourth century Phoenician carving of a woman and a priest. She is wearing the garment usually called a *himation* or *pallium*. Israelite law (Deut 22:5) makes it clear that women's clothing differed from men's. According to S. Yeivin, however, the *saddîn* (Judg 14:12) was worn by both men and women; it was not an exclusively female garment, as had been assumed.

The earliest Israelite undergarment was the kiltlike loincloth, or *ezôr* (left) The common tunic or *ketônet* was the outer garment worn by the three figures (right)

PART VI

A. THE CLASSIC PROPHETS

1. THE TRANSITION FROM THE EARLY TO THE WRITTEN PROPHETS

We have seen that traditions about the early prophets often included miraculous stories and supernatural knowledge was attributed to them in many cases. Although divination was the target of constant attacks by the later prophets, it clearly plays a role in stories about earlier figures such as Samuel and Saul.

Various examples of divination and ecstatic prophecy, known to us from the books of Samuel and Kings (see Parts IV and V), have much in common with Canaanite, Egyptian, and Mesopotamian practices. The best-known examples attested by archaeological finds are the seers and diviners of Mari of the early second millennium B.C., known as the *āpilum, muhhum,* or ecstatic prophets, and the *baru* priests, known from every period of Babylonian and Assyrian history, who specialized in liver omens. The similarity between the Mari prophets especially shows that prophecy was not native to Hebrew culture but was well known in the ancient Near East. However, while Israelite experience gave rise to the great classical prophets, the phenomenon remained basically static in the rest of the ancient world.

In the period of Samuel-Saul, ecstatic prophets appear in groups, often under the leadership of a single seer. We have no record of such appearances in the period of the monarchy, but during the reign of Ahab groups of independent prophets appeared throughout the land and may have helped in the struggle against Jezebel and her Phoenician acolytes (1 Kgs 18:19–21:27).

Charismatic personalities such as Elijah and Elisha had a great impact on the prophetic tradition, and it was because of the respect in which they were held by their audience that these "men of God" were endowed with legendary accretions of magic and divination. Elijah was the leader of a prophetic group, one among many that flourished at that time. They were located in places hallowed by tradition, such as Bethel, Jericho, Gilgal, where members lived a communal life. We learn that Elisha was a disciple of Elijah because he had "poured water on the hands of Elijah" (2 Kgs 3:11). It seems that Elisha was instrumental in promoting Jehu's excessive cruelty in dealing with his Israelite enemies (2 Kgs 9:1–10:36). While it may be true that pagan worship was eradicated from Israel, the ceaseless wars with the Arameans had killed off multitudes of people and impoverished the masses, placing them at the mercy of the rich landlords and merchants. The prophets now became the mouthpiece of the downtrodden.

In the eighth century the point of view in the biblical tradition shifts radically. Rather than stories about prophets we now have the actual utterances of famous prophets remembered and recorded. By this time prophets presented their message to their fellow Israelites in the form of eloquent rhetorical compositions which are distinguished by their high artistic and theological standards. Underlying their prophecy is a sublime moral and religious experience as well as a broad understanding of the historical situation in which they lived.

2. A UGARITIC LEGAL TERM EXPLAINS THE TRANSITION TO WRITTEN PROPHECY

A study of legal Ugaritic documents written in a dialect of Canaanite has helped S. A. Löwenstamm to correct a crucial mistranslation of a well-known verse in Habakkuk (2:3), namely that the word *c'ôd* (the adverb "yet" or "still") should be read as *'ed* (the noun for "testimony"). The line should therefore read "For the vision is a testimony of the appointed time." This explains the reason for the instruction in the preceding verse: "Yahweh answered me: Write the vision, make it plain upon tablets..." It proclaims God's will that *prophecy should be recorded*; and when it is fulfilled, the written record will prove that the "word of God" has actualized itself in history. In the preface to the Song of Moses (Deut 31:19) we find the same rationale: "That this song may be a witness (testimony) for me..." Consequently, a proper understanding of the biblical data means that at this time, it was found imperative to record prophecy in writing, with momentous implications for Israel and the world.

The rhapsodic prophets who followed Elijah and Elisha were opposed to prophetic guilds, which involved the practice of prophecy as a craft and to the idea that any person could be taught by a master to prophesy. They were not professional prophets nor were they connected formally with any shrine and its rituals. A new type of prophet appeared who objected to the mistreatment of the poor and saw the lack of social justice as a fundamental violation of the covenant between the people and their God.

3. PROPHECY RELATED TO HISTORICAL REALITY

It is important that the classical prophets set out to interpret Yahweh's commandments in terms of the historical reality of the day and observed contemporary events with great insight. This separates prophecy clearly from the pagan practices of divination and magic which were dominant in the rest of the Near East. These Israelite prophets did not set out to divine the future, but rather sought to understand and improve the present. Divination rested on a deterministic belief that what was ordained by fate or by supernatural powers would certainly come to pass and that it was the diviner's task to discover it. The classic Hebrew prophet held that the future was not foreordained but depended in large part *on the moral behavior of the people*. Hence the current situation was of vital importance for its bearing on the future. Because of this the prophets are a reliable witness to the main events of their time, which biblical scholarship and especially archaeology can illuminate.

4. GENERAL THEOLOGY OF CLASSIC PROPHECY

The prophets proclaimed that the obligations inherent in the Mosaic covenant and the commandments of the Law (Torah) were the essence of Israelite religion, but more than intellectual appreciation and assent was required to make them meaningful and significant. A commitment in faith to the God of Israel and the fulfilment in practice of his demands were the necessary ingredients. For instance, Isaiah (Isaiah 1) would not accept lip service as a substitute for active faith and an upright life. The prophets understood the Law as regulating the relations among human beings in the light of divine revelation and especially as restraining the exploitation of the weak, the poor, the downtrodden, and the defenseless. They spoke for God in behalf of the disinherited and disenfranchised. To them the viability of the state and the survival of the community depended on the response of all to the stipulations of the covenant, but especially the rich and powerful whose behavior affected the lives of so many. All of the prophets gave warning of divine judgment which would come to pass in the context of historical events, if the people as a whole failed to keep the terms of their commitment, and they summoned the people to repent before it was too late. They faced their task with a profound sense of divine vocation and an ultimate compulsion, as they had been called and commissioned by Yahweh to be his messengers.

There was a fundamental conflict between the prophets and kings, which grew more intense toward the end of the Kingdom of Judah. Although the relationship went back to the beginnings of the monarchy in Israel (e.g., Samuel and Saul and David), there were basic tensions and difficulties as royal policies and practices diverged more and more from prophetic standards of divine righteousness. While kings necessarily were concerned with political decisions, both internal and external, designed to safeguard and promote the well-being of the nation and the dynasty, they therefore engaged in the international games of diplomacy and military adventures; the prophets were more concerned with questions of ultimate morality and adherence to the religious requirements of the covenant, both in relation to other nations and to internal matters. Modification or denial of the fundamental requirements in the interest of expediency met with radical rejection on the part of the prophets and denunciation of the monarch and his aides. The prophets were equally at odds with venal priests, who were mere sycophants and retainers of the crown. They easily misled many of the religious with assurances that faithfulness and continuity in the performance of the ritual was sufficient to meet the demands of the faith. The prophets insisted on a return to fundamentals, to a reaffirmation of Mosaic faith with its emphasis on commitment and compliance with the Law of God.

These prophets transmitted the divine message, "God's word," to the people or the king in highly personalized pronouncements. They were strong-willed men and kings listened to them whether they wanted to or not; priests came seeking them, never the reverse. Championing the rights of the downtrodden on the basis of the covenant, the prophets risked abuse at the hands of those they attacked, as was the case with Amos and Jeremiah (see below).

5. PROPHECY AND PREDICTING THE FUTURE

When read by later generations under altered circumstances, the prophetic message came to be interpreted in a way that the prophets themselves may not have intended. They were primarily concerned with their own generation and what the future held in store for it, especially if it failed to heed the words of warning and the call to repentance. Since many announcements of impending doom were fulfilled, the prophets were seen primarily as predictors of the future, whose words held meaning for later generations concerning their future. In other words, hidden in the prophetic oracles of the past were secret messages about the sequence of much later events, including destruction and exile and ultimate return and restoration of the people of God. What in the prophets had been conditional pronouncements about the future, consequences being affected by behavior and responses on the part of the people, became in later times explicit predictions fulfilled as evidence of their special powers and of God's overriding control and determination of the course of history. These early biblical scholars paid little attention to the "setting-in-life" of the prophecies, namely the historical situation which was the object of their political analysis. Partly because of their literary merit, the prophets were read and increasingly investigated for these hidden meanings relevant to the new age and situation. The eschatologists and messianists, concerned with the end of time, particularly the covenanters at Qumran, carried this practice to its extreme. Warnings of defeat or destruction which were related to the time of Isaiah or Habakkuk were reinterpreted in light of the tribulations of their own lives. Even greater was the temptation to find hidden promises of imminent redemption.

To be sure, the prophets believed that Yahweh would restore Israel to the land under the rule of a descendant of the House of David, who would be "Yahweh's anointed," but they saw this as resulting from the repentance of the people of their day. The Jews of the Roman and Byzantine periods, however, read into the prophets a prediction concerning the end of the post-Temple exile and thought they would witness a third restoration in their days; this is particularly true in the time of Bar Kochba (second century A.D.) or Julian (fourth century). Similarly, the early Christians found in the Scripture predictions of the coming of Christ and his messianic role.

6. REFORMERS FROM WITHIN

The prophets should be considered conservative reformers, who wished to restore an earlier form of society, rather than as revolutionaries. They called for a radical return to, not a radical departure from, the traditions of Israel's earliest days. They sought to infuse ritual and legal regulations with spiritual integrity and a deep sense of moral justice and in this way to revitalize the existing order. They carried God's message to repent, to return to God's commandments to which Israel had bound itself at Sinai.

7. PARTICULARISM AND UNIVERSALISM

The prophets' concern did not stop with their own nation. They understood that Israel, as a small nation, was part of the complex of large nations which made up their world. They understood from the beginning that all the nations, the whole universe was under the rule and power of the one God. Therefore the other nations served his purpose and played a role in his historical plans. On the one hand, this relationship could be seen in the use of the small and great powers as instruments of divine wrath in smiting Israel and Judah. On the other hand, here was an inherent universalism which became evident in later Israelite thought.

Thus, although their words were aimed at contemporaries, the prophets' message was perpetuated through the ages: the fundamental principles governing human society were for all, and all were equal before the law and before God. The covenant expressed the justice and mercy of God, qualities which were to be emulated by human beings in personal and social relationships. The words of Micah 6:8 sum this up: "What does the Lord require of you but to do justice, and love mercy, and walk humbly with your God?"

8. WHO WERE THE CLASSIC PROPHETS?

Limitations of space preclude detailed descriptions of the numerous prophets from Amos to Malachi whose writings are found in the Bible. They represent a pinnacle of Israelite tradition not only for their lofty ethical standards but also for the superb poetic quality of their writings. Moreover, the legacy of classic prophecy, its spirit, message, and style have figured prominently in Judeo-Christian culture and is one of the foundations of western civilization.

We shall examine various prophets in brief, pointing out significant characteristics of the literary prophets, with special attention to their historical background and "setting-in-life." This will include a discussion of the relevant archaeological information available for those periods.

The first of the classical prophets were Amos and Hosea around the middle of the eighth century B.C., both of whom prophesied in the Northern Kingdom. They were followed shortly thereafter by Isaiah and Micah, who were active in Judah. Jeremiah's prophetic activity dates to a century later.

9. AMOS AND HOSEA

The great material progress under Jeroboam II (784–748 B.C.) resulted in a considerable rise in the standard of living of some, and a growing disparity between the few rich and the poor masses. This is evident from the material wealth found in Samaria, dating to the days of Omri and Ahab, and later (see V; 1, 2, Kings). At the same time, Israel's religion seems to have been corrupted by the infiltration of pagan practices (as claimed by Hosea, Amos' contemporary), particularly the fertility cult with its immoral rites. The numerous figurines of the Lady Ashtoreth found in many Israelite cities (see above) provides archaeological evidence of this proliferation. Moreover, the Samaria ostraca (in the first half of the eighth century B.C.) show that names formed with Baal (e.g. Yerubaal, Ishbaal) were almost as common as names formed with Yahweh, or the short form Ya(h)u (e.g. Šemaryau). This shows that Baalism and Canaanite customs, many of which were probably transmitted by the Phoenicians, had not been eradicated. This is the background against which we can appreciate the sayings of Amos and Hosea. Both were horrified by the selfish luxury, the oppression of the poor and the immorality they saw around them.

The horned altar of sacrifices of the sanctuary of Beersheba, reconstructed from its scattered ashlar blocks. Now on view at Tell Beersheba

B. AMOS

The earliest of the recorded prophets was Amos. His career dates from about 750 B.C., during the reign of Jeroboam II. With Amos we have direct testimony of a creative individual in Israel's spiritual life, the like of which is unattested earlier anywhere in the ancient world. What we know of the ministry of this rustic herdsman is limited to his visions and fearless preaching at Bethel and Samaria in the Northern Kingdom. His prophecy dwells on the impending judgment against the arrogant rich and the royal house. When challenged by the priest at Bethel, he defied him and asserted that regardless of other considerations, when a man is called by God and commissioned by him, he cannot submit to the rulings and restrictions of men.

1. CONTENTS

Like the other prophetic books, Amos is not a strictly coherent unity, but a series of oracles and addresses arranged in loose order. Therefore we will discuss the material according to subject matter rather than following the biblical sequence exactly.

The book of Amos opens with indictments against the neighboring nations, climaxing in 2:6–16 with an extended indictment against Israel. The next four chapters (Amos 3–6) contain oracles of judgment against Israel. Amos announces the punishment that will take place on the "Day of Yahweh" (5:18–20), a day of judgment when Israel will be oppressed, its land destroyed, and its people exiled (3:14–15; 5:3, 26–27). This material is followed by reports of five visions: the locusts (7:1–3), drought (7:4–6), the plumb-line (7:7–9), the basket of summer fruit (8:1–3), and Yahweh announcing the destruction of Israel (9:1–4). Among these visions there is also the angry exchange between the prophet and the priest, Amaziah, at the shrine of Bethel (7:10–17). Finally there is the epilogue which includes a final announcement of disaster for Israel (9:7–10) and a prediction of the eventual restoration of Israel and the prosperity which the inhabitants will enjoy (9:11–15).

2. AMOS' MESSAGE

Amos cries out against the oppresion of the poor by the wealthy and powerful (2:6–7; 3:10; 4:1; 5:11); against those who pervert justice by bribery (5:7, 10–12); against dishonest merchants (8:4–6); and the idleness and luxury of the rich of Samaria. No better description could be given of the exquisite beauty of the ivories discovered in the king's palace of Samaria and other rich homes of the capital. In retribution, the rich and their property would eventually be destroyed (3:11, 15; 4:3; 5:11; 7:11).

The famous passage in 5:21–25, censuring the popular sacrificial ritual is not a rejection of the formal cult *in toto,* but emphasizes that it is not   143 the only or most important element in the worship of Yahweh; his criticism is based in part on the corruption of the cult which was accompanied by drunkenness (2:7–8) and various Canaanite debaucheries, and more generally because the ritual was performd without regard to justice in everyday activity. Therefore Israel's shrines will be destroyed (3:14; 5:5; 7:9, and elsewhere).

Although Amos' prophecies of doom are often untempered with hope, he does include the idea that Israel would not be destroyed totally as a consequence of its sins. A "remnant" would be saved to enjoy the promises inherent in the covenant (9:11–15). This concept, along with others such as the "Day of Yahweh" and the distrust of the formal cult practices, is echoed throughout the rest of Israelite prophecy.

3. THE DISCOVERY OF THE ALTAR OF SACRIFICES AND SANCTUARY OF BEERSHEBA

The city gate of Beersheba is situated to the right. The area to the left and the bordered streets date from Solomon's time

Until recently the high-place at Beersheba denounced by Amos (5:5; 8:14) lay undiscovered, though biblical tradition stressed its importance from earliest times (Gen 21:33; 46:1–5). We have seen above (Kings) that it was customary to maintain sanctuaries at the boundaries of the country.

This is why Jeroboam chose Dan and Bethel as the sites of his high-places. Just as there was a sanctuary at Arad on the Edomite border of the Southern Kingdom, it is logical that there was another at Beersheba, the last inhabited town bordering on the vast desert which divided the land of Israel from Egypt. It took Aharoni's expedition five years of excavation at Tell Beersheba to find the first evidence of its presence. Four ashlar blocks were found in a repaired section of the storehouse complex near the city gate (see picture); they had originally been part of a large horned altar which stood in the sanctuary. These ashlars, three of which were intact, had been built into the wall. Other similarly dressed ashlar blocks of a special sandstone

Aerial view of the gate area on the left (as in previous picture) with the storehouse area to the right were found above them and in other areas. The reconstructed altar is similar in design to smaller incense altars from the period of the monarchy. This altar is now on view at the expedition camp at Tell Beersheba.

4. LOCATING THE SANCTUARY OF BEERSHEBA

The first discovery confirmed the assumption that a sanctuary had existed at Beersheba, probably more elaborate than the isolated high-place of Arad. Beersheba's altar was dismantled apparently during the reign of Hezekiah (see Kings). But where was the sacred high-place? A large public building, some 65 feet square, was uncovered near the northwestern corner of the tell. West and south of the building were rows of basements connected by subterranean doorways. It had been built on bedrock and belonged to the latest Israelite city (Stratum 2). Various details of this structure are similar to that at Arad; their areas are the same, both are oriented east to west, and both had large courtyards to the east where an altar would stand. Support for the hypothesis that this was the sanctuary was provided by the discovery of a temple from the Hellenistic period. It was built nearby and consisted of one broad room, possibly with a central niche. East of it was a large courtyard with a series of ovens along its walls and the base of an altar of burnt offerings at its center. Though the later temple was pagan, it may have preserved the location of the earlier sacred site, a common phenomenon in the ancient world, Y. Yadin, on the other hand, argues that there was no real temple at Beersheba, but only a sacred high-place, which was at a different location, with the horned altar nearby.

Ritual spouted bowl of faience from Beersheba

C. HOSEA

Hosea ben Be'eri came on the scene either at the end of Amos' career or shortly after, although the introduction to the book is not clear as to the precise dates of his ministry. Amos had lived in Jeroboam's prosperous and successful years, while Hosea lived through the years of decadence and chaos which followed. The book of Hosea, after ch. 3, reflects the chaotic situation and bewildering succession of plots and murders bringing six men to the throne within a score of years (Hos 7:7; 8:4; 13:10–11; 2 Kings 15). Hosea sneered at the dependence of these kings upon their fortified cities, impotent idols, or on the protection of Assyria or Egypt, all of which would invite disaster.

Limestone statuette of a 'Temple boy', one of the *qedešim* of a sancturay (From Cyprus)

1. THE NATURE OF CANAANITE CULTURE

The discoveries relating to Canaanite religion at Ras Shamra, ancient Ugarit, provide a panoramic view of Ba'alism, which would later be the target of Hosea's attacks. The extensive finds in the large tell have revealed, in addition to innumerable artifacts, a great collection of tablets containing mythic and ritual texts, historical and political, administrative, legal and commercial data, as well as official correspondence. Examination of the tablets indicated a close relationship with the somewhat later Hebrew writings, especially Hebrew poetry (see Psalms). Just as this classic Canaanite civilization contributed a major share to Israel's cultural heritage, we find it had a strong influence in Israelite religious ritual. The Canaanite cult included a highly developed sacrificial system, an extensive priesthood, and male and female temple servants. Early Israel was the heir of many Canaanite traditions and pratices; it is clear that they persisted among the people of Israel, in spite of the fierce hostility of the canonical prophets.

Fertility figurine pottery from Tell Megadim

2. BA'ALISM

The struggles of nature formed the basis of the plot played out among the deities in the Canaanite cult drama. Priestly men and women enacted the major roles of gods and their consorts. Actual union of the male and female actors was believed to bring about, through mimetic magic, the union of the lord of nature, Ba'al, and mother earth to ensure great harvests and herds for the community. The use of wine and beer often turned the proceedings into bacchanalian festivals. Sacred prostitutes, both male and female, were designated by the same words in Ugaritic and Hebrew, *qedašim* and *qedašot*. In Hebrew the word for a temple attendant is different from that for a common prostitute, but the distinction is lost in translation.

The prevalence of sacred prostitution called forth repeated invective from the prophets, particularly Hosea (e.g. Hos 4:13–14). The prohibition against such practices was never totally effective. Even though Josiah later "broke down the houses of the cult prostitutes which were in the house of

Before the use of coins became current, metal silver was weighed corresponding to the amount of *shekels* agreed upon

The fertility goddess symbol bears a relation to the Hosea story

Yahweh" (2 Kgs 23:7), these practices continued until the destruction of the Temple in the sixth century.

3. CONTENTS

The personal tragedy of the prophet's marriage runs through the book, which falls into two major sections. The first three chapters concern Hosea's marriage to Gomer, and its significance as a paradigm or allegory of Yahweh's marriage to Israel.

a) In chapter 1, written in third person, God tells Hosea to marry a harlot or an adulteress as a symbol of the apostasy of the people. He married Gomer and the son born to them was called Jezreel in token of the blood of the innocent victims of the ruthless kings of the dynasty of Jehu shed in Jezreel. The daughter was called 'Not pitied,' alluding to the house of Israel. A second son was named 'Not my people' to symbolize the people's breach of the covenant with God and his rejection of them. Chapter 3 continues the story of his marriage from a point subsequent to that reached in 1:9 and is written in the first person; it records a similar story: God commanded Hosea to love the adulteress, who had meanwhile sunk to the level of a slave, and to ransom her for 15 pieces of silver and a generous measure of barley. In Exod 21:32 the price of a female is 30 shekels of silver, while archaeological records reveal that the price of a slave was around 40 pieces of silver in contemporary Assyria. Hosea ordered Gomer to live in chastity for long days as though to represent the future penitence of Israel.

The two accounts can be merged into a single coherent narrative of a personal experience of the prophet illustrating the unhappy history of Yahweh's betrayal by his people. Hosea banished his wife, then ransomed her, hoping that the painful experience would not prevent them from resuming a happy relationship. In the same way, Israel betrayed God, who banished her but now is ready to take her back in the hope that she will repent. Another interpretation of Hosea's marriage is that Gomer's misbehavior triggered his prophetic mission. Through his experience, he came to a new understanding of the love of God and of the injury which Israel had inflicted by its faithlessness. This seems to be the case with other prophets whose theological insights and accompanying pronouncements were sharpened and focussed by their personal, often painful, experiences.

b) The second section of the book, chapters 4–14, contains short and separate oracles whose arrangement and connection are not obvious. Although they are mainly judgments against Israel, Hosea's message was not limited to impending disaster. Words of comfort are interspersed among prophecies of doom.

PART VII

FIRST ISAIAH

Isaiah lived during the reigns of King Uzziah, Jotham, Ahaz, and Hezekiah of Judah. When he was called to his ministry in ca. 742 B.C., Judah was a flourishing state, thanks to the aggressive policies and energetic activities of Uzziah who reigned for over 50 years. His father, Amaziah, had reconquered Edom (2 Kgs 14:7) with its copper and iron mines and, for the first time, Judah completely subjugated maritime Philistia. But the days of plenty passed as Judah was subjected to invasions which depleted her power and prestige. The first significant threat was the Aramean-Israelite invasion of 735 B.C., described below.

Isaiah saw that greed and covetousness divided the nation into possessors and the dispossessed. As urban life expanded rapidly, the nobles built up large estates, and with the help of some corrupt judges, piled up wealth in houses and land; meanwhile the oppressed and dispossessed peasantry sought legal redress in vain. Extremes of wealth and poverty, impossible under the older biblical system of land tenure, were now quickly appearing. Indeed, the prophetic writings provide evidence of land accumulation and the emergence of a royal tenantry. Landless farmers, who flowed into the cities in search of a livelihood, were surrounded by wealth, luxury, and vice, while they lived in poverty, misery, and squalor. Nevertheless Isaiah foretold better days, when settlements would extend through the lowland and the farmer would prosper without interference (32:15-20).

Isaiah stands at the forefront of the prophetic tradition. In fact, the 66 chapters collected and canonized under his name represent the prophecies of at least two different men: Isaiah ben Amoz, who lived in the eighth century B.C. and to whom most of chapters 1-39 of the book is attributed, and an anonymous prophet, now designated Second Isaiah who lived in exile in Babylon on the eve of its fall in the mid-sixth century B.C. and to whom the bulk of chapters 40-66 is usually ascribed (see Part VIII, Second Isaiah).

The prophecies attributed to Isaiah ben Amoz were not collected into a single anthology until long after his death. There are indications in the book of smaller collections which may have existed in independent form before the book as a whole was assembled.

1. CONTENTS

Although the composition of the book has resulted in a loose collection of originally unrelated pronouncements, the following groups are fairly distinct: Chapters 1-12 are generally autobiographical and deal mainly with Judah and Jerusalem; chs. 13-23 contain oracles against the nations;

Hittite version of the 'heavenly court', a symbol met with in Isaiah's vision

chs. 24–27 are eschatological prophecy; chs. 28–33 deal primarily with the relationship between Judah and Assyria; chs. 34 and 35 consist of two eschatological prophecies; chs. 36–39 contain historical narratives and can be regarded as an appendix.

a. The Call and an Ancient Image

Isaiah's career may have begun with his call which he describes in chapter 6. In a vision he finds himself in the heavenly court, in the very presence of Yahweh on his heavenly throne and surrounded by his heavenly host. Yahweh then purifies Isaiah and commissions him to carry the divine message to Israel.

The concept of the heavenly court has antecedents in Canaanite mythology. The Ugaritic texts present vivid descriptions of the meeting of the gods in the court of El. This image was adapted in Israelite tradition so that Yahweh is pictured as the king, surrounded by his divine entourage of counsellors and servants.

b. Archaeology and Isaiah's Call

Many scholars associate the seraphim of Isaiah's vision with the winged serpent or four-winged uraeus, a well-known symbol in the ancient Near East. From Egypt, there is a uraeus rising vertically from the two back corners of the seat of the throne of Tutankhamon (14th century). The four wings of the Egyptian uraeus represent the pharaoh's rule extending over the whole earth. The winged seraphim chant: "The whole earth is full of his glory" (6:3). Archaeological evidence reveals that this symbol was known and used by the Israelites, even in royal symbolism. Numerous scarabs from Megiddo, Gaza, Beth-shemesh, Lachish, some with inscribed Hebrew names, bear the Egyptian uraeus; two-winged or four-winged uraei were well known in the time of Isaiah, a period when Egyptian motifs were common in Palestinian art. An ivory handle in the form of a winged uraeus wearing the double Egyptian crown came from the floor of Ahab's courtyard in his palace at Samaria.

In the third quarter of the eighth century B.C., Judah faced political circumstances that altered her status permanently and decisively. Following

150

the war with the Arameans, Assyria regained the strength and energy to rebuild its empire. Samaria fell before the Assyrian expansion in 722/21 B.C. Though Judah managed to survive for another century and a half (to 587 B.C.), she was not to know sustained political independence again. Our major sources for this period are the books of Kings and 2 Chronicles (see chapter V above).

While it is true that neither religious decay, including wholesale apostasy, nor extreme social deterioration had gone as far in Judah as they had in the northern kingdom, Judean society was not free from these diseases, as we learn from both Isaiah and Micah. This was particularly the case during the reign of Ahaz who paid homage to the Assyrian emperor in return for the help he asked. This meant burning offerings to the gods of Assyria along with the sacrifices for Yahweh on the great altar of the Temple. There was a swell of popular discontent, inspired by dissatisfaction with national policies and promoted by the oracles of Yahweh's prophets.

Section of the Isaiah scroll found in the caves of Qumran

2. ISAIAH AND ARCHAEOLOGY

The records of the Assyrian kings illuminate the biblical narrative at many points and are cited extensively by modern historians. In addition, the Dead Sea Scrolls copied in the 1st century B.C. have yielded texts of Isaiah that are only 1000 years older than the earliest extant copies of the Hebrew Masoretic text of the 9th and 10th centuries A.D. One scroll is a complete text of Isaiah, while the other is fragmentary but in good condition. The second is practically identical with the Masoretic text, while the first, which is older (dating to about 100 B.C.), varies somewhat more, and is written with much fuller spelling, characteristic of the Maccabean Age.

Two-winged scarab with the owner's name in the lower register. Scarab seals were used to stamp the clay sealings which protected letters and containers

3. THE PROPHECY OF ISAIAH 7 IN HISTORICAL PERSPECTIVE

Isaiah 7 is one of the key chapters of the Old Testament, and it has been the subject of a great deal of scholarly debate and difference of opinion throughout the long history of biblical interpretation. It is now possible to set the record straight with the help of the new data at our command.

The first 20 years of Isaiah's career were spent during the reign of Ahaz (735–716 B.C.), namely the period of the last wars with the Arameans and the increasing aggression of Assyria. Pekah of Israel and Rezin of Aram wanted Ahaz to join them in a coalition against Assyria. Isaiah had analyzed the balance of forces for the king and his fellow Israelites. However, he did not appear before the king as a political commentator, but as a messenger of God, claiming that he and his children were appointed by Yahweh to be signs for Israel; from their names and his activities people could infer what Yahweh intended to do. Consequently, the "man of portent" asked to meet with the king "at the end of the conduit of the upper pool" (Isa 7:3). This was an outer open-air conduit running from the Gihon spring along the Kidron valley floor to a pool at the southern end of the city. It was later abandoned during Hezekiah's reign and replaced by the tunnel leading to the Siloam pool. The visible traces of this conduit mark its termination at the dry upper pool, a mute witness to the dramatic encounter between Ahaz and Isaiah.

a. *The Facts Involved*

Isaiah was sent there to expose a plot of the kings of Israel and Aram to unseat Ahaz of Judah, thus ending the Davidic dynasty. They meant to install on the throne the son of Tabeel of the house of Tobiah, which possessed vast estates in Transjordan. Another descendant of this house would appear on the scene in Nehemiah's time; still later, a third Tobiad was known as a leading Jewish Hellenizer on the eve of the Hasmonean period (Hellenizers and Hasmoneans: Part XVI).

The point of Isaiah's message was that the solution offered by the coalition with Pekah and Rezin would not prevent Assyria's eventual aggression, which was inevitable. But Judah would be saved in the end and as a sign, a son named Immanuel would be born. The symbol *Immanuel*, "God is with us," assures that Yahweh is still the God and protector of Israel. The fact that the boy "will eat curds and honey when he knows how to refuse evil and choose good" (7:15) means that the fortunes of Judah will be reversed by the time he reaches maturity so that there will be feasting in the land. The promise that a remnant would be preserved is contained in the name of the son whom Isaiah brought along: She'ar-jashub, "A remnant shall return" (7:3).

The proper sense of Isa 7:14, which has been seen as a prediction of the virgin birth of Jesus and cited in this connection in Matt 1:22–23, can now be elucidated on the basis of Ugaritic texts. The term *'almâ* refers to an adolescent woman of marriageable age, not necessarily to a virgin. In Ugaritic the goddess Anat is refered to as both *glmt* (= Hebrew *'almâ*) and *btlt* (= Hebrew *betûlâ*, "virgin"). Anat is described in the texts as both a virgin and a courtesan; she is the sister and consort of Baal. The mistranslation of the Hebrew *'almâ* as virgin may be traced to the Greek Septuagint, which rendered it by *parthenos*. Whatever may be behind that rendering, there is no historical or exegetical connection between this passage and the birth of Jesus. The connection rests rather on a spiritual and messianic interpre-

An Aramean prince or king. Ivory carving from Arslan Tash

Aramean mounted soldier; from Tell Halaf

tation, an approach to Scripture popular among different sects of the first century B.C.

Two Assyrian scribes record the spoil taken from Israelite Ashtarot, as women and children are carted away

b. *The Political Consequences*

Events proved Isaiah correct as the pro-Tabeel plot failed. Ahaz's enemies made a joint attack against him in 735, but he enlisted Assyria's help against Aram and Israel. In ca. 733, Tiglath-pileser III marched to the west, conquered Philistia, and devastated Israel and Aram. Judah maintained its position only by becoming an Assyrian vassal state. These events are confirmed by the Assyrian royal chronicles. The episode is further illuminated by a letter written by a certain Assyrian official which has been found in Nimrud advising the court that an emissary from the house of Tabeel was bringing an important message to Assyria. It must be noted, however, that when Ahaz turned to the emperor for help he also had to pay the price: official recognition of the state religion of the Assyrian overlord, along with a heavy burden of tribute. Thus Ahaz, against the prophet's vehement opposition, introduced an Assyrian-type altar into the Temple as well as other Assyrian cult practices (2 Kgs 16:10–16).

Captured cities invariably brought tribute to the Assyrian invaders as shown by the carving at the foot of a statue

4. KING HEZEKIAH

After the fall of the northern kingdom in 722/21 B.C., Merodach-baladan, king of Babylon, tried to form a coalition with Judah and organize western Asia to defy Assyria (Isa 30:1–5; 31:1–3). Again Isaiah came forth and warned Hezekiah, son of Ahaz, that he too would be trapped in the middle of a bitter struggle (39:6–7; 2 Kgs 20:16–18). He was joined in this protest by the prophet Micah. Isaiah was equally critical of any alliance with Egypt.

Hezekiah, notwithstanding the risks involved, undertook meticulous preparations for the ensuing conflict. He dug the Siloam tunnel (see Kings above) to divert the waters from the Gihon spring to a point inside the city walls in case of siege. He also built warehouses to store extra food. He hastily reinforced the walls of Jerusalem by using stones from buildings nearby (22:8–11) and strengthened his chariot forces.

Isaiah opposed a rebellion against Assyria based upon an alliance with Egypt and other neighboring kingdoms, both in 714–711 and 705–701 B.C. He regarded Egypt as a "broken reed" and argued that the kingdom of Judah could not successfully pursue a policy based upon human cleverness without trust in Yahweh (29:15; 30:1–7; 31:1–5).

a. *The Siloam Epitaph*

Many scholars relate an Isaian verse to an intriguing epitaph found on a tomb in Jerusalem. The passage in Isa 22:15–25 begins: "Come, go to this steward, to Shebna, who is over the household, and say to him: What have you to do here and whom have you here, that you have hewn a tomb for yourself, you who hew a tomb on the height, and carve a habitation for yourself in the rock?"

The epitaph was discovered on the facade of a tomb dating to the days of Isaiah and Hezekiah which reads: "This is (the sepulcher of ...) ...yahu, who is over the house. There is no gold and silver here but (his bones) and the bones of his slave-wife with him. Cursed be the man who will open this..." The owner of this tomb "who was over the house" must have been one of the notables of Jerusalem, possibly Shebna, but the beginning of the name "...*yahu*" is missing because of a hole in the surface of the tomb. It

Inscription carved in the rock wall of Hezekiah's tunnel (late 8th c.) describing the exciting moments in the hewing of the conduit as two groups of borers were about to meet each other in the middle of the tunnel

Assyrian king holding enemies by ropes (see Isaiah 19:28). Carved on the 'broken obelisk' from Nineveh (10th c.)

is difficult to decide whether this could be the termination of the full name Shebnayahu. The letters of the Siloam tomb inscription are very similar to those of the famous Siloam tunnel inscription, which belongs to the reign of Hezekiah. Both may be dated around 700 B.C.

We have mentioned and illustrated above (see Part V: Kings) the tombs of the aristocrats of Jerusalem in the days of the monarchy, discovered by B. Mazar near the Temple Mount. The burial places of ordinary people who could not afford to prepare closed rock tombs or epitaphs have been more difficult to locate archaeologically. They are referred to in Jer 26:23 as the "burial place of the common people," which B. Mazar believed was situated in the Kidron valley below the cemetery of the Mount of Olives.

b. *Sennacherib's Invasion*

The accession of Sennacherib to the throne of Assyria in 705 B.C. occasioned a series of rebellions throughout the empire. He set out on a vast campaign in 702, conquering most of Judah, including Lachish, and besieging Jerusalem where Hezekiah found himself imprisoned. This was the occasion of Isaiah's mockery of Sennacherib (37:21–29), "I will put my hook in your nose and my bit in your mouth..." (37:29), which is consistent with contemporary custom. The threat has been illustrated vividly in an Assyrian engraving of the tenth century showing a victorious king holding his defeated enemies by ropes tied to rings fixed in their noses. While it is true that Hezekiah paid a heavy tribute to the emperor, Jerusalem itself was not conquered. Though the prophet first opposed a rebellion against Assyria, he now set out to encourage and sustain the morale of the people in the beleaguered capital. His oracles express the calm assurance that Zion would be saved and the Assyrians broken by Yahweh's power.

Sennacherib's inscriptions on clay prisms describing his campaign against Hezekiah and the Philistines in the year 701 B.C. are the most detailed Assyrian accounts of an episode related in the Bible. Sennacherib boasts:

> "As for Hezekiah the Judahite, he did not submit to my yoke. I laid siege to forty-six of his strong cities, walled forts, and to countless villages in their vicinity, and conquered them... I drove out over 200,000 people... Hezekiah himself I made prisoner in Jerusalem, his royal residence, like a bird in a cage."

Prism of Sennacherib describing his campaign against Judah (701 B.C.)

A 'copper serpent' from a Mesopotamian temple, similar to the one king Hezekiah cast away from the Temple (2 Kings 18:4)

These were not empty boasts, for scenes of the Assyrian siege of Lachish were carved in the imposing panels exhibited in the British Museum.

c. *Ahaz's Sundial*

After the siege of Jerusalem and Lachish, the aged prophet drops from view, but before this we read of Hezekiah's illness and Isaiah's suggested cure for his boils: a dried fig cake. The medical use of fig cakes is attested in an Ugaritic text describing the preparation of a plaster pack for a sick horse. When Isaiah predicted that the king would live for another 15 years, the king asked for a sign and Isaiah replied: "This is the sign to you from the Lord, that the Lord will do the things that he has promised: Shall the shadow go forward ten steps, or go back ten steps? ...and he brought the shadow back ten steps, by which the sun declined on the dial of Ahaz" (2 Kgs 20:9–11). By relating this passage to a former reference to an "upper chamber" of Ahaz, Y. Yadin hypothesized that he built an upper chamber which had two stairways leading up its sides to the roof. This served as a sundial. The angle of the walls threw a shadow onto the steps and it moved along one stairway as the sun rose in the sky, and moved up the second as the sun set.

Graphic illustration of Ahaz's sundial

PART VIII

SECOND ISAIAH

There is a scholarly concensus that chapters 40–66 of Isaiah do not date to the eighth century B.C. but rather to the sixth century, the period of the Babylonian exile and after. The clearest argument for this is the two references to Cyrus (Isa 44:28; 45:10), but there are other indications. Assyria, the enemy in Isaiah ben Amoz' day, is mentioned only once in passing (52:4), while Babylon now fills that role in Second Isaiah. The exile has already taken place; the Jews are awaiting their release (40:1–11). Jerusalem and the Temple are in ruins but hope for the restoration runs through the oracles of this later prophet. Since his name is unknown and his teachings have been incorporated by tradition into the book of Isaiah, he is conventionally called the Second Isaiah or Deutero-Isaiah.

The issue of the composition and authorship of Second Isaiah is further complicated by certain important differences between chapters 40–55 and 56–66. The major theme of the latter section is the division between the two components of the community: the genuine and the spurious Israel. Chapters 56–66 may have been composed at a later time, for they suggest that the Jews had already returned to Israel, and the Temple had been rebuilt, although the walls of Jerusalem were still to be restored (60:10). Many scholars have suggested that the last section was composed by still another anonymous prophet, termed Third Isaiah. It is also possible that the 27 chapters (40–66) were written by a single prophet over a long period of time, covering both the exile and the earliest stages of the restoration. We will leave this question in abeyance and proceed with the archaeological evidence for the division of the book of Isaiah.

1. EVIDENCE OF THE DEAD SEA SCROLLS

Of the two parchment scrolls of Isaiah found at Qumran, J. T. Milik points out a significant detail in the former, more complete text (10Isa): "Chapter 33 comes to a close toward the foot of column XXVII [of that scroll, though it is not identical with the conventional chapter numbers as we know them today]. The three ruled lines which follow are left blank. Furthermore, the sheet on which it is written has only two columns instead of the four that are used in this roll. Chapter 34 begins on a new sheet of leather, and the text thereafter continues without further interruption until the end of he book [chapter 66]. This oddity may indicate that there persisted a memory of two different collections of prophecy (corresponding roughly to the modern distinction between Proto- and Deutero-Isaiah) although the two collections had been already combined in one book by the time of the copyist." There are, furthermore, differences in grammar and

157

orthography between the two parts, and the material disposition of the text in the roll is not the same. We may explain this division by the fact that there is no material in the book of Isaiah beginning with chapter 34 which can be attributed to First Isaiah. Chapters 34–35 are exilic or post-exilic in date and chapters 36–39, while a historical summary of the period of First Isaiah, are closely related to 2 Kings, which itself was part of the Primary History probably published in exilic times.

2. CYRUS AND NABONIDUS, THE FIRST ARCHAEOLOGIST

The Second Isaiah, who proclaimed his message from ca. 546 to 538 B.C., witnessed Cyrus' meteoric rise to power in the Near East. Beginning with his defeat of the Medes in 550 B.C., Cyrus never experienced a serious set-back on the way to building an empire which would eventually include Asia Minor, Syria and Palestine, Mesopotamia, and lands to the east. After the subjugation of the Median empire, he turned to the west, defeating Croesus, king of rich Lydia, and captured Sardis, Lydia, and the Greek cities on the coast of Asia Minor. He was now prepared to turn back and confront the mighty Babylonian empire.

Cyrus was able to enter Babylon without resistance for several reasons. The Babylonian government had been unstable since the days of Nebuchad-nezzar (605–562 B.C.). This instability dramatically increased under the last Babylonian king, Nabonidus (555–539 B.C.). From a number of in-scriptions which have been found, including one by his mother, we learn that Nabonidus was an antiquarian and a religious fanatic. He estranged himself from the priests of Marduk, the major Babylonian god, with his zeal for Sin, the moon god. He spent long years away from Babylon, mainly

Nabonidus states on this stele that Sennacherib was assassinated by his sons due to the god Marduk's wrath against his destruction of Babylon. This historiosophy stands in sharp contrast to Isaiah's concept of the "Day of the Lord' when all the proud and lofty rulers would be humbled

Section of Isaiah scroll from Qumran (Is. 47:1–49:8)

at the remote oasis of Tema', southeast of Palestine, a major junction on the caravan routes of Arabia. He was absent from the New Year Festival (*akitu* festival) for ten years, which further enraged the powerful Marduk priesthood. He had left as regent in Babylon his son Belshazzar, whom we meet in the book of Daniel, which describes the fall of that kingdom. Strangely enough, a scroll found at Qumran shows that the dream of Nebuchadnezzar (Daniel 4) was a story originally told of the errant Nabonidus, who is not mentioned in Daniel.

Nabonidus' other passion was for the past. His scholars sought out and read ancient cuneiform inscriptions. When he had a temple rebuilt, he directed his scholars to search for the foundation of the earlier temple: "To the right and the left, in front of and behind the chambers and in the sanctuary I made an excavation." He used a verb, which elsewhere means "to dig a ditch," specifically of digging to find ancient remains, at one point uncovering a temple foundation which he attributed to a Sumerian king who lived 2220 years earlier. Although his chronology was inaccurate (by almost 500 years), Nabonidus' find still qualifies as the first extant archaeological report.

In the Persian empire Cyrus the Great established a new policy regarding the treatment of subject peoples. The Assyrian system of maintaining domination over conquered peoples involved the wholesale transfer of populations, to break local ties and generate common loyalties to the empire. This practice was continued by the Babylonians. The Persian policy, on the other hand, was to treat their subjects kindly, allowing them to remain in (or return to) their land and to worship according to their own religion as long as it did not interfere with the political authority of the empire. Because of this more lenient policy, the Israelites welcomed the advent of Cyrus, and Second Isaiah even refers to him as "his [Yahweh's] anointed" (45:1).

3. THE CREATIVE SIXTH CENTURY B.C.

The sixth century, which has been remarkably well illuminated by archaeology, saw the eclipse of Egypt and the passing of world power to Babylonia. The Babylonian exile was a major turning point in Jewish history and religion. Under new circumstances, Israelites had to reinterpret much of their earlier tradition. Longstanding doctrines had to be rethought in a situation in which there was no king, no land, no nation, and Jerusalem and the Temple lay in ruins. This period was also a time of great literary activity, including the collection and composition of the bulk of the principal parts of the Hebrew Bible: the Primary History consisting of the Torah (Pentateuch) and the Former Prophets (Joshua, Judges, Samuel, and Kings); most of the Latter Prophets including First Isaiah and at least parts of Second Isaiah, Jeremiah, Ezekiel, and many of the Minor Prophets. Books like Psalms and Proverbs undoubtedly existed though probably in an earlier form than is now preserved in the Bible. Other books like Ruth, Lamentations, and very likely Song of Songs, were in circulation.

4. CONTENTS

Second Isaiah may be divided roughly into three sections. The first two, 40–48 and 49–55, express the hope for the end of the Babylonian exile. In the first section, the prophet relates this hope to the figure of Cyrus and also expresses deep hostility toward false gods and idol worship. They are contrasted with Yahweh, sole ruler of the universe and the Lord of history. In the second section these themes, particularly the first two, are dropped and the central theme becomes the rehabilitation of Zion-Jerusalem. The four "Servant Songs" interspersed in these two sections (42:1–4; 49:1–6; 50:4–9; 52:13–53:12) deserve special attention (see below). The last section (56–66) contains admonitions and predictions, often in a different literary style from that of chapters 40–55. Especially in chapters 60–61 there is a message of comfort and confidence in Israel's future glory.

5. SYMBOLISM AND THE ANCIENT ARTS

In his eloquent use of imagery, Second Isaiah often made reference to ancient crafts which his contemporaries would readily have understood, but are accessible to modern readers only through archaeology. In his succint picture of the "metalworker" (44:9–20), Second Isaiah describes the process of plating metal over a wooden core to produce idols. He alludes, likewise, to the smelting furnace (48:10) and the testing of metal. At high temperatures, the ore melts and the heavier lead and other impurities sink, while the lighter silver floats on the surface.

Except copper, which was mined in the Arabah, other metals such as iron, tin, silver, and gold were imported in bars and transported on heavy cargo ships (Tarshish ships) from Spain, Cilicia, and other lands. These ores were refined locally. Crucibles for smelting iron and copper, usually made of clay, have been discovered at several places in Palestine. Gold and silver were smelted in closed crucibles to prevent the loss of any of the precious metal. These crucibles were placed in a beehive-shaped furnace, with air holes at the bottom to create a draft, or so that bellows could be used. The pure metal was cast into molds, which were made in two symmetrical halves and provided with holes or small escape channels so that the excess metal could flow out. Molds for making weapons, figurines, and jewelry have been found in excavations.

In one of the poems the stained clothing of the person treading out grapes in the wine press in a metaphor for the appearance of the wrathful God on judgment day (63:2). The whole process of wine production is illustrated abudantly by the numerous examples of wine presses found in excavations. The Gibeon press has a broad surface for treading the grapes by foot, squeezing the liquid from them. The liquid flowed down through a drainage channel into collecting vats in which the precipitates settled at the bottom. From there the clear liquid flowed to a second vat where it was collected. The new wine was then transferred to vessels which were sealed and placed in a cool place to stand until the juice fermented and became wine. The

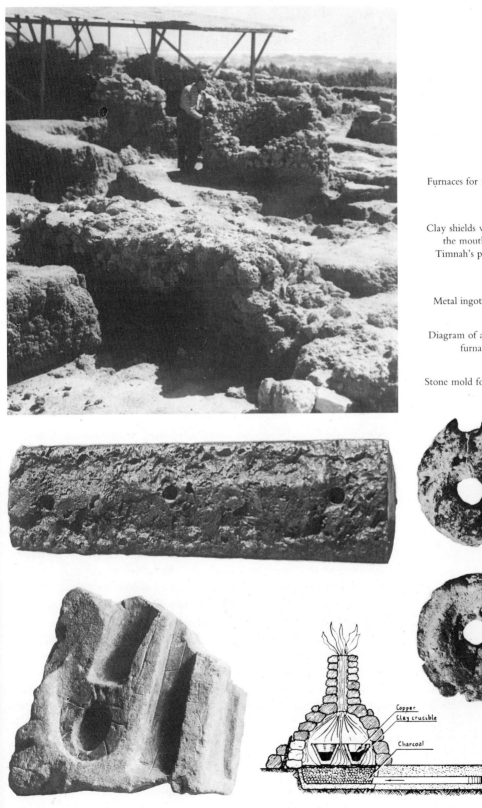

Left:
Furnaces for metal casting at
Tell Qasileh

Margin:
Clay shields which protected
the mouths of bellows at
Timnah's primitive copper
works

Center:
Metal ingot from a furnace

Right, below:
Diagram of a copper casting
furnace, Tell Qasileh

Left, below:
Stone mold for the casting of
weapons

Copper
Clay crucible

Charcoal

wine was poured into liquid measures, the *bāt* and the *hîn*, 40 and 6 liters respectively. Then these were stored in the wine-cellars of the wealthy, including royal and noble families, and sealed with their stamp.

Underground wine vats and storage cellars at Israelite Gibeon. The wine was filled into wineskins and jars and stacked in the cellars. Some 100,000 liters could be stored there

6. THE FALL OF THE BABYLONIAN GODS

One of the beliefs that was common to most of the ancient Near East was that battles on the human scale were reflections of battles in the divine world between the gods representing the two warring nations. Thus, when the Babylonians attacked Judah, Marduk, the chief Babylonian deity, was simultaneously attacking Yahweh. The notion that Yahweh leads both the divine and human army of Israel into battle permeates the military traditions of the Bible. The implications of this belief was that the god leading the victorious army had defeated the god of the conquered people. According to this traditional wisdom the Babylonian destruction of Jerusalem signaled Marduk's ascendancy over Yahweh.

Second Isaiah rejected this thinking unequivocally and argued repeatedly against any notion of theomachy (i.e. war among the gods) or even the existence of other gods. This is the occasion of his wholesale ridicule of idolatry in 40:18–20; 41:6–7; 44:9–20; 46:1–7. In Babylon the Israelites were confronted with a multiplicity of shrines, each of which contained at least one, and often a number, of idols. These idols were regarded as divine beings by the priesthood which served them. They were awakened in the morning and put to bed at night; they were royally dressed and fed. At least once a year, during the New Year's Festival, all the gods, i.e. the idols, were brought out and paraded through the city in a major procession led by the idol of Marduk. This is illustrated by a striking image whereby Second Isaiah draws a contrast between the pagan idols which cannot move

Wine vat from Gezer

unless carried, and Yahweh, who has carried Israel from its origins: "Bel bows down, Nebo stoops, their idols are on beasts and cattle; these things you carry are loaded as burdens on weary beasts. They stoop, they bow down together, they cannot save the burden, but themselves go into captivity" (46:1–2).

A procession of gods mounted on animals: A striking illustration of Second Isaiah's sarcasm against the idols (see also 2 Kings 23:11). From an Assyrian relief

7. ISRAELITE MONOTHEISM

The second line of argument used against the belief that Marduk had defeated Yahweh was Second Isaiah's explicit ethical monotheism. Yahweh is God alone, unique and incomparable in power and majesty, the Creator of heaven and earth, and the Lord of all human history. In expressing this faith, our author has produced some of the most beautiful poetry and profound theology in the Hebrew Bible.

To be sure, this theology is not a radically new development at the time of the exile; rather Second Isaiah only made explicit what was implicit in earlier Israelite tradition. In the prevaling religious climate in Palestine in the days of the monarchy, Yahweh was thought of as the one national god for Israel, powerful beyond imagination in the land he had chosen for his people. At the same time, the doctrine of Yahweh's control of the universe is already present in the creation story (Gen 1:1–2:4). The ramifications of this seminal belief were often overshadowed by concern about the unique relationship between Yahweh and Israel, but with time they became more evident in the prophetic writings.

The ethical monotheism now formulated by Second Isaiah carried with it the assurance that the people could have confidence in Yahweh and his power and authority anywhere in the world. He meant to convince his fellow exiles that the Babylonians and their gods were not the real victors over Judah

163

and Yahweh, but that, on the contrary, these heathen were no more than the rod of his anger and punishment: "I am the Lord, that is my name; my glory I give to no other, nor my praise to graven images" (42:8).

8. ISRAEL'S MISSION AND DESTINY: THE WIDESPREAD DISAGREEMENT OVER THE "SUFFERING" SERVANT OF YAHWEH

Seal impressions on store-jars or wine-jars denoting the place of origin of the wine; or identifying them as taxes paid in kind to the state. The impressions bear the seal "(Belonging) to the king/ Hebron" and (Belonging) to the king/Mmšt

The most striking passages of Second Isaiah are found in the four "Servant of Yahweh" poems (42:1–4; 49:1–6; 50:4–9; 52:13–53:12). The Servant, to be elected by Yahweh, will proclaim the message of truth and of righteousness to the world, helped by the divine spirit to overcome obstacles set in his way. Though he first meets with failure, the Servant will be helped by God to become the savior of his fellow Jews and of the whole earth. The last poem depicts him as a martyr and outcast who lays down his life for others. No concept in the Bible is stronger, more elusive, and more movingly profound than this. Its interpretation has evoked widespread disagreement among scholars.

Who was the Servant? Was it Israel as is suggested in 49:3? However, in 49:5–6 the Servant clearly has a mission *to* Israel, so it has been proposed that he represents a smaller group within Israel. On the other hand, many theologians and scholars believe that the Servant was an individual and not the personification of a group. The question then arises as to whether he is a historical figure or someone still to come. It is suggested that the Second Isaiah himself accepted his undeserved suffering meekly and thereby succeeded in sparing his contemporaries from the punishment which was their due for their transgressions. Numerous other figures from the period of the exile have been proposed as the model for the Servant.

Finally, many have seen in the Servant passages the promise of a suffering and saving messiah to come. The messianist followers of Jesus saw in him the suffering servant of Second Isaiah and the royal messiah of Israel combined in one person. This interpretation is already present in the New Testament, as can be seen in Matt 26:24, Mark 9:12, and Luke 18:13. While such an interpretation may be debated, there can be no doubt that the message of Second Isaiah had a profound effect on the formulation of Christian doctrine. At the same time, the message had a contemporary impact and effect, since it was addressed by the prophet as a warning and a comfort to his fellow exiles and it proved to be a motivating force in normative Judaism in the following centuries.

It is clear throughout these passages that the Servant's mission did not stop with Israel but extended to all the nations. This universal concern is a corollary to Second Isaiah's explicit monotheism (see above). On the basis of the latter he sounded a note of promise, for the God who created the cosmos had also committed himself to the survival and success of his people Israel, and could not rest until he had accomplished all. Thus Israel, through its service and suffering, could triumph, and the whole world would share in the salvation of God.

9. THE INSCRIPTION ON THE WALL

Another proof of Isaian prophecy seeking hidden promise of redemption beyond the immediate future was a recent discovery in the excavations of the Temple Mount: A large Hebrew inscription carved in the stone was found in the course of uncovering the Western Wall. It quoted a passage of Isaiah 66:14 "You shall see, and your heart shall rejoice; your bones shall flourish like the grass." This was the conclusion of the phrase: "As one whom his mother comforts, so I will comfort you; you shall be comforted in Jerusalem. You shall see..." This allusion illumines an obscure phase of 4th century A.D. Jewry. This inscription was made in the days f Emperor Julian "the Apostate" who promised the resettlement of Jeru- !em by Jews, whereupon work on the restoration of the Temple had ɔegun and the inscription carved. But when Julian died in 363 A.D., the ˈope and the dream had to be abandoned.

וראיתם ושש לבבכם
ועצמותם כדשא

Carved inscription on an
ashlar of the Western Wall
of the Temple Mount,
quoting Isaiah 63:13–14

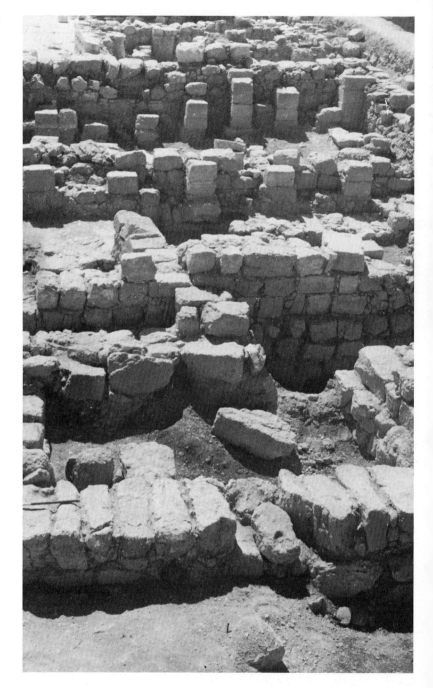

The Israelite wall surrounding the 7th c. fort-palace of king Jehoiakim at Ramat-Rahel is seen in the foreground. The structures in the background were Byzantine halls

PART IX

JEREMIAH

Jeremiah is an invaluable source for the historical background of the period leading up to the Babylonian exile, as are the books of his contemporaries — Zephaniah, Nahum, Habakkuk, and the young Ezekiel. Jeremiah's career began in the year 627 B.C. during the reign of Josiah and lasted for over 40 years, until some time after the destruction of Jerusalem in 586 B.C. He was active during the reigns of Josiah, Jehoiakim, Jehoiachin, and Zedekiah, the last king of Judah.

Jeremiah lived in a period when the tottering Assyrian empire relaxed its grip on its former holdings. In the next 40 years, under the rule of Josiah, Judah passed through a period of independence, only to fall victim to the imperial ambitions, first of Egypt, then of resurgent Babylon. It was finally overrun by the Babylonians in two campaigns, in 598 and 586 B.C., as a result of Judah's futile attempt to throw off the yoke of Nebuchadnezzar. Every act of the tragic drama is reflected in Jeremiah, with all its pathos and anguish.

1. GENERAL CONTENTS

The book of Jeremiah, consisting of 52 chapters, makes extremely difficult reading, yet it is replete with historical material which can be illuminated by the results of archaeology. This book, as we know it today, is not a single composition, but is composed of three shorter "books" which at one time had circulated separately. These shorter sections are themselves collections of oracles, which are sometimes arranged chronologically, but often are organized according to subject matter. As with the other prophetic books, the completed work is the result of a long and intricate process involving the gradual coalescing of various streams of the Jeremianic tradition. The major sections are:

a. Chapters 1:1–25:13a; 34–35, a collection of oracles, dictated to Baruch (cf. Jeremiah 36), uttered between his call (627 B.C.) and the days of Zedekiah; 1:4–6:30 are from the time of Josiah; 7:1–20:18, 35 from those of Jehoiakim; 21:1–25:13; 34 from the time of Zedekiah. They contain words of censure, warning and judgment for Judah and Jerusalem, and to a lesser extent, oracles of hope: 3:11–18; 16:14–15; 23:1–8.

b. Chapters 26–29 and 36–45 relate the story of Jeremiah's suffering. They show Jeremiah's personal anguish as he is confronted with a stubborn people led astray by false prophets and corrupt priests.

c. Chapters 30–33, sometimes referred to as the Book of Consolation, were originally a separate section, containing many different promises concerning salvation, extending from the time of Jeremiah to the post-exilic period.

d. Chapters 46–51, oracles directed against foreign nations. The conclusion of Jeremiah, chapter 52, is a historical appendix, like the appendix to Isaiah ben Amoz in Is 36–39.

It has often been pointed out that there are three major types of material in the book of Jeremiah. They are broadly classified by modern scholars into the following categories, each of which has its own history of transmission: Type A consists of poetry. This is primarily the prophetic oracles, i.e., public preaching and brief addresses in which the prophet acts as the direct messenger of God, delivering the divine words. Type B or prose biography comprises the bulk of Jeremiah 26–29 and 36–45. Type C material is prose discourse cast in verbose and highly rhetorical style. This may be presented in an autobiographical framework in which God addresses Jeremiah and tells him what he is to say or do; or the material may be presented as prose sermons (e.g. Jer 16:1–13; 18:1–12; 33). A rapid perusal of the book shows that the three types of material are widely scattered throughout the book.

a. *Ancient Deeds of Sale*

The passage in Jeremiah 32:6–15 is of particular interest in that it affords the clearest extant description of the way in which property was conveyed, i.e., bought and sold in ancient Judah (in this case the property was purchased by Jeremiah). Seventeen silver shekels were paid, meaning weighed-out silver as coined money was not yet in use. The deed was written in duplicate on two halves of a single sheet of papyrus or parchment, as we know from one such deed from Elephantine, a Jewish colony in Egypt. One leaf of the sheet was then rolled up, tied with strips running through holes in the middle of the sheet, and sealed; the other half was then loosely rolled for ready reference while the sealed copy protected the document from fraudulent alteration. They then "put them in an earthenware jar" (32:14) and placed them in a safe, dry place. Y. Yadin found some "tied deeds" in the Judean desert caves. This method of securing documents is well known to us from the preservation of the Dead Sea Scrolls in jars hidden away in the caves at Qumran.

Right:
Legal document and its clay envelope

b. *Jeremiah and Common Pottery*

Chapters 18–20 form an editorial unit containing examples of all three types of material: poetic oracles, prose discourse, and biography. They were originally independent but probably placed together because of the "potter-pot" motif that runs through both. They both involve symbolic actions: as the quality of the clay determines what a potter can do with it, so the quality of the people determines what Yahweh will do with them.

In chapter 18:1–12 he tells how he visited the potter's house, watching the potter working at his wheel. If he was not satisfied with the first pot he could reshape the soft clay into another pot. The potter's wheel was made with two stones on a vertical axle. The lower stone disk was spun by the feet, while the upper supported the clay which the potter shaped as the wheel revolved.

The manufacture of pottery was the principal industry of the ancient world, involving a highly sophisticated and advanced technology. It was used in every phase of man's life from cradle to grave. For example, the household items made of clay were cooking pots, bowls, cups, plates, bottles, jugs and juglets (juglets with perforations were used for sprinkling), cruets, pitchers, and larger jugs for wine, oil, and water storage. Pottery was also used for cheap jewelry, gaming pieces, molds, and for scoops to carry live coals. Finally, broken sherds of pottery were occasionally used as scratch paper for writing accounts or quick messages and letters. These inscribed sherds, called ostraca, make up much of the surviving extra-biblical Hebrew texts, such as the Samaria and Lachish ostraca.

Pottery was cheap and easy to make. The raw material, clay, was available everywhere and the techniques of pottery-making were well known since at least the fourth millennium B.C. Pottery is both friable and indestructible, ubiquitous and distinctive in its styling and decoration, thus furnishing the archaeologist with the chief tool by which he can date ancient history. Broken pots were so common that nobody bothered to repair or remove them, so they provide unerring clues to the history of their occupation.

c. *An Archaeologist Corrects a Misconception*

In chapter 19:1–12, Jeremiah relates that he went outside the so-called "Potsherd Gate" and there, before witnesses, smashed a clay bottle, proclaiming that so would Zion be smashed beyond repair. This symbolic action

The potter and his wheel

Revolving stone tournette of the potter's wheel. The cone-shaped piece fits into the stone base and is turned

Opposite page:
Clay served every household purpose, from a pilgrim flask (left) to pottery cult-stands (right). Excavated at Tell Zofit and Tell Amal, 11th–10th c. B.C.

Right:
Cross sections of a potter's oven

Left
Potter's oven at Tell Qasileh

is particularly terrifying considering the spot where it was performed: the valley of Hinnom, where child sacrifice to the god Molekh had been practiced in the days of Manasseh (2 Kgs 23:10). *Topheth*, in the valley of Hinnom (renamed the "valley of Slaughter" in Jer 7:32) lay just outside the ancient gate leading to this southern valley. Some scholars believe that there is some relation between the gate leading to the Tophet, called the Potsherd Gate in Jeremiah and the Dung Gate (*ša'ar hā-'ašpot*) which is located in the same area in Neh 2:12 and 3:13. B. Mazar has recently pointed out that the word *'ašpot* is derived from the root Š-P-T, having the sense of "hearth" or "burning place" and that it may be an archaic by-form of Tophet. He concluded that the southern gate, erroneously called the Dung Gate, led to the burning place of Tophet in the valley. Furthermore, this gate should not be confused with the present-day Dung Gate, situated on Mount Moriah in the late Turkish wall of the Old City, near the Temple Mount area.

d. *The Abominable Tophet and Josiah's Reform*

The practice of sacrificing children, which surfaced during the reign of King Manasseh, but was suppressed by Josiah, was a Phoenician custom. The most important evidence for this ancient practice comes from the sanctuary of Tanit at Salambo, Carthage, built by the Phoenicians; the finds there prove conclusively that the Greek and Roman stories of Phoenician infant sacrifices to Molekh were only too true. The excavators uncovered thousands of urns containing the cremated remains of small children mostly under the age of two. The lowest strata of the large sanctuary consisted entirely of these urns of burnt children's bones. The urns were covered by little cairns of stones. At Canaanite Gezer, similar urns were found, dating to the Middle Bronze Age.

2. JEREMIAH AND JOSIAH'S REFORM

Jeremiah's poetic addresses to the people of Judah are filled with his intense hatred of paganizing ritual and all kinds of cant, particularly the conventional exaltation of the Temple and its sacrificial rites, which were mere lip service at the expense of kindness (*hesed*) and elementary justice (*mišpāt*; cf. Jer 7:21–23). Since he was a contemporary of Josiah,, we would expect Jeremiah to have supported Josiah's reform movement, with its emphasis on the election-covenant faith of the Mosaic age, God's love for Israel, the demand for reciprocal love on the part of Israel, and the need for responsible and humanitarian behavior. Unfortunately, it is uncertain whether we have any record of Jeremiah's activity in the years following the reform. It may that Jeremiah 11 gives an authentic account of Jeremiah's early support for the movement. His general silence, however, suggests that the reform did not appear to have affected the people or to have halted the moral deterioration and so the prophet dissociated himself from it.

Josiah's revival was made possible by the death of Ashurbanipal in 627 B.C. and the subsequent decline of Assyrian power. For a short period of time Judah had a respite from external pressures, allowing Josiah to effectuate a thoroughgoing religious reform in the country, and enabling him to eradicate pagan practices throughout the land. This power vacuum was temporary, however, as the Babylonians and the Medes split up the Assyrian empire and the Egyptians sought to become an international power again. The year 609 witnessed the tragic death of Josiah in battle, as he attempted to halt the forces of Pharaoh Necho which were marching north to the Euphrates to assist the Assyrians. Necho deposed Joahaz, a son of Josiah, and elevated Jehoiakim, another son of Josiah, to the throne as his vassal, although the latter was utterly unfit to rule.

3. JEHOIAKIM'S PALACE

Having decided that his father's palace in the city was not good enough for him, he sent out to build a new and finer one, and imposed forced labor on the local population for this purpose. This provoked Jeremiah to one of his most scathing denunciations (22:13–23), contrasting Jehoiakim's desire for a fine house with Josiah's desire for justice and righteousness.

A fine complex of buildings, probably similar to Jehoiakim's proposed palace, was found at Beth-kerem, south of Jerusalem, a site founded during the Judean monarchy. There was a wide house with large chambers; the facade of the main building was decorated with conspicuous ornamental windows (cf. Jer 22:14). The imposing palace, surrounded by a lower citadel extending over an area of five acres, resembles the one which was unearthed at Ramat Rahel. The palace walls were constructed of ashlar blocks, similar

Right, below:
Urns containing the incinerated bodies of sacrificed children. From the Carthaginian cemetery near Tunis

Left, below:
Entrance to a secret passage found in the Israelite wall of Jehoiakim's fort-palace (see p. 166)

to Ahab's palace at Samaria. It was decorated with proto-Aeolic capitals. Among the other finds were window balustrades of the main palace. The remains of the balustrade indicate that the capitals supported cedar beams. Traces of red paint still are visible on the stones. A painted potsherd was also found there, depicting a king seated on his chariot or throne.

4. THE IMPENDING BABYLONIAN THREAT

Jeremiah had become increasingly convinced that the Babylonians were to be Yahweh's agents of judgment upon his people. Some of his oracles telling of the "foe from the north" were uttered as the conquerors swept south to quell the rebellions of Phoenicia, Israel, and Philistia (cf. 46:2–12). By 605 B.C. the Babylonian army had rolled onto the Philistine plain, which they ravaged, carrying off many prisoners. An Aramaic letter found in Egypt contains a desperate plea for help from the king of Ashkelon to the Pharaoh. It failed, as we know from the Babylonian Chronicle, for Ashkelon was captured and destroyed by Nebuchadnezzar's army in December 604 (cf. Jer 47:5–7).

The last years of Judah's independence were overcast by a sense of inescapable doom, as King Zedekiah followed a suicidal pro-Egyptian course against Babylonia. Town after town fell to the Babylonians on the coastal plain and in the Negeb, as we learn from passages in Jeremiah, and as is vividly illustrated by the Lachish ostraca (see below). The excavations of Debir and Lachish show how impoverished these cities had become in the last decade before the final destruction in 586.

During this catastrophic period Jeremiah attacked the prevailing view that the physical presence of the Temple brought protection. Belief in the inviolability of Zion had long since hardened into dogma, and the notion that the city could fall and that the Davidic dynasty might end was simply not entertained in many circles in Jerusalem. Yahweh would not allow it! Secure in this confidence, the state marched blindly to disaster. When defeat and destruction came, the popular religion was powerless to explain it: The national-cultic community disintegrated. The state was at an end, and its people scattered. One era had ended and another begun. The idea of Israel, while permanently linked with a land and a tradition, would never again be limited to a political unity or geographic area.

5. JEREMIAH'S ULTIMATE INFLUENCE

If Israelite faith had been no deeper than the popular religion, it never would have survived such a disaster; it would have sunk into oblivion like the religions of the other peoples of the Near East, when their states were destroyed by the might of Assyria and Babylonia. And when those great empires fell, their religions collapsed as well. This did not occur in Israel due in great measure to men such as Jeremiah, Ezekiel, and the anonymous biblical historiographers who explained the tragedy in terms of Israel's faith. The prophetic oracles enabled the people to survive the

Stone balustrade from Jehoiakim's palace, Ramat Rahel

dark days facing them, and to put their hopes in a brighter if more distant future.

The characterization of Jeremiah as the weeping prophet is little better than a caricature. He was a failure as the world might judge such matters. His words could not deter the people from the suicidal course that they followed, yet after his death his prophecies served as guarantee and promise of God's eternal faithfulness to even an undeserving people. All that was needed was a genuine change of heart and mind, a renewal of faith, commitment, and a future greater and more marvelous than any past would be their lot. Jeremiah's ultimate and continuing influence can hardly be exaggerated.

6. THE ARCHAEOLOGICAL EVIDENCE OF THE BABYLONIAN VICTORY

The fifth paragraph of the Babylonian Chronicle for 605–594 B.C. relates the first capture of Jerusalem in 597, the exile of Jehoiachin and appointment of Zedekiah as king

The publication in 1936 by D. J. Wiseman of additional tablets of the roughly contemporary "Chronicles of Chaldean Kings" provided a much fuller picture of the course of events in the Near East in the period preceding the destruction of Jerusalem than had previously been available. These clay tablets, inscribed in Babylonian cuneiform, describe the political and military developments in the years 616–595 B.C. They tell of the fall of Nineveh, the Assyrian capital, to the Babylonians and Medes in 612 B.C. and document Babylonian relations with Necho of Egypt. They continue with Nebuchadnezzar's conquest of Syro-Palestine as implied in 2 Kings 24 and list the tribute received from the kings of these lands. Among those giving tribute is Jehoiakim, who remained loyal until the Babylonians were defeated by the Egyptians in 601 B.C. Spurred on by the pro-Egyptian false prophets who saw in this Babylonian setback confirmation of their predictions of well-being, the king of Judah rebelled openly against Babylon. The inevitable response came as soon as the Babylonians were able to settle problems elsewhere in the empire. The fifth paragraph of the chronicle relates the capture of Jerusalem in 597, the deportation of Jehoiachin (the young son and successor of Jehoiakim who was killed during

Trephinated skull found among the remains of Lachish

the siege). His uncle, Zedekiah, another son of the great Josiah, served as the last reigning king of the house of David.

a. *The Evidence from Lachish*

The archaeological finds at Lachish (Tell ed-Duweir) vividly confirm the upheavals and crises that lay behind Jeremiah's writings. These finds fully support the biblical evidence of the Assyrian campaign of Sennacherib (ca. 701 B.C.) and the Babylonian campaigns of 598 and 587 B.C. As a result of the Assyrian campaign the town of Level III at Lachish was utterly destroyed. In a last effort to prepare the town to withstand the coming assault, the defenders attempted to ensure the water supply by excavating an enormous rock-cut shaft connected to a spring or reservoir. Unfortunately it was not completed at the time the city fell.

The debris which covers Level III shows evidence of appalling destruction. In the gateway, eight feet of burnt debris separated the floor of Level III from that of Level II. The citadel was ruined completely as is shown by heaps of calcined bricks over its stone foundations. The rooms of nearby shops were filled with objects of daily use, storage jars for corn, and the remains of a weaving establishment. Two thousand skeletons with some of the bones calcined were found in a tomb outside the city. Among the skeletons were three skulls from which a square of bone had been removed by a saw to reduce pressure in the head. This rather crude surgical procedure is known as trephination and apparently was a part of recognized medical practice in Judah.

After Sennacherib's withdrawal, the town was rebuilt in the seventh century. Its defenses were reconstructed and the gates were placed so that any intruder would have to pass through an outer gate on the west side of the city and then through an inner gate beyond the outer bastion. In the final Babylonian assault against Judah, Lachish is listed by Jeremiah (34:7) together with Jerusalem and Azekah, "for these were the only fortified cities of Judah that remained."

Lachish Letter IV of the days of the Judean Monarchy (586 B.C.)

b. *Tale of the Lachish Letters*

In a guardhouse between the outer and inner gates of the city, in a layer of ashes, a collection of 18 ostraca was found, of which eight are sufficiently legible to make connected sense. These letters are probably all from Hoshaiah who was in command of a garrison stationed outside of Lachish, to his superior Ya'osh in the city itself. Letter 4 is particularly interesting in the light of Jer 34:7 cited above. Hoshaiah informs Ya'osh that he has carried out his orders and ends: "We are watching for the fire signals from Lachish, according to all the indications my Lord had given, because we do not see (the signals of) Azekah." This line suggests impending tragedy: Azekah may already have fallen, and as we know, Jerusalem and Lachish would soon follow.

The military correspondence found at Lachish seems to have covered an appreciable period of time. Throughout the letters Hoshaiah insists that he has been carrying out Ya'osh's orders in full. In Letter 3 he tries to justify or excuse himself in the face of insinuations or accusations that he had read some secret documents, sent from Jerusalem to the commander at Lachish, and revealed their contents to others. The letter then tells of a warning brought by an unnamed prophet from Tobiah, a royal official. Perhaps in relation to this prophet, the ostracon reads "The army commander Koniah, the son of Elnathan, has gone down to Egypt..." This in turn may be related to Jer 26:20–24 where Jehoiakim sent certain men, including Elnathan, to Egypt to bring the prophet Uriah back to Jerusalem.

c. *Letter 6 and Jeremiah*

The best course to avert total disaster, Jeremiah said, was to compromise with Babylon and bow to its yoke, awaiting a brighter day (Jeremiah 27). This was the voice of moderation — the will of God, but the priests and other prophets opposed him and treated him as a coward (Jer 27:9–22). The royal officials, *sarîm*, denounced him to Zedekiah "for he is weakening the hands of the soldiers" (38:4), and demanded his execution. In Letter 6, however, there is a complaint about the messages circulated by the *sarîm* because "they weaken the hands of the people." The same expression is used here as in the biblical text, although it is the officials, not Jeremiah, who are accused of sedition.

Excavations at various Judean sites prove that they all suffered total destruction at this time. This is the case at Lachish, Eglon, Beth-shemesh, Gibeah, Ramat Rahel, Beth-zur, En-gedi, and Arad.

7. THE AFTERMATH

After the destruction of Jerusalem in 587/6 B.C., the leading figures of the community had either been carried off in exile in the two major deportations to Babylon, or had fled to Transjordan or Egypt. The land was in shambles and its economy wrecked.

Gedaliah ben Ahikam was appointed governor. He belonged to a very

Defenders of Lachish fight from a tower as women remove their belongings from the town. From the vast bas-reliefs found in Sennacherib's palace at Nineveh

The two upstanding pillars
must have supported the roof
of an Israelite house of ca.
800, judging by the pottery
found there

Remains of Israelite houses
demolished during the siege
of 586 B.C.

prominent family in Jerusalem, which had been closely associated with the reform movement in the time of Josiah. Gedaliah's grandfather, Shaphan, was a principal scribe, according to M. Weidenfeld, who played an important role in the discovery of the Book of the Law in 622 (see II Kings). The family was friendly to Jeremiah and protected him at critical points in his career. It may also have had a hand in the preservation and compilation of some of the prophetic literature, including an edition of Jeremiah's oracles. It has also been suggested that the scribes from this family residing at Mizpah were responsible for the final edition of Deuteronomy. Gedaliah was murdered at Mizpah by a survivor of the royal house, with obvious intentions to restore the monarchy. Despite Jeremiah's urging to remain in Judah, a group took him forcibly with them to Egypt (Jeremiah 41–43). Among the numerous seal impressions found at Mizpah, one bore the inscription "Jaazaniah, servant of the king." This is probably the Jezaniah who met with Gedaliah at Mizpah according to Jer 40:8 (see Part IV, 8).

Tablets found in Babylon, dated 595 and 570 B.C. list rations of oil and barley delivered by the royal storehouses to the deposed Jehoiachin and his entourage, held as prisoners

8. JEHOIACHIN IN BABYLON

When Nebuchadnezzar laid siege to Jerusalem for the first time (598 B.C.), Jehoiakim was assassinated and replaced by his son Jehoiachin. Almost immediately he surrendered the city, possibly to appease the pro-Babylonian faction that had killed his father. The Babylonian Chronicle records the capture of Jerusalem and then describes Nebuchadnezzar's deportation of Jehoiachin and his retinue: "The king of Akkad (= Babylon) ...laid siege to the city of Judah (*iahudu*) and the king took the city on the second day of the month of Addaru. He appointed in it a new king of his liking, took heavy booty from it, and brought it to Babylon." The new king was Zedekiah. The deposed king, Jehoiachin, was well treated; a list of foodstuffs found in a storehouse near the Ishtar gate in Babylon details the rations issued to his household and refers to him as "Yaukîn, king of Judah." This agrees with the biblical account of his treatment in 2 Kgs 25:27. Jehoiachim was released by Evil-merodach, Nebuchadnezzar's successor, in the 37th year of his captivity (561 B.C.)

The search for traces of the destruction of Jerusalem in 586 B.C. has produced scant evidence. One explanation for this is that the same area was thoroughly destroyed by the Romans in A.D. 70. But the remains of homes destroyed by fire have been found on the eastern slopes of the Ophel. Among these was a structure with three halls, divided by partitions made of monolithic pillars resting on their sockets. There is an abundance of sherds and other artifacts discovered on that hill and around the Temple area which date to the last years of the Judean monarchy (see page 176).

LAMENTATIONS

The small book of Lamentations follows directly after the book of Jeremiah in the standard Bibles, because traditionally it was thought to have been composed by him. Actually, it is of anonymous authorship and dates from exilic times. Five successive dirges relate and bemoan the disasters that befell the country at the hands of the Babylonians in the sixth century B.C., including the destruction of the Holy City, the captivity of the people of the land, and the subsequent invasion of the country by its southern neighbors, the Idumaeans. In this last respect, it is reminiscent of Obadiah 1:10–14 (see Part XI). The book is read to this day in the synagogues on the eve of the date when both the First and Second Temples were destroyed. Much of its interest lies in the vivid picture the book provides not only of the devastation wrought in the city, but of the soul-searching and agonized questions which the fall of Jerusalem provoked in the minds of the survivors. It seems to have been composed, and certainly was used, in the liturgy for the days of fasting and lamenting. Formally, the poems in chapters 1–4 are composed in an acrostic pattern in which the first verse begins with the first letter of the alphabet, the next verse begins with the second letter, the third with the third letter, and so on through the rest of the alphabet. The poems do not give a connected story of the last days of Judah and Jerusalem, but rather evoke the terrible experience, and reflect the agonized thinking of those who were left. The poetic style and acrostic arrangement of the lamentations, all of which contribute to fixing the text of the poem, thereby ensures effective memorization of the composition. It seems clear that from the beginning the poems were intended for use in public mourning observances.

The literary type represented by Lamentations is one of the oldest in the repertoire; an excellent example is provided by N. Kramer in his publication of the Sumerian Lamentation Tablets over the Destruction of Ur. They were found in the excavations of Nippur in Mesopotamia. This form of ancient lamentation has been preserved for millennia in Babylonia right down to the fourth-third centuries B.C. There is little doubt that the biblical book of Lamentations owes much in this way of form and content to its Mesopotamian forerunners. Thus the expression, "He has made my flesh and my skin waste away, and broken my bones" (Lam 3:4) is typical of the physical sufferings endured by the conquered people at the hands of the Babylonians who followed the same general policy of the Assyrians. Their atrocities were a byword in antiquity. Their artists proudly commemorated them in stone as shown in the reliefs in the palace of Ashurbanipal at Nineveh.

In conclusion, Lam 5:13 draws attention to the fate of young men drawn into forced labor, carrying beams and gravel.

Hanging above the Assyrian siege-engine are nude figures impaled on poles

PART X

EZEKIEL

Ezekiel ben Buzi, of the priestly family of the Zadokite line, was exiled to Babylon, probably as early as 597 B.C. shortly after the deportation of Jehoiachin. The Judean exiles were not dispersed throughout the Babylonian empire, but settled in towns like Tell-abib on the river Chebar near the holy and prestigious city of Nippur (Ezek 3:15), as well as Tell Melah, Tell Tarsha, Kerub, Adan, Immer, and Casfiah. They were able to assemble and to continue a communal life (8:1; 14:1; 33:30–33). They observed their religion in the first synagogues, and such communal centers helped them maintain their identity. In the course of time, many Jews entered trade and some grew rich.

1. LIFE IN NIPPUR AND TEL-ABIB

Apart from a fragmentary cuneiform record listing rations provided to the exiled Jehoiachin in Babylon (see A, 8 in the previous chapter) and Jeremiah's injunctions to the exiles to establish a normal community in exile (e.g. 29:4–7), little is known of the Jewish diaspora there. In the course

The ziggurat, or sacred temple-tower of Nippur (see Tower of Babel in Genesis)

One of the Murashu documents mention two witnesses to an agreement over the cultivation of leased land

of two generations, some Jews specialized in banking in the rich city of Nippur and are known to have amassed great wealth, laying the foundation for the long-lived and well-educated Jewish community located there in the following centuries (see Esther). An archive containing over 700 tablets, known as the Murashu documents, provides a significant glimpse into the social and commercial activities of a Jewish business family in Nippur in the fifth century B.C. The tablets record varied commercial and real estate deals, including business contracts, land leases, and loans and payments. Judging from the non-Hebrew names in this corporation, the Murashu family had adapted itself effectively to the local community, thus fulfilling the commands of Jeremiah, perhaps more thoroughly than he would have wished, since partial assimilation may also have taken place.

2. CONTENTS

The book falls into three major parts which roughly reflect distinct phases of the prophet's varied activity:

Chapters 1–24 are oracles of doom, pronounced between 593 and 586 B.C.

Chapters 25–32 are oracles of doom awaiting the nations which had contributed to Israel's fall: Ammon, Moab, Edom, the Philistines, Tyre, Sidon, and Egypt.

Chapters 33–48 are discourses of promise and consolation. Ezekiel's concern is with the revival of the nation through collective action, both in exile and in the land of Israel. Chapter 37 contains the vision of the valley of dry bones, an allegory of the people's resurrection after the exile.

Chapters 38–39 describe the apocalyptic wars of Gog of Magog.

Chapters 40–48 present an elaborate description of the restored nation, including the future organization of the cult, and the plan of the ideal Temple (see below). The basis for this vision of the future was Ezekiel's first-hand knowledge of Jerusalem before the exile.

a. *The Trauma of the Exile; A Coherent Explanation of the Tragedy*

The events of Judah's last years sent shock waves through Israelite society. The popular belief that Yahweh would not let Jerusalem fall on any condition had to be abandoned. The reliability of God's ancient promises was put in question. The despair that spread through the people is reflected in Jer 18:25: "Yet to say, "The way of the Lord is not just.'" The leaders had to supply a theological explanation of the national disaster in terms understandable and acceptable to the exiles! They had to resolve this problem or the community would disintegrate from despair. By incessantly announcing the righteousness of Yahweh's judgment against the nation, Jeremiah and Ezekiel gave the tragedy coherent explanation. They viewed it as the vindication of Israel's historic faith, not as a contradiction. The exile was a merited punishment, but also a purge preparing Israel for a new future. While they demolished cheap or false hopes, they affirmed the ultimate triumph of Yahweh's redemption and provided the people with a hope they could cling to while the future remained obscure.

Ezekiel stood like a watchman over his people (3:17–21), announcing Yahweh's righteous decision with the authority of ancient tradition. Judah and Jerusalem had fallen because the people had trusted in false doctrines and false prophets, thus failing their obligation to God, to obey his commands and to listen to the words of his true servants. Knowing that Yahweh's decree of destruction against the city was fixed (Ezekiel 9–11), he likened the prophets who gave hopeful oracles to fools who try to save an old, bulging wall by daubing it with whitewash (13:1–16). Judah had brought disaster upon itself by its political machinations. Henceforth he advised the exiles to submit to the Babylonians and bide their time. God's indefeasible righteousness would bring deliverance to the faithful and observant members of the community.

There is no inconsistency between Ezekiel's harsh announcements of doom before the destruction of Jerusalem (Ezek 1–24) on the one hand, and his subsequent visions and messages of consolation and eventual restoration (33–48) on the other. Once the great tragedy had occurred, he naturally turned his thoughts to salvage and salvation. Now hope was the order of the day, and steadfast reliance on the divine promise.

The Mesopotamian winged sphinx evokes Ezekiel's symbolism of 28:14

b. The Cherubim

In Ezekiel's inaugural vision of the throne/chariot (Ezek 1:4–2:8) there is a detailed description of the "four living creatures." They are cherubim, guardians of God's throne, symbolizing mobility, intelligence, and strength. The image may go back to the winged deity, called *karibu*, "intercessor," in Mesopotamian texts and represented in art by a sphinx, griffin, or a human figure. Winged sphinxes and griffins are found in the iconography of the Samarian ivories, as well as at Carchemish, Nimrud, and Aleppo. In Ezekiel's vision, the traditional image of the cherubim is combined with several other concepts, including the wheels symbolizing God's mobility, the all-seeing eyes, and the four faces reflecting God's dominion over the animal, as well as the human world.

c. Mimetic Symbols

During the initial phase of his prophecy in Babylonia, which lasted for about two decades, Ezekiel resorted much more than his predecessors to symbolic imagery and mimetic acts. Whether driven to it by inner or outer compulsions, these strange demonstrations underscore the prevailing setting-in-life confronting his audience.

Drawing a diagram of Jerusalem on a clay brick, Ezekiel laid mock siege against it (Ezek 4:1–11). Drawing city maps on clay bricks is a Mesopotamian practice, as is demonstrated by a number of such maps discovered at Mesopotamian sites. In one of his more histrionic actions, he swallowed a scroll on which God's word for his people was written on both sides (2:8–33). This would not be a piece of parchment, made of animal skin, as it could only be penned on the side where the hair was shaved. It was probably common papyrus which could be inked on both sides.

Shaving his head and beard, Ezekiel burned some of the hair in the

181

Ezekiel's mockery of the king of Tyre who identified himself with the god Melkart (Ezek 28) finds an apt parallel on an incised stone bowl from Sidon depicting the ritual burning of a god. The rite, apparently connected with the Melkart cult, depicts (in scenes 1–4) the "awakening" of Melkart as a solar deity and his resurrection celebrated by burning him in effigy on a pyre

fire, hacked at some with a sword, scattered some to the winds, and tied only a few wisps to the bottom of his robe, symbolizing a similar fate for his people (5:1–4). He once made a hole in the brick wall of his house, passed through it at night, carrying his pack on his back, and thus enacted the role of the wandering exile. This scene also has a Babylonian background as houses there were built of brick, while Israel houses were built of stone.

3. EZEKIEL'S IMPACT ON FUTURE JEWISH THOUGHT

Ezekiel has frequently been misunderstood as a strange figure of fantasy, a visionary priest remote from reality, and regarded as a psychologically abnormal person. His prophecy stands at the dividing line between the pre-exilic covenant community of the land and the post-exilic legal community without the land. This emerges in chapters 33–48 where he begins laying blue-prints of a restored cult, government, and Temple. The life of the new community was shaped by Ezekiel's representation of the ancient faith.

One of Ezekiel's most interesting discourses, which can be illuminated by archaeology, is against Tyre (28:1–20), still the queen of the seas in the sixth century B.C. The prophet mocks and denounces the king of Tyre because he identified himself with the god of the city, Melkart, either directly or symbolically. The bejewelled sphinx is the emblem of Melkart in Phoenician art. Perhaps the association between the sphinx and the god explains the reference in v 14: "With an anointed guardian cherub I placed you..."

Tyre, shown as a fortified island surrounded by water, ferries tribute to Shalmanser III on the mainland (From the Assyrian Tell Balawat bronze bands, 9th c. B.C.)

Tyre was first built on a narrow coastal strip and subsequently expanded to include an island separated from the mainland by a strait half a mile wide. It reached its zenith in the ninth century B.C. when Carthage was founded as a daughter city. After that period, the Assyrians extended their sway to the Mediterranean coast, and Tyre had to pay tribute to them. Later Nebuchadnezzar besieged Tyre for 13 years (585–573). While he was not able to conquer it, he wrecked its commerce, cutting off its sources of trade and wealth. It never truly recovered and ultimately was captured by Alexander the Great.

In the description of proud Tyre riding in the harbor like a great galleon soon to be shipwrecked in the political storm (27:32), Ezekiel draws upon knowledge of the city, its trade, and its monuments. Tyre is portrayed in an Assyrian maritime scene, with Phoenician vessels drawing logs from Tyre and Sidon to Khorsabad. There is another Assyrian relief which depicts the escape of Luli, king of Sidon, from the city of Tyre, an event mentioned in Sennacherib's annals.

Ezekiel was well aware of the great wealth and power of the merchant city and the wide range of its commerce (27:27). In the same passage he refers to the sources of ivory tusks and ebony: "The men of Rhodes traded with you; many coastlands were your own special markets, they brought you in payment ivory and ebony" (27:15). There were two main sources of supply of elephant tusks: one was Africa; the other was from northern Syria and Mesopotamia where a kind of pigmy elephant survived until the eighth century B.C. The latter was apparently the more common source of the small carvings and inlays found in rich homes of Syria, Mesopotamia, Samaria, and Judah.

Finally there is the reference in 28:3 to the claim by the Tyrian king that he was "indeed wiser than Daniel..." We now know that Danael was a legendary king and that his wisdom was proverbial. In the Ugaritic texts, *Dn'l* (= Danael) is the hero of an epic cycle in which the central theme is the king's quest for an heir, realized in the birth of Aqhat. There is no apparent connection between this ancient king and the biblical Daniel, reputedly a contemporary of Ezekiel. On the contrary, Ezekiel refers to the ancient Danael as a contemporary of figures like Noah and Job (chapter 14).

a. The Ideal Temple

Ezekiel stressed the role of the destroyed Temple in the worship of Yahweh. In his picture of the future, the restoration of the people to their land and the renewal of life there were principal features. But at the center was the new Temple, the ultimate symbol and guarantee of God's eternal presence with his people.

An Assyrian scene depicting the escape of king Luli from Tyre (Ezek 27:32)

Comparison of the extended descriptions of the Temple in 1 Kings 6–8 and 2 Chronicles 2–4 with Ezekiel's vision of the future Temple (40–48) reveals so many discrepancies and differences that scholars have been hard put to explain the variations. As a young priest in Jerusalem, Ezekiel obviously was familiar with the first Temple, before its destruction. There is a general resemblance between it and his vision of the restored Temple, and while many details of the latter are imaginary, some correspond to the reality of Ezekiel's earlier experience.

b. *Ezekiel's Altar*

In his description of the great altar in 43:13–17, Ezekiel relies on his remembrance of the altar at which he served in his youth. This may well have been the one which Ahaz had copied from a model in Damascus (2 Kgs 16:10–16). The impression is supported by the Syro-Mesopotamian influence evident in some of its features, especially the storied structure resembling the Babylonian temple tower. The uppermost tier of Ezekiel's altar was called *har'el* or *'ariel*. The fact that it was to be made of wood suggests that Ezekiel is describing the altar after it had been stripped of its gold by Nebuchadnezzar in 597 B.C. (2 Kgs 34:13).

c. *How Did the Priests Dress?*

Phoenician carvings and statuary provide significant clues to the appearance of the garments mentioned in Ezek 44:17 and 42:14 as the vestments of the high priest: the breeches, robe, waistband, coat, girdle, and headdress. There were four outer priestly garments: the robe of the breastplate, the breastplate itself, the ephod, and the embroidered sleeveless garment falling from the shoulders to the heels. The head of the high priest was covered wth a miter decorated by a blue band, while the priests wore a "decorated turban" (24:17).

Reconstruction model of the storied altar of sacrifices envisioned by Ezekiel

PART XI
MINOR PROPHETS

A. MICAH

Micah, as a product of rural Judah, was particularly critical of the urban society that arose in Jerusalem: "What is the sin of the house of Judah?" (1:5). He goes on to place the blame on the leaders of the people, the "rulers of the house of Israel," the priests, judges, and prophets. A century after Micah died, Jeremiah (26:18–19) recalled that the earlier prophet had forecast the destrucion of Jerusalem, but instead of provoking angry retaliation by the king, his words inspired a popular repentance led by the king, and resulted in a general reformation.

The book has been arranged into four sections which alternate between doom and promise. Chapters 1–3 contain prophecies of judgment and punishment over Samaria, Judah, and Jerusalem. The opening chapter may reflect the prophet's lament over the destruction of the cities of western Judah in the days of Sennacherib's campaign against Hezekiah (701 B.C.), including the siege of Lachish (v 13), near the prophet's home of Moresheth. Chapters 4–5 consist of promises for the future when "the remnant of Jacob" shall flourish among the nations. Micah 6:1–7:6 is an indictment against the people for not responding properly to God's gracious acts on their behalf. The final poem in Mic 7:7–20 returns to the theme of hope and has affinities with exilic poetry such as Second Isaiah.

THE DOMESTIC CULTS

Micah foresaw Yahweh's violent eradication of idol worship with the accompanying sorcery, images, and pillars (*massebôt*). He was referring in part to the domestic cult performed at home with small images of the goddess of fertility, which were also used as talismans against barrenness. These Canaanite practices were widespread as is demonstrated by the presence of representations of nude goddesses with elaboraely dressed hair in excavations of Palestinian sites dating from the end of the second millennium to the eigthth century B.C.

Micah was able to define the essence of biblical religion in a classic question. He asks: "What does the Lord require of you but to do justice, and to love kindness, and to walk humbly with your God" (6:6–8). He echoes the injunction in Deut 16:20: "Justice, and only justice, you shall follow..."

Like the other great prophets, he condemned those seers who had become mere professionals and hangers-on at the local shrines. Many of them were interested chiefly in their fee (3:11) and did not feel impelled to criticize the king and society which were bound by the ancient covenant.

Sorcery and the 'science' of divination, through the inspection of livers, required the use of clay models to guide the adepts (From Mari, Mesopotamia, early 2nd millennium)

The books of the Minor Prophets are presented in what has been determined to be their chronological order, and not according to the traditional arrangement in Jewish and Christian Bibles.

B. NAHUM

NAHUM ON THE ASSYRIANS

Nahum of Elkosh prophesied in Judah probably after the middle of the seventh century B.C. about the impending fall of Nineveh, the Assyrian capital (which occurred in 612 B.C.), an event that shook the ancient world. Nahum adopted it as his leading theme to demonstrate the justice of Yahweh (1:2–3), ending his oracle on a somber, almost elegiac note (3:14–19). The body of the poem is a triumphal ode, which recalls Isaiah's mockery of Sennacherib when he failed to capture Jerusalem almost a century earlier.

The prophet paints a vivid picture of the destruction of Nineveh as an act of vengeance by Yahweh with a few powerful strokes (3:2 ff.). The description of the opposing armies and their equipment reflects the Assyrian annals in which battle and conquest were constant features. The bronze gates of Balawat (ninth centurp B.C.) show the Assyrian chariot force in action as it destroyed the fleeing forces. Only this time it was Nineveh which suffered the fate of all its own victims.

Additional light has been thrown on the oracles of Nahum by a Babylonian record known as the Gadd Chronicles, which recounts the victories of Nabopolassar, founder of the neo-Babylonian empire. It asserts that a decisive part of the overthrow of Nineveh was played by his allies, the Medes who "made a great slaughter of the princes... They took a heavy weight of booty from the city and the temple (and turned) the city into a mound and a ruin..."

The Gadd Chronicles relate how the Median allies of Babylon defeated Assyria

C. ZEPHANIAH

King Manasseh had gone overboard in complying with Assyrian orders to recognize Assyrian deities. Local shrines flourished where pagan practices were given free rein. Even within Jerusalem followers of Ba'al were prominent (1:4). In addition, there was a general aping of foreign fashions and ways (1:8) and enormous interest in the occult arts. The inevitable result of this widespread disregard of covenant law was social injustice and violence (1:9; 3:1–7).

Zephaniah's pronouncement of the coming destruction of the Philistine cities, Gaza, Ashdod, and Ekron, reflects the ancient enmity between them and Israel, once more fanned by the attempts of the Philistines to encroach upon Judah in the eighth and seventh centuries B.C. The capture of Ekron by the Assyrians is depicted in a relief from the palace of Sargon II, identifying the name of the city. *Amqaruna*, in cuneiform characters. Zephaniah continues with a curse on the seagoing "nation of the Cherethites" (2:5–7), a synonym for the Philistines derived from an old tradition which attributed their origin to the island of Crete (cf. Ezek 25:16). There is another archaic allusion in this passage that is misinterpreted easily. In speaking of "Canaan, land of the Philistines," Zephaniah is referring to the merchants (= Canaanites) among the Philistines, a synonym for teeming Ashkelon, the leading emporium.

There is a sharp contrast between the dire predictions of the first two and a half chapters and the concluding eschatological vision of the third chapter. In this section (3:8–20) Zephaniah looks forward to a time when the guilt of the nation is removed and Yahweh shall rule as the King of Israel.

Oil press built in a 7th c. B.C. Israelite habitation of the Mishneh, the Upper City of Jerusalem

THE MISHNEH AND THE MAKHTESH

There is an interesting reference in the prophet's predictions of doom to the sections of Jerusalem which have been excavated recently: "On that day... a cry will be heard from the Fish Gate, a wail from the *Mišneh* (Second Quarter), a loud crash from the hills. Wail, O inhabitants of the *Makteš* (the Mortar or Vale...; 1:10–11).

Several sections of the Mishneh have been uncovered by N. Avigad's excavations of the Western hill or Upper City, which overlooks the Temple Mount area. It was populated by the upper class people and lay close to the city's main commercial center, as shown by the finds illustraed here. The Makhtesh is probably the lower area later known as the Tyropean Vale which separated the Upper City from the Temple Mount.

D. HABAKKUK

The short book contains no information about the prophet's life. It consists of three chapters, the first two containing a dialogue between the prophet and God about the rule of iniquity in the world. The second chapter also contains a series of five woes against the wicked nation. The third chapter is a prayer in the form of a liturgical psalm. It is quite different from the preceding material, evoking the imagery and style of some of the most ancient Israelite poems.

1. ORACLE

Habakkuk lived during the time when the Babylonian empire was at the height of its power, in the sixth century. In his oracle he expresses amazement at the doom in store for the suffering and defeated people. There is an interesting pictorial representation in Mesopotamian art of the theme of the net mentioned in Hab 1:15. Pictures of the victor carrying away captives, shown wriggling in a fish-net, are found in murals from the 24th century B.C.

While Habakkuk's prophecy concerned the Chaldeans (or *kasdîm*), it was later adapted to apply to other hated enemies. Thus in the commentary on Habakkuk found at Qumran (from the first century B.C.), the term *kasdîm* was interpreted as Kittim, that is, the people of Kition (Cyprus) but really

The king of Lagash holds a mace and smites the nude figures contained in a net (Mesopotamia, mid-third millennium B.C.)

applied to the oppressive Romans, who had moved into the area in force, replacing the equally hated, if somewhat less powerful, Greeks.

2. ARCHAIC SYMBOLS

The psalm of Habakkuk (chapter 3) contains archaic material reminiscent of the old poetry in the Primary History. For example, the land of Cushan mentioned in 3:7 is probably the ancient name of Gilead in the Late Bronze Age when the Cushites were in possession of southern Transjordan and possibly the Negeb. The Ishmaelites traded and transported goods there in the Late Bronze Age and the Iron Age. The "sons of Sheth" appear in poetic parallelism with Moab in Num 24:17 (the Oracles of Balaam) and in like manner Cushan is parallel to Midian in Hab 3:7. Evidently, these passages preserve the ancient names of nomadic peoples in these regions (see Part II: Numbers — The Land of Shutu and Archaeology).

Habakkuk 3:10 preserves the memory of the ancient Semitic creation stories in which the world was created out of the body of the conquered god, either from "Tehom" (the primeval Flood) in Babylonian epics or from "Yam" (Sea) in the Ugaritic texts. Here this pagan motif is used as a metaphor of Yahweh's historical victories over the enemies of Israel.

In Hab 3:5 the prophet alludes to the calamities and plagues to befall Yahweh's enemies. The image still contains overtones of the Canaanite use of the word rešep, "pestilence", which was the name of the god of war as he defeats his rivals. This god was also worshiped in Egypt, as is illustrated by a relief from the second half of the second millennium B.C. The symbols help to convey the prophet's message.

Stele of Resheph, god of war and pestilence. From an Egyptian engraving

E. OBADIAH

Containing only 21 verses, Obadiah is the shortest book in the Old Testament. His vision expresses the age-old hostility of Judah toward Edom, its southern neighbor. This feeling was heightened dramatically when Edom took advantage of the Babylonian capture of Jerusalem in 597 to exploit Judah, rejoiced in its plight, and occupied the Negeb (Obad 10–14; Ezek 35:10). Edom's territory was particularly attractive to Israel and Judah because the lucrative trade from the exploitation of ore in the Arabah valley passed through Edom. In the final section (19–21) Obadiah promises the return of the scattered Israelite exiles and the restoration of Israel to its former glory, including dominion over Edom. The Judean exiles, who will join the ingathering, will come from as far as Sepharad, most probably the city district of Sardis (Persian *Sapparda*) in western Asia Minor, famous for its great wealth.

F. JONAH

The book relates an episode of Jonah's life, including the well known incident of Jonah and the great fish, but unlike the minor prophets, it does not contain prophetic oracles. Rather it is a narrative with a message, like the book of Ruth and some of the stories in the historical books of the Bible. It is a parable which illustrates the power of repentance and divine mercy for all living creatures. Here there is emphasis on God's concern for all men, not for Jews alone, the universalism so important to Second Isaiah.

1. THE PURPOSE OF THE BOOK

It is important to dissociate the popular concept of Jonah and the fish from the modern historic view underlying our understanding of the book.

There is no need to discuss the physical possibility of the fish swallowing Jonah. The miracle in the parable of Jonah is on the same order as those of the prophets Elijah and Elisha. Few would argue that the book was written before Nineveh's destruction (612 B.C.) or that it is the record of a personal experience of a prophet by this name mentioned in 2 Kgs 14:25. It is difficult to date, but there is nothing in its contents or style to suggest a date later than the sixth or fifth century B.C., namely within the range of the Minor Prophets. The author may have chosen the eighth century prophet because he lived when Nineveh was still standing and anti-Assyrian feelings were strong in Israel.

The places which are mentioned in the story have symbolic importance: Nineveh typifies all the great ancient cities filled with iniquity; Tarshish is a remote harbor beyond the seas. Therefore we do not need to try to associate the allegorical material with any particular archaeological background but to place the work in its proper setting.

2. CONTENTS

The narrative consists of three sections. In chapters 1–2 Jonah is commissioned by Yahweh to go to Nineveh and proclaim its destruction. He refuses to commit himself to a prophecy which he does not believe Yahweh will fulfill so he flees in the opposite direction by taking a ship from Jaffa to Tarshish. As a result of the storm, the sailors throw him into the sea where he is swallowed by a fish. At this point a hymn of praise is inserted (2:1–9) which was originally unrelated to the narrative. At the end of chapter 2 the fish vomits Jonah on an unspecified shore and Jonah proceeds to Nineveh. There he proclaims the city's imminent destruction but God relents when the people repent. In chapter 4, the prophet argues with God, sulks in a booth, and finally learns the meaning of pity. The metaphor at the end of the book expresses its central theme: God's compassion for all his creatures. Nineveh was not destroyed because its people repented, showing that it is never too late to repent.

3. THE PARABLE

Although the anonymous author drew on myth and folklore, essentially the story is a moral tale. It says nothing of the fate of Nineveh after it was saved or of Jonah's future career. The book ends with God's question to Jonah and the audience is left to find the answer for itself. More specifically, this is a parable of two conflicting attitudes, one seeking the punishment of the pagans: people like Jonah would be outraged if they were not destroyed for their sins. The other view is that of the author himself, who contrasts Jonah unfavorably to his gentile shipmates and has the concept of a compassionate God who is willing to forgive even the hated inhabitants of Nineveh if they repent. The author rests his case on the ancient formula, attributed to Moses in Exod 34:6–7, and cited in Jon 4:2: "I know that you were a compassionate God, slow to anger..." A further indication of the broad-mindedness of the book is that it makes no mention of "gentiles" or "the people of the land," terms denoting a sharp distinction between Jew and non-Jew. The New Testament makes further reference to Jonah when Jesus guarantees the truth of the story concerning him (Mat 12:40).

The first narrative section describes two natural disasters, a plague of locusts and a drought, and then there is a call for repentance (1:13–2:17). It closes with a promise of God's blessing (2:18–27).

Joel then proceeds to describe the coming of the Day of Yahweh. The imagery shifts from the natural as in the first section to the supernatural events of the apocalypse. On the Day of the Lord there shall be an outpouring of charismatic gifts together with fearful portents (2:28–32). Chapter 3 is full of military motifs in the description of the eschatological conflict between Yahweh and his enemies. God intervenes with terrifying disasters, defeating the foe with great slaughter and establishing his people forever in peace.

As with many of the Minor Prophets, the composition and date of Joel are unresolved problems. Some authorities believe that the material in Joel 2:28–3:21 comes from a later period than the rest of the book although most are satisfied with the essential unity of the book. The question of date has occasioned much speculation by biblical scholars with opinions ranging from the ninth to the second century B.C. Most indications point to the early post-exilic period when the Temple had been rebuilt. The reference to the Greek in 3:6 clearly points to a time prior to the conquests of Alexander the Great. Thus a date in the late sixth century or around 500 B.C., corresponding to other Minor Prophets like Haggai and Zechariah, is enirely reasonable.

H. HAGGAI

1. DEVELOPMENTS IN JUDAH

We know little of the conditions of the land during the latter part of the sixth century B.C., when Sheshbazzar, the first Jewish ruler of the Persian province of Judah, returned to Jerusalem to rebuild the Temple (see part XIV: Ezra) and Haggai and Zechariah appeared to exhort the people. The land was in no condition to support a significant restoration. Among those who had never left the land, few evinced great enthusiasm for a return to a way of life since abandoned.

Haggai's prophecies may be dated to the early years of Darius' reign, or some 18 to 20 years after the edict of Cyrus allowed the return of Jews from Babylonia. Shortly after 522, the Persian empire faltered and some subject provinces revolted. Believing that there was a chance to restore Judah's independence, the Jews named Zerubbabel, a descendant of the royal line, God's chosen one (Hag 2:20–23). But Darius crushed the rebellion in the empire, and Zerubbabel was not heard of any more. The glory of Darius' reign is memorialized in huge reliefs and inscriptions at Behistun (Iran), where he is portrayed sitting in judgment over those who had rebelled. The inscription corroborates the date of the restoration of peace cited in Zechariah (1:7).

It was during the time when Judean hopes were running high, stimulated by a change of Persian kings, that Haggai urged the Jews to begin work on the Temple. In his four prophecies, dated to 520 B.C., he accuses the people of being too concerned for their own welfare to help with the Temple. He claims that once the work started, their prosperity would return.

CONTENTS

The message of the book is contained in four oracles: The first, following the introductory verses, describes lamentable conditions in Judah and tries to arouse the people from their passive attitudes (1:3–11). The second oracle (2:1–9) speaks positively of the rebellion in progress and the hopes of a new Jewish commonwealth. The third (2:10–19) argues that sacrifices without a central sanctuary would be valueless and that the people would remain ritually impure. The fourth oracle proclaims the overthrow of the nations and declares that Zerubbabel is to be the messianic hero.

Darius' reliefs and inscriptions
at Behistun as he is sitting
in judgment of rebels

I. ZECHARIAH

Zechariah was one of the heads of the priestly families that returned to Jerusalem with Zerubbabel (Neh 12:4). He began his prophetic mission in the same year as Haggai and prophesied over a period of two years (520–518 B.C.). His oracles reflect the situation in Judah when Darius the Persian strengthened his hold over the vast empire. The Jews, however, were left alone and the community stagnated for decades before the arrival of Nehemiah and Ezra (see part XIV).

It is surprising that neither Zechariah nor Haggai mention the other, as both were active in Jerusalem at the same time, urging the population to begin working in earnest on the Temple. However, they are mentioned together in Ezra (5:1). Considering the breadth of Zechariah's concerns versus Haggai's narrow focus on the Temple, of the two Zechariah reflects more accurately the important spiritual and historic trends of the time. Messianism is the dominant note in the book, but messianism had become strongly apocalyptic, one of the mainsprings of thought in subsequent centuries.

The returnees, as mentioned, found communities of foreigners settled in Judah. Some, like the Edomites, had encroached on Judah's southern territory; others were scattered throughout the land. A ray of hope appeared in the wake of convulsions against Darius' rule, accompanied by the commencement of work on the Temple and rising expectations of the reestablishment of the Judahite commonwealth under the leadership of Zerubbabel. This, Zechariah proclaimed, would entice the gentiles to join Israel: "And many nations shall join Yahweh" (2:11) and "many nations shall come to seek Yahweh in Jerusalem..." (8:22). This is an indication of the readiness of some of the people to encourage the fusion of disparate elements such as the Samaritans, the Philistines, and the Ammonites into the community. Thus, Zechariah seems to be on the side of the proselytizers and universalists. His attitude was countered by the exclusivist trend which we will see in Malachi's writings. Ezra and Nehemiah, a few decades later, would lend their authority to the exclusion of foreigners from the Jewish community.

1. VISIONS

The book of Zechariah has two major sections: chapters 1–8 contain oracles of Zechariah delivered between 520 and 518 B.C.; chapters 9–14 are quite different, but whether they are by Zechariah or date to the same period is uncertain and the subject of much dispute. Much of the material in the first section takes the form of night visions or visual allegories. These eight visions, which are unique to Zechariah, are said to have taken place on a single night in 519 B.C.

The first (1:7–15) and eighth (6:1–8) visions contain numerous references to horses and riders. The use of this symbol may be explained by the prominent part played by horses in the lives of the Persians, who were great horse breeders; the cavalry was the mainstay of the Persian army at all times. Representations of horses are well known in Iranian art, as the Iranian plateau was ideal for raising horses.

The third (2:1–5) and fourth (chapter 3) visions refer to the rebuilding of Jerusalem and the anointing of Joshua as High Priest. The fifth vision (4:1–5, 10b–14) uses the symbol of the gold menorah (seven-branched candelabrum) of the Temple to represent the omniscience of God. We now have two of the more ancient examples of this symbol before A.D. 70: one appears on the relief of the Arch of Titus in Rome and the other is in a fresco uncovered under the plaster of a priestly house in the Upper City of Herodian times. The sixth (5:1–4) and seventh (5:5–11) visions depict the elimination of evil from the new Jerusalem.

Horses played an important part in the lives of Assyrians and Persians.

2. ZECHARIAH 9—14

Of the book's 14 chapters, the first eight can be ascribed without question to Zechariah ben Berechiah, the contemporary of Haggai. There is little in chapters 9–14 to indicate the date of composition or the author, but in view of the general uncertainty it is perhaps best not to speculate. The mysteries of the messianic chapters (9–11) and the heathen assault on Jerusalem (12–14) have not been resolved satisfactorily so far. Much of the difficulty in interpreting and assigning this material may be attributed to the use of apocalyptic imagery whereby historical references are now cloaked in obscure symbols.

J. MALACHI

Malachi lived in Judah during the first half of the fiifth century B.C., i.e. in the Persian period, when the fortunes of Judah were at a low ebb. We are given no biographical material about the prophet and it is possible that the name Malachi, meaning "my messenger," is not a personal name but a title. Unlike the earlier prophets who simply presented the divine message, Malachi states his argument in a question-and-answer method. The prophet picks an opinion that is opposed to his own, making it the basis of a dialectic comment.

1. JUDAH AND THE IDUMAEANS

The hopes for the restoration of the kingdom and the rebuilding of the Temple had faded in the century after the return from Babylon. Taking issue with the prevalent mood of defeatism and indifference, Malachi endeavored to raise the people's spirit by explaining that Yahweh had not ceased to love Israel any more than he had ceased to despise Edom. The latter had expanded northward and settled at Hebron in the more fertile southern Judah, thus restricting the settlement area of the Jews. The Greek and Roman name for this part of the country, Idumaea, is derived from the name Edom.

2. MALACHI'S ETHNIC EXCLUSIVENESS

Malachi contains one of the most frequently quoted and erroneously interpreted verses in the Old Testament: "Have we not all one father? Has not one God created us?" (2:10). He does not refer to all mankind is is commonly assumed; indeed he opposed the trends of co-existence between Judahites and their neighbors which would lead to the mutual assimilation of their cultures. It is clear that Malachi directed the question to his fellow Jews only, in order to point out their mutual commitment not to injure the community by introducing foreign ways. This interpretation is supported by the reference to a foreigner in 2:12 as "the daughter of a foreign god." Malachi insisted on exclusivist Jewish nationality to protect the feeble community from disappearing under the twin pressures of hostile threats on the one hand, and the friendly danger of assimilation on the other.

PART XII

A. PSALMS

Though Jewish tradition ascribes the composition of all the hymns of the book of Psalms to David, the results of scholarly investigation make it clear that most of them could hardly have been composed by the king. Rather they were attributed to him because he was considered the father of Israelite music. Just as Moses was traditionally the author of the Law (the Pentateuch), and Solomon of Wisdom, so the musical traditions were gathered under David's name.

Recent study has shown that the psalms were intimately related to the forms of worship in pre-exilic Israel. In the main, they had their origin in cultic circles and are much older than has been assumed by many modern scholars. Originally they were not so much expressions of personal piety as they were hymns intended to be chanted as part of the ritual of the pre-exilic sanctuaries or high-places: Shiloh, Bethel, Dan, Beersheba, Hebron, Gibeon, Arad, and of course, the Temple in Jerusalem. At one time, each type of psalm was probably related to some specific act in the ritual of the sanctuary.

1. THE MORNING RITUAL IN THE HERODIAN TEMPLE COURTS

According to the Mishna, before the break of day, the voice of one of the Levites who attended the altar of Holocausts would ring out: "Out of the depths, I cry to thee, O Lord, Lord hear my voice! ...my soul waits for the Lord more than watchmen for the morning..." (130:1, 6). Early in the morning lots were cast to determine which of the priests would perform the sacrificial rites. The lambs were brought up, examined by the priests, and then immolated while the 93 officiating priests stood around the altar and blessed the worshipers in the ineffable name of God: Yahweh. As one priest bent to pour the libation and offer the oblation, another priest raised the standard and signaled ben-Arza, the leader of the levitic band, to strike the cymbals, and the priests to blow the silver trumpets. The Levites read the prescribed daily psalm and portions of the Law to the accompaniment of musical instruments. As they finished each verse, they stopped and the priests repeated the blowing of trumpets, while the worshipers bowed in prayer (Mishna, Tamid 7:13).

2. ARCHAEOLOGY AND THE PSALMS

With the help of archaeology and the resulting epigraphic finds, we now know that the Psalms represent a cross-section of Israelite religious life from the earliest period onward (12th century to approximately the 4th

The legend of Al'in (the mighty) Ba'al, from Ugarit, is a saga of the mightiest of heroes, scion of Dagan, the primordial western-Semitic deity

Ba'al Haddad, the god of thunder, illustrated by appropriate symbols, including the might of the bull (reminiscent of 'the bull of Jacob' in Genesis)

century B.C.). The discovery of Canaanite hymns and epic poems has proved the antiquity of many of the linguistic forms found in the Psalms, as well as many of the other books of the bible. They demonstrate conclusively that there was a well-established literary tradition in greater Canaan and Syria before the Israelites settled in what was the southern section of Canaan. This literary tradition provided the earliest Hebrew poets with a highly-developed literary heritage which they drew upon freely as they created their own poetry.

3. THE LITERARY TREASURE OF UGARIT

The 70 acre tell of Ras Shamra on the north Syrian coast concealed the ancient city of Ugarit, destroyed by fire in the 12th century B.C. In the spring of 1928, a Syrian peasant was plowing his field when his plow jammed against a stone slab which formed a tomb ceiling. As a result of this accidental discovery, some 30 archaeological campaigns were conducted there under the leadership of C. F. A. Schaeffer. The many discoveries at this site, and particularly the thousands of texts uncovered, make this site a rich source of information for the biblical scholar and archaeologist. The discoveries include temples, palaces, private houses, sanitation systems, statuary, and jewelry. As may be gathered from Part I, 4, the Semitic civilization of Ugarit was but a province of the early great Canaanite kingdom centered at Ebla in northern Syria, which had preceded it by several centuries.

The tablets from Ugarit date from the last two centuries of the city's existence (15th–13th centuries B.C.), but much of the epic poetry goes back to an earlier time. There are three major compositions which have relevance to Hebrew psalmody. The first is the Ba'al cycle of poems which describes how the storm-god gained ascendancy over the Canaanite pantheon by defeating Prince Sea ("Yamm") and then had his palace built on Mount Saphon. The Legend of King Keret may be a semi-historical epic, describing the varying fortunes of Keret of Hubur. The third major composition is the Epic of Aqhat, son of Dan'el. Another text worth mentioning is the poem of the Beautiful and Gracious Gods concerning the birth of the twin deities, Dawn and Dusk.

4. THE OLDEST PSALMS IN THE PSALTER

On the basis of recent cholarship, it is altogether likely that Psalms 29 and 68 are among the oldest Psalms in the Bible. This conclusion is based on a comparison between the biblical poetry and the Canaanite poetry from Ugarit, which is archaeologically datable. The similarity between the Canaanite and Hebrew poetry is most striking in the areas of the use of imagery, and literary devices.

One of the essential features of both is the use of parallelism: symmetry in pattern of both content and form between two lines of poetry. For example, using capital letters to indicate parallel units of each line, we may analyze the opening lines of Psalms 29 as:

$h\bar{a}bu/layhwh/ben\hat{e}\ 'elim$ (ABC)
$h\bar{a}bu/laywh/k\bar{a}bod\ wa'oz$ (ABD)
$h\bar{a}bu/layhwh/kebod\ \check{s}em\hat{o}$ (ABE)

A slightly different example comes from v 6:

$wayyarq\hat{i}d\text{-}mi/km\hat{o}\ 'egel/leb\bar{a}n\hat{o}n$ (ABC)
$wesiry\hat{o}n/kem\hat{o}\ ben\text{-}re'em\hat{i}m$ (C' B')

Here the second members of the parallel units are marked as being synonymous but not identical. These two patterns are only examples of parallelism found in both Hebrew and Canaanite poetry. The first type is called repetitive parallelism because the terms are identical. This pattern is characteristic of Canaanite poetry while its use in Hebrew poetry decreased over time. Thus it is far more common in the oldest Hebrew poetry.

Psalm 29 has so many features characteristic of Canaanite poetry that many believe that it was originally a hymn dedicated to the Canaanite storm-god, Ba'al, which was adapted to Yahweh. For example, according to M. Dahood: "Virtually every word in the psalm can now be duplicated in older Canaanite texts." The antiquity of the poem is also indicated by the use of repetitive parallelism, not only in v 1 as seen above, but also in vv 4, 5, 8, and 10. The use of imagery in this psalm is also highly reminiscent of that of the poetry from Ugarit. Here Yahweh is described in terms which resemble the descriptions of Ba'al-hadad, riding the great storm-wind blowing from the sea and giving forth peals of thunder. Another similarity is the invocation of the *benê 'elim*, who are lesser gods in the pantheon at Ugarit, serving the chief god, El. In biblical theology they become the angels who wait upon Yahweh and carry out his orders.

Psalms 68 has many of the same archaic features that are found in Psalm 29. There is repetitive parallelism in vv 8 and 15. Once again the imagery describing Yahweh echoes that of the storm-god Ba'al The epithet of Yahweh in v 4 is identical to a title used for Ba'al at Ugarit. There is more archaic material in v 23, which M. Dahood translates: "The Lord said: 'I stifted the Serpent, muzzled the Deep Sea.'" In the Ba'al cycle we read: "I indeed muzzled Tannin (in Hebrew, the sea monster), I silenced him; I smashed the twisting Serpent."

These examples are but a few of the thousands of poetic parallels between biblical and Ugaritic hymnody. The discovery of the Ugaritic material has supplied biblical scholars with a standard to analyze the grammar and vocabulary of old Hebrew poetry, which is more helpful and productive than trying to make Hebrew poetry conform to the rules of classical biblical prose.

5. THE GRADUAL AMALGAMATION OF THE PSALTER

It is generally admitted that Psalms 29 and 68 derive from a Canaanite background, and in their present form they come from the earliest period of Israel's history — the 12th–10th centuries B.C. It is probable, according

Stele of Ba'al, from Ugarit, carrying the thunder in his left hand, the mace in the right, flowing water beneath and the horns over his head symbolizing fertility; a faithful representation of his designation as the 'rider of the winds', the god of the thunder, the rain and the fertility of the earth, as he is alluded to in Psalm 68:4 or 29. (14th c. B.C.)

Inscribed ashlar stone from a niche of the northwestern parapet of the Temple Mount, reading: "To the Place of Trumpeting... to herald..." It indicates the site from which the priest blew the shofar or the trumpet to signal the holy day

to Albright, that other Canaanizing psalms, like Pss. 18, 45 and 89, were written in the tenth century B.C. In the light of available evidence, it is entirely reasonable to assign a pre-exilic date for most of the psalms, leaving only a few from the period of the Exile or later.

Many attempts have been made to group the 150 psalms into various divisions, whether according to their superscriptions or the use of the divine names, or by some other principle. But the timeless quality of many of the psalms and the varied nature of the individual poems makes it difficult to trace the history of these collections or the process by which they were combined. Nevertheless, it is probable that the various collections had been gathered by the end of the Persian period (fourth century B.C.). The inadequate knowledge of the language and images of the Psalter displayed by the third and second century translators of the Septuagint points to a long gap between the original composition of the psalms and their translation into Greek. Even the later psalms (e.g. 1, 19, 112, and 119) are clearly much older than the second century Hymns of Praise (Hodayot) from Qumran.

6. THE SETTING-IN-LIFE OF THE PSALMS

a. *Psalms to David:* The superscriptions of 73 psalms contain the phrase *leDavid*. In fact, the historical significance of his title is still a matter of dispute. These psalms may have been "dedicated to David" by later composers or they may have been written "in the Davidic manner." The Ugaritic material may provide a significant parallel in titling a number of hymns with *lb'l*, "concerning Ba'al."

b. *Festivals:* The title of Psalm 92 indicates that it was a psalm for the Sabbath. In addition, the Septuagint notes that other psalms were to be used for certain days of the week: Psalm 24–Sunday; Psalm 48–Monday; Psalm 93–Friday; Psalm 94–Wednesday. Psalm 81 was composed for a major festival, either for the Passover or the Feast of Tabernacles as shown by v 3: "Blow the trumpet at the new moon, at the full moon, on our feast day." We also know that Ps 30 was intended for the Dedication of the Temple. Finally Psalms 78, and 106–107 are didactic psalms, drawing salutary lessons from Israel's history, composed for use at major festivals.

The shofar (ram's horn)

c. *Liturgical Prayers:* The hymn book of the Second Temple is the Psalter; both Jewish and Christian prayer books are based upon it, and have adopted specific passages for use in their liturgy and hymns. It is often hard to distinguish between individual and collective prayers, and between private and corporate liturgical prayers. Psalms which are placed in the mouth of an individual were sometimes included in the Psalter for use in Temple services; others were adapted for liturgical use by the addition of doxologies (praise of God). Psalm 44, one of the finest expressions of supplication of the Psalter, ends with a fervent appeal for help. Worshipers who presented their entreaty went down on their knees as is illustrated in our picture.

d. *Pilgrim Songs:* The Songs of Ascent or Pilgrim's Psalms were used in connection with pilgrimages to sites hallowed in Israelite tradition, such as Bethel, Gilgal, and Jerusalem. Prayers uttered by pilgrims as they entered the holy place are found in Psalms 15 and 24:3–6: "Who shall ascend the hill of the Lord? And who shall stand in his holy place?" (24:3). There are references to the happiness of the pilgrims in Pss 27; 42–43; 84; 122. The Songs of Ascent (Psalms 120–134) may have been used by pilgrims on their way to Jerusalem. They include archaic material as can be seen in 132:5 which refers to the "dwelling place of the Mighty One of Jacob." The use of the archaic appellation of God may indicate that this phrase

"Thou preparest a table before me... my cup overflows" (Ps 23:5). The obscure allusion may bear a relation to the ancient clay cup on its stand (Exhibited at the Israel Museum)

Left: The wide stairway uncovered south of the Temple Mount and leading to the Hulda Gates (walled up as seen in the corner) is an apt illustration of the Song of Ascent. This is the stairway pilgrims ascended on their way to the inner courts of the Temple

Man making an offering

Sistrum with metal bow and jingles

Man and woman playing the tambourine

originally referred to the portable tent-shrine, like the desert sanctuary at Timnah (see part II: Exodus). When the pious pilgrims came to the Temple with their fruit offerings, they sang as they deposited their baskets at the foot of the altar: "I shall exalt you, O Yahweh, for you drew me up."

e. *The Musical Giulds:* The superscriptions of the Psalter ascribe psalms to musical guilds named for their eponymous founders: Heman, Korah, Ethan, Calcol, and Asaph. 1 Kings 4:31 refers to Heman, Calcol, and Darda as "sons of Mahol," i.e. members of the choir. The names are not typically Israelite. Heman was one of the legendary wise men of Israelite tradition. Calcol is found in an Egyptian inscription from Megiddo as the name of an Egyptian woman from Ashkelon. The name Ethan is apparently of Canaanite origin. R. de Vaux and B. Mazar believe that the first choir singers at the Temple were recruited from among the indigenous Canaanite families who joined the community at David's time (see I Kings).

One of the most interesting illustrations reproduced above is the drawing of a musician playing a lyre as he marches (11th century B.C. pottery from Megiddo). Psalm 150 provides us with a list of the various instruments used by the Levites in the Temple courts: trumpets, ram's horns, the drum and timbrel, cymbals, and portable harps. Some of the instruments named are still not identified. Many of them, however, decorate numerous Assyrian and Egyptian reliefs.

f. *Psalms* 105, 106, 111–117, 135, and 146–150 are Hallelujah Psalms. In them God is praised for his mighty deeds and for his great promises. The Chronicler shows how these psalms were used in the Jerusalem cult. "Hallelujah" is sung as the antiphon by the different choirs of Levitical singers (Ps 135:19 ff.) or by the congregation (1 Chr 16:25).

g. *Royal Psalms:* The Jerusalem sanctuary, being the royal shrine, was where the royal psalms were sung. These psalms (2; 18; 20; 21; 45; 72; 101; 110; 132; and 144) are rooted in the theology of the Davidic kingship and were composed and sung on the most solemn occasions. For example, Psalm 45 was composed for a royal wedding.

In Psalm 2 Yahweh declares that it is he who has anointed his king on Zion, whereupon the king reads the divine decree (*ḥóq*), a declaration of a covenant between Yahweh and the House of David.

In Ps 18:37–42 the king's victory over his foes is described as though it were his own personal achievement, with no mention of the role of the army. This description is derived from traditional modes of thinking in the ancient Near East. The pattern is reflected in other forms of oriental art, especially in painting and sculpture. A striking example is seen in Egyptian art, in the stele commemorating the victory of Rameses II over the Hittites, where the king is enlarged to superhuman proportions.

In Psalm 110 Yahweh seats the king on his right and declares: "You are a priest for ever after the order of Melchizedek," the pre-Israelite high priest of Jerusalem. This verse serves not only to combine both the priestly and royal functions in the person of the king, but also to legitimate Davidic claims to the city of Jerusalem (see Genesis C, 3, b.) These psalms suggest that every king of the Davidic line foreshadows the ideal king, and express the hope that the enthroned king might fulfill the promise.

Some Scandinavian scholars have proposed the theory that the royal Psalms, including 47, 93, 96–99 celebrate the mythical enthronement and reign of Yahweh on the pattern of the well-known Babylonian cultic practice. While there are certain similarities and Babylonian influence can not be ruled out, they are nevertheless distinctly Israelite, stressing Yahweh's permanent enthronement on Zion, his kingship over Israel, and his promise to David of an eternal dynasty.

Trumpets, stamped on a coin

Below:
Musical instruments of
ancient Israel. Cymbals

Left:
Hebrew captives of Assyria
playing lyres

B. SONG OF SOLOMON

"A garden locked, a fountain sealed. Your shoots are an orchard of pomegranates" (4:12–13). A gazelle head, two amphorae, two pomegranates, two doves, are grouped on a ring base found at Megiddo (12th c.)

Pottery incense burner, with figures of musicians, one playing the lute. From Ashdod, 10th c.

The book is a collection of erotic lyrics which are connected by common themes and characters, but do not form an integrated work with a consistent plot-line or narration. Part of the difficulty lies in its complex structure and the abundance of sophisticated poetic devices. Tradition assigned the authorship to Solomon, who is mentioned in the work. Its unsurpassed beauty led early rabbinical scholars to present it as an allegory of the love of God for his bride Israel. Early Christians also read it as an allegory, but for them it applied to the relationship between Christ and the Church, his bride. Aside from the tacit agreement among interpreters, there is no basis of support for such an allegorical approach to the Song of Songs. The whole collection has been divided into eight chapters.

Most modern scholars regard the material as a collection of Hebrew love poetry, including bridal songs, similar to those sung at Palestinian and Syrian village weddings to this day. In the last centuries B.C. and the first centuries A.D., Jewish wedding guests used to dance before the bride (Ketuvot 16; 17a) and sing verses from the Song of Solomon. The early Egyptians serenaded lovers, referred to as brother and sister, and used similes much like those in the biblical book. The pastoral background of these similes also suggests that some of the songs were sung at harvest and other communal gatherings. It is evident that the collection was made at a rather late date (after the Exile) but that the bulk of the material comes from earlier times, reflecting traditions about romantic episodes in the life of Solomon. This nucleus served as the basis for the anthology which grew throughout the biblical period using poetry from both the Northern and Southern Kingdoms. Some of the earlier poetry was reworked in later times, and updated so that it would be comprehensible to the postexilic Jewish community.

1. TIRZAH

One of the poems speaks of the loved one as "beautiful as Tirzah... comely as Jerusalem" (6:4). The comparison probably reflects the period from the end of the tenth century B.C. when the two cities were capitals of the rival kingdoms of Israel and Judah. In the Iron Age city of Tirzah, which was excavated by R. de Vaux, there are three well-defined strata. In the lowest and earliest of these levels, dated to the tenth and early ninth centuries B.C., the houses erected over the remains of the former Canaanite town were built on a completely different plan: the four-room Israelite house. The plan of this house is nearly square; the inner portion consists of three oblong rooms and another room running along the width of the building. The old city gate was still in use, and close to it a small shrine was constructed. The excavators assumed that Canaanite cults still prevailed, to the chagrin of the prophets. In the later layers of the city gate (eighth century B.C.) a stone bench is visible along the length of the wall. This was probably the site of formal gatherings of the elders "at the city gate," to conduct the affairs of the community. Other buildings attest to the wealth of the fortified city, which remained the capital of the kingdom until Omri transferred the seat of government to the newly built Samaria early in the ninth century. Tirzah was destroyed by the Assyrians in 732 B.C.

Reconstruction of a perfume workshop at Ein Gedi

2. EN-GEDI

The oasis known in ancient times as Hazazon-tamar (2 Chr 20:2) was settled and built up in the later Israelite period, as shown by the excavations of Stratum V conducted at Tell el-Jurn by B. Mazar and I. Dunayevsky. In antiquity the district of En-gedi was already known for its aromatic plants: e.g. "the camphire in the vineyards of En-gedi" (Song 1:14). It became still more renowned for its groves of palms and balsam in the period of the Second Temple.

The earliest period (Stratum V) is attributed to the days of King Josiah and his successors (7th–6th centuries). To this period belong several houses in which large rough storage jars were found, as well as a variety of other pottery vessels. There were also metal utensils. The excavators believe that these houses were connected with the perfume industry and that the pottery and metal objects were probably used in the extraction of essence from balm.

Clay barrels from a workshop for the manufacture of perfumes at Ein Gedi. Israelite period

"The king has brought me into his chambers... (Song 1:4). Reproduced here is a section of a relief from the Pharaoh's palace at Tell el Amarna, depicting the women's house, enlivened by music and dance

C. RUTH

The book tells the story of Ruth, a Moabite girl who married into a family from Bethlehem. She is widowed in her homeland, then returns to Judah. Ruth is noticed by the landowner, Boaz. As a kinsman, he agrees to act as *go'el* or redeemer of her late husband's estate and marry her.

There has been considerable discussion of the date of the book, but no firm decision has been reached. On the basis of recent research, it may plausibly be placed in the time of the monarchy. In any case, it faithfully reflects the way of life in a provincial Judahite town, which probably did not change greatly from the time of Ruth and Boaz until the time the work was written. The details of the story illustrate village practices from earliest times: The legal transaction before the elders at the gate (Ruth 4) is typical.

A TALE OF COMMUNAL EXISTENCE

It is often suggested that the book was written as a protest against the exclusivist policy of Ezra and Nehemiah in the fifth century B.C.; they forbade intermarriage between Jews and Gentiles and even forced those already married to be divorced. It is possible that the book of Ruth was cited for its remarkable portrayal of a gentile woman as a model of faith and good works. But the story itself has nothing to say about the question of intermarriage, and Ruth is a bad example of a gentile wife, since she would qualify as a convert and proselyte to the Jewish faith, which would give her equal standing in the Jewish community with the native-born. Just as Ruth does not deal with intermarriage as a religious problem, so Ezra-Nehemiah does not mention the question of conversion in dealing with the foreign wives of members of the Jewish community. Some believe that it is more reasonable to see in the book of Ruth a story about the royal house of Judah, and the remarkable personality of one of the ancestors of the founder of that dynasty, David the son of Jesse of Bethlehem.

PART XIII

A. WISDOM

The tradition of wisdom literature, which is found in the Bible, chiefly in the books of Proverbs, Job, and Ecclesiastes, came into existence many centuries before the Hebrews arrived in Canaan. We learn from the Bible that Israelite wisdom was similar to that of neighboring peoples like the Edomites, and the sons of Qedem ("people of the east"). The biblical material also reflects the wisdom tradition in the far older cultures of Canaan (Phoenicia), Egypt, and Mesopotamia. Only fragments of the Canaanite wisdom literature have come to light in Ugaritic tablets from the Late Bronze Age. They must represent an extensive and influential literature, which finds echoes in the biblical book of Proverbs. Ezekiel (28:3) attributes to a Phoenician king a wisdom greater than the prestigious Dan'el, a royal hero of Canaanite legend. Indeed, Sanchuniaton of Tyre and Mochos of Sidon are quoted by later writers as famous Phoenician sages.

The most extensive non-biblical wisdom literature comes from Mesopotamia and Egypt. The wise men of Egypt are mentioned in the stories of Joseph (Gen 41:8), Exodus 7:11, and in Isaiah (19:11–12). A section of Proverbs (22:17–24:11) is based on the Egyptian work *Amen-em-ope*. The international nature of wisdom may also be seen in Esther (1:3) with its reference to the soothsayers and wise men of the Persian court, and in the intertestamental book of Tobit (1:21–22) where the Assyrian sage Ahiqar is represented as the nephew of the Jewish story teller.

Thus, wisdom literature was the product of an intercultural and international school of thought.

There are two major tendencies within the biblical wisdom tradition. On the one hand, the book of Proverbs embodies the practical worldly wisdom of men of wide learning and experience: conservative, didactic, pragmatic, optimistic in spirit. On the other hand, there are the books of Job and Ecclesiastes which express the questioning side of wisdom: they are skeptical and pessimistic, introspective, independant, challenging traditional values and views.

THE COSMOPOLITAN NATURE OF ANCIENT WISDOM LITERATURE

In Egyptian wisdom writings, the conservative and didactic type predominates and persists from 2600 B.C. to some time after 500 B.C. Among earliest examples are the *Instruction of Ptah-hotep* and the Instruction to King Meri-Kare, both of the third millennium B.C., containing precepts which the king passes on to his successors. The *Dispute over Suicide* is more questioning in its dialogue and resembles Job in this attitude. Other important compositions are the *Instructions of the Scribe Ani,* the *Instruction of Amen-em-opet* (18th–16th centuries B.C.), and the Instructions of *Oneh-sheshonqy* (fifth century B.C.).

The wisdom tradition in Mesopotamia had its origin in the Sumerian culture and was expanded, but not radically changed, by the Babylonians and Assyrians. In Mesopotamia, wisdom is found in the form of adages and maxims or short fables and illustrative anecdotes, or even in parts of epic cycles such as *Gilgamesh and the Land of the Living,* which deals with the search for immortality. A fragment of the *Instruction of Šuruppak* seeks to explain the suffering of man, much as in the book of Job. Other works which deal with this theme, according to the interpretation of S. N. Kramer and W. G. Lambert, are *I Will Praise the Lord of Wisdom,* (1500–1200 B.C.), the *Dialogue about Human Misery,* a discussion between two sages, and the Dialogue of Pessimism. A series of precepts similar to Egyptian and biblical proverbs and laws are contained in the *Counsels of Wisdom* from the Early Babylonian period and the later *Words of Ahiqar* (an Assyrian scribe), known from an Aramaic copy of the fifth century B.C.

In sum, wisdom in Israel was part of a much wider and older tradition which extended throughout the Near East. But biblical wisdom is distinctive in its emphasis on the unitary divine source of all knowledge and comprehension, in its ethical awareness, its great breadth, and accommodation of widely differing and conflicting attitudes.

B. THE BOOK OF JOB

The Wisdom movement produced also a second type of literature, more speculative and radical, among which are Job and Ecclesiastes. The former, one of the indisputably great classics of world literature, undertakes a vigorous and vehement examinaton of the doctrine of reward and punishment and the eternal problem of suffering, as taught by Jewish tradition and by its conservative sages. The book, as we know it today, presents the argument in a unique literary framework: The prosperous, happy and just man, Job, is presented dramatically in a prose introduction or Prologue which tells how Yahweh permitted the hero's piety to be put to the tests of disaster, the loss of his family, and a loathsome and painful disease. The root problem is then explored in a poetic colloquy between Job and three friends, Eliphaz, Bildad, and Zophar, who try to comfort him but aggravate him as they expound the traditional viewpoints. The dramatic confrontation culminates in the great intervention of God, in which he defends himself against the charges of injustice and indifference proferred by Job. The great poetic interlude ends with a second prose Epilogue which restores Job's fortunes and happiness.

The occasion — if not the contrived reason — for these undeserved calamities of Job is Satan's challenge to Yahweh to test the sincerity of Job's faith. It is traditional to refer to Job's patience, but that factor is only in evidence in the Prologue and Epilogue of the book. In the former, Job accepts his ordeal with equanimity as he refuses to blame God. In the Epilogue, he is restored abundantly and his endurance is rewarded. The ancient Job, emerging out of hoary antiquity, is anything but patient. His complaints crash like thunder: He attacks his creator and accuses him of being insensitive to man's suffering and even the wilful cause of it. His outcries raise the question of divine providence and justice which occupies the greater portion of the poetic dialogue between Job and his three companions.

1. THE TWO STRATA OF THE BOOK

The contents of the book may be summed up as follows (and readers are advised to read it and rediscover an exceedingly eloquent masterpiece) as it falls into five unequal parts.

a. The prose Prologue: Chapters 1–2
b. The poetic Dialogue or Colloquy: Chapters 3–31
c. The Elihu speeches: Chapters 32–37
d. The Theophany or the Voice from the Storm: Chapters 38–42:6
e. The concluding prose Epilogue: Chapter 42:7–17.

We will discuss below the connection with archaeology and the ancient world, but we should precede this by pointing out that the book is a composite as it is made up of two distinct strata: the prose sections which are Israelite in origin and date to post-exilic times, and the forty chapters "how much more those who dwell in houses of clay, whose foundation is in the dust" (Job 4:19). So is this miniature model shrine house from Beth-shean

forming the poetic colloquy where sources are far older, often archaic and of external origin, as has been demonstrated.

The anonymous poet of this composite work was familiar with the archaic mythological motifs which abound in the poetic sections constituting the core of the book, while the prose sections represent the later stratum, i.e. the period of its writing, and the cultural and historical background. What setting-in-life in Palestine could account for the acceptance, not to speak of the popularity of so speculative and radical a book compared to orthodox works, which were canonized as sacred literature? Was it the period of the classic prophets or was it after the Exile?

2. THE BOOK REFLECTS A COSMOPOLITAN POST-EXILIC OUTLOOK

We have already seen that the religious and social tenets which animated post-exilic Judaism as exemplified in Ezra and Nehemiah (cf. Part XIV) did not reflect solid and monolithic orthodoxy in the days which followed them, when other, far more cosmopolitan views, were aired.

Job, according to A. Schalit, is one of the biblical works which attest to the existence of differing views among post-exilic Jews, namely that the separation of Israel from other peoples was the all in all of Judaism, as was the belief of Malachi, the late prophet, or of Ezra and Nehemiah. In fact, it may be assumed that the general oulook of the book of Job reflected the thinking of people after the reforming attempts of Ezra and Nehemiah. Hence, apart from the cosmopolitan literary composition of the book, it is generally assumed that the work in its present form dates to the late fifth or early fourth century B.C. Even if we grant that the poetic colloquy originated in an external and more ancient source, its popularity became manifest during the post-exilic period under discussion. The universal humane problem which animates it not only proves that it was familiar to the people after the time of Ezra and Nehemiah, but that it summed up their world philosophy. The book deals with neither Jews nor gentiles; it has no dispute with the God of Israel, but with a universal godhead. Its

210

central problem is that of universal justice and of man's suffering or success wihout reference to race and creed. God's answer to Job from the storm (38:1) proclaims its application to one and all throughout the world: The same sentiment is voiced by Elihu, "whether it be a nation or man" (34:29). In this respect the outlook bears comparison with several Psalms which reflect similar views (to quote some among many, 22:28; 34:1; 67:6, 8; 72:11, 17; 82:8; 145:9).

Hence we meet again the two opposing tendencies, exclusivism and communal co-existence which polarized post-exilic Jewry for centuries. Neither viewpoint finally prevailed, as is evident from a study of the literary products of the later intertestamental period (see Part XVI).

3. PARALLEL AND MORE ANCIENT SOURCES UNDERLYING THE BOOK

The problems with which the book of Job are concerned also exercised the sages of Egypt and Mesopotamia. The text having the most striking affinities with Job is that of a Sumerian lament excavated at Nippur, as well as the tablets in Akkadian, *ludlul bet nemeqi,* "I will praise the Lord Wisdom" which describes sufferings even more gruesome than Job's. They date from the second millennium B.C., and there is every reason to believe that a similar story about an ancient Job circulated in Palestine-Syria in pre-Israelite times. The outline, at least, has been incorporated in the biblical work. The locale of the story of Job is in Transjordan, among the "children of the East."

4. THE EPILOGUE

Major assistance in understanding the many obscurities in the book of Job has come from the Ugaritic texts discovered since 1929, and deciphered and interpreted in the decades following. Difficult terms, mythological allusions, archaic usage and construction have been clarified in a remarkable way by these alphabetic inscriptions in a Canaanite dialect closely related to biblical Hebrew.

5. THE REMOTE MYTHOLOGICAL BACKGROUND OF THE POETIC COLLOQUY

As Job's three friends come to console him, he breaks the silence with bitter complaints and curses evoking the help of the master curser among the gods. By comparison, in *Ba'al's* battle with *Prince Sea* in the Ugaritic myth, the weapons by which Sea was defeated were rendered effective by incantations by the god *Koshar* who specialized in magic as well as metallurgy. The versatile Koshar fetched a weapon while pronouncing incantations; then a second weapon toppled Prince Sea (3:8). In Eliphaz' response to Job, he avers that man is born for trouble "as sparks fly upwards," or in better, modern, translation as "Resheph's sons wing high" (5:7). The al-

Representations of gods warring against mythical monsters are found on Mesopotamian cylinder seals. One of the gods is shown drawing his sword into the mouth of a horned 'serpent' while two other deities hack him up. This is suggestive of the primeval monsters Yamm or Leviathan of early legend echoed in Job

lusion is to Resheph's mythological children who fly up from the nether world to plague mankind. *Resheph* is a god of fertility as well as of pestilence. In his reply (7:12) Job refers to the mythical Sea who is closely guarded. In the Ugaritic texts, the conflict between the sea god *Yāmm* and the god of lightning, Ba'al, results in the defeat of Prince Sea, who is captured and muzzled (like Job in his complaint). The theme recurs in the mythological allusion 38:8–11 of "who shut in the sea with doors... when it burst forth from the womb," as clarified in an Ugaritic text which mentions swaddling cloths in connection with the birth of certain bovine monsters. The god El contrives a diabolical plot to undo his enemy, Ba'al, when he sends divine handmaids into the wilds equipped with obstetrical instruments, there to give birth to monsters called *Eaters* and *Devourers*. When Ba'al goes out to hunt them, he is incapacitated; whereupon drought and infertility ensue for seven or eight years. The great monsters Behemoth (40:15) and Leviahan (41:1) both have mythological backgrounds and identities, the hippopotamus and the crocodile being only pale reflections on earth of their supernatural dimensions and powers. *Leviathan* is the great sea monster with seven heads (Hydra) whose body girdles the world, while *Behemoth* is the great *Bull of Heaven,* of whom the rabbis spoke as comprising the chief dish (*shor habār*) for the messianic eschatological banquet.

Right:
"Worthless physicians are you all' said Job (13:4). Ancient medicine resorted to exorcism and this Assyrian tablet depicts priest–doctors, masked as fish, trying to exorcise the evil spirit from the prone figure

Below:
A Sumerian medical tablet prescribing treatments. This dates some two millennia before the days of Hippocrates

Let us mention in passing that in Job's reply to Eliphaz (14:16) he does not admit guilt commensurate with his suffering and he hopes for a fair reckoning eventually, when he alludes to a count of his steps. Light on ancient methods of accounting has been shed by cuneiform documents excavated at ancient *Nuzi* (Kirkuk) whereby pebbles placed in a shepherd's pouch were transferred to different accounts, i.e. "deposited," "removed," or "transferred" in, from, or to various receptacles to represent the actual movements or changes in status of the animals being counted.

In Job's rebuttal of Bildad's second discourse, he pleads that his words be engraved (probably in copper) or carved in rock for all time (19:23–24). The use of copper or bronze for writing material was fairly common in antiquity. The now famous copper treasure scroll from Qumran is an illustration of what Job was presumed to have had in mind: a record for posterity. Similarly, the carvings on rock are a common feature seen along the paths of the caravan routes in Sinai since early Nabatean times, as illustrated.

This passage is followed by another significant symbol: "For I know that my Redeemer (vindicator) lives..." (19:25). The agent in question is not God against whom Job rails, but a remote mythological figure, a member of the divine court who acts as legal advocate and defender of accused men before the great god who sits in judgment.

In Bildad's third discourse, verse 26:7 should be translated "He stretches *Zaphon*" (not "the north") over the void. Since the discovery of the Ugaritic myths about Ba'al and his holy mountain, Zaphon (= Mount Casius in Lebanon), it is clear that the allusion here is to the storied mountain of the gods, the Mount of Assembly. It is on top of this mountain that the great palace of Ba'al is erected by the god *Koshar wa Hasis,* who formed it of gold, silver and lapis lazuli.

In the poem on the inaccessibility of Wisdom (28:13), a comparison is made with the remoteness of mining operations, whether in or out of Palestine. Such activity has been uncovered at Timnah and the Arabah near Edom, at the turquoise mines of Serabit el Khadem in Sinai, or overseas at Ophir, the source of gold (see Part V: Solomon).

In Elihu's final speech (37:18), the sky is likened to a molten mirror. Ancient mirrors were made of polished bronze. The sky (cf. Genesis) was thought to be a solid dome-shaped vault, separating the two primeval reservoirs of water.

"Who has let the wild ass go free?" (39:5). Assyrian relief portraying an ass-hunt

C. PROVERBS

The book of Proverbs expresses wisdom in brief adages and maxims, or in longer admonitions suited to the instruction of young men in the discipline necessary for a happy and profitable lfe. The contents range from folk sayings to lofty speculation on the nature of wisdom and its relationship to God, man, and the universe. The first major unit (chapters 1–9) begins and ends with the same summary statement, embodying the essence of biblical widom: "The first principle of knowledge is to hold the Lord in awe" (1:7; 9:10). Although the books of Job and Ecclesiastes share this fear of the Lord, the book of Proverbs does not contain the poetic dialogues and theological skepticism which characterize these other wisdom books.

1. GENERAL CONTENTS

The introductory section of Proverbs, chapters 1–9, consists of a series of ten admonitory discourses, two allegorical poems in which wisdom is glorified as the first of all creations, the companion of God, and the true guide of men, and some additional miscellaneous material. In the admonitions, young men are warned to live according to moral standards, to shun evil personified as a wicked woman, and to follow wisdom represented as a beautiful woman of sublime virtue.

Chapters 10:1–22:16 present a long series of proverbs, attributed to Solomon. For the most part, they are in the form of a single balanced line using poetic parallelism between the two halves of the line. The sayings revolve around a group of basic practical issues, but shift from one to another without a clear principle of organization. Apparently this section is the end result of a long process of accumulating couplets, derived from the instruction in the wisdom schools.

Chapters 22:17–24:22 form the "thirty Precepts of Sages,'" a compendium of thirty longer exhortations, modeled on the Egyptian *Instruction of Amen-em-opet* which contained 30 chapters. The close similarities between this section and the Egyptian work enabled scholars to interpret the appearance of the strange word *šališom* in Prov 22:20 as a corruption of *šělošim* meaning "thirty," rendering the proper translation as: "Have I not written for you thirty sayings...?" This is one of the very few cases of confirmed borrowing in the Bible, and it illustrates the international and cosmopolitan nature of wisdom literature in the ancient Near East.

Chapters 25–29 contain proverbs similar in style to those in chapters 10–22. The heading, however, is of special interest: "These are further wise sayings of Solomon transmitted by the men of Hezekiah, king of Judah" (see below).

In chapters 30–31 there are four separate appendices ending with the famed acrostic poem describing the virtues of the ideal housewife (Prov 31:10–31).

214   The book of Proverbs is more than an anthology of wise sayings, which

circulated in Israel, although the "Proverbs of Solomon" in chapters 10–25 represent this type. It is also a text-book of instructional materials for the young to inculcate practical wisdom and cultivate personal morality. Many of these aphorisms and folk sayings which were in common use in ancient Israel have passed into current use in Europe and America. We need only cite a few: "A poor man is better than a liar" (19:22b); the antithesis between personified Wisdom and Dame Folly (9:1–6, 13–18), one of the most picturesque figures of the book; or the saying: "A soft answer turns away wrath, but a harsh word stirs up anger" (15:1).

2. *MĀŠĀL*: A PROVERB AND OTHER CONNOTATIONS

The Hebrew word *māšāl* has the basic meaning of a comparison or similitude. It may simply be an extended metaphor, or as much as a parable. The English word "proverb" does not cover as much ground, but in general a *māšāl* is a wise saying with some special literary feature. It could be said of Balaam's oracle (Num 23:7), a mysterious utterance backed by effective power or of a prophetic utterance (Jer 24:9). Ezekiel's observation: "The fathers have eaten sour grapes, and the children's teeth are set on edge" (Ezek 18:2) is called a *māšāl*. Finally there are lengthy discourses in the book of Proverbs which are considered *māšāls*, such as the description of the virtuous wife (Prov 31) or the invitation of Wisdom in chapter 7.

In Proverbs 7 and 8 Wisdom is personified as a female figure addressing men on her own behalf. It is true that Wisdom is regarded as a distinct deity in the pagan cultures as we see in the Egyptian Maat, goddess of truth and order, or Ishtar, the Babylonian "creatures of wisdom," the personified genius of life and wisdom consulted by the legendary Gilgamesh. The biblical passages reflect this mythological usage and portray Wisdom as a divine being, though created by and subordinate to Yahweh. It is to be remembered, however, that the passages are examples of poetic imagination and embellishment rather than serious statements of theological doctrine. Biblical monotheism remains intact.

3. SOLOMON'S PROVERBS

The traditional ascription of the book of Proverbs to Solomon (specifically Proverbs 10–17 and 25–29) is based on the tradition in 1 Kgs 4:29–34 and elsewhere, emphasizing his great wisdom, intellectual brilliance, and cosmopolitan culture. Actually, certain sections of the book are ascribed to anonymous sages (22::17; 24:23) or to Agur (30:1) or to Lemuel (31:1), mysterious figures of non-Israelite origin.

There is something to be said, however, in favor of Solomon as a great patron of the arts and culture. In the chapter on the historic Solomon (Part V: Kings), we traced the rapid cultural development of the United Kingdom in his time. The rich cultures of Egypt and Phoenicia (Tyre) made a great impression on Israel at that time, both of these lands being famous for their wisdom traditions (cf. Isa 19:11–12; Ezek 28:3–5). Although

First columns of the papyrus containing the Instruction of Amen-em-opet in hieroglyphic script. It was written in the first half of the 1st millennium B.C. but it dates to the 12th c. or before and is remarkably similar to some biblical proverbs the amount of actual participation by Solomon in the dissemination of wisdom is debated, it is likely that moral instruction of the upper class had begun in Solomon's day or soon after (see below). It is also probable that wisdom literature, and not only royal annals and histories, was composed and compiled at the royal court. The truth behind the Solomonic tradition is that he promoted a school of wisdom teachers on the Egyptian model; it is plausible to think that the pithy sayings contained in a single balanced line, which constitute the bulk of the two collections specifically associated with his name, were characteristic of the Solomonic period.

4. PROVERBS "WHICH THE MEN OF HEZEKIAH COPIED"

There is extra-biblical evidence of the wisdom movement which is associated with the royal court in the eighth and seventh centuries B.C. W. F. Albright has suggested that renewed activity in this respect finds a parallel in a Phoenician literary renaissance at the same time. The fourth collection (Proverbs 25–29) is distinguished by its headings: "These are further wise sayings transmitted by the men of Hezekiah," the king notable for the reformation which he instituted (ca. 715–687 B.C.). These "men" must be understood as "professional servants," a school or guild under his patronage. To these men the king assigned the task of collecting and recording the traditional wisdom of Israel. In line with his reforming zeal, he apparently undertook the great enterprise of assembling, organizing, editing, and publishing the literary legacy of Israel.

5. ANCIENT SCHOOLS

The acceptance of practical responsibility for the instruction of youth characterized the wisdom tradition in the Near East long before the emergence of Israel. From the collections of teaching materials such as Proverbs, R. B. Y. Scott and others infer the existence of schools in Israelite cities. Further and final compilation of older collections of proverbs must have taken place in the Persian period producing the long prefatory section (chapters 1–9) as a guide to the interpretation and understanding of the remainder of Proverbs.

From later records and the Talmud, we can reconstruct ancient schools: the teacher was seated on the floor or stone bench with his students seated on straw rugs around him. The teaching of the law consisted of an oral recitation accompanied with admonitions in the general manner of chapters 1–9, and an interpretation of the law. The first of the admonitions in Proverbs calls on the youth, when tempted by bad companions into a life of crime as an easy way to wealth, nevertheless to cling to the moral training received at home.

The Audience

Formal education was intended for young adults rather than children as in the modern world. This is shown by the maxims against marital unfaithfulness, prostitution, the "adulteress," the foreign woman with her seductive wiles (2:16 ff.). The teacher thus underscores the traditional condemnation of the law of sexual aberration and marital infidelity (Exod 20:14; Lev 20:10; Deut 27:20–23). Similar language is used in the Egyptian *Instruction of Ani*:

"Be on thy guard against a woman from abroad... Do not know her carnally; a deep water... is a woman who is far away from her husband... She has no witnesses when she waits to ensnare thee" (J. Pritchard, *Ancient Near Eastern Texts*, p. 420).

Also condemned were the six, even seven vices hateful to Yahweh (6:16). The use of numerical pairs, in succession, is characteristic of traditional poetry in the ancient world. This pattern appears also in the proverbs of Ahiqar:

"Two things are meet, and the third pleasing to Shamash:
one who drinks wine and gives it to drink,
one who guards wisdom, and one who hears a word and does not tell (*ibid.* p. 428b).

6. THE IDEAL HOUSEWIFE

The last unit in the book is the famous praise of the ideal housewife, well known to many modern readers. It is an acrostic where the initial letters of the 22 lines follow the order of the Hebrew alphabet (cf. Lamentations). It is interesting not only for the light it throws on domestic activities, but it indicates the extraordinary scope of managerial responsibility assumed by the Israelite wife. The picture of the woman in her role as wife, whether well-to-do or peasant, contrasts with traditional notions of the servility of women in the Near East.

The Aramaic parallel, in the Proverbs of Ahiqar, of the Hebrew proverb 23:14 "If you beat him with the rod you will save his life from Sheol". The copy, preserved in papyrus and reproduced here, was discovered at Elephantine, where a Jewish military colony was established in the 5th c. B.C. The Proverbs of Ahiqar, however, go back ultimately to an Assyrian book of wisdom of the early 7th c.

D. THE BOOK OF ECCLESIASTES

Ecclesiastes is the most radical work in the biblical wisdom tradition. It consists of a series of soliloquies on the main theme: Man's existence and his struggle to comprehend the meaning of life or to achieve anything of permanent value are futile, for the conditions of life are determined by an inscrutable power. The best course for man is to learn from each experience life affords. The opening verse: "Vanity of vanities, all is vanity" exposed the writer's major thesis: he goes on to consider the question of how men should live in a world where all experiences are fleeting and all efforts produce no lasting result.

1. CONTENTS

Chapters 1:2–18	There is nothing new under the sun; the futility of human effort and wisdom.
2:1–26	The illusory satisfactions of pleasure seeking; the wise man is better off than the fool; death robs man of the fruits of his labor.
3:1–4:3	Everything happens at the time God decrees for it; the existence of injustice proves that man is only a mortal animal.
4:4–5:9	A life of sheer toil is profitless; advice about religious observances.
5:10–6:12	Wrong and right attitudes toward wealth; contentment is life's highest good; man is at the mercy of fate, which is incomprehensible.
7:1–9:12	Short comments: no man can be perfect; the frustration of seeking wisdom; the proper attitude towards civil authority; wickedness goes unpunished; man's mysterious fate.
9:13–12:14	Pessimism about wisdom in practice; the joys of youth; biographical footnotes and summation.

2. THE LEAST ORTHODOX BOOK OF THE BIBLE

The book of Ecclesiastes, dating from the latter part of the Persian period (fourth century B.C.), embodies a different philosophy of life from that set forth in Proverbs. It is openly speculative, far more radical, penetrating, and

A fragment of Ecclesiastes 6:3–4 found among the Dead Sea Scrolls. The elegant script suggests that the complete scroll was written in the middle of the 2nd c. B.C. The book was in circulation a long time before pessimistic. From the didactic elements of the work, it is evident that the author, referred to as *Qohelet,* "one who conducts an assembly," was a renowned wisdom teacher. It appears from the biographic notes (12:9–12) that he won a following among the Jews of his time. The period in which he lived is marked by the beginning of Greek influence in Judea, whereas in the coastal cities of Phoenicia and Egypt there is widespread evidence of Greek influence since the end of the fifth century B.C. There was a dramatic increase in Greek penetration of Western Asia after Alexander the Great's conquests, and the subsequent division of his empire into three great Hellenistic kingdoms. Greek officials, merchants, travelers, and soldiers went everywhere, and Jews, for their part, migrated or traveled to foreign lands. Alexandria had such a large population of Greek speaking Jews that a translation of the scripture into Greek, the Septuagint, was made for them.

3. THE AUTHOR

The reason for the association of the book with Solomon, the traditional patron of wisdom, is not stated explicitly in the book. However, the author is identified in the opening verse as "son of David, king in Jerusalem," as though he were the famous successor of the founder, but this is a device adopted by the author for purposes of his argument or for literary effect. The author assumes the role of Solomon, not only because of his wisdom, but also because a king can do as he pleases, and is free from the obstacles that beset ordinary men, and can thus exercise a wide range of options, explore many lfe styles. He was a professional sage and teacher and his precepts and proverbs, which were teaching tools in the schools, were obviously popular. The background of the book appears to be a stable and stratified authoritarian society, engaged chiefly in agriculture and commerce.

In his list of the human activities that have preordained times, Ecclesiastes indicates that there is "a time to mourn, and a time to dance" (3:4). Greek art, contemporary with Ecclesiastes, illustrates ancient forms of these expressions of human emotion. The Attic vase above shows men and women mourning according to prescribed gestures. Below is a statuette of a dancing girl swaying rhythmically with her arms raised and head thrown back

4. THE IMPACT OF FOREIGN CULTURES

The book is far more worldly-wise and cosmopolitan than other post-exilic books of the Bible. Its Hebrew is significantly different from the classical Hebrew of the pre-exilic period, with linguistic features resembling the Mishnah (completed by A.D. 200) and the Copper Scroll from Qumran. There are so many similarities to Phoenician inscriptions that M. Dahood has suggested that the author was either a Phoenician himself or living in a Phoenician city. Finally, the use of Persian loan words indicated that it could not have been composed before the fifth century B.C., but not as late as the Greek period. These linguistic arguments point to a date toward the end of the Persian period, when Jews lived in a wider world whose doors had been opened by commerce, foreign conquest, and more direct relations with other nations. An example of non-traditional biblical theology is the attitude toward God: in Ecclesiastes Yahweh is not only unknown to man through revelation, he is unknowable through reason, the medium by which Qohelet believes knowledge is attained; this doctrine is similar to the views of the Greek Stoic philosophers, and derives from earlier Phoenician thinkers.

Our author shares the questioning spirit of the Stoic and Epicurean schools of thought. In common with Ecclesiastes, Epicurus of Samos (340–270 B.C.), an expositor of Hellenistic hedonism, praised physical comforts. The author also has much in common with the Stoics, who maintained that man's strivings are foolish, and for peace of mind one should cultivate virtue instead.

When and why Ecclesiastes was included in the authorized canon has been a persistent subject of debate. The Alexandrian Jews admitted it in their loosely defined scriptures, the Septuagint, and the Mishnah says that it was retained "because its beginning is religious teaching and its end is religious teaching" (Talmud, Shabbat 30b). The book shows that wisdom teachers were individualists and not subservient to orthodox theologians and priests; the same is true of Job, which was written earlier.

5. ECCLESIASTES AND JOB

Ecclesiastes denies the possibility of man knowing God through revelation or by reason. His analysis goes beyond that of the book of Job, because his concern is primarily intellectual, while Job's is moral and religious. Just as in Job, the author denies the traditional dogma that virtue is rewarded and that vice is punished, and that suffering is inevitably the consequence of sin. He breaks away from tradition in understanding God as an incomprehensible power which has determined man's fate and conditions forever.

Clay cylinder of Cyrus
(538 B.C.) sanctioning the
return of Jews to Jerusalem

PART XIV

A. EZRA AND NEHEMIAH

1. THE TRANSITION PERIOD DURING THE EXILE

Thanks to archaeological discoveries, it is possible to reconstruct the situation of the Jews in Palestine during the exile after 586 B.C. Practically all the fortified cities in Judah had been razed to the ground, as we know to be the case from systematic excavations at Jerusalem, Lachish, Debir, Beth-shemesh, Ramat Rahel and Beth-kerem, as well as a host of others known from soundings and surface explorations. The poor were left to harvest grapes and make wine since they constituted no threat to the ruling power. The Edomites were allowed to settle in Hebron and other centers of southern Judah, while large communities in Samaria and Transjordan, partly assimilated with non-Jewish groups, were able to survive. The inhabitants of former Northern Kingdom towns such as Bethel and Tell en-Nasbeh had remained under Babylonian control, and thus were saved from the fate of the Judean towns which resisted the onslaught. Curiously, a number of settlements were left intact in the Negeb.

B. Mazar calls attention to the fact that Jews still came down in pilgrimage from the north to the ruined Temple. bringing cereal offerings and incense (Jer 41:5). A significant archaeological discovery is a contemporary carving on a tomb near Lachish which reads: "I am Yahweh thy God; I will protect the cities of Judah and will redeem Jerusalem." A century and a half later, Nehemiah (1:3) comments with feeling about the Judahites who had not been exiled: "The survivors there in the province who escaped exile are in great trouble and shame." The classic Hebrew tradition paid little attention to them but thir influence prevailed as we shall see.

2. SPIRITUAL AND SOCIAL ATTITUDES WHICH FACED EZRA AND NEHEMIAH

We have noticed (Part XI: Malachi) that the Jewish population — both old residents and returnees from the exile — in the early part of the fifth century, had polarized into two camps. One hewed to orthodox ethnic and religious exclusivism, the other was more cosmopolitan in its social attitude and was led by the high priest, Eliashib, the Assembly and the upper class.

This is the situation Ezra and Nehemiah confronted when they came from Babylon. Ezra's initial efforts were to alter the people's attitude and way of life, involving their dealings with their gentile and Samaritan neighbors, and intermarrying with them. Ultimately with the backing of the more practical administrator, Nehemiah, Ezra's plan was carried through, and orthodoxy was established firmly in the land. They did resist, however, the attempt of certain Judean fanatics to revive messianic pretensions in a

221

scheme to establish an independent state with a scion of David to occupy the throne, as had been proposed and perhaps attempted in the days of Zerubbabel, who took steps to rebuild the Second Temple, with the encouragement of the prophets Haggai and Zechariah. But that attempt, if it was made, failed.

3. CONTENTS

The books of Ezra and Nehemiah were originally one book, then separated. We shall deal with them as a unit concerned with the same historical situation during Persian times.

a. *Book of Ezra*

Chapter 1:1–2:70	The decree of Cyrus in 538 B.C. permitting the return of exiles to Jerusalem eighty years before Ezra's time.
3:1–13	The work of restoration begun.
4:1–24	Progress brought to a standstill.
5:1–6:22	The building of the Temple resumed and completed.

Chapters 7–10 deal with the situation some sixty years after the events described in Chapter 6.

7:1–8:36	Ezra comes to Jerusalem and faces an almost hopeless situation described in his prayer of confession.
9:1–10:44	The problem of mixed marriages and Ezra's inquiries.

b. *Book of Nehemiah*

The thirteen chapters of Nehemiah's memoirs constitute the autobiographical account of the governor appointed by Artaxerxes I of Persia (464–424 B.C.) and his mission to Jerusalem, together with his achievements, as well as passages derived from other sources and inserted in the book.

Chapter 1:1–11	Nehemiah hears of the distress in Jerusalem. His confession and prayer.
2:1–3:32	His arrival in Jerusalem; the king's commission to rebuild the city; his secret survey of the damaged walls; the people's readiness to undertake the work. A list of the builders.
4:1–7:4	The work completed in spite of the mockery of Sanballat and Tobiah; the workmen armed against a surprise attack; social injustices remedied; further attempts to trap Nehemiah; arrangements for the guarding of the city.
7:5–73	An old register of returnees from Babylonia.
8:1–10:39	The Law read and expounded; national repentance and a covenant of obedience.

4. EZRA

The first verse of Ezra (1:1–2): "In the first year of Cyrus king of Persia, that the word of the Lord by the mouth of Jeremiah might be accomplished, the Lord stirred up the spirit of Cyrus king of Persia so that he made a proclamation throughout all his kingdom and also put it in writing: "Thus says Cyrus king of Persia: 'The Lord, the God of Heaven, has given me all the kingdoms of the earth, and he has charged me to build him a house at Jerusalem, which is in Judah.'" This echoes the wording of the proclamation of Cyrus (538 B.C.) sanctioning the return of Jews to Jerusalem, as it was publicly announced by herald and then circulated by royal messengers throughout the new empire. Similar terms are used by Cyrus himself in an inscription on a clay cylinder.

The decree granting royal sanction for the rebuilding of the Temple was deposited at Ecbatana (modern Hamadan) and it was found there after a diligent search when, in the reign of Darius I, officials in Palestine questioned the right of the Jews to do so. This scroll also authorized a grant from the royal treasury and specified the plan of reconstruction including the use of cedar timber. These planks were inserted at intervals horizontally into the stone walls to reinforce the structure, as may be seen in walls at Megiddo, Beth-shean and, later, at Masada where charred pieces of wood were found in the space at the bottom of the stone wall of the palace. Actually, Nehemiah's memoirs mention a letter the king gave Nehemiah ordering the keeper of the royal forest (apparently in Lebanon) to supply him with cedar for the gates and walls of Nehemiah's home (Neh 2:8).

Ezra had come from Babylonia earlier (458 B.C.) with a contingent of Jews (8:15 ff.) to join the community and strengthen its numbers and improve its status. Ezra found, however, that many of the established people lived on intimate terms with those outside the fold, and with the Samaritans

Charred remains of wood found in the space at the bottom of the stones forming the palace-wall of Masada, show that it had once contained courses of timber

Coin of Judah inscribed
YHWD to the right of the
Athenian owl

who followed heterodox Israelite rites as a separate community. Ezra initiated a drastic reform that involved an end of such liberal behavior, especially in requiring that the Jews divorce their foreign wives and religiously illegitimate offspring. This brought on the hostility of those who were excluded and it became imperative to rebuild the walls of Jerusalem (Ezra 4:13, 21) against the possibility of attack. The effort was nullified by the intervention of Rehum, the governor of Samaria, who reported it as a prelude to rebellion.

5. NEHEMIAH

Shortly after (445 B.C.), Nehemiah, an official in the court of Artaxerxes I, arrived in Jerushalem as *peha* or governor of the *medinta* of Judah. The Persian realm was divided into satrapies, each governed by a Persian commissioner, the biblical *Ahašdarpan*. These were subdvided into smaller units called "provinces" in the Bible, which in turn were made up of districts such as Judah and Samaria, each of which was under the direction of a governor or his subordinate.

Of the two districts in Nehemiah's time, Samaria was the larger and more wealthy. Bronze fragments of the lower part of a ceremonial chair were found there, probably related to the gubernatorial seat. The original chair was patterned apparently after the throne of Darius I, found on a relief at Persepolis, as illustrated.

a. *YHWD and Y-R-Sh-L-M*

Silver and gold coins first made their appearance in Judah in those days (Ezra 2:69). They were coins issued by Darius I following the example of Lydia which first issued coins in the seventh century B.C. The Greek states likewise issued coins in the eighth–sixth centuries B.C. The Judean coins were simply a copy of the Attic drachma which was common currency in the eastern Mediterranean in the fifth and fourth centuries. It bore the emblem of the owl of Athens and an imprint of the letters YHWD (Yehud – Judah). Many jar handles were also found bearing this imprint. Furthermore the letters Y-R-Sh-L-M (Jerusalem) were impressed between the points of the star of David.

Impression on a jar handle
bearing the imprint YHWD
(4th c. B.C.)

b. *Which Walls Did Nehemiah Repair?*

After examining the dilapidated walls (which were not completely destroyed, see below) he summoned the leaders of the people and inspired them to begin the arduous task of reconstruction, namely the repair of various sections of the wall by different teams of builders. Rich and poor responded to the call, even the high priest Eliashib who had opposed Ezra's reform, and the work was completed in fifty-two days in 445 B.C. — clearly devoted to intensive repair rather than basic reconstruction, as confirmed by B. Mazar's review of the background (*The Mountain of the Lord*, p. 193 ff.). In any case, this work was restricted to the southeastern ridge (or City of David, unchanged in Nehemiah's time). He reduced Jerusalem's area of occupation within the walls in comparison to the larger city in the time

MEDITERRANEAN
SEA

ACRE
GALILEE
QARNAIM

Sea of Galilee

GELIL-HAGOIM

ASHTAROTH

DOR

MEGIDDO

D O R

BETH-SHEAN

GILEAD

Jordan

SAMARIA

SAMARITANS

JAFFO

AMMONITES

BEIT-TUVIA

LOD

BETHEL

JERUSALEM

ASHDOD

JUDAH

ASHDOD

ASCALON

MARESHA   HEBRON

M O A B

GAZA

DEAD
SEA

EDOMITES

ARABS

BEER-SHEBA

KIR-MOAB

Left:
The 'medinta' or district of
Judah in Nehemiah's time
formed a small part of the
Persian satrapy of Eber-
Nahara (west of the
Euphrates)

Above:
Fragment from a ceremonial
gubernatorial chair found at
Samaria

Below:
The legs of King Darius'
ceremonial seat served as a
model to the Samarian
governor

of the Monarchy, thus leaving the Upper City (the *Mishneh*) unfortified. His other building enterprises were (a) the Birah or citadel and seat of civil government situated at the northwestern angle of the Temple Mount; (b) his own residence, the governor's mansion. This evaluation fits well with the results of recent archaeological excavations. They show that his repairs were concentrated on the western "Ophel" wall (3:24 ff.) of the City of David and along with it, the Valley Gate. A section of the western wall restored by Nahemiah, later expanded by the Hasmoneans into a fortified complex, is shown in our illustration. Nehemiah 3:8 states that the Jerusalemites abandoned the depleted outer areas as far as the wide wall, this being the wall built by King Hezekiah in former days, and recently discovered by N. Avigad in the Upper City (see II Kings: Hezekiah).

One of Nehemiah's major achievements lay in persuading a tenth of the population of Judah to move into Jerusalem, thus strengthening the city in the face of threats and encouraging the growth which made it the metropolis of Judah at the end of the Persian period.

Right:
Section of the defenses at the crest of the Ophel hill behind which Nehemiah rebuilt the wall. In the foreground are steps which presumably led to the roof of a house destroyed by the Babylonians. The Hasmoneans built there strong defenses in the 2nd c.

Above:
The inscription found in Goshen of Egypt settles the debate over the identity of Geshem, the Arab ruler of Nehemiah's time

Persian figurine from the Persian period. Tell Zippor

Nehemiah gained considerable popular support among the poor by proclaiming a remission of debts. Again the Samaritans tried to block the reconstruction program. Sanballat the governor of Samaria and Tobiah, a powerful noble in Transjordan (see below), led the opposition. Both were connected through marriage with influential Jewish families and were allied with Geshem, the Arab ruler (Neh 6:6). The identity of Geshem of the Negeb and Sinai and the land of Goshen has been settled by the discovery of an inscription on a silver dish found at Tell el Mashkuta (the Pithom of Exodus) in the Land of Goshen. It reads: "Which Qainu the son of Geshem the king of Qedar brought as an offering to Han-Ilat" (fourth century B.C.). Qainu's father, Geshem, reigned in the second half of the fifth century, in the time of Nehemiah.

c. Nehemiah's Convocation

Nehemiah's aim was to enforce the law of Moses; we may single out the following prescriptions: a) To prohibit business on the Sabbath and on holidays; b) to enforce the sabbatical year with its remission of debts (a boon for the poor); c) to have each citizen contribute a third of a shekel head tax to the Temple; d) to render first fruits and other emoluments to the priests, and tithes to the levites (cf. Neh 13:16–22). Acting tactfully but forcefully, as a representative of Persian rule, he achieved this by renewing the ancient covenant, an agreement between God and his people: on one side were the priests, the levites, the singers, and the *nethinim,* the temple servants (Neh 10:1–28). On the other was the God of Israel to whom his people, "the holy seed," owed allegiance (9:5–37). The people as a whole undertook to abide by the written undertaking of their representatives. This agreement confirmed the unique status of Israel before God. In this way also, Nehemiah was able to establish an autonomous community within the larger sovereignty of the Persian Empire, and thus put off for a time the aspirations for political independence and the restoration of the Davidic monarchy. For the time being, Judah would content itself with a theocratic state, as defined by the historian, Josephus.

Ruins of the Samaritan temple and abutting structures atop Mt. Gerizim. The structure in the back is an Arab tomb.

Pottery figurine of a bearded priest (Persian period in Palestine)

6. THE JEWISH COMMONWEALTH AND THE SAMARITANS

It would be erroneous to believe that Nehemiah's reform sealed Judah off from all other contacts: After all, the numerous non-Jews who had adopted Judaism were entitled to the same privileges as the native. Thus a latent liberalism remained and would take on more serious proportions. First, Nehemiah's work proved to lack sufficient momentum. Before or after his return to Persia in 433 B.C., public laxity set in, and upon his return in 432 he tried to disrupt the family ties of the Jews, on the one hand, and the Samaritan hierarchy on the other. This led to the rupture between the two communities which became irreparable. Though the Samaritans observed the same Law, faith and ritual, the difference between them was the identification of God's Holy Mountain as Mount Gerizim, not Jerusalem's Temple. The temple on Mount Gerizim enjoyed the favor of foreign suzerains from Hellenistic times onwards (second century B.C.). Nevertheless, Samaritan Shechem was destroyed and rebuilt four times, the last time by the Hasmonean John Hyrcanus (128 B.C.). The site was not occupied in the Roman period. Its ruins were covered by a Roman temple, and ultimately by a Byzantine church.

The history of the Jewish people, shaped largely by the reforms of Ezra and Nehemiah, as well as by the priests during the rest of the Persian period, was soon to enter a new stage in the Hellenistic period which followed, when the theocratic community was replaced by a commonwealth in the early third century B.C., and when the rigid Torah precepts were reinterpreted by the liberal rabbis (Pharisees) in accordance with later contemporary conditions (see Part XVI).

7. THE TOBIADS SPAN THE INTERTESTAMENTAL PERIOD

Though the Bible, the books of Chronicles in particular, provides lengthy genealogies of important families or clans, few have left physical remains which archaeology can identify. A notable exception is the prominent house of Tobiah, known since the days of the Judean monarchy. In the days of Nehemiah this house was represented by Tobiah the Ammonite (fifth century B.C. cf. Neh 2:10; 13:4–8). Later princely Tobiads of the third and second centuries B.C. are mentioned, before and during Hasmonaean times. The epigraphic remains found in their ancestral domain at 'Araq el Emir about eleven miles west of Amman, suggest a continuous occupation of the site from before the exile until the second century B.C., when the Tobiad John Hyrcanus was governor of the area (187–175 B.C.). In the papyri of the Egyptian Zenon, who visited Palestine in the third century B.C., the Tobiad center is referred to as *Birta* (fortress in Aramaic). Further chronological data is supplied by inscriptions carved on the rock in the caves above 'Araq el Emir, where the name Tobiyah appears twice, as illustrated. When John Hyrcanus fell out of favor in Jerusalem, he retired and built himself a splendid castle called *Tyros* in the heart of his principality. The castle's remains are located at Khirbet es Šār, a high point some ten and a half miles west of Amman. The most interesting find of the excavations was a fountain carved in the rock with a relief of lions and tigers in the lower part of the eastern wall of the fort. Excavations in nearby 'Araq el Emir in 1961–62 by P. W. Lapp have confirmed that the ruins of the large building on top of a hill (Kasr-el-'Abd) are those of a Jewish temple erected by Hyrcanus early in the second century B.C., as shown in the reconstruction. It is of white stone and decorated with colossal figures of lions in relief. It is rectangular in outline with four corner rooms, one of which was a staircase tower opening into a gallery and leading to a terrace. The portico is near the tower; then follow the entrance porch, the shrine (*naos*) and a storehouse at the rear of the temple.

B. ESTHER

Opposite page:
Above, right:
Remains of the facade of a
vast structure, probably a
temple, built by Hyrcanus of
the House of Tobiah at
Kasr-el-'Abd

Above, left:
Inscription on a funerary
monument bearing the name
TOBIYA

Second from top:
Reconstruction diagram of
the facade

Third from top:
Plan of the temple at 'Araq-el-
Emir; the reconstruction is
based on findings from
excavations of the site

The book of Esther is a vividly told story about the miraculous deliverance of the Jews of the Persian diaspora from extermination. Though it does not lack touches of satire at the expense of the natives, the story illustrates the insecure position of the Jews living at the mercy of arbitrary whims of princes; they depended for their very existence on the good offices of influential courtiers. The first two chapters relate Esther's success in winning the king's favors. A certain Haman, a high official in the empire, persuaded his master to hand over to him for spoil ("and destruction") the Jews of Susa and the empire. He pointed out that they were unassimilable, their laws totally different from those of other people, and they were therefore not to be tolerated (chapter 3).

In spite of this extraordinary offer, Haman was thwarted by Ahasuerus' favorite, the new Jewish Queen Esther. Under the guidance of her astute cousin, Mordecai, she outwits Haman and brings about his downfall. Indeed he is hanged from the gallows he erected in order to hang Mordecai, and his henchmen were killed as well (chs 4–8). The Jews, the book says, "did not lay hands on the spoil" of the Persians (cf. 9:15–22; 3:11, 13) in fulfillment of the law of Holy War, and to show that they did not fight for material profit, but only to preserve themselves and their religion.

The book, as most critics have pointed out, is too neatly organized and contrived to be accepted as historical. Nevertheless, it is known that Jews achieved positions of wealth and influence throughout the Persian empire and this prominence no doubt provoked the envy and hostility of the gentile population, thus providing the background and setting for the story of Haman and Mordecai, and above all Esther.

Nevertheless, although no confirmation has yet been found in Persian sources of the historicity of the events related in the book of Esther, the descriptions of court etiquette and the actual setting accord with what we know of the imperial court of Susa (the summer capital) and its parallel winter capital at Persepolis (Parsa). Ahasuerus is identified with the Xerxes of Greek tradition (485–465 B.C.) who fought the Greeks. They describe him as a temperamental sovereign ruling over a vast empire and still greater wealth. His figure is sculptured in stone on reliefs of his second capital, Persepolis.

1. THE ABUNDANT WEALTH INVOLVED

The palaces of the Persian emperors were renowned for their splendor and magnificence. Though very little has survived of the brick palace at Susa at the eastern end of the empire, archaeologists have unearthed at Persepolis an elaborate complex of stone palaces dating to those times, among them the Hall of Pillars or *apadana*, and its seventy-two pillars, the royal throne rooms, the harem and the treasury.

One of the most piquant and historically significant elements in the story

229

Compared to the splendors of Persepolis, the winter palace of the Persian emperors (right), little has remained of the summer palace at Susa (left) beyond the tiled floor and the bases of many columns

is the reference to the sum of 10,000 silver talents paid by Haman in return for the royal assent to the destruction or despoiling of the Jews. A talent is the equivalent of 125–130 lbs. of silver, and the sum offered approximated a ton and a quarter of silver, an important share of the total revenue of the Persian empire (Herodotus estimates Darius' revenues at 17,000 talents; Alexander carried off 50,000 talents of silver from Susa alone and 120,000 from Persepolis, the richest city on the face of the earth; the treasury of Persepolis was a vast fortified structure).

2. ANOTHER VIEW OF HAMAN

The usual explanations of the story and its background are rooted in the traditional motives of Haman's intrigue. It is also worth considering another theory suggested by G. Cornfeld. The key to this is the offer of a large sum by Haman for a concession to despoil the Jews as an ethnic group, and in return a far greater sum would be paid into the king's treasury. Shorn of its antisemitic trimmings, this could well have been a transaction between the emperor and one of the powerful "tax-farmers" who bid the large sum for the privilege of bleeding the Jews, and whom the latter regarded as an extortionist and an enemy.

It is known that in this and the following century, the system of tax collection during the rule of the Hellenistic Ptolemies in Palestine (or their predecessors), was based on the system of tax-farming by concessionaires. The collection was farmed out to the highest bidder, usually a man from the upper classes who would pay an annual lump to the central authority and then proceed to extract as much as possible from the populace. The difference between what they paid the king and what they got out of the people netted them a substantial profit (cf. Part XV: The Hasmoneans).

The Haman intrigue may well have started along such conventional lines, later encountered bitter opposition in Jewish ranks, then flared up into the threat of pogroms which was averted by the clever diplomacy of Mordecai, helped by Esther's wiles, consummate artistry and bravery.

A procession of lions on the multi-colored tiles was discovered outside the *apadana* (audience halls) of Susa

PART XV

DANIEL

A. WRITING UNDER AN ASSUMED "CLASSIC" NAME

It is general practice in the intertestamental period for writers to cast history in the form of prophecy by attributing a contemporary account of the past to some great figure from earlier times, noted for his piety and vision, who thus "foretells" the events from his standpoint until the time of the actual author. In this way the writer accomplished two goals. First he achieved status and authority for his work by attaching a highly regarded name of the past to it, and second, the reliability and accuracy of the "foretold history" established the credibility of the new prophecy about the actual future which the writer himself wished to contribute, still in the name of the ancient hero.

The writer of Daniel did not invent the setting of the stories, but took well known traditions of saints and martyrs which originated in the time of the Babylonian and Persian empires and were handed down for centuries. By the time they came to the writer, they had already been fixed in tradition in the days of the Babylonian exile. He then adapted the stories to his own situation in the time of Greek Seleucid rule in Palestine (second century B.C.), retold the history of the world and his people from those days to his own, disguised in the form of visions with all kinds of animal and cosmic symbols, and wove them into an account of the career and prophecies of Daniel.

Daniel himself is presented as a hero of faith, a wise man favored by God, who interprets dreams and foresees the future according to the plan of God. By appealing to the authority of such a figure of the past, and showing how Daniel not only saved his people and the nation which ruled over them, but was able through faith in God and loyalty to him to save himself and others, the author, combining stories of miraculous deliverance with visions of historical fulfilment, could convey not only a solemn message of warning in times of great trouble, but also one of great hope for the future of the hearers and readers would only emulate the faithful obedience of the godly Daniel and his true-hearted companions.

Stone capital of a column topped by two bulls joined together to support the roof beam (center) at Susa

Bas reliefs of winged sphinxes on colored tiles. The winged disk was a Persian emblem

B. A CLANDESTINE ANATHEMA OF HELLENISM

Bronze mask of Antiochus IV found near Susa

We have noticed (cf. Malachi) how the exclusivist strain in post-exilic Judaism expressed by some of the last prophets combated the more tolerant co-existentialist stream. The struggle between exclusivism and cosmopolitanism flared again as Hellenism became fashionable among the upper classes in Jerusalem early in the second century B.C., as we find in contemporary literature (cf. Part XVI: Maccabees) which refers to overt acts against hallowed Jewish tradition on observance of food laws, deportment, and worship. Then intercommunal tensions between the groups increased and culminated in the ferocious persecution of the orthodox by the Greek Antiochus IV, who sided with the Hellenizers. His atrocities, on the other hand, provoked the armed rebellion of the faithful Maccabees, who attacked Hellenists and Hellenizers with equal fervor. A protest by the orthodox, veiled enough not to arouse police action, had to be written and circulated among the faithful. This is the credo of the anonymous author of the book of Daniel, who tells how his hero and friends avoid impure food, refuse to bow to idols, live apart from gentiles or those who befriend them (meaning the cosmopolitan Jews), cf. 1:8; 11:32; 12:3, 8–13.

Hence, Daniel, which is chronologically the last book of the Old Testament, is in its present form a product of the second century B.C. It tells a dramatic story of the purported career of a Jewish youth and his companions living in the Babylonian exile in the days of Nebuchadnezzar, a period which symbolized the pit of despair, but it actually concerns the even more desperate period of religious persecution by Antiochus IV (ca. 167–165 B.C. cf Part XVI).

C. THE BOOK'S CONTENTS AND ARCHAEOLOGICAL BACKGROUND

The book of Daniel falls into two parts which, while distinct in form, i.e., stories and visions, nevertheless are linked by a common theme and common subject matter.

Chapters 1–6 relate Daniel's early career in the Babylonian court and his symbolic dreams with veiled allusions to the persecutions of the Jews in the days of Antiochus IV.

Chapters 7–12 follow, in the form of apocalyptic visions of the end of days. Thus the two phases refer in dramatic manner and literary rhythm all its own both to the fate of Babylon (which occurred in the sixth century B.C.) on the one hand, and to the impending divine victory over Antiochus IV of Syria about 165 B.C., with the consequent establishment of the eternal kingdom of God.

The framework of later history with the passing of the Babylonian empire, already in the remote past, is apparent in text from the accurate descriptions of administrative and historical data pertaining to the Persian empire, i.e. the division into satrapies, 3:2–3, 27; 6:2–7, and from the use 8:21 refers to Alexander the Great and to the divisions of his empire. It is interesting to note how the prestigious figure of Alexander was treated in ancient art and legend. He is called "Alexander of the double horns" and a Ptolemaic (Egyptian-Hellenistic) coin portrays him as a god, with a covering of elephant's hide over his head and "horns" protruding from his forehead, as from the forehead of the ancient gods of Mesopotamia.

Right:
Marble statue of Aphrodite found in the fields of Tell Dan, probably belonging to the last days of the use of the High Place in Hellenistic times

Left:
Head of Alexander the Great on a Ptolemaic (Hellenistic) coin, portrayed with a covering of elephant's hide and horns protruding from his head

D. THE PRESUMED BABYLONIAN PHASE

In comparison with the Persian shekel, the Isrealite stone shekel weight (11.4 grammes) was used for weighing silver and gold of the corresponding weight. The stone was incised with the sign 𐤀 signifying 1 shekel, or by another numeral such as 𐤀𐤃 = 4 shekels. Most of the marked weights date to the 7th c. B.C. the period of the *lamelekh* seal impressions reproduced above, indicating a standardization of royal weights and measures

The heterogeneous composition of the book becomes apparent from its peculiar stylistic patterns. It starts in classic but stilted Hebrew, breaks off at 2:4 into idiomatic literary Aramaic, then resumes (ch 8) in Hebrew until the end of the book. It seems clear that the author's language of preference was Aramaic, but that he felt obliged to use the classical language of Scripture (Hebrew) for the opening and closing sections of the book. The language division does not correspond exactly to the organization of the book into stories and visions, leaving some unanswered questions as to the author's purpose and objectives.

1. SYMBOLS AND DREAM INTERPRETATION

Chapters 1–5 relate how Daniel and his friends, presumably Judean exiles, were trained in the lore of "wise-men" or diviners, termed "Chaldeans," and his growing reputation as an interpreter of dreams. Throughout the years they remained steadfast observers of Jewish law though living in the seductively pagan Babylonian court. Daniel rose to power through his interpretation of the king's fantastic dream of the fallen statue (chapter 2) by an accepted system of correlation, similar to Joseph's interpretation of Pharoah's dreams in Genesis. Thus, the statue represented a succession of kingdoms: The head of gold was the Babylonian empire, to be follower by the Median, Persian, and Greek empires, represented by the lower parts of the body, until the last one would be destroyed by a great stone which symbolized the kingdom of God and his saints, which would endure forever (2:36–45).

For a contemporary Jewish audience, living in what were believed to be the last days of the Jewish kingdom, the principal message was in the form of an eschatological vision: In the end of days, God's kingdom will smash the tyrants of this earth and abide forever. Apocalyptic expectations were fostered in Jewish circles, especially in times of persecution, to comfort and encourage the faithful in the blackest times of despair.

2. THE WRITING ON THE WALL

Toward the end of Chapter 5, the familiar story of Belshazzar's feast, there is the ominous account of the hand-writing on the wall. The words are interpreted by Daniel as a prophecy of doom on the kingdom: The Aramaic "*Menê, menê, tekêl upharsím* (= and *parsím*)" may be rendered, "Counted, counted, weighed and divided," to signify the approaching end of Babylon, i.e. God has counted out its days, weighed the king in the scales, found him wanting, and divided up his dominions. On the other hand, the words taken literally are simply various weights which were employed as units of exchange before the introduction of coinage, and subsequently gave their names to coins: *manêh* or the Babylonian *mína* weighing sixty shekels (*shekels* both a basic weight and coin); *pérês*: half of any previously mentioned weight, or a shekel as shown in the illustration of Babylonian measures. These weights or coins then refer to the kings of the Babylonian dynasty: possibly Nebuchadnezzar, Nabonidus, and Belshazzar.

3. THE FATE OF BABYLON — NABONIDUS' ARCHAEOLOGICAL INCLINATIONS

When Nabonidus of Haran seized power in 556 B.C., he challenged the religious monopoly of the priests of the god Marduk, by devoting himself to the revival of ancient gods, especially the moon-god Sin. He was an early antiquarian and archaeologist (see Part VII, 2). When the danger of Persia became acute, he moved his capital to the oasis of Teima' on the Arabian border, where he stayed until 545 B.C., while his son Belshazzar managed affairs at Babylon (Daniel 5) until its capture by Cyrus in 539. The biblical text errs factually by naming Belshazzar the son of Nebuchadnezzar, but this slip has been clarified by one of the Dead Sea Scrolls closely related in style and content to the biblical cycle of Daniel. It relates that Nabonidus contracted a "dread disease by the decree of the Most High" and was "set apart from men." The biblical source transfers this affliction of madness to Nebuchadnezzar and the change of names may have come about during the course of the transmission of the tradition. Hence Nabonidus belongs apparently in the cycle and has been inadvertently displaced by Nebuchadnezzar in Daniel 4–5.

Persian shekel

The Babylonian *mîna* (which brings to mind *menê, menê*...) was the equivalent of sixty shekels in weight. Metal ingots served as currency before the advent of coins

E. THE HISTORIC MEANING OF THE BOOK

The second part of Daniel is a veiled reference to the persecution of Antiochus. His kingdom is represented by a horrible beast (7:7–24) which devours and tramples everything. From it ten kings will arise, each one worse than the other. According to the usual analysis of the last verse (7:25), the tenth horn in the vision, with human eyes and a boastful mouth, uttering blasphemies, is none other than Antiochus.

On the river of Ulai, near Susa, Daniel has a vision of the struggle between Persia and Greece. The first is represented by a ram (a favorite subject of Persian art) with two horns (Media and Persia) and the Greeks by a he-goat. The symbolism of the visions is based on an established ancient pattern. The he-goat charged the ram and trampled him (8:7), an allusion to Alexander's victory at Issos in 333 B.C., described in the illustration.

In the vision of Chapters 11–12, Daniel foretells the later history of the two Hellenistic successor kingdoms of Alexander's empire, which were of most concern to the author, Ptolemaic Egypt and Seleucid Syria. They fought intermittently over the territory between them with first the Ptolemies and then the Seleucids controlling Palestine. The ultimate fate of both kingdoms and of the Jews caught between them is the subject of these chapters, a re-markably detailed account of the period down to 165 B.C.

F. A FORERUNNER OF APOCALYPTIC WRITING

The book of Daniel with its dreams and visions, its stories and exhorta-tions, became the model for apocalyptic books, or supernatural revelations, which appeared first in Jewish and then in Christian literature (see Part XVII). In the present instance the inspiring tales of faithfulness under duress, and of miraculous deliverance from tribulation, were intended to strengthen the resolve of the faithful Jews, so that they would not collapse under pres-sure, or abandon their religion, since in the end God would save them, and destroy the wicked enemy.

In Daniel the angels who are anonymous agents of God in the stories of the earlier books of the Bible, have names, ranks, dominions, and duties, constituting a complicated hierarchy in heaven and destined to play a major role in Judaism, Christianity and Islam, with belief in a final judgment for all men, resurrection and eternal life for the just, and damnation for the

wicked.

PART XVI

A. INTERTESTAMENTAL PERIOD

1. THE GAP BETWEEN THE OLD AND NEW TESTAMENTS

In spite of the many historical and theological links between the Old and New Testaments, there are significant divergences and differences, many of which are attributable to special developments during the period between the Testaments. The recognizable gap between the two was caused, on the one hand, by the process of canonization of the Hebrew scriptures and, on the other, by the emergence of a varied extracanonical religious and historical Jewish literature. Though they represented important trends in Jewish life between late post-exilic times (fourth–second c. B.C.) and the first century A.D., they were not canonized by the rabbis and sages of that period and incorporated in the scriptures. Those were the apocryphal, pseudepigraphical and apocalyptic writings, to be described briefly below. Yet these writings exerted an important influence on early Christianity and left their mark on the New Testament especially in respect to its apocalyptic eschatological expectations (see Part XVII)

a. *Canonization*

The canonzation of the Old Testament was the end result of a process which lasted throughout post-exilic and Second Temple days and produced in effect two different but overlapping bodies of scripture, one Hebrew and Palestinian, the other Greek and Alexandrian, both entirely Jewish. They incorporated most trends in Jewish life, exclusivist and cosmopolitan alike, as is evident from the inclusion of writings as diverse in spirit an Ezra-Nehemiah or Malachi, and Job, Jonah and Ecclesiastes, not to speak of the addtional books in the Greek canon. The canon of biblical books initially included the Torah, to be followed quickly by the Prophets, Former and Latter. The scope and status of the Writings were a matter of discussion for many years, not finally resolved until the Council of Yabneh around A.D. 100. The process with regard to the Greek canon, and the organization of the parts are somewhat different, yet the Greek Old Testament included all of the books in the Hebrew Bible, plus some others composed in Persian and Hellenistic times. The only such work included in the Hebrew Bible was the book of Daniel, all others being relegated to non-canonical status. The Greek canon was more expansive, and when the Christian Church was established, it adopted the Greek Old Testament as its scripture to which were added later the books of the New Testament. It should be added that for all Jews the Torah (the five books of Moses) are paramount, and *halakha* (rules of practice) had to be based on it.

b. *The Apocrypha*

These are books which were rejected by the Palestinian rabbis and scholars as not manifstly inspired works and written mostly by unknown men. Fourteen of these were included in the Greek canon, among them such works as I and 2 Maccabees, Ecclesiasticus (Ben Sira), Judith, Tobit, Wisdom, and additions to Esther, Daniel and Jeremiah. They constitute a central element in the progress of contemporary Jewish intellectual life.

c. *Pseudepigraphia*

These books were composed under an assumed name, the choice of which was dictated by theological reasons. To give these books both the aura of divine sanction and the patina of antiquity, the actual authors assigned their work to great heroes of the faith, known for their piety and intimate relationship with God, e.g., Enoch, Moses, Baruch, Ezra. These books purported to be forecasts of the future delivered by these ancient worthies, but were thinly disguised historical works, interlaced with moral warnings, and exhortations to hold fast to the traditional faith.

d. *Apocalyptic Literature*

The apocalyptic literature consists of the revelation of secret information about God's plan for the world generally and Israel in particular. The revelation is couched in colorful often bizarre imagery, and is set down as a series of extraordinary visions, the meaning of which is revealed only to the visionary and by him to the faithful. The book of Daniel in the Old Testament is a prime example, as in the Book of Revelation in the New Testament. Using symbolic language full of fantastic figures, the texts allude to mysteries beyond the reach of man, but revealed and explained by God through helpful angels to his chosen few. It seemed to them that the present world was passing while the new eschatological age was about to begin. The details were worked out with an agonized blending of history and this world, with idealized pictures of the world to come, recapturing the vision of the Garden of Eden and combining it with that of a heavenly paradise. The present crisis would be resolved in a final Day of Judgment when the worthy could inherit eternal life and the wicked corresponding damnation. These ideas are reflected in New Testament writings, particularly the Book of Revelation. Strikingly similar literature before the New Testament has been found among the famous Dead Sea Scrolls (see below). Other apocalyptic works are: Enoch, Testament of the Twelve Patriarchs, Second Baruch, Fourth Ezra, The Assumption and Testament of Moses, and Third Baruch.

2. THE JEWISH HISTORICAL SOURCES

The fullest direct accounts concerning the period from 175 B.C. to the first century A.D., i.e. including the rule of the Greek Ptolemies in Egypt, the Seleucids in Syria, and the Hasmoneans in Palestine, which ended in Roman domination and the puppet reigns of the Herods, are found in

"Antiquities of the Jews" by the Jewish historian, Josephus Flavius (in Books VII–XX of this monumental work).

The other dependable accounts, aside from Josephus, are found in 1 and 2 Maccabees. 1 Maccabees traces the growth of Jewish independence from the revolt of Judas Maccabaeus to the reign of John Hyrcanus. Its author was a devout and patriotic Jew and, while the book reflects this commitment to the Maccabees, it is one of the most reliable authorities for the intertestamental period. 2 Maccabees covers a briefer portion of the same period, ending with the death of the Syrian general, Nicanor (161 B.C.). It is a digest from an older work by Jason of Cyrene (North Africa) who wrote in Greek and stressed the supernaturel aspects of the deliverance of his people by Judas the Maccabee. Nevertheless, it supplements 1 Maccabees at a few points where the latter is deficient, and corroborates it at others. There are many differences in detail, but these are rarely of significance, except for historians.

3. DIVERGENT SPIRITUAL AND SOCIAL TRENDS — FOURTH CENTURY B.C. TO FIRST CENTURY A.D.

a. *Israel and the Nations*

Several of the biblical works already considered reflect a basic problem of post-exilic Judaism, namely the sharp division between Israel and the nations, and varying views on its position in the world. The two groups were in opposition from the time of the Babylonian exile, and that tension persisted throughout all the days of the Second Temple. Whereas the prophets Zechariah and Haggai saw no harm in peaceful coexistence with non-Jews, the anonymous Malachi hewed the line of strict exclusivism. Two principal social trends appeared in these times (cf. Part XI), but while Ezra and Nehemiah were dominant in their time (Part XIV), exclusivism did not win the day. A more liberal view, evident in Job and Jonah, and a more cosmopolitan outlook as in Ecclesiastes, were preserved through public recitation and reading, and finally, in canonical scripture. Thus the two attitudes continued side by side for centuries without either completely dominating the other. The tolerance Jews enjoyed in the world impelled them to adopt a more cosmopolitan outlook, akin in some ways to Hellenistic philosophical thought, which was popular among the educated and sophisticated circles in the Near East, and not unknown in Judea (as southern Palestine became known in post-exilic times).

b. *Hellenism and Judea*

Hellenism swept the east through the conquests of Alexander the Great, which extended from Greece to India. It was split into three powerful kingdoms after his death in 323 B.C.: the *Ptolemies* in Egypt who also controlled Palestine until 200 B.C., the *Seleucids* in Mesopotamia with headquarters in Syria, and the European domain centering on Macedonia.

The high priest of the hereditary house of Zaddok presided at the Temple in Jerusalem. He was also the leading political authority and levied taxes for the Egyptian overlord, though the actual collection was delegated to local tax-farmers (cf. Esther), usually recruited from leading Jewish families. A prototype of such a tax-farmer was Joseph ben Tobiah in the mid-third century B.C., a scion of the powerful dynasty which had established itself in Transjordan as far back as the days of Nehemiah (cf. Part XIV). By that time (early 3rd c.) Greek and Macedonian settlers had come to Palestine, forming islands of Hellenistic civilization, complete with all the architectural, social and political forms of the self-governing *polis* (city) and the polytheism to which it was bound. Their rulers encouraged mutual exchanges between Greek and Semitic civilization and their interpenetration created a symbiotic Hellenistic-Oriental culture, characterized by the graceful Greek styles in art and architecture, tempered by traditional Oriental spirit and manners.

Judea proper was surrounded by a ring of such states and modelled its own municipal governments on Greek patterns, including their elected town councils, clearly an innovation in oriental cultures. The more exclusivist and pious Judeans looked upon this as a necessary evil, while the more cosmopolitan-minded Jews prospered in the new climate; this was particularly true of the class to which the Tobiads and their contemporaries belonged, as well as the powerful priesthood. The Tobiads provide a classic example of the attraction and advantage of Hellenization which was a useful and effective instrument in the drive for greater wealth and power. Contemporary conditions are described graphically in the non-Jewish Zenon papyri (late third century B.C.).

c. *New Western Institutions Come to Jerusalem*

As the Hellenistic way of life first infiltrated, and then shaped urban life in Judea, the people of Jerusalem and other cities became familiar with the ubiquitous Greek institutions for the physical and moral training of young men. Many attended the gymnasium and ephebeion (for athletic

240

games). The first to endorse the new culture were those already in close contact with the authorities, the landed gentry, rich merchants, officials, and the priestly aristocracy. Large elements among the masses did not become Hellenized and the more traditional and exclusivist elements bitterly resented the new cosmopolitan way of life.

d. *The Hellenistic Reform*

In spite of growing tensions within the Jewish community, the situation remained relatively calm at the end of the third century B.C. But in 198 B.C., Judea — heretofore under Ptolemaic rule — was annexed by Antiochus III, the Great, the Seleucid king. While autonomous Jewish life was not disturbed under the new foreign ruler, strife intensified when the Tobiads, now loyal to the new overlords, succeeded in deposing the high priest, Onias, and replacing him by his pro-Hellenistic brother, Jason. Onias retired to Egypt with many other refugees who fled from the distasteful religious and social climate. He then built a Temple at Leontopolis in northern Egypt to rival that of Jerusalem.

One of the halls of the 2nd c. B.C. Hellenistic *gymnasium*, part of the *Xystos* place of public assembly. It lies underground, close to the Western Wall bordering the elevated Temple esplanade. The upstanding column supported the roof of the hall

Unlike the ancient prestigious *soferim*, the present day *sofer* or scribe is a professional copyist of Torah scrolls

The right of succession to the high priesthood of the house of Zaddok had never before been challenged. It was almost as sacrosanct as the tradition of the house of David. Now the usurper Jason gave the Seleucids the privilege of appointing future high priests when it suited their political or financial hellenized and the more traditional and exclusivist elements bitterly resented needs. From 2 Maccabees we learn that Jason established a *gymnasium and ephebeion* in Jerusalem, virtually turning it into a Hellenistic *polis*. This construction, identified by Josephus with the *Xystos,* seems to have been an open-air porticoed plaza paved with large polished flagstones, and used for public assemblies. It faced the Temple Mount on the west and lay therefore in the busy Tyropoean vale, the busiest throughfare of the Lower City. One of the halls of this complex has been uncovered, as described. By that time cosmopolitan Jews began to adopt Hellenistic names, either by Hellenizing their Hebrew names or by coupling their own with a Greek sounding name.

4. THE HASSIDEANS

Thus far, Hellenization trends had not affected directly the religious faith of the people. Its real purpose, according to 1 Maccabees, was to end the exclusiveness of the Jews and to open their way to membership in the commonwealth of Hellenistic peoples. But the erection of the gymnasium was a radical and treacherous step, in the opinion of the orthodox; this explains the hidden meaning of Daniel 11:30–33, as well as 1:5; 12:3, 8–13; 7:13–14, which refer to the underlying resentment and ground-swell of protest. Its apocalyptic viewpoint reflects the appearance of a new movement in Judaism led by the exclusive *Hassideans*. It believed that secular rule was granted by God to the nations according to a predetermined plan which controlled the course of world history. Israel, the chosen people, must also conform to this plan, and be subject to pagan empires until the end of time, when God would destroy the kingdoms of the world and replace them with his own kingdom, made up primarily, if not exclusivsely, of the faithful among his people. According to the Hassideans and the author of Daniel, that day was fast approaching and therefore it was all the more important for Jews to cling to their faith in the face of enticements on the one hand and persecution on the other. This secret was known to the elect, the apocalyptists, and such other pious people who adhered to a strict observance of the priestly Code of Holiness and Levitical purity (see Part II, Leviticus). According to historic Jewish sources, the early Hassideans split up later into the sects of the Essenes and the Pharisees (see below, Conflict with the Pharisees).

Besides being strict upholders of the Law, the Hassideans also instructed the people in its observances. Many illustrious scholars belonged to the group, including the *soferim* (scribes) who were responsible for the transmission of holy scripture. 1 Maccabees (7:12) refers to a company or synagogue of scribes involved in a conflct with Alcimus, another usurping high priest, in the days of Judas Maccabaeus.

According to historic Jewish sources, the early Hassideans split up later into the sects of the Essenes and the Parisees (see below, conflict with the Pharisees).

5: THE HASMONEAN WAR OF INDEPENDENCE

Antiochus IV, who acceded to the Seleucid throne in 175 B.C., was a firm believer in an ecumenical Hellenistic religion which would embrace all the peoples in his vast kingdom. A few years after his accession, in 171 B.C., the Tobiads and their allies in Jerusalem successfullly promoted Menelaus, a relative of theirs and an extreme Hellenizer, to the high priesthood. He used the appointment, obtained through bribery, for political and material ends. He supported Antiochus IV's disregard for Judaism and plundered the Temple's treasure on the king's behalf. His unrestrained personal behavior, coupled with growing class conflicts between the wealthy Jewish Hellenizers and the masses, resulted in riots and street fighting. Two years later, when Antiochus suffered reverses in Egypt, the priest Jason returned from exile and executed a number of Menelaus' followers. Antiochus then occupied Jerusalem with his troops to suppress the civil disturbances and in the process massacred 80,000 people. He profaned and pillaged the Temple and took away a treasure amounting to 1800 talents (approximately seven million shekels of silver). The king instructed his officers to carry through the Hellenization of the Jewish religion. In 167 B.C. he forbade the observance of the Jewish faith, a religious policy hitherto unknown in Hellenistic annals. Instead, he ordered the worship of the Greek, Zeus in its oriental form, i.e. Ba'al Shamêm (the Lord of Heaven). The process om identifying similar gods in different Pantheons had been going on for millennia in the Near East, and it was accelerated by the introduction of Greek and Roman deities during this period. Thus Melkart of Tyre was identified with Heracles; Ba'al Shamêm was represented in Baalbek in Lebanon as Jupiter Heliopolitanus. For Antiochus the equation of Yahweh with Zeus = Jupiter = Ba'al would be entirely appropriate, though utter blasphemy to all but the most radical and emancipated Jews. Though Menelaus was reinstated as High Priest, the Temple had been so desecrated that pious Jews avoided worshiping there, even before it was officially closed to them.

a. Restoration of the Kingdom

Fidelity to the Law of Moses finally led to rebellion. Holy war against Hellenism was proclaimed in 166 B.C. by the Hasmonean priest, Mattathias, and his sons and bands of valiant men who rallied around him. Judas, surnamed Maccabaeus, the third of the five sons, took strategical command. He was killed after six years of fighting. Under Jonathan and Simon (161–135 B.C.), who secured the high priesthood, the territory of the Jews was recognized as independent and was greatly extended north and west to include Samaria and the coastal plain. By the time of Simon's violent death, the dynasty was firmly established. During the reign of Hyrcanus, 243

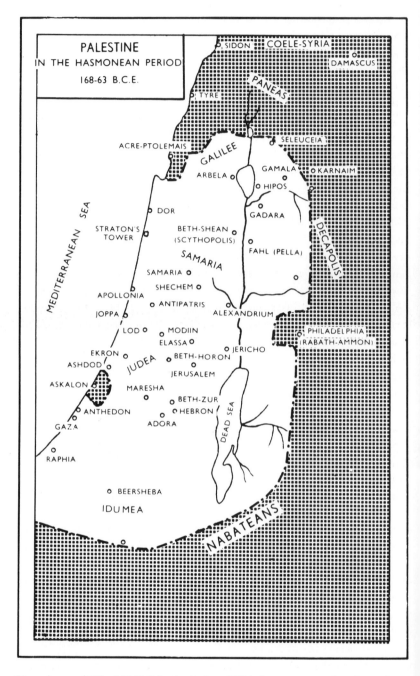

Simon's son (135—104 B.C.), Antiochus VII led an army against Jerusalem; he imposed a tribute on Judea, took John as hostage, but the latter escaped and succeeded in restoring the independence of his country and even considerably enlarged its territories.

b. *Conflict with the Hasmoneans*

The Hasmonean leaders, once independence had been won, began a process of secularization of national life. This seemed to the Hassideans, their allies in the struggle, a betrayal of their faith and commitment to God. When Jonathan had assumed the high priesthood in 152 B.C., he compounded the offense with a disavowal of Hassideans tenets of priestly succession, as he was not of the ancient priestly house of Zadok established since the days of Solomon. When this office became hereditary in the Hasmonean line under Simon, the act displaced the Zadokites from their preeminent position. The Hassideans had expected the eventual restoration of the ideal kingdom, but the historical success of the Hasmoneans only alienated them. After political independence had been gained, the Hassideans broke away from the Hasmoneans, giving up their participation in political life and emphasizing instead religious observance, and faithful adherence to the ancient ways. They became rigorous critics of the Hasmonean establishment but preferred prayers to protests, and rather than fight against the Maccabees chose, non-violent forms of resistance. A group of Essenes, an off-shoot of the Hassideans went out into the Judean wilderness, there to build a new society based strictly on the most ancient traditions of the Bible, to be the nucleus of a new pure Israel which would one day inherit the kingdom prepared by God for his elect. This event was never recorded in contemporary annals, and it would have been lost forever but for a chance discovery by a Bedouin shepherd, of one of the greatest finds of modern archaeology. The discovery of the *Dead Sea Scrolls* at *Qumran* and nearby localities — so essential for the study of contemporary Judaism and early Christianity — has identified a religious and social group of Covenanters associated with the Essenes, if not the central group of Essenes themselves (see below, Qumran and the Dead Sea Scrolls).

Syrian Jupiter Heliopolitanus
(from Baalbek)

c. *The Pharisees*

On the other hand, larger numbers of the Hassideans chose to unite, instead, in active opposition to the Hasmonean dynasty, because its claims and behavior ran counter to their theological outlook. In time they were organized as the powerful *Pharisaic* party backed by the masses, and eventually became the dominant force in normative Judaism.

d. *The Sadducees*

Unlike the other sects, the supporters of the Hasmoneans, devout, conservative and commited to the strict observance of the Law of Moses, were bent on consolidating the new idependence of the nation. They were quite willing to maintain contact with their neighbors in Palestine and Trans-Jordan, and as the occasion warranted, to negotiate with them, or fight with them and forcibly Judaize them. This pragmatism, coupled with their support of the new Jewish power, kept them busy with mundane matters and led them away from eschatological visions of the Day of Judgment. Organized as another sect around the Hasmonean hierarchy, the *Sadducees* were represented in the main by the aristocracy, the numerous and rich priesthood, and their own scholarly leaders.

6. THE PHARISEES AND THE HASMONEANS

The early Pharisees, concerned with the practical interpretation of the traditional Law in relation to everyday problems, also took an active part in teaching the people. They shared the Hassidean contempt for secular politics and for years maintained the same objection to Hasmonean usurpation of the high priesthood. Later, as members of the Assembly of Notables, they supported the new government out of patriotic motives. However, as king John Hyrcanus' international status grew, so did the pomp and ceremony of his court, as when Hyrcanus appeared before his people in splendid imitation of a Hellenistic oriental monarch. Though Hellenization had lost its potency in the country, the Hasmonean monarch behaved as a secular dynast. Although theoretically restricted in his authority by the Assembly, his rule became increasingly autocratic. Disaffection stemmed from the Pharisees who, up to now, had been inclined to support the government. Their deepest wish was to let Hyrcanus exercise only civil authority, and even that on an interim basis, until "a priest descended from Zadok and a savior or king from the house of David could be reinstated." Eventually their insistence turned Hyrcanus against them and he adhered firmly to the aristocratic Sadducee party. It must be noted, however, that his reign was a period of prosperity and expansion of Jewish interests in Palestine, so no serious opposition could crystallize (see below; Numerous Remains of Jerusalem in Hasmonean Times). In fact Josephus speaks glowingly of him, saying that in John the roles of prophet, priest, and king were combined.

a. Rise and Fall of the Hasmonean Dynasty

John Hyrcanus was succeeded by his sons, *Judah Aristobulos* (105–104 B.C.) and *Alexander Yannai* (graecisized as Jannaeus), who were bidden to make peace with the Pharisees. Judah died after a year and was succeeded by Alexander, who adopted the royal title and reigned until 75 B.C. He assembled a professional mercenary army and conquered Transjordan, Idumaea in the south, and the coastal plain, carving out a large kingdom. His antagonism to the Pharisees, who opposed his expansionist war policy, led to civil rebellion which he suppressed after a bloody struggle. His cruelty was notorious, and he was remembered for his practice of crucifying his enemies. Nevertheless, the Pharisees gained influence and power during the reign of his widow, *Salome Alexandra* (76–69 B.C.). Hasmonean rule began to decline with her death, due to the strife between her sons, *Hyrcanus II* and *Aristobulos II*. This led to the intervention and eventual domination of the state by *Antipater,* a Judaized Idumaean, and his son Herod, who were abetted by the Romans, the new super-power on the scene. The Roman general, *Pompey,* who had invaded the country, captured Jerusalem and entered the Temple precincts in 63 B.C. The last Hasmonean princes had frittered away the remnants of their power and authority through internecine feuds. Hyrcanus remained a puppet in Antipater's hands. Meanwhile, the efforts of Aristobulos II and his sons, *Alexander* and *Antigonus Matathias II,* proved unsuccessful. The latter disappeared after his defeat by Herod and the capture of Jerusalem in 37 B.C. This spelled the end of the Hasmonean dynasty.

b. The Tomb of Matathi, Son of Judah

A rock-tomb was uncovered in recent years on Mount Scopus, east of Jerusalem. It bore a monumental inscription and contained a sumptuous ossuary. The inscription proclaims that Abba, descendant of the High Priest Aaron, who had been persecuted, had brought back the bones of Matathi, son of Judah, and that he buried him in his cave-tomb. The discovery has aroused considerable speculation, as Matathi is presumed by some to be the last Hasmonean prince, Antigonus, who was deposed by Herod. No conclusion has been reached as yet, however.

The startling inscription over the loculus where the bones of Mathati had been buried

7. NUMEROUS REMAINS IN JERUSALSM OF HASMONEAN TIMES

The Hasmoneans effectively ruled in the land for one hundred years (163–63 B.C.). Herod took the throne from the last Hasmonean prince, Antigonus, and killed off most of the surviving Hasmoneans to insure that there would be no political threats from that quarter. Then he embarked on a vast building program in Jerusalem and other urban centers in Palestine.

Regret is often expressed that very few Hasmonean buildings and monuments have survived, especially since theirs was the last Jewish kingdom in the Holy Land, and they devoted a great deal of time and effort, and the royal exchequer to reconstructing the city of Jerusalem which served as their capital. But this is a misreading of the available evidence, based on a series of archaeological discoveries during the last century, and more particularly in the decade since 1967. These remains are not less important than those surviving from the days of the Monarchy (cf. Part V) and are second in significance only to those dating to the Herodian period (see below).

The monumental remains illustrate how the Hasmoneans fortified the expanded area of Jerusalem and built its walls and palaces; and how this expansion and increased population encompassed the commercial centers to the east and north, and particularly the Upper City (the present Jewish Quarter). The evidence consists both of massive walls, monumental biuldings, stone carvings, and rock-tombs on the one hand, and small finds in great quantity including pottery and coins on the other.

a. The Walls and Fortifications

Beneath the ramparts constructed by Herod or later builders, archaeologists have uncovered in various locations, solid Hasmonean foundations and stretches of massive wall which help to explain the ancient plans underlying Jerusalem's defense. Let us examine them at the west, south, east, and north: The excavations at the Citadel on the west, and since 1976 along the entire lengths of the western wall of the Old City, which faces modern Jerusalem, have uncovered the thick walls built apparently by John Hyrcanus and Alexander Jannaeus. The line of walls and adjacent towers at this lower level

247

interlock with the massive Herodian walls and towers built above them. It is not difficult to distinguish the different styles of stone carving and jointing throughout the length of the walls. This is one of the most spectacular discoveries in Jerusalem, along with those made at the Temple Mount and on the slopes of Mount Zion, as illustrated by Magen Broshi's dramatic excavations since 1976.

One of the key achievements of the Hasmonaean kings was to fortify various sections of the capital so that each could stand on its own in time of war. The Hasmonean wall of Jerusalem is built mostly of large rocks, squared roughly and uncarved, in contrast to the characteristic finely chiselled and embossed Herodian ashlars. The earlier line of walls was built hastily under military pressure and threat of imminent attack.

The second most imposing fortification was erected on top of the Ophel, the site of the ancient City of David, in later times the Lower City, about 220 feet west of the Gihon spring and several hundred feet east of the Temple Mount. This wall was flanked by two towers and protected on the eastern side by a sloping ramp faced with stepped masonry, to prevent the approach of besiegers trying to scale the walls and of siege engines to batter them.

The fortifications were erected by the Hasmoneans during the second century B.C. and rested on an earlier wall and houses erected in the days of the Judean kings (ninth–eighth centuries B.C.). The latter had been repaired by Nehemiah (cf. Part XIV); a section of it is still visible in the rear of the structure illustrated here. It is one of the oldest surviving structures of biblical Jerusalem, which suffered more than its share of attacks and destructions. Another segment of Hasmonean wall has been located near the southeastern corner of the ramparts of the Temple Mount esplanade. This section, dating to Hasmonean times, made of roughly cut square stones, stands out in sharp contrast to the abutting larger ashlars carved in characteristic Herodian style.

Pediment of a 40 foot column (Attic style) in the Upper City

b. The Upper City and the Aqra

A large number of Hasmonean remains have been uncovered in the Jewish Quarter through excavations conducted by Professor N. Avigad on the occasion of its reconstruction. It is now definitely identified as the Upper City described by the historian, Josephus, the aristocratic quarter of the capital in which the Hasmoneans erected their palace, and where the elegant homes of the nobles, military leaders, and high priests were built. It overlooked the Temple Mount esplanade, the scene of solemn daily ritual, and the great festive occasions. The settlement and expansion of this quarter followed the capture of the Akra, the last stronghold of the Hellenizers. The exact location of the Akra is disputed, some scholars holding that it was in this quarter, while B. Mazar, in charge of the excavations of the Temple Mount, believes that it stood further south, on top of the Ophel ridge facing the southern gates.

Evidence of extensive Hasmonean construction in the contemporary Hellenistic style is offered by broken columns and the Corinthian or Ionian capitals which topped them. They were scattered about in the wreckage, but some have been reset on their bases. The standard size was about forty feet high and six feet in diameter, used in the construction of large and impressive buildings. The excavations carried out have uncovered, in addition, vast quantities of pottery and other ceramic remains dating to the third and second centuries B.C. Some of their handles bear the *Yhwd* impression in archaic Hebrew letters characteristic of Hasmonean ware.

Under the floor of one of the contemporary houses, a rich treasure of coins was found, some belonging to Alexander Jannaeus or Antigonus, and

The Hasmonean fortifications of the Ophel, with ramp and glacis on the right. The ramp meets a square tower at the left

The name of Jonathan
(Alexander Jannaeus) is
spelled between the horns
on the Hasmonean coin
Below:
Stone relief of cornucopia
depicting a pomegranate
between the two horns of
plenty

others to Herod. The excavation of a lower layer revealed only Hasmonean coins. Another important find in this building was a stone relief of a cornucopia and pomegranates, a motif found only on Hasmonean coins and familiar as the emblem of the royal house.

c. *The Gymnasium, Xystos and Wilson Arch*

Another fascinating relic of Hellenistic and Hamonean days is a small hall found in the Tyropoean vale facing the western ramparts of the Temple Mount, with the remains of a column which supported the roof, and the carving of a winged lion at the upper corner. The underground hall lies below the present level of the Old City of Jerusalem. According to B. Mazar, it is related to the Xystos, the site of the Hellenistic gymnasium famed for athletic games and other entertainment held there before the Hasmoneans banned them (*The Mountain of the Lord*, p. 215). The site abuts on the lower ruined arch (named the Wilson Arch after its discoverer) supporting an aqueduct which brought water to the Temple Mount from distant springs in the south.

d. *The Stairway and the Pools*

A further reminder of the times was a cache of weights dating to Hasmonean times found at the top of a long stairway, beginning in the grounds of the Church of Gallicantu. It connected the western quarter on Mount Zion with the Siloam pool situated at the outlet of the underground aqueduct dug by King Hezekiah (cf. Kings).

e. *The Hasmonean Pool of Bethesda*

This double pool which has since dried up was discovered just beyond the northern end of the Temple Mount esplanade. It was about 400 feet

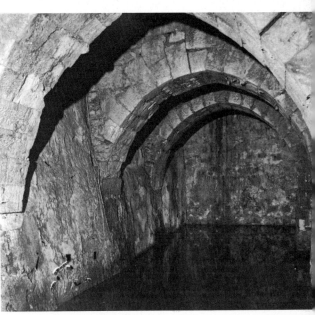

long, 200 feet wide, and 33 to 50 feet deep. At least a section of the pool was cut in the rock in Hasmonean times. Five rock-cut rooms in Hasmonean style were found there, to which access was gained by a flight of stairs which led to immersion rooms. A monument in honor of Alexander Jannaeus had been erected near the Bethesda pools. These pools, lying just outside the Temple area esplanade, adjoin a large number of other underground pools, passages, and corridors to the south, under the upper esplanade on which stands the Moslem shrine (the Haram es-Sherif).

f. Family Tombs in the Kidron Valley

Further evidence of the city's splendor, as attested in 1 and 2 Maccabees and Josephus, are the underground family tombs, cut into the bedrock of the Kidron Valley east of the Temple Mount, and the monumental mausoleums surmounting them, such as the priestly *Bnei Hezir* tomb. It consists of a porch and sepulchral chambers decorated with motifs borrowed from the Greco-oriental (Hellenistic) art of the time. The facade is decorated with Doric columns and a Hebrew inscription on the upper panel, identifying it with the distinguished priestly house.

g. Extent of the City in Hasmonean Times

These extensive finds attest to the rapid growth of Jerusalem in Hasmonean times and its economic prosperity. Greek historians who visited there say that its populaton exceeded 120,000, and that it was protected by three city walls. Its streets were paved and its markets packed with people and merchandise, a far cry from its diminished state in Nehemiah's time. The population estimate may be too high, however, although in the opinion of B. Mazar, it would suit the still greater city in the time of Herod the Great.

Above:
Lower reaches of the Pool of Bethesda, dating to Hasmonean times

Left:
The columned part of the Bnei-Hezir rock tomb in the Kidron valley (left) over the burial chambers

Ancient stairway descending from Mount Zion (Upper City) to the Ophel

B. HEROD'S PERIOD

1. DEVOUT AND RUTHLESS

Antipater's ascent to power, with the direct help of Julius Caesar, was accompanied by a division between the religious establishment under the Hasmonean Hyrcanus II, who bore the title of "High Priest and Ethnarch" and the civil government, with power vested in Antipater the Idumaean, who was named Epitrophos (Procurator). After his defeat of Matathias Antigonus, Antipater's son, Herod was enthroned king in 34 B.C., with Mark Anthony's backing. The Jews labelled him as the "King of the Jews," to distinguish him from a "Jewish King." His reign was immensely successful by the standards of the day, being long and prosperous; but his character, made up of ruthlessness, cunning and courage in equal parts, left something to be desired, and those who wrote about him reflected the fear and hatred he inspired in his people as well as grudging admiration for his magnificent achievements, which included the greatest building program in Jewish history. He favored the Hellenizing elements in Jerusalem society and the Jewish Diaspora, for administrative, diplomatic and military purposes. At the same time, he observed Jewish ritual closely and devoted great efforts and sums to the renovation of the Temple, his most notable accomplishment. His purpose, apparently, was to win over the disaffected rabbis and scribes who rejected his royal claims because he was not a descendant of David, or even of Jewish descent. Like his illustrious predecessor, he was a great leader and complex personality, whose commitment to the Jewish faith should not be discounted simply because his hands were stained with blood and his crimes so great. He safeguarded his position as a faithful vassal and ally of the Roman empire, and maintained close cultural and commercial ties with the countries of the eastern Mediterranean world. Ambivalence in his loyalties met different responses among the people: The more orthodox, and certainly the Essenes, distrusted him (as attested in traditional Hebrew writings and the Talmud), while the more cosmopolitan circles who were exposed to Hellenistic cultural influence, as well as the wealthier classes and Pharisees, appeared to appreciate both sides of the complex picture. He strengthened his ties with patrician Jewish families in the Hellenistic Diaspora and appointed successively high priests from such families as the House of Boethus. The period from his death in 4 B.C. until A.D. 70 witnessed the rivalry of two great priestly houses —Boethus and Hanan. It appears that Joseph Caiaphas, who collaborated with the Roman authority, was related to Hanan the First (i.e., his son-in-law, cf. John 18:13–14). Herod's family life was a disastrous combination of lust and jealousy, intrigue and suspicion, resulting in the murder of his sons, and the execution of his favorite wife. In his last years the alienated maddened tyrant wandered from one mountain fortress to another seeking peace and respite from a host of real or imagined enemies. He would then retire to the beautiful winter palace he had built on top of the mountain-rock of Masada (whose monumental structures were revealed by Y. Yadin's excavations) or he would seek water cures in the elegant baths of Calirrhoe, on the east of the Dead Sea.

2. HEROD'S MONUMENTS AND CITIES

By the second decade of his reign, Herod had expanded his kingdom to northern Palestine and large parts of northern Transjordan. Having secured his borders and increased his revenues, he undertook a vast building program. Around 20 B.C. began the reconstruction of the Temple. He enlarged the esplanade by building new retaining walls of huge trimmed ashlars, still visible at the lower levels of the Temple Mount on its western, southern and eastern contours. He rebuilt the fortress at the northwestern

The Courts of the Temple
and the Sanctuary

Above, right:
The Antonia Tower;
according to M. Avi-Yonah's
model of Jerusalem (Holyland
Hotel park)

Above:
Inner courts of the Hasmonean
palace facing the western
retaining walls and the Temple
site on the esplanade

end of the Temple esplanade, and named it Antonia in honor of Mark Anthony. He also erected a great palace on the western side of Mount Zion, which consisted of two main structures resting on a large podium, surrounded by elevated gardens and courts, and flanked by three massive towers. This royal administrative complex was also the headquarters of government throughout the Herodian era, and later it became the seat of authority of the Roman Procurators during the first century A.D. This is the actual site of Pontius Pilate's *Praetorium* referred to in the Gospels (though Christian medieval tradition places it at the head of the Via Dolorosa on the opposite side of the city).

South of the palace area rose Jerusalem's richest quarter, already known to us from Hasmonean times. It expanded south and east over the slopes of Mount Zion, as revealed in excavations conducted since 1976 by M. Ben-

Dov. The clearing of the lower slopes of the western walls of the Old City by Magen Broshi has exposed the enormous walls reconstructed in Herod's time. The city itself contained an amphitheater, a hippodrome, a theater, public squares and new paved streets, and colonnades which covered acres of ground, all of which still await the spade of the archaeologists. During the period in question, Jerusalem doubled in size and population, as a result of Herod's building operations and the increasing prosperity of city and country. In addition, tens of thousands swelled the population of the city at the annual festivals, especially Passover. In all respects, the remains and small finds in the Upper City (Mount Zion) of Hasmonean levels are surpassed in wealth and extent by the Herodian materials. Furthermore, a number of magnificent mausoleums were erected by priestly and patrician families in the Kidron valley and the increase in family-tombs around Jerusalem created an ever-widening necropolis. These are uncovered constantly as bulldozers clear the ground of expanding modern Jerusalem.

Herod enlarged the city of *Samaria* (which was called Sebaste, Greek for Augustus), and built in it a temple to Augustus Caesar. He dedicated other monuments to the Emperor, and paid an annual tribute estimated in millions of dollars in silver and gold pieces paid from the royal treasury. He reconstructed a sumptuous winter palace at Jericho. At a former Phoenician town on the coast, called Straton's Tower, he founded the city of *Caesarea,* and formed an artificial harbor by breakwaters, surmounted by towers. He built a great aqueduct to lead spring water into the city; he also improved the aqueduct which brought water to the reservoirs in Jerusalem. He fortified his borders with castles and strongholds, and donated funds for public buildings in many cities outside his own realm, including Antioch, Rhodes, and Pergamum. His winter palace at Jericho and his summer palace were marvels of architecture, as the excavations by J. L. Kelso and R. de Vaux have shown. The synagogues at Herodion and Masada, both constructed under his orders, are the oldest so far discovered.

3. HERODIAN STRUCTURES UNCOVERED BY THE EXCAVATIONS SINCE 1968

The excavations conducted by B. Mazar since 1968 around the Temple Mount — the most important archaeological undertaking in Israel — have helped to reveal many unsuspected aspects of life in first century Jerusalem before its destruction by the Romans. In addition, they have confirmed the extraordinary accuracy of architectural and topographical detail conveyed in Josephus' "Antiquities of the Jews" and "The Jewish War."

a. *The Tyropoeon and the Lower City*

The *Tyropoeon* vale which crossed the lower part of the city west of the Temple Mount and the paved road uncovered in sections amid remnants of municipal institutions, shops and arcades, were at the center of the daily life of the capital city, teeming with crowds and commerce of all kinds. The Tyropoeon road is shown skirting the gigantic supporting walls of the high Temple Mount esplanade and the gates which led through rising ramps to the Temple Mount courts. The road then ran under the aqueduct which passed over the Wilson Arch, branched south to the other gates and descended southeast to the ancient *City of David* or the *Ophel* built over the ancient Millo terraces. It then reached the Siloam pool at the southern end of the city, in the valley. Contrary to what was believed for a long time, this road did not pass under a viaduct which spanned the Tyropoeon vale from west to east, i.e. from the Upper City to the Temple Mount; instead, it led to the foot of a great stairway which rose to the so-called Robinson Arch and entered the Temple esplanade through a wide gate facing the southern,

Royal Portico or Ḥanuyot built by Herod (see Part XVII: Jesus at the Ḥanuyot).

The paved road which turned and rose eastwards to reach the southern gates met the southern approaches to the Double and Triple Hulda Gates, the plaza at the top of the Ophel and the great stairway (since reconstructed) over which the worshipers and pilgrims flocked daily, and in greater numbers on the holidays. On the way up the worshipers performed their purification rites in the numerous *mikvehs* or immersion baths carved into the rock of Mount Moriah (see Part XVII, 3).

Many sewers, gathering rainwater and refuse from the Temple grounds, were uncovered at the lowest levels and several underground passages were found in the lower levels under the esplanade. The network of ramps leading to the other Porticoes has been analyzed as well as its relation to the vast underground stores of the Temple built by Herod over the southern slopes of Mount Moriah (illustrated by the jacket picture of this book). Several inscriptions, stone fragments and ritual artifacts, as well as thousands of coins and other fragments attest to complex activity relating to the formal acts of worship and at the meeting places on the Mount (*The Mountain of the Lord,* New York and Jerusalem, by B. Mazar, D. N. Freedman and G. Cornfeld).

Below, left:
Subterranean chambers which lay beneath the wide stairway to the Hulda gates (the walled triple gate)

Below:
Ritual slaughter of a heifer

C. THE DEAD SEA SCROLLS

1. THE SETTLEMENT AT QUMRAN

The Dead Sea Scrolls are one of the most dramatic archaeological discoveries of the present century. The first seven scrolls were found in 1947 above the banks of Wadi Qumran near the northwestern shore of the Dead Sea, as a Bedouin shepherd chased a goat up the marl hill into a cave containing half-buried jars and scroll fragments. Several scrolls were acquired by E. L. Sukenik (father of the famed archaeologist, Y. Yadin) for the Hebrew University during the War of Independence in 1948; the rest were brought to the United States and were ultimately acquired by the government of Israel. They are all kept in the Shrine of the Book adjoining the Israel Museum of Jerusalem. Shortly after the first discovery several scholars and larger numbers of Bedouin, began the hunt for other scrolls; some were found in other caves to the north of that site, along with large numbers of fragments, and the largest single collection turned up in Cave IV, in the vicinity of Khirbet Qumran, the ancient settlement established by the sectaries who wrote and guarded the scrolls.

The site of the settlement was excavated by R. de Vaux in 1951–56. It is situated on the terrace of marl facing the wadi and caves. The 250 square foot enclosure and buildings used by the Qumran sectaries since the Second century B.C. had been incorporated into earlier remains of an old Judahite fort, built around the time of Josiah, in the seventh century B.C. and abandoned since the destruction of the Judean state by the Babylonians. It seems to have been part of an ancient town, "the City of Salt" (Josh 15:62).

The Qumran enclosure was entered from the north, protected by a massive three-story tower; a narrow court led from the gate to various parts of the enclosure. The other important rooms lie south of the tower. One hall is identified as the *scriptorium* where the scrolls were copied. To the east is another small court and around it were the kitchen, laundry, and some large reservoirs made watertight by several coats of plaster. A dam was built across the wadi from which an aqueduct and channels led to each cistern. South of this complex was the assembly hall, measuring 67x35 feet, a pantry still containing sets of dishes, more reservoirs, and a potter's workshop with two kilns, one for firing large jars of the kind used to store away the scrolls, the other for small vessels for daily use. The western part of the settlement contained workshops, stores, silos. Separated by a stone wall, a cemetery with at least 1,100 burials lay to the east of the settlement.

Qumran was resettled in the days of John Hyrcanus (135–104 B.C.) by the Dead Sea sectaries, probably a branch of the Essenes. It was destroyed and burned as the result of an earthquake in 31 B.C., then rebuilt in 4 B.C., and finally destroyed by the Romans in A.D. 68 at the time of the Jewish Revolt (Josephus, War IV, 449 ff.). A Roman garrison occupied it for another twenty years. The sectaries raised their food supply and tanned skins for leatherware or parchment at Ein Feshka, one and a half miles to the south.

The Covenanters were ruled by a council of twelve "princes" or lay leaders and three priests. Their affairs were administered by a *mebaqqer* or *paqid* who was regarded as the shepherd of his flock, and performed many of the same duties as the bishops of the early Church. The Essenes rejected private property in favor of the communal sharing of goods. The central group practiced celibacy, but other adherents of the community did not.

Ruins of *Qumran*, home of the Essenes. Some of the caves are seen above

2. THE SCROLLS

Most of the scrolls were made of animal skins and were written on the smooth side in the Hebrew square script with ink made from charcoal or iron. A few papyri fragments also were found. One scroll consisted of copper sheets riveted together, with the letters incised on the metal. Some were written in pre-Hasmonean, and other in Hasmonean times, and the last date to Herodian times up until A.D. 68. A number of documents, including the books of the Pentateuch and Job were written in the paleo-Hebrew script imitative of pre-exilic writing and Phoenician. The largest single document in this script is a partial manuscript of Leviticus. In a number of manuscripts in square script the word YHWH (the Tetragrammaton or sacred name of God) is written in the old script. About a quarter of all the manuscripts and fragments are biblical texts, which date between the middle of the third century B.C. to the middle of the first century A.D. They are earlier by a millenium than any previously known copy of the Bible (i.e., the Aleppo Codex of the ninth century A.D.), and as a group are an invaluable witness to a much earlier stage in the transmission of the biblical text.

The Aleppo Codex (Bible featuring 2 Chron 2:26–3:4) dates to the 9th c. A.D. and was written on parchment a thousand years after the Dead Sea Scrolls

In addition to the Old Testament books in Hebrew, all of which are represented at Qumran with the single exception of Esther, many of the Apocryphal and some of the Pseudepigraphic books are also present, including The Wisdom of Ben-Sira, Tobit, Jubilees, Enoch, parts of the Testaments of the Twelve Patriarchs, etc. (see above). Known heretofore from translations, the Apocrypha copies were in the original Hebrew and Aramaic. In addition to these, there were commentaries such as the Habakkuk *Pesher*, and elaborate paraphrases such as the Genesis Apocryphon (in Aramaic).

3. THE WRITINGS OF THE DEAD SEA SECT

For information about the sect itself and its organization and life-style, the best source is a collection of their manuals, hymns, and other edifying works, which may be classified as follows:

a. *The Sectarian Scrolls*

The Manual of Discipline from Qumran

Three main works may be considered under this heading: the "Manual of Discipline" — the most important — contains prescriptions for the annual ceremony at which the Covenant between God and the sect was renewed: the ideology of the Covenant sect; its laws and regulations, its principles of religion and law and rules of conduct. It concludes with a hymn of praise. The other composition in the Manual is a Rule for "All the Congregation of Israel in the Last Days," which will carry out the sect's precepts, and with an eschatology peculiar to the people of Qumran. The concluding composition is a collection of Psalms of Thanksgiving, *"Hodayot,"* to be included in a certain mystic ritual in the Last Days.

b. *The Damascus (Zadokite) Document*

This document, containing exhortations to the people to return to the true faith, is interwoven with the history of Israel, while it alludes also to the history of the sect. It reiterates many of the principal stipulations of the Manual of Discipline and formulates rules for the government of urban and rural societies, both of which were affiliated with the central group. The document avers that it was written by pious Jews who remained more faithful to tradition during the exile in Babylon. It mentions three classes: the priests, the levites, and the sons of Zadok, the traditional line of high priests. The "priests" were those Jews in Israel that repented and departed from the land of Judah; the "levites" were their associates, whereas the "sons of Zadok" were the Elect of Israel that were designated for the exercise of authority in the last days. They firmly believed that while prophecy and direct revelation from on high ceased, they, the *elect*, were blessed with a continuing revelation. The conviction that they were the elect remnant of the people of God, gave them an enormous self-confidence, and a dynamic optimism about the future in spite of present hardship and suffering. The document ends with rulings which correspond generally, though with important exceptions, to standard *halakhot* (rulings) of the Mishnah. A book similar to the Essene manual had been found in 1896 among ancient texts preserved in the *genizah* (depository of old and worn-out manuscripts) of the Cairo synagogue. It is commonly called the Damascus Document and indicates that there was a community in Damascus affiliated to the sect, with the same general rules. However some prominent scholars feel that the mention of Damascus is a disguised allusion to the Qumran community.

c. *The Commentaries*

Once the biblical books were canonized, it was imperative to have an authoritative interpretation for the use of later communities, and each of

Left:
Section of the *Pesher*
(commentary) of Habakkuk

Right:
"Thanksgiving" Scroll before
unrolling

these naturally interpreted the biblical oracles as it saw fit, using a variety of methods to arrive at the applicable truth. Thus at Qumran there were found a number of *pesharim* (commentaries) which provided contemporary applications of prophetic and poetic passages of the Bible. There are similarities between the sectarian approach and that of the early Jewish-Christians (see Parts XVII–XVIII). Both groups believed that they were living in the times of fulfilment of Old Testament prophecy and interpreted the older materials accordingly. There were distinct differences as well: Normative Jewish exegesis of a later period differed from both in important respects. Each of the scrolls begins with a biblical passage, followed by its commentary, then the next passage from the Bible was quoted, and another comment added. The ancient history of the original text was brought up to date by allusion to contemporary circumstances and in this way the background and experience of the sect and its principal leaders can be recovered to some extent.

The Commentary on Habakkuk is the most important among these works, and accords in general with the allegoric rabbinical style which attempts to translate the obscure oracles of this prophet into terms of the contemporary conflict between the faithful remnant and the unbelieving world (cf. Part XI; Minor Prophets: Habakkuk). The oblique references to the "wicked priest," his arrogance and materialism, are too vague to pin down the identity of that figure, though it applies only too well to the Hasmonean high priests from Jonathan, the brother of Judas, to Alexander Jannaeus.

The Nahum, Hosea and Micah Commentaries, on the other hand, are fragmentary and ambiguous, but their pattern of interpretation is similar.

d. The Teacher of Righteousness

This dominant but enigmatical figure in the community is described in the Habakkuk Commentary as having unique divinely given powers to interpret Scripture, and reveal the true meaning of the message of the pro-

261

phets (like Habakkuk). While it is clear that the Teacher was in direct opoosition to the then Heigh Priest and his Jerusalem establishment, and suffered along with his fellow Covenanters as a consequence of the persecution carried out by the former, there is no justification for identifying the Teacher as a messianic figure, or in speaking of a crucifixion or resurrection in connection with him. There are similarities with the figure of Jesus in the Gospels, but they have been exaggerated by sensation seekers. The correspondences can be explained in terms of their common background in the Jewish community and their instruction in the Old Testament. The differences are pronounced: Jewish-Christians and Essenes shared this common heritage, but parted company over the difference between Jesus and the righteous Teacher, and proceeded to diverge from that point.

e. *The Thanksgiving Scroll*

This scroll is a collection of hymns expressing the conviction of the Covenanters that in spite of their imperfections and sins, they belong to the elect of God, and in the great division between righteous and unrighteous, they will be saved from the fate of the wicked. The religious lyrics resemble the Psalms of the Old Testament, and often interweave words and phrases, sometimes whole verses from the earlier anthology. The Qumran Psalms are a link between the biblical psalms and the poetic elements of the New Testament, though no direct link between the Jewish-Christians and the Qumran sect can be demonstrated. The Teacher has been identified as the author of the Hymns, and they have been interpreted autobiographically by some scholars. It is more likely that, as in the case of similar usage in the canonical psalms, the use of the pronoun "I" is representative of the group, or simply collective.

f. *War of the Children of Light against the Children of Darkness*

For the Qumran sectaries, the world was divided in a cosmic struggle between the forces of good and evil, in which men and angels were ranged on both sides. This composition contains a prophecy of the coming war to be waged between the nations which rule the world, called *Kittim* of Ashur and of Egypt, the children of darkness, and the people of faithful Israel, the *Children of Light*. While the original setting, as in the book of Daniel, reflected the precarious position of the Jews in the time of the Ptolemies and Seleucids in the second century B.C., the present form of the composition points to the Roman period, because the description of military equipment and tactics seems to be derived from the manuals of the Roman army rather than any of its predecessors in the Near East. This is followed by regulations for the enrollment of the warriors in the *Holy War*, the strategy and ritual of the war, supplemented by a timetable indicating the vicissitudes of the Children of Light until they are triumphant over all the forces of darkness. Specific details are given about the trumpet calls, the signals to be given to the troops, and the arms and tactics to be used in the great battles. Its extant part concludes with prayers to be said before, during, and after the battle. The end is missing.

g. *The Copper Scroll*

Two rolls originally riveted together were discovered in another cave (III), one of the few finds made by archaeologists in the scroll hunt. They contain a list of hiding places containing fabulous treasures with instructions for reaching them. It is the opinion of most scholars that the treasures are imaginary, and that the list belongs to a genre well known in Jewish and pagan tradition in which great treasures of the past are described in elaborate detail, with descriptions of their hiding places. In the present instance, no reference is made to heroic figures of the past, and the treasure itself is not identified. But the amounts of silver and gold, and precious garments seem exhorbitant, and the locations, while identifiable in part, are too vague to permit actual search. The date of the Copper Scroll can be fixed around the middle of the first century A.D.

Perhaps the most important of the sectarian writings so far discovered is the famous *Temple Scroll,* which has been prepared for publication by Y. Yadin, and is now in press. It presents the sect's views on cultic and ritual matters, especially with regard to the Temple, that is a new Temple to replace the present one in Jerusalem. In this respect it resembles the last chapters of the book of Ezekiel with its visions of a new Temple, but according to Y. Yadin, the picture is both complicated and different. Another important find was a complete phylactery, which differs in important respects from the standard type.

The outer sides of a leather phylactery box after opening. The boxes were fastened to leather straps laid around the arm and forehead and contained portions of the Pentateuch written on parchment

4. BIBLICAL AND APOCRYPHAL BOOKS

Complete scrolls or fragments of all the books of the Old Testament were found, except the book of Esther. Cave I contained the most complete scroll, almost the entire book of Isaiah; another copy of Isaiah, less complete, was also found. In Cave VII was found a copy of the two books of Samuel (in a single scroll) but in very dilapidated condition. Since its text differs significantly from the standard Hebrew text, but resembles the Greek translation, it is regarded as perhaps the most important of the biblical manuscripts at Qumran. On the basis of its readings it is possible to recover an earlier and more reliable form of the text than hitherto has been possible. (See p. 259 on Apocryphal scrolls).

D. OTHER BRANCHES OF THE ESSENE MOVEMENT

1. IN THE REGION OF DAMASCUS

Before leaving Qumran, let us mention other groups of a similar nature. First of all, various scattered groups and their way of life are described by Josephus and the Alexandrian Jewish philosopher, Philo, but they were unaware of the existence or writings of Qumran and their specific way of life. Another important group had retired to the region of Damascus between 31–4 B.C., when they lived in camps or in the city. The region south of Damascus was fairly densely settled by Jews in the Greco-Roman period, and until the fourth century A.D. many Jewish, Jewish-Christian, and Gentile Christian sects were to be found there.

Prescriptions concerning family life in the Damascus group, their Sabbath rest and ritual purity are characteristics which reveal religious links with the Pharisaic groups or *habûrot* ("fellowships"). There are some differences between the rules for organization and practice between this group and the sectaries of Qumran, but they can be attributed to the historical development of the groups and their geographical displacement.

During this period there was also a lessening of eschatological tension in the Qumran community, superseded by a greater emphasis on the daily observance of the Law, as determined by the sect's priestly specialists. The apocalyptic community continued to wait for the *Messiah of Aaron* and the *Messiah of Israel,* the anointed ones who were to preside over the banquet of the end of the age that was prepared for the congregation. The presence of so many sets of plates and pots in the storerooms of Qumran indicates that outside devotees came there on pilgrimages.

2. OTHER HETERODOX SECTS OF SPLENDID ISOLATION

Besides the Syro-Palestinian branches of the Essene movement, we learn from Philo and Eusebius of Caesarea (fourth century A.D.) of the *Therapeutae* whose way of life was analogous to that of the Essenes. They were Jewish solitaries who lived in the region of Lake Mareotis near Alexandria. They had a religious feast of an unspecified type every few years, no doubt similar to the Covenant renewal festival of the people of Qumran. In addition, the *Ebionite* movement had developed as another offshoot of Essenism. From its modest beginning in the second century B.C. the Essenic movement and heterodox forms of Judaism spread throughout the Jewish world, reflecting the power of the "splendid isolation" which gave rise to the Hassidean movement. They and associated and derivative groups served as catalysts in each crisis that developed under religious and political persecutions (by the Greeks and later the Hasmonean princes). Being born out of an intense ideological crisis posed by the Hasmonean priest-kings, they persisted through the power struggles which followed the fall of the Hasmoneans and the Herodians. They were caught up in the great independence movements of the Jewish people in A.D. 66–70 and 132–135, and suffered the same fate as their counterparts. Only remnants survived, and these ultimately disappeared, merging back into Judaism or one or another of the Christian groups (cf. Parts XVII–XVIII). After the suppression of Jewish resistance in Jerusalem in A.D. 70, and Masada in A.D. 73, and the utter destruction of the short-lived independent Jewish State established by Bar-Kochba in A.D. 135, the rabbinic successors of the Pharisees alone enjoyed authority in the religious and social sphere, and were active in stabilising the form of Judaism that persists until today.

3. THE DEAD SEA SCROLLS AND THE NEW TESTAMENT

a. *Are There any Links between Them?*

Pharisaic Judaism and early Christianity represent different offshoots of Old Testament religion. The one emphasized the Law of Moses but in terms of oral tradition and the adaptability of ancient revelation to contemporary conditions. The other places stress on prophecy, on the fulfilment of divine promises in the messianic figure of Jesus and of divine sovereignty in the last days. It is clear that some Jewish-Christians, along with the Essenes of Qumran, stressed obedience to the Law of Moses as much as any other group of Jews, whether Sadducees, Pharisees, or Zealots, and in fact adhered more closely to the written code than the Pharisees who combined oral and written tradition and exhibited remarkable flexibility in applying the Law (Torah) to given situations. At the same time it is clear that the Essenes were closer to the Jewish-Christians in terms of messianic expectation and eschatological fulfilment, although they were at different points in the timetable. Thus the people of Qumran awaited both royal and priestly messiahs, while in the New Testament the term "Messiah" is clearly the Davidic king. At Qumran all is still future; only preliminaries have occurred, and the major events and people are yet to appear. For Jewish-Christians, the process of fulfilment is in full tide. The Messiah had appeared; he has been put to death and raised from the dead. Resurrection is not just a hope, but a reality, though not a historical fact.

Another historical line of development from the Old Testament is represented by Pharisaic and Rabbinic Judaism as the contemporary Mishnah and Talmud passages depict it. It is true that eschatological theology is already becoming stronger in the later books of the Old Testament (cf. Parts XIII–XV). We are aware that Old Testament apocalyptic writings share the specific Essenic doctrine of the end of days as well as dogma of the *Gzera Kedumah* ("foreshadowed fate") whereby God ordained the fate of every man for good or for evil, while the Covenanters of Qumran were chosen as "God's elect." Finally, the Pharisaic establishment respected and tolerated the visionary mystics and Essene sectaries, for they too believed in the eventual coming of the messiah. They deprecated, however, the extreme hopes of the visionaries and criticized those who "hasten his coming": They believed that the Kingdom would come when the people obeyed in spirit and in truth the Law and the Word of the Prophets.

b. *Conclusion*

There does not seem to be a direct derivation of early Christian doctrines or rites from the sectaries. Many of the parallels between Qumran and early Christianity can be explained from the apocalyptic materials in the Old Testament and the intertestamental literature (see above, A). Both early Christianity and Qumran had something in common with the early Pharisaic *habêrim*; like the Hassideans, they accepted the authority of Moses, were messianically inclined, and believed in the ressurection of the dead and final judgment. The Qumran teacher, however, made no claim to messiahship.

PART XVII

NEW TESTAMENT

A. INTRODUCTION

Restoration of the position in which an unknown first century Jew — with the legs adjacent — was crucified. This was determined from the skeletal remains found in his tomb in the northern necropolis (Giv'at Hamivtar)

The emergence of the Christian community in the first century is a distinct historical, cultural, and religious phenomenon for which the great bulk of the available evidence is to be found in the New Testament. The writings of Josephus and other historians provide useful background information, and occasional inscriptions shed random light on the movement in various parts of the Roman empire. The Jewish literature of the intertestamental period, as we saw yields substantial links between the Old Testament and the New Testament writings, and show how Jewish experience and thought produced significant modifications in traditional beliefs and patterns of practice, thus opening the way for the even more radical departures of Christianity. In this respect a significant forerunner of the Christian community was the Qumran settlement on the shores of the Dead Sea. The latter, however, had advanced beyond that stage to the moment of truth, when the Messiah had come, and his kingdom had appeared, consisting of disciples and followers of the way he had enjoined and by which he had lived and died, and been raised again to life. In addition to the new literary evidence for the background and origins of Christianity, recent archaeological excavation has brought to light a great deal of data bearing on the Jewish-Christian community in Palestine, its emergence, its differentiation and ultimate separation from the parent body. Eminent Franciscan and Dominican scholars have corrected earlier misconceptions and have contributed much to an understanding of the beginnings of the Christian movement in Galilee and other parts of the country. Recognition of this development and the information about it now available is indispensable for a comprehension of Christianity as the more radical offshoot from the trunk of post-exilic Judaism, the other being Pharisaic and Rabbinic Judaism which represented a creative version of a more orthodox line.

1. THE SETTING-IN-LIFE AROUND A.D. 1

Herod's kingdom was divided among his sons (4 B.C.–A.D. 6) but this seeming independence was short-lived. Herod's son, Archelaus, who ruled Judea, was disgraced and deported, and the government transferred to Roman procurators in A.D. 6. Their autocratic and arbitrary treatment of the Jews only emphasized the dramatic change in fortune that had overtaken the Jewish community since the days when they were an independent nation, ruled by a man of their own stock.

The only Jewish princeling who held out was Herod Antipas, another of Herod's sons, whom we meet in Jesus' story (Luke 12:32). He ruled in

Stone bearing the inscription mentioning Pontius Pilate, found in the Roman theatre at Caesarea

Right:
Northwestern side of the
Lake of Galilee (top left)
scene of many Gospel stories

Above:
Remains of the pagan shrine
at Caesarea-Philippi devoted
to the pastoral god Pan

No gentiles could pass beyond
the low balustrade *(Soreg)*
which encrircled the inner
Temple courts. Warning
inscriptions in Greek were set
there to that effect

northern Palestine. The general political situation outlined in our map is
the background of the events related in Gospels. On the whole, Roman rule
was regarded as the ordeal preceding the advent of a messiah. While the
Pharisaic and Sadducean majority maintained a shaky balance and prevented
an explosion against Rome — which came a few decades later under the
leadership of the Zealots — a minority of people, inspired by Hassidean and
Essene ideals (see Dead Sea Scrolls), faced the future in a different way. The
present world had to be endured, but their commitments, hopes and expectations were on the world to come. Again the eschatological visions of the
"End of Days" inspired many to repentance, and a renewal of vows of
obedience to God and his revealed will. A movement of this type was led
by John the Baptizer who preached in the Jordan valley (ca. A.D. 27). It
was a significant development as events proved, and though this activity
was not of a revolutionary type, it provoked the last of the pro-Roman
Herodian rulers and their Jewish allies to persecute its leaders, John and
Jesus, both of whom were put to death, and their adherents.

While these people suffered at the hands of their fellow-Jews as well
as the Romans, they evoked and expressed a feeling shared by most, against
the established authorities, a deep unhappiness with their present lot and
an irresistible longing for the days of the messiah, when everything that
was upside down would be righted. This was no less true of Palestine
than of the Jewish multitudes in the Greco-Roman Diaspora.

2. JESUS

These conditions provide the ideological background of Jesus' youth
and subsequent career. Though he was a fervent lover of his people and
his country, and would rather die than hurt the national interest, he was
not a revolutionary or Zealot as the Gospels and Paul explicitly describe him.
Jesus was born in Bethlehem, according to the Gospels, some time before
4 B.C., during the reign of Herod the Great. His home was in Nazareth
of Galilee, where he grew to manhood. His baptism by John was to trans-
form his life, and he retreated to the wilderness near Jericho (no contact

with nearby Qumran being known). The following years of his career in Galilee, as described in Gospels, were central. Though revered by some and rejected by others, he was both prophet and healer, the leader and teacher of a band of followers. His travels outside of the country or to Caesarea-Philippi in the north were apparently intended in part as escapes from the persecution of Herod Antipas' agents. When he ventured in his last journey on a pilgrimage to the Temple, he traveled through Peraea, east of the Jordan, to avoid setting foot on Samaritan territory, so as not to have any contact with the Samaritans, customary practice on the part of the Jews. He proceeded from there to Jericho and came to Jerusalem where he was met by an admiring crowd, which provided a triumphal welcome.

a. *Jesus at the Royal Portico and Hanuyot*

Jesus stayed in the house of Annas on the Mount of Olives and went down to preach in the southern Royal Portico. The majestic halls created by Herod were built, according to Josephus, of 162 monolithic columns, each 4.6 feet in diameter, with a Corinthian capital and rows of acanthus leaf decorations. The columned structure was three stories high and served several functions. It housed the section of the Ḥanuyot (= halls) to which the Sanhedrin moved in the days of Rabbi Gamaliel (known as Paul's teacher). Other public halls of the Ḥanuyot were used by money changers and dealers in ritual objects. These auxiliary precincts were probably differentiated, in the public eye, from the truly sacred areas within the *Soreg*

Left:
The earliest vestiges under the church of St. Joseph are remains of a Byzantine cathedral built over cisterns (right) stairs and a baptismal fount (center) situated in the ancient crypt. It was apparently used by the early Jewish-Christians for the mystic initiation rites of neophytes (see Part XVIII: Jewish Christians)

Above:
Ancient underground cave and silo situated under the Church of St. Joseph built over the biblical village of Nazareth

Left:
Reconstruction model of the Temple facade, seen from the historic Women's Court (The Holyland Hotel park)

Below:
Before entering the gates Jesus immersed himself in one of the *mikvehs* (ritual baths) situated nearby

(balustrade) beyond which no pagan was allowed to pass. Jesus, like other puritanical Jews, regarded their presence there as an intrusion of commercial affairs into places dedicated to the service of God, so he drove away the dealers. Christian tradition maintains that James, the brother of Jesus, was an ascetic Nazirite (not to be confused with Nazarenes or natives of Nazareth, which he happened to be, along with the rest of the family). He spent his days in devout seclusion, prayer, and study in the Temple precinct (though not in the inner Temple where the daily rites of sacrifice were conducted).

A large number of decorative columns and architectural fragments recently uncovered in the excavations of the Temple Mount, attest to the magnificence of the Ḥanuyot. These have been replaced by the vast El-'Aqsa mosque and its substructures.

b. *The Crucifixion and Site of the Praetorium*

In connection with the Passover festival, Jesus partook of the ritual supper with his disciples in the house of a notable on Mount Zion in the Upper City. It was the place of residence of the wealthy burghers of Jerusalem, as the excavations in progress there have revealed. He was betrayed and arrested shortly afterwards in the garden of Gethsemane, the site of olive groves and oil presses in the valley east of Mount Zion. The high priest refused to try him as a rebel and transferred his case to Pontius Pilate, the Roman procurator, then resident in Herod's former palace in the Upper City. Jesus was tried in the Praetorium hall for sedition as the alleged "King of the Jews" and ordered by the procurator to be crucified. The manner of execution, which was prescribed for crimes against state and emperor, is illustrated by a picture and diagram of a contemporary crucified Jew, later buried on Mount Scopus.

Unbiased scholarly opinion, convincingly presented by Père B. Benoit, maintains that Herod's palace situated in the Upper City, was the official residence of the Roman procurators in Jerusalem. Hence Pilate's Praetorium referred to in the story of the Passion of Christ was situated here. The street along which he carried the cross must have started from that point and led to the site of the crucifixion outside the city. walls (John 19:20b; Heb 13:12). However, medieval Christian tradition placed the *Via Dolorosa* at the opposite, eastern end of the Old City, and reinforced the choice by instituting the annual procession along the Way of the Cross for the benefit of the pilgrims. In view of the conflict with the archaeological evidence about the location of the Praetorium, questions have been raised about the traditional site of the crucifixion on the rock at Golgotha.

c. The Burial Site at Golgotha

According to the Gospels, Joseph of Arimathea, a member of the national asembly (*buletheros*) in Jerusalem and a believer in the "Kingdom of Heaven" removed Jesus' body from the cross and buried him in his family tomb. His followers, the first Jewish-Christians, believed that Jesus was raised from the dead the third day thereafter, and appeared to his disciples around Jerusalem, at Emmaus, and the Sea of Galilee. They also believed that some time after the Resurrection he ascended into heaven. This event was represented by inscriptions and art found in contemporary graves in Jewish cemeteries (see: What Are the Jewish-Christians?).

d. The Debate about the Burial Site

Regarded from the viewpoint of historical and archaeological data, the following is to be said: From early times Christians regarded the Holy Sepulchre as the site of Christ's crucifixion and burial. The place had been desecrated by the Romans who erected there a statue of Jupiter-Serapis,

Left:
Roof plan of the fourth-century Holy Sepulchre:
(1) Ambulatory; (2) Rotunda;
(3) and (4) lateral vestibules;
(5) southern atrium; (6)
courtyard of the Rotunda;
(7)Baptistry (8) Church of
Golgotha; (9) the Cross;
(10) Basilica of Constantine;
(12) eastern atrium; (13)
entrance; (14) Cardo
Maximus; (15) site of
Hadrian's Forum

In the middle:
The basilica which Constantine
erected prior to the
construction of the Anastasis
(Rotunda). An adjacent tomb
venerated under the open
sky, preceded the Rotunda

Right:
Reconstruction of the 4th c.
Rotunda

thereby making it impossible for believers to come there and worship, as
had been their practice. Though they kept away from the place, the Jewish-
Christians preserved the memory of the site until the time when Constantine
decided to erect a shrine to mark and protect the place of Christ's burial.
The tomb was exposed during A.D. 326/7 and work on the Church of the
Holy Sepulchre began. In the course of the church's reconstruction in
recent years, excavations conducted by V. Corbo uncovered a number of
important artifacts. They shed new light on the edifice erected there by
Constantine and his successors (fourth century A.D.) and put an end to
a century of debate over the true nature of the original shrine, the Anastasis (in Greek, resurrection) and the Rotunda over Christ's tomb. However, apart from authenticating the fourth century building, the question
of the burial site, of the crucifixion and burial remains unsettled.

It is known that in the days of Constantine the tomb stood uncovered
in a court and only was covered towards the end of the fourth century, by
a *Rotunda* or circular church 37 feet high and 40 in diameter. Independently
of this, Constantine erected a *basilica* over the bare rock of Golgotha. The
two construction sites stood apart until the tenth century.

A remarkable discovery in the excavations at the foot of the Temple
Mount deserves mention. A golden ring was found, with what appears to
be a representation of the dome of the original tomb shrine, the *Anastasis*.

As Jesus' crucifixion took place outside the walls, the identification of
the site depends first of all on locating accurately all the city walls then
in existence. No final agreement has yet been reached on this subject.

In conclusion, the different approaches of the traditionalists and the
scholars on the debated points may be summed up as follows:

1. The traditional view identifies the medieval "Via Dolorosa" in eastern
Jerusalem as the "Way of the Cross" to the place of crucifixion and burial.
The place of Golgotha and the tomb of Jesus are memorialized by the
Church of the Holy Sepulchre (see b. c. and d. above).

2. One scholarly view, taking into account the presence of the Third
Wall of Jerusalem several hundred yards east of the Church of the Holy
Sepulchre, regards the traditional location as doubtful at best.

3. A rival of the Catholic Golgotha is a rock tomb or the "Garden

In this map of Jerusalem, the Third Wall (No. 15, built in A.D. 41) stood far north of the ancient Second Wall (No. 14) near which stands the traditional site of the Tomb and Golgotha. Scholars argue over the relevance of these two walls to the point at issue: Was the Second Wall the northern limit of Jerusalem at the time of Christ? It must be observed that the city had expanded far north in Herodian times and King Agripa I built the Third Wall only a decade after the Passion. The problem cannot be resolved to the satisfaction of all

Left:
The excavations of the Third Wall proved conclusively, from finds at the foundations, that it was built in A.D. 41 as the northern city wall

Below:
Representation of the dome of the Anastasis on a gold ring discovered in the excavations at the Temple Mount (4th c. A.D.)

Tomb" which was "discovered" near the Damascus Gate, but still within the area circumscribed by the Third Wall; this is in all likelihood a Jewish family tomb dating to the days of the Second Temple or possibly the days of the First (see Map of Jerusalem; diagram of the Third Wall).

4. The most recent discovery bearing on this subject is that of a large group of cave-tombs, dating to the time of the Judean monarchy, underneath the Dominican cathedral of St. Etienne, which was built in the Byzantine period outside the Old City. These tombs seem to be part of the Jewish necropolis outside the walls of the city for several centuries B.C. As new evidence piles up, none of it decisive, traditionalists and skeptics will continue to argue these various points. It is not likely that the problem will ever be resolved to the satisfaction of all.

B. THE GOSPELS

1. THE CANONICAL TEXT OF THE NEW TESTAMENT: A SUMMARY

The only significant direct source for the beginnings of Christianity, apart from isolated references in contemporary literature and rudimentary archaeological data cited above, is the text of the New Testament itself. It is also the main source of our knowledge of the relationship between the Jews and the Jewish-Christians (the primitive church).

The four basic classes of literature in the New Testament are: The central message in the four *Gospels*; the history of the early church: the *Acts of the Apostles*; the Apostolic correspondence: the *Pauline and other letters;* and apocalyptic literature: the book of *Revelation*. This grouping corresponds to the order of books in the New Testament, but it does not reflect the chronological order of composition. While the Gospel traditions go back to earliest experiences of the disciples, the canonical Gospels did not appear in their present written form until a generation or two after the events they describe. It is generally agreed that the earliest documents of the New Testament are the Pauline epistles dating from the 50's and 60's of the first century.

a. Of these assorted documents the four Gospels deal with the life, death, and resurrection of Jesus, called the Christ.

b. The book of Acts is an account of the early Christian movement, emphasizing the missionary achievements of the followers, chiefly Peter and Paul. It closes with Paul under house arrest in Rome, awaiting trial before Caesar.

c. Thirteen books of the New Testament are letters attributed to Paul. Of these, the four great epistles: Romans, 1 and 2 Corinthians, and Galatians, are universally regarded as being authentic, while opinions differ about the others. Many scholars accept ten as genuinely Pauline, excluding the three Pastoral Epistles (1 and 2 Timothy and Titus) which seem to have been compiled by a follower on the basis of Pauline ideas and attitudes. Varying degrees of doubt are expressed about Ephesians, 2 Thessalonians, and Colossians, but Philippians, 1 Thessalonians and Philemon are almost certainly genuine.

d. The general or catholic epistles number seven, and are attributed to various disciples and followers: John (3), Peter (2) James, the brother of Jesus (1), and Jude, the brother of James (1).

e. The epistle to the Hebrews, has traditionally been assigned to Paul, but there is no basis for this opinion, as the work differs markedly from all of the Pauline letters. It is an anonymous work of the latter part of the first century stemming, as does the book of Revelation, from Jewish-Christian cicrcles.

f. The last book of the New Testament, like Daniel, is an apocalyptic work which forecasts the sequence of events in the last days, which are now coming upon the world. The great struggle between the forces of good and

Opposite page:
Below, left:
Entrance to the 'Garden Tomb', presumed, since 1882 to be the tomb of Christ, according to General C. G. Gordon's theory

Below, right:
The inner tomb. This may also be part of the northern necropolis ringing Jerusalem since the latter days of the Judean Monarch. Notice the bench on which the body was laid

Above, right and the two, middle, left:
A cistern and wine press discovered near the site by Dr. Schick in 1890, dating to Second Temple days. The cistern, marked by a cross, may have been used as a meeting place of early Christians

Above, left:
One of the tombs of Jerusalem's necropolis, dating to the end of the Judean Monarchy, found near the St. Etienne cathedral. Notice the characteristic stone bench and 'pillow'

light, and the forces of evil and darkness, will culminate in a complete triumph for God and the Lamb, the crucified and risen Lord.

2. THE SYNOPTIC GOSPELS

The principal source for the life and ministry of Jesus is the four-fold Gospel. These documents in turn were dependent on older sources and represent a series of reworkings and restructuring of the earlier traditions.

a. *Sources*

What led to the writing of the books that are called Gospels, meaning "good news"? Modern Bible study stipulates the existence, prior to the written Gospels, which we now possess, of comparatively early Palestinian and other tradition-cycles, some oral, some written, of the "Sayings of Jesus," the so-called "Q" source, and stories about Jesus, especially the narrative of his last days on earth. Their purpose was to bear witness to Jesus Christ. Hence, they told the story of the coming of Jesus among men, his words and deeds, his suffering and death, his resurrection and exaltation. The word Gospel became established in the vocabulary of the early church as the technical term for the message of salvation proclaimed by the evangelists.

b. *General Plan*

Due to the marked similarity of the subject matter, the order in which their material is presented, and their language, the first three Gospels of the New Testament are generally referred to as *the synoptic* (Greek: having or taking the same point of view) Gospels. If the data in these three Gospels were to be arranged side by side in parallel Columns so as to be seen at a glance, the inter-relationship among them would be clearly visible. The agreement among them can extend to the smallest details, as for instance:

Mark 12:36–37	Matthew 22:43–45	Luke 20:42–44
6:41–43	14:19–20	9:16–17
2:10–12	9:6–7	5:24–25

In fact, practically all of the contents of Mark can be found in Matthew, and much of it in Luke, because they share some common sources. Equally impressive, however, is the element of divergence. For example:

Mark 10:17	Matthew 19:16	Luke 18:18
8:29	16:15–16	9:20
10:46	20:29–30	18:35
1:12–13	4:1–11	4:1–12
6:8–9	10:10	

The distinctive style and special purpose of each Gospel cautions one against superficial blending or harmonizing of the three synoptics. The differences are at least as important as the similarities in analyzing and evaluating the material and in determining such questions as date, authorship, provenance, objective, and the like.

In fact, practically all of the contents of Mark can be found in Matthew, differently by different traditions, and that each author would record the material either in the words which were handed on to him or in his own words, in order to express more clearly his understanding of the tradition. In addition, the material has been transferred from a Semitic context in which Aramaic and Hebrew were used, to the Greek language which was common to the Mediterranean world.

For well over a millennium, the opinion expressed by St. Augustine, that the canonical order of the Gospels likewise reflected their correct chronological order, held sway in the scholarly circles of the church. However, as the synoptic Gospels were subjected to closer scrunity, their parallelisms analyzed and their relative contents compared, it became increasingly evident to many scholars that the Gospel of Mark predated those of Matthew and Luke. It was argued as well that both Matthew and Luke were acquainted with Mark, and adopted or adapted his materials in their Gospels. Since Matthew and Luke have material in common which is not found in Mark, it was deduced that they used another source, Q (which consisted mostly of sayings). Finally Matthew and Luke each have materials not found in the other Gospel, and these are regarded as deriving from separate sources or the evangelist himself. The four-document hypothesis: 1) Mark; 2) Q (material not in Mark common to Matthew and Luke); 3) M — Matthew, special source; 4) L — Luke, special source — is still held by the majority of New Testament scholars, but in recent years, especially, there have been numerous challenges, and different scholars argue for the priority of Matthew, and the independence of Luke; but nothing has yet displaced the Markan-Q Synoptic hypothesis.

c. Differences with Matthew and Luke

There are, nevertheless, certain significant differences between Mark and the other two, mainly in relating the words of Jesus, Matthew's Gospel is arranged around five discourses, the rest and most familiar being the Sermon on the Mount. There is a familiar discourse in Luke, but not in Mark. Accordingly, most scholars have distinguished in the Gospels between the *narrative* and the *discourses* (what Jesus *did* and what he *said*). It is an accepted tenet of New Testament scholarship that the Gospels are not intended as a biography of Jesus in the modern sense, but rather reflect the apostolic teaching of what Jesus did and what he taught (Acts 1:1). They are a statement of the faith of the early Christians, founded on the historical fact of Jesus, and preached as a lesson to the world.

The generally accepted assumption that Mark preceded Matthew and Luke is, however, only a partial solution of the synoptic problem, for Matthew and Luke have some two hundred verses of material which they share in common and which is not contained in the Mark Gospel. These passages consist largely of the sayings and teachings of Jesus, including for instance the Sermon on the Mount (Matthew 5–7). The fact that this also appears in Luke (in a different form and arrangement) but not in Mark points to the existence of another literary source aside from Mark. Though

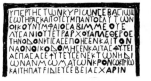

Luke twice attempts to provide a chronology for his story. He names "Lysanias the tetrarch of Abilene" (3:1) one of the contemporary governors, identified by a votive inscription found near Damascus. He mentions also Cyrenius, governor of Syria (2:1–2) apparently identical with Quirinius referred to in the broken Roman inscription

A page of Papyrus Bodmer II containing John 11:31–37

the source is no longer extant in an independent form, it is commonly referred to as Q, as mentioned above. Another significant difference between Mark and Luke has been noted by D. Flusser in determining the origin of the so-called Synoptic apocalypse in Luke 21:20–24, (paralleled by Mark 13:14–26, and echoed by Matthew). This will be discussed below.

Eusebius (*Ecclesiastical History* iii. 39, 15; fourth century A.D.) quotes Papias, Bishop of Hierapolis, ca. A.D. 140, as reporting that Matthew composed the *Logia* (source or tradition) in Hebrew (i.e. Aramaic) and that "everyone interpreted them" (i.e. translated them) into Greek. For some time it was assumed that these Logia represented the Q document but modern scholarship is growing increasingly skeptical of this theory. The "Logia" (words about rather than of Jesus) may be an original Semitic Gospel of Matthew. Scholars today are also inclined to believe that the language behind Matthew was probably Hebrew, not Aramaic, and they accept Papias' statement as literally exact, although it is still not certain just what the Logia were.

d. *Mark and John*

The relation of the fourth Gospel to Mark is more difficult to assess. John has a different outline. Where there is common ground with the three Synoptics, there are some striking phrases not in Matthew and Luke, but common to Mark and John, e.g. loaves costing 200 dinarii (Mark 6:37; John 6:7); pure nard (Mark 14:3; John 12:3); pallet (Mark 2:11; John 5:8).

The accidental discovery of Christian papyrus fragments, namely Papyrus 52, Egerton Papyrus 2, John Rylands Fragment, Bodmer papyri, has shown that the Gospel of John circulated in Egypt early in the second century A.D. It is once again acceptable to hold to a comparatively early date for the composition of the Gospels, especially Mark and Luke, though it is generally agreed that the evangelists were not themselves Apostles or directly involved in the events described.

e. *Christian Writings of the Second Century*

We find in extant Christian writings of the first half of the second century A.D. many indications of knowledge of the Gospels, especially the teachings recorded in them: In the period A.D. 90–120, Clement of Rome (96), Ignatius (ca. 115), Polycarp (ca. 115). In the period A.D. 120–150: The "Didache" (which has many primitive elements and in its original form much older), Papias, "Shepherd" of Hermas. At mid-century: Justin Martyr probably refers to Peter's "memoirs which, I say, were composed by His apostles and those who followed them." Tatian (ca. 170), in his "Diatessaron," made a harmony of the Four Gospels, while with Irenaeus (ca. 180), Clement of Alexandria (ca. 200), and others begins the period of clear citations and quotations from the four canonical Gospels.

278

C. RECENT DISCOVERY AND GOSPELS

1. THE MYSTIC GROTTO OF BETHLEHEM

For purposes of worship, the Jewish-Christians of Palestine availed themselves not only of the synagogues, but also developed their ritual in certain "sacred and mystic grottoes" as reported by the ecclesiastical historian, Eusebius of Caesarea. In their worship in this "Lord's house" in Bethlehem which was carried on there till the fourth century, they celebrated two of the "three mysteries" par excellence: Mary's virginity and her bringing forth the Christ child; the third mystery was the death of Christ. Because of its mysteries, this Bethlehem grotto, though dark, was bound up in the minds of the Jewish-Christians, with the concept of light, i.e. the effulgence which filled the place at the birth of Jesus. They had a deep devotion to the grotto for yet another reason, at it represented the incarnation or first descent of Christ to earth from heaven.

The mystic grottoes were associated with their doctrine of the "descent" and "ascent" of Christ and his initiated ones. He descended from heaven and rested in Bethlehem under the earth. For them the Bethlehem grotto became a symbol of the passage of the soul from darkness to light. Beth-

Inscriptions found in Peter's house. 1–6 name Jesus and Peter. 7–8 derive from an eschatological citation of 3 Baruch

The octagonal Byzantine church (foreground) standing on the site of Peter's house (1st c. A.D.) was used as a cult place in the second century. It is related historically with the Capernaum synagogue mentioned in Gospels. Remains of the hall of the later third-century synagogue appear in the background

The Bethlehem grotto. The niche on the left is the birth place of Jesus and the manger is on the right. The grotto became a symbol of passage from darkness to light

lehem also came to stand for the church of the gentiles, in the person of the Magi, to whom the star appeared. On the other hand, Jerusalem was the symbol of the Church of the Circumcision, as the Jewish-Christian community was known. Hadrian profaned the site by planting a wood over the grotto, but this helped to maintain the tradition of the birthplace of Jesus.

2. CAPERNAUM AND ITS REMOTE TRADITIONS

a. Peter's House

Considerable material was brought to light at Capernaum, some of which bore on the location of Peter's house, and his association with the mission among his fellow Jews. The house was built about the first century B.C. It became a center of religious activity, i.e. a house-church or meeting house, already in the second half of the first century A.D. *Minim* (as the Jewish-Christians were later called) were numerous and lived continuously in Capernaum and kept alive this tradition; their graffiti on the plastered wall of the place of worship testify to their faith in Jesus, the Christ, the Lord, the Most High and Good, and to their veneration for Peter, the local saint. Non-Jewish Christians took over the sanctuary in the middle of the fifth century and built the splendid octagonal church with baptistry, which was uncovered in 1971 and 1972. A Spanish pilgrim, Aetheria, states "that the house of the chief of the apostles has been turned into a church." The pilgrim of Piacenza (ca. A.D. 570) also relates that the house of Peter had given way to a place of worship.

Rooms south of the house of Peter with stone pavement (1–2). Foundations of the octagonal church (3–4)

b. The Synagogue

The well known synagogue of Capernaum was built in the 3rd or 4th century as a rectangular basilica as attested by a hoard of some three thousand coins found under the mortar of a pavement and another of six thousand found in the courtyard. It has been restored in recent years by Father G. Orfali, with additional work in progress, or being planned.

Though Capernaum is a holy place for Christians and not for Jews nowadays, it may be noted that Jewish and Jewish-Christian communities had lived side by side and constructed their religious buildings in the same quarter. The two Jewish communities differed in personality and spirit and had different "committees" There is no written evidence of their rivalry, though this was possible.

3. THE ROCK OF CALVARY AND THE MYSTIC GROTTO

What, archaeologists ask themselves, was the rock of Calvary in fact? It is almost completely enclosed by the exiting Byzantine monument, but Father C. Couasnon gives us some new clues based on the 1961 excavations conducted by V. Corbo. A quarry bed was found below the mystic Adam's Chapel (see below) west of the rock, with an ancient cistern nearby. This suggests that the rock of Calvary was an isolated vertical block in the ancient quarry. A cavern which communicated with the underground cistern could, in relation to the vertical block, have been a tomb. Couasnon suggests that the vertical block was the *nephesh* (funeral monument) of a Jewish tomb similar to those erected in the Kidron valley in the second and first centuries B.C. In time, a mound was formed through the accumulation of earth around the rock, while only a bare rounded tip emerged, like a skull-cap or Golgotha. A stone's throw away, the tomb of Joseph of Arimathea had been cut into the rock face of the quarry.

4. THE MYSTIQUE OF THE TOMB OF ADAM

In the second century or possibly before, mystical speculation born of the Jewish-Christian milieu of Jerusalem, had transferred the legend and site of the presumed "tomb of Adam" from Mount Moriah to Golgotha. The crack in the rock below the top of Calvary, still visible and venerated today, the belief that Jerusalem was the hub of the world, the siting of Adam's grave there, and the localizing of the deeds of the patriarchs, all contributed to the formation of a mystique centering on the spot. The second Adam was to make good all the damage brought about by the first Adam, even to triumph over death. This tradition is not far removed from Paul's theology who saw in Christ the "New Adam" taking the place of the former Adam, and atoning for his original sin (Rom 5:12 ff.).

This train of thought around Calvary was far earlier than the neo-Christian fervor of the fourth century, which caused and witnessed the exposure of ⁻⁻⁻⁻⁻⁻⁻⁻⁻⁻⁻ist and the erection of a shrine over Calvary by Contanu... ......s. On the other hand, this idea of Golgotha as the place of the skull of Adam, which lent itself to enriching spiritual consequences, pleased the Fathers of the Church and the devout penitents and pilgrims to the Holy Sepulchre. In any case, without regard to the Jewish-christian mystique of the Cosmic ladder, the legendary myths about the grotto of Calvary have been preserved by Catholic and eastern churches to 's day (see below: First Century A.D. Jewry and Jewish-Christianity).

D. THE EVANGELISTS: EDITORIAL STAGES AND ARCHAEO- LOGICAL BACKGROUNDS

In the process of the formation of the Gospels, two distinct stages must be recognized: (a) The transmission of the oral tradition by the early religious community, and (b) the editorial redaction by the evangelists. In the earlier stage, the community provides the setting in which the different units of tradition are shaped, in terms of its needs and purposes, while the role and impact of the creative individual are diminished. In the latter stage, the community tradition is reworked by the evangelist, who, while bound by the common creed, the common commitment, and the common interpretation and who is a member in good standing of the group, nevertheless exercises his own judgment, puts his own stamp on the material, and formulates the essential "good news" in his own way and after his own word. Comparison of the resultant Gospels shows the range of divergence resulting from the differences among the communities by which the Gospel tradition was given form, and the discretion exercised by the individual evangelists in setting down their version of the message.

Distinguishing the effects of the different stages of development is not easy, but the particular contribution of the evangelists can be identified in terms of interpretive comments, selection, modification, ommissions and additions of material, summaries and conclusions, reflecting a long process of editing and revising.

The limited compass of this book does not permit a detailed analysis of the Gospels, and we must limit ourselves, therefore, to recent discoveries bearing on the interpretation of the Gospels and new assessments emerging from recent investigation. We will see below (Jewish-Christianity) that the material remains provide authentic background for the central tradition of Gospels and the life of the early church in which it received its basic shape.

1. MATTHEW

In relation to the Gospel of Matthew, we have selected the following topics for discussion:

a. *The* ~ *on the Mount*
    three chapters (5–7) that make up the "sermon on the mount" are not considered the transcript of a discourse delivered all at one time by Jesus, but rather are a collection of sayings pronounced at different times and under varying circumstances drawn from a number of partly written and partly oral sources. In spite of its heterogeneous origin, it constitutes a remarkable compendium of the ethical teachings of Jesus, giving a very clear impression of the style and content of his message. The end result is the work of Matthew who was not simply an amanuensis, but an imaginative and creative editor, concerned to present the tradition in a specific way to a specific audience. According to W. D. Davies, it was the church which "took what was radical,

modified it, and made it regulatory" and that this process "is contained and continued in the Christian-Rabbinism of Matthew, where we see slowly emerging a neo-legalistic society." (W. D. Davies, *The Setting of the Sermon on the Mount,* New York, p. 701). Moreover, in support of his doctrine of messianic fulfilment, Matthew cites the Old Testament at every turn, often quoting verses out of context or imposing a meaning upon them that seems forced, to illustrate and emphasize the central idea that in Jesus Christ all the lines of prophecy and promise have come to fruition. The Old Testament is understood to be predictive in all its parts, everything in it (explicitly, implicitly, or presumably) pointing to the figure of the Messiah, Jesus. While from the point of view of scientific, historical, and linguistic exegesis, such an approach gives a distorted picture of the material in the Old Testament, and derives from Old Testament passages meaning and implications which the authors did not intend, the purpose of Matthew and the community must be understood and respected. Once it had been established that Jesus was the messiah (chiefly because of the resurrection attested by eye-witnesses apart from scriptural references and arguments), then it was both permissible and desirable to read this *datum* back into and out of the scripture upon which they relied as the bed rock of their faith: the Old Testament. In short, the Old Testament was not used to prove Jesus' messiahship, which was established on other grounds, personal and group experience, eyewitness testimony; but once it became an article of belief, then the Old Testament was ransacked to illustrate, elaborate and articulate that conviction.

b. *Matthew Modifies the Older Source*

As an illustration of this tendency, modern scholarship has noted that Matthew took liberties in changing and modifying the Old Testament Scriptures quoted. But he went further by using an ever freer hand in modifying and rearranging documents not protected by Jewish scriptural sanctity, namely sources of a popular character like Q and Mark, in putting together his gospel. His account of the triumphal entry changes Mark's record. The result is that Jesus rides on two donkeys into Jerusalem. In the sequel he changes Mark's account (Mark 11:1–11) of the return to Bethany, with Jesus coming back the next day to drive the traders from the Temple. Matthew, on the contrary, states that Jesus drove them out immediately after his arrival at the Temple (Matt 21:12–17; Mark 11:15–19; Luke 19:45–48). In his account of the resurrection (Matt 28:1–12 in contrast with Mark 16:1–8), Matthew says the women ran and told the disciples what they had seen, while Mark recounts that they came to the tomb early that Sunday and were frightened when they found it empty. Out of admiration for Peter, Matthew transferred the saying (Matt 18:8 ff.) to a new context and to rewrite it so as to give Peter alone authority which Jesus gives to all the disciples alike.

2. MARK

In the Gospel of Mark, the following historical and archaeological items deserve notice:

a. Nazareth, from the First to the Fourth Century A.D.

What do we know concretely about first century Nazareth? In the first two centuries A.D., it was a modest village built on rocky soil in a valley far from the main trade routes. By the third century, however, there was a revival of interest in the town on the part of Christians, who knew it as the home town of the family of Jesus, where mementoes and memorials were preserved. Two excavations, one led by Father P. Viaud, the other by Father Bagatti, led to the discovery of the traditional site of the Annunciation to Mary and the places which Jesus frequented as a growing lad. Other discoveries included a large complex of caves, silos, cisterns, oil vats, wine presses; of mosaic floors, numerous graffiti, inscriptions, drawings and symbolic signs. These constitute important evidence of the religious life of the Jewish-Christians, preserved beneath the foundations of the two later shrines in Nazareth, as they were described in a report to Constantine. Ancient inscriptions and archaeological discoveries at Nazareth bear witness to a Jewish-Christian cult of Mary there, at a very early time. The primitive shrine was erected by Jewish-Christians who used it for worship. They were natives who remained in the area, holding on to the property, and preserving the traditions about the family of Jesus and the shrines of Nazareth. They were followed in the third and fourth centuries by the faithful of Gentile origin. The magnificent basilica of the Annunciation is late Byzantine.

b. Interpreting the Last Supper

According to the Synoptic Gospels, the Last Supper was the Jewish Passover meal, while according to the Gospel of John, it preceded the Passover by one day. While there has been considerable debate as to which tradition is correct, and no final resolution has been reached, there can be no doubt about the paschal overtones of the meal. While none of the accounts provide details of the Passover celebration, and the correlation between the Last Supper and the Passover meal are inexact at best, there is a strong emphasis on Jesus' role as the mediator of a new covenant who offers himself as the paschal lamb. It is a witness to the "Christ, our Passover sacrifice for us."

c. Genuine Holy Places and Later Christian Monuments

It has been observed that the early Jewish-Christians (until the fourth century A.D.) marked sites sacred to them by modest monuments, rather than impressive buildings. Examples of this practice are found in the oldest foundations of the Church of the Holy Sepulchre in Jerusalem, in Nazareth, in Bethany, and in the Tomb of the Virgin in Jerusalem. The erection of a modest baptistry without a church structure identified it as a holy place.

Other topographical points of reference have been preserved in the traditions surrounging the "holy places" in Israel. They were "rediscovered" by the official church during the era of Constantine. Previously, the information and traditions about them had been kept by the native Jewish-Christians. Among them, the mystic grottoes very early became places of worship: Eusebius lists Bethlehem, the Mount of Olives, and Calvary. These were not

Christianized pagan shrines, but ancient Jewish-Christian sites associated with memories of the life of Jesus. Some of them were profaned by Romans who had used them for their own cults, and were then "rediscovered" at the time of the Constantinian restoration. Since that time the Christian monuments have been embellished, extended, and restored by different groups at different times. Since the Middle Ages especially, competing Christian communities have attempted to control the holy places, and thus benefit from the steadily increasing flow of pilgrims to the Holy Land. As a result, identifications of sites became confused, sacred traditions were transferred from place to place, and in the process authentic memorials and attested locations were lost. Had it not been for the emergence of modern scientific archaeology, the confusion of conflicting claims and the multiplication of spurious sites and manufactured traditions would have been complete and permanent. Thanks to controlled excavations, and dispassionate evaluation of data, it has been possible to sweep away the cobwebs of prejudice and sentimentality, and to recover authentic data from the earliest days of the Christian community in the Holy Land.

d. The Jewish-Christian Character of the Pre-Constantine Era

The Jewish-Christian nature of these and other sites has not been widely recognized, because the data have been available for a relatively short period of time, have been treated in piecemeal fashion, and have been the object of study of a very limited group of Jewish and Christian scholars. Moreover, pilgrims and tourists are usually shown the more spectacular post-Constantinian "holy places" thus perpetuating the errors of earlier times. The archaeological discoveries, however, have been confirmed by literary sources which attest to the existence in these early times of Jewish-Christian culture, as shown by J. J. Danielou, L. Bagatti, and Father Testa, in their research. A comparison of the symbols drawn on the ossuaries and those found in the literary texts of the early church shows that they belong together: e.g., the cosmic ladder, the eight-pointed "ogdoad" stars, the plow, the palm, and others. The strange sects described by Epiphanius, Eusebius, Jerome were Jewish-Christian communities living on the fringes of the "Great Church" (cf. Part XVIII, C).

3. LUKE

a. What Kind of Jew Was Jesus?

Let us begin by asking what the Synoptic Gospels suggest by their general content to have been the prevailing interests to which the words of Jesus were directed or responded, and how these words define the person who uttered them, or convey his central thoughts. Among them certain statements and expressions of attitude stand out.

b. Luke's Attitude to the Gentiles

In Luke 4:25–27 there is an anticipation not simply of the Gentile mission, much less of God's rejection of Israel and turning to the Gentiles, but rather of Jewish-Gentile reconciliation, i.e. the consecration of Gentiles which will make it possible for faithful Jews and Gentiles to live and eat together in the new age. How does this passage fit with the painful Nazareth episodes and, incidentally, with Luke's attitude to the Jewish-Gentile question? In his treatment of the problem, Luke takes the position that despite what happened at Nazareth, and the continuing hostility between Jew and Gentile, the destiny of both groups is bound up with Jesus; it is God's intention to save and heal both together through him.

c. *Jesus' Attitude to His Fellow Jews, and the Eschatological Discourse*

In the eschatological discourse, Jesus prophesies with deep anxiety about the impending destruction of the Temple (Luke 21:20–28). This, in fact, provides one of the most important clues to the significance of the Gospels and Acts, as it illustrates the social and religious situation of the groups who are at the center of the New Testament (see below).

The suggested attribution of Luke to an earlier date (before the destruction of the Temple) stems, among other things, from the eschatological discourse cited above. In the view of R. S. Lindsey and Professor D. Flusser, Luke's rendering is more original and much nearer to the earliest written sources than that of Mark. (R. Lindsey, *Novum Testamentum* VI, 1969, pp. 239 and 243–444; D. Flusser, *Israel Exploration Journal*, 1971, pp. 226–236). There is reason to believe that in essence, passages about the eschatological deliverance of Jerusalem represent Jesus' own words. Even in its earliest stages, the Lukan discourse was apparently a collage of various "sayings" of Jesus. Jesus is quoted as saying that "Jerusalem will be trodden down by the Gentiles until the times of the Gentiles are fulfilled... when these things begin to take place, look up and raise your heads, for your redemption is drawing near."

For Jesus and Paul nothing less than the total salvation of their people was in mind, as the New Testament documents show. The word "redemption" is to be understood in the specifically Jewish sense of liberation from Roman rule and the restoration of sovereignty to Israel. In Jewish eschatological thought the idea that the darkest hour must come before the brightest was deeply rooted; before the Messianic Age must come the messianic woes. Jesus' disciples shared the same hopes and fears as other Jews of the period. Jesus himself felt closely bound to the emotions of his compatriots. His disciples were committed to him personally and to the Jewish people. Thus, the prophecy seems to fit the Jewish context and adheres to the scheme of similar prophecies in the Old Testament. It also has a parallel in Revelation 11:1–2. In Acts 1:6–8 the hope for the restoration of the kingdom of Israel is also expressed. The resurrected Jesus there states that it is not possible for his disciples to know the time of the national liberation; their mission impossible is simply to bring Christ's message "to the end of the earth." Behind Luke's story lies the hope that the kingdom will yet be restored to Israel. But until that happens "this gospel of the kingdom will be preached throughout the whole world, as a testimony to all nations; and then the end will come" (Matt 24:14).

There are good grounds to believe that Paul was aware of the Lukan form of Jesus' words concerning Israel's doom "until the times of the Gentiles are fulfilled' and that he and his contemporaries understood Jesus to be saying that Israel would at last attain complete salvation, after the Gentiles had been converted to the message of the Gospel. Hence his famous words, "A hardness has come upon part of Israel, until the full number of the Gentiles come in; and so all Israel will be saved (Romans 11:25-26). In this way, apparently, the original prophecy of the final liberation of Jerusalem from the yoke of the Romans and the eschatological redemption of the people was eventually interpreted as a prophecy of the acceptance of faith in Christ by both the Gentiles and Israel. This is essential to an understanding of Paul's thesis.

d. The "Witness" Function in Luke

Why did Luke expand the travel account from Galilee to Jerusalem, as compared to Mark's brevity? In this story, the witness function is attested in Acts 13:31, which defines those witnesses who went up with him and to whom he appeared for many days. This accords with Acts 1:21 ff. for the prerequisites for selection as an apostle, i.e. "all the time that the Lord Jesus went in and out among us, beginning from the baptism of John until the day when he was taken up from us" (Luke 24:6 ff.; 23:55; Acts 10:37-43). Thus for Luke, the Christian witness was based on the testimony of those: 1) who were present during Jesus' Galilean ministry; 2) who followed Jesus on the trip to Jerusalem; and 3) who witnessed the resurrection.

4. JOHN

For John the following points are noted:

a. Prologue

The book of John begins with the well known *Logos* prologue on the Incarnation of the Word which sets the tone for the whole book, and presents Jesus as the heavenly messenger and transcendental messiah, a part of the Godhead itself.

It is basic to the concept of the Logos as a divine personality that the spirit received by the believers is to be identified in one way or another with Jesus himself. Paul attests to such a doctrine by assuring the Galatians that their adoption as sons of God had been secured through the indwelling of the Spirit, the Spirit of God's son, in their hearts. Where does this stem from? The origins and elaborations on the theology of the *name* found in both orthodox and gnostic Christian writings, are ultimately rooted in Jewish esoteric speculation (as shown by G. Scholem and J. Danielou).

b. His Theology

The Gospel of John differs markedly in language, concepts and theology from the three Synoptics. As the reader proceeds from them to the fourth Gospel, he finds himself in another world. For example, the Synoptics place the ministry of Jesus mostly in Galilee, whereas the Gospel of John divides 287 it between Galilee and Jerusalem. The cleansing of the Temple is dated at opposite ends of Jesus' ministry: John at the beginning, the Synoptics initiating Holy Week. This accords different interpretations to the Lord's Supper, and John's presentation of the resurrection appearances diverges widely from that of the other Gospels. John reveals or reflects an earlier tradition that the first followers of Jesus did not understand him as royal messiah, at least not in the same way that later ones did.

c. *The Earlier Date of John*

While the differences between the Synoptics and John are striking, basic elements in common also should be recognized. The story of Jesus' ministry, culminating in his trial, execution and resurrection, is basically the same, though details vary. The conviction that Jesus was the Christ, the son of the living God, and the commitment to him as divine leader is essentially the same as well. But why the drastic difference in tone and style, in vocabulary and the articulation of doctrine? It has been supposed widely that John was not interested in historical and chronological accuracy, and also that he wrote the Gospel at a much later date than the Synoptics. These views can no longer be taken for granted; distinguished scholars have defended an early date for the Gospel of John, at least the initial composition, and reconsideration of the narrative details indicates that he had reliable information about matters of fact. It is true that his vocabulary and ideas show the influence of Philo, the Hellenistic Jewish philosopher of Alexandria who tried to harmonize orthodox Jewish thought with Greek philosophy, or at least originate in the same world of discourse. It is noteworthy that similar ideas and terms have turned up at Qumran among the writings of the sect there.

A fragment of an Egyptian codex containing John 18:31–33, 37–38 was found in 1935, dating to the first half of the second century A.D. This is the oldest extant fragment of the New Testament and tends to support an earlier date for John, in the first century.

5. ARCHAEOLOGICAL CONTEXT FOR UNDERSTANDING JOHN

a. *Encounter with the Samaritan Woman*

Some ruins on Mount Gerizim would have been visible to Jesus when he talked to the Samaritan woman at Jacob's well in Sychar (John 4). These have been identified through archaeological research. The woman was pointing to Mount Gerizim where the Samaritan temple had stood. It was destroyed by John Hyrcanus in 128 B.C. In the time of the emperor Hadrian (A.D. 117–138) the Romans built a great temple to Jupiter on the same site. The Samaritans maintained their faith and their existence, and to this day worship and celebrate the biblical festivals. They still perform their Passover sacrifice nearby (see Part II: Samaritan Sacrificial Ceremony). Elsewhere on the mountain is the fortification of Justinian enclosing the octagonal Theotakos church (see also Part XIV on the Samaritans).

The Twin Pools of Bethesda

The authenticity and significance of the twin pools in John 5:1–9 is highlighted by the excavations at the back of Saint Anne's Church on the northern edge of the Temple Mount courts. The rectangular pools were surrounded by porticoes in the account of John. In the process of excavation, remains of a fifth century century basilica of the Paralytic (traditional site of the cure by Jesus) were uncovered. According to B. Mazar, the ancient pools at the lowest level originated in the days of Simon the Just in the early second century B.C.: "In his days the great water reservoir was dug, a deep pool as extensive as the sea" (Ben Sirah, in the extracanonical Ecclesiasticus). We have already discussed the pools in Part XVI: Remains of Hasmonean Times. According to Père B. Benoit, the pools are identical with the *Eshdatayim* (twin pools) mentioned in the Copper Scroll while treasure was concealed in the smaller of the two. The Romans who were garrisoned in the nearby Tower of Antonia in the early second century A.D. had built a ritual bath there dedicated to Jupiter Serapis (as they did at the Holy Sepulchre). This was under the vaulted halls of the pool, over

Marks of Roman games are visible in the flagstones. The Antonia has been erroneously identified with Pilate's Praetorium as explained above

The Herodian steps leading to the Gihon spring, scene of the Tabernacles water ritual

the original Jewish site. The ancient pools, on the other hand, had been abandoned as a reservoir when the nearby larger installation, the Pool of Israel, was dug apparently in Herodian days to service the Temple area. Hence, Jesus' miracle of a later time must have occurred at the cave situated east of the twin pools. A small pool forms there from a nearby spring; the water's reddish color was credited with curative power. This factor was secondary to the main object which was to have pure fresh water in the vicinity of the *mikveh* (immersion purification bath) conveniently placed in the immediate neighborhood of the Temple Mount. Several mikvehs were excavated by B. Mazar along the ascent leading to the southern gates of the Temple Mount. They were a major facility provided for worshipers and pilgrims entering the holy precincts.

c. The Feast of Tabernacles

John 7:37–39 suggests an organic relationship between the Feast of Tabernacles (*Succoth*), which occurs around the beginning of the Jewish calendrical year (September or early October), as observed by the Jewish-Christians, and ancient messianic associations reminiscent of the eschatological visions of the prophet Zechariah (the line of continuity is suggested in Part XI, above). In fact, Zechariah 14 is probably the background not only for John 7 but also for Revelation 22 (see below, Part XX). Tabernacles was the occasion for mass pilgrimage to Jerusalem and the autumn harvest week-long festival. It was characterized by solemn but joyous ceremonies. Processions went down to the sacred Gihon spring whose waters led to the Siloam Pool (cf. Part V, Hezekiah's Tunnel). A priest filled a golden pitcher with water and the choir intoned Isaiah's song of the water (12:3); then the procession went up to the Water Gate as crowds carried the symbols of Sucoth, the palm fronds, myrtle, willow and citron, as signs of the harvest. R. E. Brown also deduces from the story of Jesus at Tabernacles that he

emained a long period in Jerusalem area between Tabernacles and the following Passover, in contrast to the crowded Synoptic picture of the Passion, in which Jesus comes to Jerusalem a few days before his capture.

d. Caiaphas and the Trial of Jesus

The high priest Caiaphas (A.D. 18–36) who held office when Pilate was procurator, lived in the aristocratic quarter on Mount Zion. The remains of his house were excavated in very recent times. Some vaulted rooms have been exposed and several interesting artifacts uncovered by Magen Broshi.

With reference to the trial (John 18:31) there is a Jewish tradition that about the year A.D. 30 the Romans took away from the Sanhedrin the right of imposing capital punishment; this is substantiated by John though the other New Testament writings do not mention the point. In any case, Caiaphas, with an acute sense of political expediency, was anxious to be rid of a troublesome messianic figure in time of tense revolutionary agitation. Anything was better than an uprising which would jeopardize the lives of the multitude in Jerusalem, whereupon he placed the decision in Pilate's lap. He could hardly have foreseen that Jesus would become a martyr on behalf of the true Israel of which his sectarian followers regarded him as the king.

e. The Lazarus Story and the Grotto

A grotto at Bethany was found in 1950 near the Franciscan olive grove, marked with graffiti (scratchings). The place must have been sacred to Jewish-Christians, where they commemorated the last supper of Jesus and his disciples. The nature of the grotto is established by the symbols employed: the cosmic ladder, the triangle, and various eschatological designs on the walls. The cosmic ladder symbolizes the journey which the soul must make from the grave to God, and it appears often in the writings and on monuments related to the Jewish-Christians. The grotto was abandoned about the fifth century A.D., when the Jewish-Christian communities also disappeared.

The tomb of Lazarus in its natural state was pointed out by the faithful at the beginning of the fourth century. It was quarried out of rock and composed of a vestibule and a burial chamber, and faced with stone or marble-work in the Byzantine period.

6. THE CHRISTIANIZED VERSION OF THE MESSIAH

Among the shifting views of the royal Messiah in Judaism, there were three constant elements: that he was human, that he was a scion of David, and that he would rule a political kingdom. Such a view falls short of the apocalyptic hope in the cosmic Son of Man who will establish an eternal heavenly kingdom. Both kinds of expectations were present in the Jewish community, and are reflected in the New Testament. Although Jesus was no Zealot, and though he never aimed at establishing a political kingdom, he was condemned as messiah in the basic sense of that title, i.e., royal pretender. Accordingly, the political concept of kingly Messiah was avoided by the oldest Jewish-Christian community. They adopted instead a spiritualized version of messiah, whereby the exalted Lord was already seen to be ruling as king, and the authoritative acts of his earthly ministry could be attributed to him as messiah on earth. Jesus was believed to be of the Davidic line, so that it was a simple matter to ascribe to him the messianic title, even though that created a tension between woldly messianism and Jewish apocalyptic hope. The resurrection of Jesus marked the temporal turning point from humiliation to exaltation. This two-stage Christology aided in the transformation of the "Son of God" from a messianic designation in the Jewish sense to its meaning in the Hellenistic-Jewish church, where the title is used of Jesus as the Lord, the all-powerful agent of God's will during his earthly ministry. Finally in the Hellenistic-Gentile church, Son of God is conferred upon Jesus as a divine title. This development culminates in the doctrine of pre-existence and incarnation.

In the Palestinian Jewish-Christian comunity, *kyrios* was used as a title for Jesus, not as divine, but as a man of authority, in keeping with the Old Testament connotations of *ādôn*. Later, this became a true Christological title by virtue of the unique authority of Jesus. This view was then extended to his coming manifestation in power, and finally transmuted under Hellenistic influence so that Jesus is thought of as divine, superior in potency to the gods of the mystery religions and the deified emperors.

PART XVIII

THE ACTS

Another important source for primitive Jewish-Christianity is in the Acts of the Apostles, which preserves central traditions of the apostolic age. The value of the accounts given there can be demonstrated by comparing and integrating them with those in the other sources: the Gospels and the material remains of Jewish-Christianity.

A. HISTORIC BACKGROUND OF THE ACTS OF THE APOSTLES

Acts offers the extant "official" account of the beginnings of the new Christian church, as seen by an early witness of the movement. It is a chronicle of events in the biblical pattern, with a broad historical perspective based partly upon personal reminiscenses of the author who, according to unanimous tradition, was Luke, the contemporary and companion of Paul.

1. THE EARLY JEWISH-CHRISTIAN COMMUNITY OF ACTS

As is shown by the preface to the book of Acts, the history of the first Jewish-Christian community is a sequel to the Gospel of Luke. It carries on the story of the disciples and followers of Jesus from the time of the resurrection and ascension, describing the community in action, and the principal events of those early creative, formative, and decisive days: e.g., the replacement of Judas to reconstitute the Twelve; Pentecost; the emergence of Peter as the leader of the community; and the martyrdom of Stephen, the ardent preacher and leader of the "deacons." Then the scope broadens: Philip, on a journey, meets and converts a eunuch. Peter's vision and the conversion of Cornelius and his household represents a further dramatic step in the same direction. It is with the appearance of Saul of Tarsus that a fateful turning point in the story is reached.

Acts can be divided into two main sections: Chapters 1–8 describe the growth of Jewish-Christianity in Palestine under the leadership of Peter. This was the early church, "the Way" or the Nazarene sect in Jerusalem and elsewhere in Palestine. Chapters 9–28 describe the spread of Christianity, Jewish and Gentile, throughout the Mediterranean world through the efforts of many missionaries, the most important of these being Saul/Paul and his close associates. The author seems intent on showing that the propagation of the gospel was accomplished without hindrance from the Romans.

2. THE SYNAGOGUE-CHURCH ON MOUNT ZION

It was in the "upper room" that Jesus celebrated the Last Supper, instituting at the end of the meal a solemn covenant with his followers, which as the Eucharist became the central rite of Christian worship. Beneath this chamber is the Jewish holy place identified erroneously since the Middle Ages as the Tomb of David, which was once a church-synagogue. This has been demonstrated by a close examination of its masonry, especially the details of the apse behind the present cenotaph of David. Equally important are some inscriptions on the walls, one of which connects the homage to David with the memory of the Patriarch, illustrating the meaning of the reference in Peter's first sermon after the Pentecost: "Brethren, I may say to you confidently of the patriarch David that he both died and was buried, and his tomb is with us to this day" (Acts 2:29). It has been noted that the organization of the early Jewish-Christian group, as it appears in Acts and the Pauline Epistles (see below) shows striking resemblances to the structure adopted by the Essenes at Qumran. Thus, in the summary of the activities of the first Jewish-Christians (Acts 2:42–47), we find reference made to the "community of property," "prayer," and "teaching." Likewise, the Qumranite sacred meals, especially the liturgy for the messianic banquet, notable affinities with the meal fellowship described in Acts, and the ordinance for the *eucharistia* and the *agape* (the joyous communal meal connected with the eucharist), reported by Paul in 1 Corinthians and in the Didache.

The activities of the apostles aroused the opposition of the Jewish establishment of Jerusalem, mainly of the Sadducees who had opposed Jesus. His followers were brought before the Sanhedrin (Supreme Council), but there opinions were divided. Rabbi Gamaliel defended them judiciously. He was a scion of Hillel the Babylonian, a notable Pharisaic thinker and leader (as Paul was first called). He held firmly to the tradition of humility and leniency in the application of the Law advocated by the school of Hillel. The decision of Gamaliel that the community be left alone (5:33–40) initiated a period of more tranquil relationship with the Sanhedrin, and allowed the Christian group to increase its membership and solidify its position. It is true that Acts 8:1 reports a persecution against Hellenistic Jewish-Christians who voiced their opposition to the Temple. There were isolated acts of violence like Herod Agrippa's execution of James, son of Zebedee and his imprisonment of Peter, but otherwise the Jerusalem community seems to have lived in peace wtih the Jerusalem authorities. In A.D. 58, when Saul came to Jerusalem (Acts 21:18 ff.), it was still customary for Jewish-Christians to offer sacrifice in the Temple. The subsequent execution of James, the brother of Jesus, marked the opening of a new period of hostility.

Although the Sanhedrin had refused to condemn the Apostles, the zeal of Stephen, the deacon, especially in condemning the Temple and its worship, aroused the congregation of one of the more fanatically orthodox synagogues to prosecute him for blasphemy and to stone him, as prescribed by the ancient legal sanctions (Lev 24:14).

Recess or apse of the 2nd c. A.D. synagogue on Mount Zion and a cenotaph which is erroneously identified as the 'Tomb of David'

3. CONTEMPORARY SYNAGOGUES

Although we are inclined to think of the synagogue as primarily an institution of the Jewish Diaspora, the truth is that they were very numerous in Palestine. One example is the synagogue of the Freedmen mentioned in Acts 6:9, whose existence has been authenticated by a dedicatory inscription (in Greek), reproduced here. It was discovered in the Ophel, the southeastern part of the lower town. This is the inscription of Theodotus, son of Vattenos, the head of the first century A.D. synagogue. The synagogue was founded by former freed slaves repatriated to Palestine and still linked to the Diaspora. While the national ritual was performed at the Temple, congregations attended the synagogues for their morning and evening prayers. There was also a *bêt midrāsh* or school for the instruction of the young, and to provide refresher courses for adults. Hebrew and Aramaic were the basic media, but Greek was also used by Jews both abroad and in Palestine.

Two other contemporary synagogues have been dicovered: at Masada, Herod's private desert resort, and at Herodion, Herod's summer palace. Both are distinguished by their simplicity. The small Masada edifice, in its original Herodian phase, had two rows of three columns, which supported the roof, while the main entrance was on the east side. Benches were built

Cross sections of the synagogu
of Masada built in Herodia
times (right) and that whic
Herod erected in his palati
summer retreat at Herodic
(le

along the walls in later years by the Zealots who took refuge in Masada during the revolt against Rome (A.D. 70–73). An auxiliary room was built into the northwestern corner during the Revolt.

4. THE HISTORICAL PROCESSES OF JEWISH-CHRISTIANITY

Since the author of Acts was primarily interested in describing the rapid spread of the Gospel throughout the Roman empire, and brings his story to a climax with Paul's arrival in the capital city, Rome, after devoting the better part of his life to other missionary enterprises, it is understandable that the author passes over many interesting and important aspects of early Christian history. His account of Jewish-Christianity is largely limited to the earliest period in Jerusalem, for which he provides excellent data; but once Paul enters the scene, the author follows him on his travels and adventures in the empire, touching home base in Palestine and Jerusalem only on the rare occasions when Paul does. As a result, the story of Jewish-Christianity beyond the remaning decades of the first century has not received the attention it deserves, either in Acts or in subsequent studies down to the present.

5. THE MOVEMENT OF "THE WAY"

The people of "the Way" — the Jewish-Christians — remained part of the larger Jewish community during the decades following the death of Jesus. The men of "the Way" still were faithful to Judaism and engaged in the traditional forms of worship (Acts 3:1; 21:20; 22:17; 23:1; 24:11–18).

The picture preserved in Acts of the early Jewish-Christian community in Jerusalem manifests significant differences with first century Jewry, long before the separation of the two communities confirmed the fact publicly. The Jewish-Christians proclaimed that Jesus was Messiah and Lord, and that salvation for the individual and the world was available through him (2:38–40). The adherents attended the Temple, but in addition they had their own meetings, celebrated meals which commemorated the Last Supper, to which only those who had been baptized were admitted, and developed their own system for caring for the poor (2:44–46). What differentiated them theologically from the other Jews was their expectation of the coming of the crucified and risen Jesus in glory as the Royal Messiah, and as the Lord of the world. Nevertheless, they regarded themselves as Jews and were considered so by others. They met publicly in "Solomon's Porch" and their members grew daily; actually this site was the *Royal Portico* or the *Hanuyot*, mentioned in connection with Jesus' experience there (see Part XVII). Then, concurrently with Paul's appearance on the scene, the missionary zeal for the movement of "the Way" resulted in the conversion of proselytes, God-fearers, and pagans, and their incorporation into the community, thereby producing additional strains between it and traditional Judaism. Acts describes in rapid sequence the steps by which "the Way" was separated from the parent religion and set out to conquer the world "in the name of Jesus."

B. PAUL'S LIFE AND MISSION

According to Acts, Paul studied under Rabbi Gamaliel, the great Pharisaic leader, in Jerusalem, and he became an active supporter of the Jewish establishment in the growing controversy between the Sanhedrin and the Jewish-Christians, which ended in the trial and stoning of Stephen, in which Paul is said to have participated. Shortly thereafter Paul led a punitive expedition against the pernicious Christian movement which had appeared in Damascus; on the road to Damascus he underwent a dramatic conversion experience, and from having been a vehement persecutor he became an ardent follower of "the Way" (cf. Acts 22:6–16; 26:12–18). We have noted the presence of an Essene messianist movement in Damascus, which doubtless was related to the contemporary community of Essenes of Qumran. The group in Damascus may have provided recruits for the nascent Christian community there. Following his extraordinary experience, Paul retired into Arabia, i.e., the Nabatean kingdom in the arid parts of eastern Palestine, an area in which another form of messianism is also attested by recent discovery. He returned to Jerusalem and was accepted by the leaders of the Jewish-Christian community (Galat 1:18 ff.); at the same time he asserts the independence of his message, saying that he did not derive his gospel from their instruction. He was certain that he received it from Jesus himself.

1. RESURRECTION AND THE JEWS

Jesus was sinless, had suffered and been crucified in atonement for the sins of mankind. Jesus' resurrection was the guarantee of salvation for mankind which is extended to Jews and to Gentile equally. It has been said that for Paul, the resurrection had the importance which earlier sectarian thought had attached to baptism. It also supplied the vital element in his eschatological teaching. In the life of the risen Christ he saw the prototype for the future life of all who were "Christ's" (Philip 3:21). In speaking to the Gentiles, it became the beginning, the goal and the manifestation of the new life (Romans 6). Paul joined the Christian community in Antioch, apparently the first Gentile Christian group to be affiliated with the Jewish-Christian community with its headquarters in Jerusalem. The leading figure of the Antioch church was Barnabas, an early adherent and dedicated supporter of the faith. He enlisted Paul as his associate, and together they served as apostles and missionaries for the church there. They were sent to Jerusalem to bring a donation to the leaders of the movement, and to confer with them. Following this venture, the Antiochians commissioned them to preach the gospel abroad. Their first journey took them to Cyprus, Perga, Antioch in Asia Minor, and finally the cities of Lycaonia (ch. 13–14) where they met with open hostility. At this phase of the story, the basic controversy concerned the obligation of the converted Gentiles to observe Jewish law. Paul endorsed the position that Gentiles did not have to become Jews (i.e., be circumcised and accept the burden of the Law) in order to become

Paul's overland journeys
through Syria and his second
journey by sea to and through
Asia Minor

Christians. This decision was appealed to Jerusalem, but Paul was able to win the approval of the Jerusalem leaders to his tolerant outlook; James issued an edict in the name of the Jerusalem church, which exonerated and confirmed Paul though at the same time urging compromise and good will on all parties. From Paul's Epistles (which precede Acts in date of composition) we learn that the ruling was not universally approved and that many Jewish-Christians in the Diaspora resented both the argument and the arguer (see Part XIX: Pauline Letters).

The second and most significant journey was begun shortly after their return to Antioch (15:36–18:21). After passing through Cilicia, Lycaonia, Phrygia, and Galatia in Asia Minor, Paul preached the gospel on the continent of Europe, in the Macedonian cities of Philippi, Thessalonica, Beroea, Athens and Corinth, where serious clashes ended in his arrest and trial.

2. PAUL AND THE JEWISH-CHRISTIANS OF PALESTINE

According to C. H. Kraeling, the Jewish-Christians of Palestine in the first century "did not make the death of Jesus on the cross as central a factor in their interpretation of his significance as Paul did, for instance. For them, Jesus was the bringer of the New Law, the Holy One who taught the higher righteousness that exceeded but did not abolish the Mosaic ordinances. We can still sense the differences of outlook that existed between the Jewish-Christian communities of Palestine and Paul on this matter, in Galatians 2:21 where Paul says for the benefit of those under Jewish-Christian influence, 'If righteousness comes by the Law, then Christ is dead in vain.'"

298

3. SALVATION FOR GENTILE AS WELL AS JEW

Paul's liberal approach earned him the opposition of the old guard of the Jerusalem church who still refused to make concessions on the question of Jewish observances. A good deal of the opposition to Paul among the Jewish-Christian communities of Palestine apparently was rooted in bitter memories of the part he had played as a persecutor. Although the leaders accepted him, there were many who remained skeptical about his conversion. The "Judaizers" with whom he came into conflict were an extremist group who did not belong to the central party in Jerusalem (see below: The Pauline Letters). Paul saw much more clearly than they that it was impossible to require slaves and hired workers in the Hellenistic world to keep the Jewish Sabbath and festivals, or to abide by the food laws. Nor could grown men, however close to Judaism, accept circumcision. Paul did not deliberately seek a solution for them. He had no desire to make things easy. He himself had been a strictly observant Diaspora Jew and, with certain exceptions related directly to the mission to the Gentiles, continued to be so. But he was concerned with questions of theology, and it seemed to him that with the coming of Jesus, the Messiah, a decisive change in the nature of the holy community had taken place, and that with it, the place and function of the Law had also changed drastictally.

In his travels in the Roman province of Asia, Paul worked mainly in cities where there were Jewish communities and through them he may have reached sympathetic Gentiles, i.e., "godfearers," who were interested in biblical religion, sympathized with Jews and frequented the synagogues. Modern pilgrims and tourists hoping to follow in the steps of the apostle through Asia Minor (modern Turkey) or Greece find very few authentic traces in the Hellenistic towns in which he preached. All that is left in most of them are the remnants of temples, forums, theaters, and occasional traces of ancient synagogues. Excavations have been conducted in a number of important cities such as Ephesus, Sardis, Pergamon, Lystra, Derbe, Perga, Iconium, and Antioch.

Elevated porch at Ephesus, somewhat similar architecturally to the Royal Porches around the Temple

Ruins of Pergamon

A glance at the map shows the great distances covered by Paul and his companions. Paul seems to have equally at home with Jews and with gentiles, and was one of the most cosmopolitan figures of the Bible, entirely at ease in the cities of the Mediterranean where on accasion he also earned his living as an artisan (usually but certainly described as a tent-maker). There is a sharp contrast between the rural and village quality of the Gospels,

and the urban atmosphere of Paul's Epistles, which reflect the hustle and
bustle of the cities which he visited and where he lived.

4. THE CONTEMPORARY ANCIENT SYNAGOGUES

What interests us particularly are the synagogues and communities of
Syria and Asia Minor. Outstanding examples are Antioch in Syria, Sardis,
and Dura-Europos. The earliest Jewish-Christian community in Antioch, one
of the great cities of antiquity, dates approximately to A.D. 40 and numbered
among its leaders Barnabas and Paul. It was there that the Jewish-Christians
became known by the Greek name *Christianoi* (Messianists) and it was from
Antioch that the mission to the Gentiles began. The city rivalled Jerusalem
as the center of early Christianity.

The beginnings of Jewish-Christianity in Asia Minor are bound up
closely with the numerous and wealthy Jewish communities. The most
striking example, verified by archaeology, is that of Sardis. Built in the
third century A.D., it was a beautifully ornamented basilica with two ritual
focal points: a permanent place for the Torah shrine (Ark) in front of
the central entrance in the wall facing toward Jerusalem and, at the other
end, a raised *bemāh* (altar) from which the Torah was read and the
sermons preached. In this manner the congregation seated on the benches
lining the long walls could face both the Ark and the altar.

The synagogue was established in the area of the public buildings of the
city, and was next to the gymnasium and Roman bath. The influential Jewish

Main hall of the Sardis
synagogue (right) and
eastern end of the hall (left)
and site of the Ark

community maintained the synagogue along with their civic privileges even during the centuries which followed the establishment of Christianity as the official religion of the Byzantine empire.

5. PAUL'S THIRD JOURNEY

A gold and metal artificer at work

The third journey was begun shortly after a stopover in Antioch, with a visit to Phrygia and Galatia and the establishment of a church in the large and important city of Ephesus. Ephesus was the chief city of the Roman province of Asia, a wealthy, highly cultivated metropolis with a temple to Artemis (Diana), one of the seven wonders of the ancient world. The town boasted a number of silversmiths who specialized in pagan images. One of these, Demetrius, provoked a riot against Paul, who ridiculed his craft as part of a biblical polemic against idolatry (Acts 19:29). His hostility was provoked by his loss of business as a result of Paul's success in undermining popular confidence in the efficacy of idols and the religion associated with them.

6. PAUL'S TRIAL

Paul's experience in Corinth (18:12-17) is characteristic of the difficulties which he encountered, important because it came to an end in a way that distinguishes it from the Jerusalem trend. The Jews were the persecutors (9:22-25, 29-30; 13:50-51; 14:2, 4-6, 19) and the conflicting statements and bitterness led to a break between Paul and the synagogue and to his making plans for an intensive mission among the Gentiles (18:6). But the Roman court refused to interfere with long-standing Jewish privileges.

After the third journey, Paul returned to Jerusalem where he clashed openly with the Jews on the Temple Mount. He took refuge in the Antonia Tower which Herod had built and which was garrisoned by the Roman troops. The cliff on which this historic fortress was built can still be identified, but the only vestige of the building are parts of a wall in and near the Arab Ommariyeh school at the north of the Temple Mount. Ultimately Paul was arrested and brought to trial on a variety of charges, chiefly that he attacked the established order and violated the basic laws of Judaism.

With Paul's trial in Jerusalem and in Caesarea, and his later appeal to the court of Caesar in Rome, the account in Acts reaches its climax. The book closes with Paul awaiting trial before the emperor, and in the meantime proclaiming the gospel even to the limited audience available under the terms of his house arrest.

7. PAUL, MESSIANISM, AND NATIONALISM

As the center of gravity of the new church shifted from Palestine to the Diaspora, and eventually to the great cities of the Roman empire, east and west, the messianic ideal on which Palestinian Jewish-Christianity was based underwent a change. Traditional Jewish expectations had been of a purely national "Messiah of David." But the humiliation of Jesus' crucifixion made it essential that any idea of Davidic kingship or suspected political rebellion must be removed from the picture of him as a messiah. In a brilliant tour de force, Jesus' submission became the mark of his messiahship, and instead of the reigning monarch, he was perceived as the "Suffering Servant of the Lord" (as in Isaiah 53). Only when he had borne the sins of the world and endured its wickedness, could he be raised to power and glory, as the triumphant Son of God. Of fundamental importance in shaping the message of the gospel was the attitude to foreign rule over the Jews. For a long time after the Exile is was accepted fact and doctrine that God had transferred sovereignty to a foreign empire, and that the Jewish community must submit patiently and penitantly until God acted in some decisive fashion to change the situation and reestablish an independant Israel, or bring the empires of the World to an end and reign as Lord over all. The alternate view, expressing the longing of many, was politically oriented and aimed at seizing territory and independance and reviving ancient monarchy.

A Jew of the Diaspora, Paul was inclined to ignore nationalist elements in messianism and the details of Jesus' life in the land (which were preserved nonetheless in the traditions of the local Jewish-Christians as seen below (C). Instead, he concentrated on the universal aspects of Jesus as the "Son of God," the pre-existant eternal instrument of divine revelation. According to W.D. Davies, "Christ has become for Paul the 'locus' of redemption here and in the world to come. The 'land' has been for him 'Christified.' It is not the land promised, much as he had loved it, that became his 'inheritance,' but the Living Lord, in whom was a new creation... And once Paul had made the Living Lord rather than the Torah the center of life and in death, once he had seen in Jesus his Torah, he had in principle broken with the land... His geographic identity was subordinated to that of being 'in Christ' in whom he was neither Jew nor Greek." (W. D. Davies: *The Gospel and the Land,* 1975).

In any case, the final break between Judaism and Christianity did not come in the late first century A.D., but only in the late second century or even after depending on the locality as well as local, social, and economic conditions. By that time the Jewish synagogues began to force Jewish-Christians out of their precincts, as may be seen from the fact that among the "Eighteen Benedictions" which is an obligatory synagogue liturgy, is a curse on the *minîm* or Jewish-Christians. As Jews who believed in Jesus refused to recite such a prayer, they could be identified and driven away. Thus they began to worship in their own synagogues. This is probably the origin of the prayer house built over Peter's Capernaum house in the second century A.D. in the quarter occupied by Jewish-Christians (see Part XVII).

C. FIRST CENTURY A.D. JEWRY AND JEWISH-CHRISTIANITY

The early Jewish-Christian community came into existence after the life and death and resurrection of Jesus, and lived side by side and in conflict with the rest of Judaism, including Sadducees, Pharisees, Essenes, Herodians, and Zealots. It was also the era of the great teachers (rabbis) who flourished before and after the fall of Jerusalem in A.D. 70.

1. THE DIFFERENT ASPECTS OF JEWISH-CHRISTIANITY

Hence, Jewish-Christianity during this period manifested itself in a variety of forms. There was the basic Palestinian stratum, close to Pharisaism and adhering to rabbinical legalistic *halakhot* (rules). There were also apocalyptic and messianic groups in Asia Minor, tending to zealotry. Reflecting a more contemplative or mystical community were written compositions like the *Shepherd* of Hermas (Rome) or the *Ode of Solomon* (Antioch of Syria). The common link among these groups is the original Christian theology expressed in Jewish or Semitic terms. They are post-biblical, belonging in the main to the sub-Apostolic period, and are described in the extant writings of Irenaeus and Clement of Alexandria; they are represented in such works as the Ascension of Isaiah, and the Epistle of Barnabas. Material remains of these groups have survived, and have been discovered in recent archaeological excavations, as presently described. It is important to define these categories of Jewish-Christians:

a) It may designate the Jewish-Christian community of Jerusalem led first by Peter, then by Jesus' brother James. It was the mother church, with the prestige and authority of the Twelve Apostles, and the family of Jesus. It was in the main an orthodox group, described in Acts 2:42–47, worshiping at the Temple and observng Jewish law, and recognizing no mandate to propagate their faith among the Gentiles. It retained the primacy until the 60's, even when the gospel had spread through the Roman empire, and churches had been founded in the principal cities. There was continuing tension between Paul, the great missionary to the Gentiles, and the central Jewish-Christian community in Jerusalem, but no resolution was achieved until the principals all died in the decade before the fall of Jerusalem (A.D. 70). When the Jewish-Roman war broke out, the Jewish-Christians fled to Pella in northern Transjordan for safety, and settled there temporarily. Many of the exiles returned to Jerusalem afterwards and stayed there. Later evidence locates them on Mount Zion. The community was led by Simon, son of Cleophas, who was related to the family of Jesus. The bishops who followed, according to Eusebius, were all of the *Church of the Circumcision*, the so-called Judaizers. The term is used to distinguish the Jewish-Christian community from those early Christians who did not practice circumcision or observe the laws of Moses.

b) It may designate Jews who recognized Jesus as a prophet or even messiah, but not as the Son of God. They constitute an intermediate group between Jesus and Christians, like the Ebionites, the "poor," who did not accept the divinity of Christ. They are not an isolated case, as witness the influence of revolutionary and messianic Jewish propaganda, which spread throughout the Jewish world and affected the young Jewish-Christian communities during the period between A.D. 40–70. Among them were the groups with whom Paul clashed in Corinth, Colossae and Galatia. This time of Jewish-Christianity, living side by side with strictly observant Jews, is syncretistic in nature, influenced by native Asiatic cultures, which we meet in the person of Simon Magus, and the like. Jewish-Christian communities flourished in Palestine, Transjordan, and Syria. Here and there, they came into touch with churches founded or influenced by Paul, and the resultant conflict over issues such as circucision (of Gentiles) and observance of the Law brought angry responses in the Pauline Epistles where he warned his followers against the Judaizing zeal of his opponents.

Other branches disappeared after the fall of Jerusalem. Their spirit is reflected in the Epistle of Jude, and they are the source of the Gospel of the Hebrews, originally written in Aramaic. Unable to return to Jerusalem, they assimilated with other sects in the Near East, probably in Egypt or in eastern Syria, where remnants persisted for many decades.

c) Finally, one can define Jewish-Christianity as a pattern of Christian thought which does not imply a direct link with the Jewish community but which expresses itself in a religious framework borrowed from Judaism. This definition has a wider scope and would comprise the former two categories as well as groups which broke away from the Jewish community but continued to think along the same lines. This would be the case with Paul and other leaders of the early church. Such Jewish-Christianity is identical with early Christianity, the origin of which was Jewish, but which had moved away from Judaism to accomodate large numbers of Gentile converts.

2. COMMUNITIES OF JEWISH AND PAGAN ORIGIN

In the course of the second Jewish revolt against Rome, led by Bar Kochba in A.D. 132, and crushed by Hadrian in A.D. 135, the Jewish-Christians who did not recognize his claim to be the Messiah were forced to flee. The leadership of the Jerusalem "church" and probably those of Jaffa, Lydda and Pella founded after A.D. 70, passed to converted Gentiles, who became Jewish-Christians. It appears that they wanted to change certain rules such as the date of the Passover celebration. Endless discussions were held between Jews and Jewish-Christians, termed *minim;* the most important of these took place in Caesarea and Tiberias. Constant friction led to the eventual separation of Christians of Jewish origin, from those of pagan origin. Churches made up of the latter were established in Caesarea and Acre, Ashdod, Neapolis (Shechem), Bosra, and Philadelphia (Amman of today). These grew rapidly and spread, reaching a peak in the third century A.D. when there were Christian communities in most Palestinian cities with the exception of the thickly settled Jewish areas of Galilee: Zippori and Tiberias. The Council of Caesarea, in 196, decided that the Passion should

The Amwas 'lamella' (metal-foil inscriptions) placed under the head of the corpse. The idea behind this was that the soul came out by way of the mouth, and in need of help. The Aramaic characters and designs (serpent as a snare laid by a demon) suggest a talisman, together with exorcisms of the demon Shamadel. The designs were obscure and assumed that only the initiates would grasp them

Jewish–Christian symbols: The fish, anchor, the cross

be observed on Easter Sunday. This was one of the signs of the eventual separation of the Jews and Christians; Jewish-Christians maintained their identity for two centuries or more, as shown by material evidence they left behind.

3. JEWISH-CHRISTIAN LITERATURE

There is close historical connection between the Jewish-Christians and a large group of extra-canonical writings, attributed to them and considered apocryphal (heterodox or doubtful authorship) in Apostolic and sub-Apostolic times. The only one which was included in the New Testament is the Epistle to the Hebrews. It expresses the thought of new Christians involved in the Jewish milieu. The Jewish-Christian *Gospel according to the Hebrews* was popular in Egypt; it is to be distinguished from the *Gospel of the Ebionites,* a later heterodox work. There are apocryphal works which deal with celestial mysteries and the end of days. In imitation of other Jewish pseudepigraphic writings (see: Intertestamental Period), which were attributed to great figures of the past like Noah, Enoch, or Abraham, these are accredited to prophets and apostles, e.g., the Gospel of Peter and the Apocalypse of the Twelve Apostles, or liturgical works like the Ascension of Isaiah, with its doctrine of the seven heavens leading to the eighth which is Christ's domain, and of *sheol,* the realm of the dead. The *Didache* (see below) the *Ode of Solomon,* the *Epistles* of *Ignatius* and of *Barnaby,* the *Pseudo-Clementine homilies,* all date to the first and early second centuries A.D. The second part of the Didache consists of ecclesiastical regulations regarding baptism, the Eucharist and the worship, as well as the appointment of bishops and deacons along with prophets and teachers. The book is of special interest, since it comes from an early period when rules of faith and practice were just being adopted by the Gentile church. Few extra-canonical books are more important than the Didache, since it contains an early and alternate version of a group of dominical sayings, when compared with the canonical Gospels, and the first instructions on the sacraments and early church procedures.

4. DISCOVERIES OF CHRISTIAN ARCHAEOLOGY

The diligent work of B. Baggatti, E. Testa and I. Mancini has provided archaeological documentation of such Christian symbols as the cross under the axe, the six-pointed star, the Christ-angel, the plow as a sign of Christ, and other examples.

a. *Sacred Letters, Numbers and Cross Signs*
There was a secret language expressed in mystic Hebrew letters and words, and in special numbers which had a symbolic and theological meaning (e.g. 1000 meaning a period of prosperity); seals which consist of designs (plow, tree, etc.); the sacred names of God and Christ which were believed to have miraculous power, and were written in the form of monograms; the

drawing of the trinitarian sign (a triangle); the *wāw* cross; the cross with two, three or six horns as dynamic signs, developing the Jewish-Christian teaching on the angels as outward manifestations of the power of the Trinity; prophetic signs derived from the Old Testament and transmuted into eschatological terms, such as the Ark of Noah, Jacob's Ladder, the bloodstained lintels of Jewish homes on the eve of the Exodus from Egypt; the serpent of Moses mentioned in Numbers; the star of Jacob; and the tree of life.

The Jewish-Christian theology glorified Christ and his Cosmic power; this is related to the mystery of the cross. On the one hand it evokes the

Graffiti on the wall of a tomb
at Bethphage near Bethany

crucifixion of the historic Jesus on earth. On the other, its symbolic double form + and the sign × emphasize Christ's redemption and the realization of the eschatological drama. The other symbols include the luminous cross of the Apocalypse, which represents the attributes of God, the all-powerful creator.

b. *Graffiti as Symbols*

In the burial ground of Dominus Flevit on the Mount of Olives, the WAW in the form of a monogram is the sign of the cross. Other signs denote the "centenarian" Abraham mnemonic substitutions for Christ, the Dove (corresponding to the symbolic 801) and the Fish symbolized by the number 29. This has thrown new light on the buildings used by the Jewish-Christians, such as the church-synagogue of Nazareth and the one on Mount Zion, with the signs and symbols used to express their religious beliefs and the initiation rites (see above: The Gospels in the Light of Recent Discovery).

The letters XE MAPIA, "Hail Mary," and a second graffito, "holy place of M" attest to the worship of Mary in Jewish-Christian times. The symbols found around Nazareth and on the ossuaries of Dominus Flevit were identical. The sign of the triangle on amulets discovered near Hebron have the same meaning; graffiti on the wall of a grave at Bethphage can be compared with Jewish-Christian belief in the future life or in the journey which the soul had to undertake to gain heaven. That journey is symbolized by the cosmic ladder sketched in the tombs and in an ornate building at Beit-Hashitta.

There is other evidence: the tablets of lead or 'lamina', copper, silver or gold refer to the oil of Faith whose meaning only the initiated could understand. They consisted of magic formulas and strange symbols with mystical interpretations (suggestive in a way of cabbalistic signs). They are Jewish-Christian amulets.

5. CONCLUSION

a. *The Church of the Circumcision and the Church of the Gentiles*

In most parts of Palestine, mainly in the mountain areas, the Church of the Circumcision led an active life until the end of the fourth century A.D., and continued on in a state of decline for more than another century. For a long time they existed side by side with the orthodox Jews, worshiping in the same synagogues, until they were forced to leave. The Jewish-Christians had their own liturgy, expressive of Christian teaching with its roots in Judaism, their own literature, buildings, worship and customs. Archaelogical evidence from neighboring countries shows that their influence was widespread, especially in Asia Minor or the famed cities of the Seven Churches of the Apocalypse (see Rev 1:12).

This background throws light on the origin of the recognized holy places. The documentation of the tradition helps to trace them back to the beginning, thus bridging the gap from the period of the Apostles to Constantine, when Christianity became the official religion of the empire. A striking example is Nazareth with its Jewish-Christian worship of Mary already in the very first centuries. On the other hand, these discoveries help us to understand some obscure New Testament passages of the Apocalypse. There, the five elements of the Jewish-Christan system of symbolism appear together (see Part XX: Revelation).

In the course of their history, some Jewish villages and towns of the second to the fourth centuries are referred to as "swallowed up" according to the Jews, that it, lost to the land of Israel. Some of them were occupied by the Jewish-Christians. Based on information provided by the historians Epiphanius and Eusebius and the debates between *mínim* (i.e. Jewish-Christians) and the rabbis in the Talmud, it is possible to draw up a map showing the centers where Jewish-Christians lived. The latter lived in the same places as Jews but, due to their *habdalāh* (separation), they dwelt in a separate quarter of the town, apart from those faithful to the synagogue. Traces of this separation were evident, until recent centuries, in the village of Beiʻna in Galilee, as well as Kfar-Kana (ancient Cana) and el-Jish (Gushhalab) where two synagogues had served the separate communities.

Bloodstained marks of a slaughtered lamb on a wall to protect the house against evil

b. *The Lesson of Archaeology*

The observations should therefore be borne in mind as a proper guide to the historical background of New Testament literature and, more specifically, as a help in understanding key passages and events in Gospels, Acts, the Pauline Letters, and with regard to the social and religious situation out of which Christianity in its various forms and types arose.

c. *The Christian Holy Places and Archaeology*

Another question arises in trying to connect the obscure and forgotten traces of primitive Christianity, described above, with over two hundred churches (many of them already in ruins) which arose presumably, over or near the ancient sites of early Christianity. The most important were built in Byzantine times, or later, hiding what lay beneath. With the possible

Facade of the synagogue of Barʻam

Below, right:
The cosmic cross on a mosaic of the Jewish-Christian synagogue at Nazareth, symbolizing the celestial abode

Graffito KE MAPIA 'Hail,
Mary' discovered in the lower
levels of the Church of the
Annunciation, Nazareth,
indicative of the worship of
the mother of Christ

exception of the lower reaches of the Holy Sepulchre (built in the 4th c.),
the prayer-house over Peter's house at Capernaum, or the chapel of Dura-
Europos (see Part XIX, A, 9), they have no more archaeological significance
than "David's tomb" on Mount Zion. Tourists, however, are not aware
of the facts and the voluminous illustrated literature on the Christian
Holy Places is of no help in trying to guide the innocents abroad in the
steps of Jesus.

d. *The Post-Apostolic Age of the Synagogue*

Traditional Jewish life survived the Bar Kochba debacle and continued
in a dynamic development throughout the second century and afterwards.
There was a renaissance of the Jewish community and its culture in Galilee,
the heights of Golan, Transjordan, and other parts of Palestine where remains
of dozens of magnificent synagogues have been discovered: Capernaum,
Meron, Chorazin, Barʿam, Ḥammath (Tiberias), Beth-shean, to mention
a few.

The style of the synagogues and neighboring patrician homes derives
from classical Hellenistic--Syrian architecture of late Herodian times, but
with the addition of decorative motifs which are plainly Jewish, i.e., the
palm and bunch of grapes (symbols of fecundity), the acanthus, rosettes.
Traditional motifs are found in the mosaic floors, on tombs, sarcophagi and
ossuaries, as in Beth-shearim and in eastern and northern Jerusalem. Where
the same motifs, as in Shafarʿam also bear symbolic invocation of Christ,
they indicate both continuity of the same culture, and distinctive Jewish-
Christian elements. Galilee has provided the most numerous examples.
Kaukabe (Star) in Syria was a village inhabited by Ebionites and Nazarenes
(a community whose name is derived from Nazareth), according to Epiphanius.

e. *Older Synagogues*

The best evidence of dynamic Jewish culture were the synagogues spread
over the whole country between the second and eigthth centuries A.D. The
early type — besides the Herodian synagogues found at Masada, Herodion,
and an inscription from the synagogue of the Ophel — was mostly in Galilee
during the second and third centuries. Their main characteristic are: the
decorated facade flanked by three portals facing Jerusalem. As worshipers
were not allowed to have their backs to Zion, they sat on benches stretching
along the walls and facing each other. Only the elders and the *hazān* (cantor
who stood before the Ark) faced the Holy City. The main hall was divided
by two rows of columns along its length and one row along its width. The
building was faced with wide stone slabs and its walls were decorated by
reliefs representing at times animals and occasionally human beings. The
outstanding inner decoration was the frieze of the balcony. A court or portico
stood outside the synagogue. The celebrated synagogues of Capernaum and
Chorazin belong to the third–fourth centuries A.D.

PART XIX

A. PAULINE LETTERS

The most important source about relations between the Jews and the Jewish-Christians outside of Palestine are *Paul's Letters,* as they were written at almost the same time as the events with which they deal. They are also the earliest literature in the New Testament canon. The letters were of a practical and occasional nature, responding to specific situations in the mission churches, affirming essential truths of the gospel, explaining mysteries of the faith, coping with problems of policy and practice, answering critics, and exhorting the faithful. Paul had established the legitimacy of gentile Christianity at the Council of Jerusalem (ca A.D. 48) and subsequently had spread the gospel in Galatia, Asia Minor, Macedonia, and Achaia in Greece. Whether Jewish-Christians or Gentiles, these new converts were often in need of guidance about basic issues, e.g., the proper observance of the Lord's Supper, the return of Jesus, organizational matters, and lines of authority. The letters actually served a wider audience and larger purposes than originally intended, and were saved, circulated, and ultimately assembled as a vivid witness to the life of the churches outside of Palestine and the genius of the great missionary apostle. They are historically of the greatest value for the light they shed on the life, customs, and problems of the early Christian communities. In them are defined the major theological issues confronting the church: the conflict with Judaism over the status of Jesus, and the place of the Law in the emerging community. While Paul's views are definitely his own, and he makes no effort to give a balanced treatment of the issues, the great debates in the early church come alive in his letters.

The letters can be grouped by their approximate dates, between A.D. 50–64, as follows:

1 and 2 Thessalonians, in which Paul defends his mission against Jewish opposition. The setting is Corinth between A.D. 50 and 52, after his second jorney.

Galatians, written to his followers in Iconium, Lystra, Derbe, and Antioch in Pisidia. Again Paul is mainly concerned to defend himself against the claim of the "Judaizers" (Jewish-Christians of Jerusalem), that Gentiles must be circumcised to become Christians.

1 and 2 Corinthians, written from Ephesus during Paul's third journey. Paul rebukes the Corinthians for their divisions, calls on them for unity, and gives them instructions regarding belief and practice.

Romans, written to the church at Rome before he had ever visited there, is more in the nature of a theological treatise or formal presentation of his understanding of the meaning of the Gospel and the significance of Jesus Christ.

Philippians, Colossians, Philemon, written during Paul's imprisonment (perhaps in Rome, perhaps in Ephesus, ca. A.D. 60–64, though scholars are

311

divided as to the exact dates). The letter to Philippians describes his condition and his hopes for release, and in Colossians, Paul sets out his philosophy of religion.

Ephesians and the Pastorals, Epistless 1 and 2 Timothy, and Titus, although traditionally attributed to Paul, are questioned by many scholars. E. J. Goodspeed has suggested that Ephesians was written by a follower of Paul's, taking the letter to the Colossians as a model, and giving a summary of Pauline thought. The Pastorals, a later collection of letters, show the influence of some of the other letters. E. F. Scott believes that they were edited by a Paulinist from some genuine fragments and published under Paul's name.

1. THESSALONIANS, THE EARLIEST DOCUMENT IN THE NEW TESTAMENT

Paul's oldest surviving letter (and so the earliest document in the New Testament) is 1 Thessalonians; the point of origin probably was Corinth in the early 50's A.D., after his second journey. On his second campaign, Paul had crossed over from Troas to Macedonia and then preached in Thessalonica (modern Salonica), Beroea, and Athens. He had been joined in Athens by Timothy who had brought a report from Thessalonica. Paul's letter is in response to that situation. He praised them for their constancy and warns them against faintheartedness, fair-weather loyalty, and sexual immortality, i.e., of the kind popular in Greece and condemned by Judaism. He defends his mission against the Jewish-Christian opposition, and closes with a word of encouragement for those who mourned their bereaved.

2 Thessalonians, a second letter to the Thessalonians, is included in the New Testament canon, but many scholars question its authenticity.

2. GALATIANS

The most spirited of Paul's letters was addressed to the Galatians, his Gentile followers at Iconium, Lystra, Derbe, and Antioch in Asia Minor. Some Jewish-Christians from Jerusalem had entered among these Gentile converts, claiming that Paul's gospel was illegitimate, and that he discouraged his converts from observing the traditional Jewish Law. They claimed that a Gentile had to be circumcised before he could be accepted as a follower of the Messiah, Christ.

In defending himself against these "Judaizers," whose doctrine differed from his, he explained that his own apostleship was "from God and not man." Then, in chapter 2, he described the conference at Jerusalem, which he had Barnabas had attended, accompanied by Titus, an uncircumcised Gentile. In that debate with the apostles, Peter and James, Paul has used Titus as a test case of a bona-fide Christian though uncircumcised. If Titus was accepted, and it was impossible to deny his qualifications, and the manifest presence of the sins in his life, then concerns about adherence to Jewish Law, especially circumcision were irrelevant to the main issue, the new creature in Christ. While agreeing with Paul in principle, the church leaders attempted to smooth over the differences between Paul and those who insisted on adherence to the Law of Moses on the part of all Christians, and imposed a compromise solution (cf. Acts 15) requiring minimal observance on the part of Gentiles, so as not to offend the sensibilities of the Jewish-Christians. As a temporary expedient the decision may have been successful in keeping the diverse groups under one roof, but the dynamics of the situation did not favor compromise. Given the potential for Gentile conversions, and the extraordinary skill and drive of Paul and his associates, the issue was bound to become more and more acute for the Jewish-Christian component of the church, and the ultimate triumph of Pauline doctrine on the subject could hardly have been in doubt. No hindrance should or could be placed in the way of the Gentiles for whose salvation Christ had died, and their entry into the church in large and increasing numbers was evidence of the overriding power of the Holy Spirit in bringing new things to pass, but also shifted the balance of power and decision away from the original Jewish-Christian community to the new Gentile majority. For a while they lived side by side symbiotically and sympathetically, but in the end the Jewish-Christians were engulfed.

3. CORINTHIANS

When Paul reached Ephesus on his third journey, word came to him of trouble in Corinth, due to factional disputes. He had apparently addressed the Corinthians earlier (cf. 2 Corinthians is thought to contain parts of more than one letter), and he now rebuked them for their divisions and spelled out the official doctrine of the Lord's Supper, and the apostolic testimony to the resurrection, along with personal advice on the subject of marriage and private morality. The letters reveal the acute problems of the community and Paul's methods in handling them (cf. 1 Corinthians 1:10 ff.).

The statements in 1 Corinthians 15:3-8 and Galatians 1:11-17 reflect essential components of the apostolic preaching, which may be culled from the Gospels and Acts. The proclamation of the Good News included the following points: a) the age of fulfillment has dawned; b) this has taken place through the ministry, death, and resurrection of Jesus; c) by virtue of the ressurection, Jesus has been exalted at the right hand of God; d) the Holy Spirit in the church is the sign of Christ's present power and glory; e) the Messianic age will shortly reach its consummation in the return of Christ; and f) an appeal for repentance, the offer for forgiveness, and the promise of salvation are extended.

4. BACKGROUND

a. *An Inimical Graffito*

The Christian doctrine that the Son of God became the means of salvation of mankind through his crucifixion was unacceptable both to the Jews to whom it was a "stumbling block" (1 Corinthians 1:23) as well as to the 313

Bronze mirror from Azor; 11th c. B.C.

Roman calumny suggesting the worship of an ass; drawn in a palace guardroom

Gentiles to whom the idea of God suffering the ignominious death of a felon appeared ludicrous. Statements to this effect appeared in polemics against Christians. A graphic illustration of the hatred evoked at times by the new faith was found in one of the guardrooms of the Roman imperial palace, the Palatine, in Rome: a crude third century A.D. graffito showing a man kneeling to a crucified figure with an ass's head, worshiping his god! Similar calumnies regarding the worship of an ass had already been uttered by the enemies of Judaism in the Hellenistic period.

b. *Mirrors*

Before glass, backed with tinfoil, began to reflect a clear image in later centuries, common bronze mirrors were used in Palestine and they reflected imperfectly the features of those looking into them, as expressed in Paul's immortal simile: "For now we see in a mirror, darkly..." (1 Cor 13:11–12).

c. *Aretas*

The Aretas referred to in 2 Corinthians 11:32 is Harethat IV, well known from coins and inscriptions bearing his name, found at Avdat in the Negeb. Paul hid from the *Nabatean* rulers of Damascus whose kingdom extended from the Negeb to Syria.

5. PHILIPPIANS, COLOSSIANS, EPHESIANS, AND PHILEMON

The Epistles are also known as "the letters of the captivity," because they were written during Paul's imprisonment. This may have been in Rome in A.D. 60–64, though he had been a prisoner for two years in Ephesus, and the letters may derive from the earlier experience.

The first three letters contain some of the loftiest teaching in the New Testament as they define once and for all the nature of the Christian life. *Philippians* is the most intimate and affectionate of them, as he tells his friends of his condition and hope of release. He then describes his experience of oneness with Christ and admonishes them to preserve their unity "for me to live in Christ..." (1 Phil 1:21; 2:1; 3:7, 13–14).

Colossians, Ephesians and *Philemon* are linked together by the mention of Onesimus and Archippus in Philemon and Colossians, and Tychicus (the Messenger) in Ephesians and Colossians.

Ephesus was the center of one of Paul's most extended and successful campaigns. He established a firm loyal community there and made many friends. Nevertheless, the Epistle to the Ephesians is a general tract and does not reflect Paul's close attachment to the church there. It should be noted that the best and earliest manuscripts do not have the word "Ephesians" and it is widely believed among scholars that it was not addressed to the Ephesians but to another church; or it may have been a circular letter which was passed from church to church. Many scholars also feel that the letter was written by a follower of Paul, rather than the apostle himself.

Colossians is similar to Ephesians in many ways, emphasizing Christ's role and status as *Kosmokrator* (ruler of the universe), and as head of the church, but there is a special emphasis in the latter on false Gnostic teaching which has penetrated the church at Colossae. Paul opposes the esoteric, elitist pretensions of the Gnostics with the true knowledge of God revealed in Jesus Christ. He points to the central experience of the believer, who achieves reconcilation with God by dying and rising with Christ. This pattern reflects the vocabulary and some of the teachings of the mystery cults, including those of Jewish-Christians.

Paul authenticated his letters by adding a "salutation in his own hand" as did other letter writers whose epistles have been preserved on papyrus. An example of a letter written in two hands is one dated 24th August, A.D. 66, on behalf of a peasant to a governor; the main part is written in a formal scribal hand, with additions in another less elegant script.

The letter to *Philemon,* while very short, is an important and intriguing document. It is the only personal letter in the Pauline corpus, being addressed to the owner of a runaway slave, Onesimus, whom Paul had converted in Rome, and whom he was now sending back to Philemon with this message. Paul has no revolutionary political objective such as abolishing slavery. On the contrary, he insists on obedience to the law. Onesimus must return to his master. At the same time, a new element has been introduced into the relationship — Christianity — which should effect a profound change in attitude and behavior on the part of both men. The operative words are love and brotherhood. While ostensibly they remain master and slave, in fact they become brothers in Christ, and must demonstrate this fact in their lives.

6. THE NEW TEMPLE

The wide diffusion of the idea of a new temple as an early Christian theme is indisputable. There are many passages in the New Testament which identify the new temple with the Jewish-Christian community. Paul lectures the Corinthians about the new temple as if it were a basic well known feature of early Christian theology (1 Cor 3:16; 6:19; Ephes 2:21). Moreover, the first Epistle of Peter expresses a similar viewpoint (1 Pet 2:5). Similar allusions to this doctrine appear in extra-canonical Christian literature which reflect the Jewish-Christian theology. The Ephesians are addressed by Ignatius, bishop of Antioch, as "temple-bearers." The extra-canonical *Epistle of Barnabas* devotes chapter 16 to the way in which the Jewish-Christian community has taken the place of the old temple by becoming a spiritual temple being built for the Lord. Another of the early witnesses to the new temple is the *Didache,* whose allusions to the theology of the new temple amplify the material in 1 Peter, i.e., the eucharist of the Didache community is a sacrifice for which new rites of spiritual purification are required.

7. ROMANS

Romans is unique in the Pauline canon in that it was written, probably from Corinth in about A.D. 56, to a church neither founded nor yet visited by the apostle. It falls into three major sections: Chapters 1–11 comprise a treatise on the need for salvaton through Christ. Chapters 12–15:13 give practical directives for living a Christian life. Chapters 5:14–16:27 consist of personal messages and salutations.

According to Paul, sin and death entered the world through the first man, Adam (5:12–14) but righteousness and life have been brought into the world through Christ (5:15–21). The central importance of Adam in the development of Christology is characteristic of Jewish-Christian thought, as we saw in the symbolism of Adam's Chapel at the Church of the Holy Sepulchre (see Part XVII).

The term "rghteousness" is used by him in the special sense of a satisfactory relationship with God: a righteous man is one who will be found "not guilty" (*saddîq* in Hebrew) at the Last Judgment. This, in a quintessential way, illustrates the unbroken line of thought which runs through Hassidean thought, Essenism, the Dead Sea Scrolls, and Jewish-Christianity, as shown in the previous chapters (Parts XVI–XVII).

Throughout the Pauline letters two Pauls seem to be revealed: Paul the practical preacher of the Gospel, and Paul the theologian. Romans is not a manual of Pauline doctrine. It was an attempt to clear up the main problems of the Jewish-Gentile confrontation within the early Christian church and the friction between synagogue and church, or put into other words, the relationship between Jew and Gentile in the new dispensation (see Part XVIII), and the conflict between ancestral Jewish Law and Faith in Christ as a means of achieving "righteousness."

8. THE LOGIA AS COLLECTIONS FOR THE "SAINTS"

The core group of early Christians in and around Jerusalem symbolized the whole movement in their lives of devotion by their own efforts. Their co-religionists in the Diaspora recognized it as their duty to supply the needs of the mother church in Jerusalem. Paul went to great lengths to raise funds for the support of the Jerusalem community which, in his time, was small and living in hostile surroundings. Collections for the "saints" in Jerusalem are referred to in Romans 15:26 and in 1 Corinthians 16:1, where they are called *logia*. The same term is used in the ostracon dated 4th August, A.D. 63, in which a Gentile Greek, Psenamunis, the son of Pekysis, acknowledges receiving four drachmas, one obolus, as a contribution for the worship of Isis. This type of collection was a common practice in antiquity.

9. TIMOTHY AND TITUS

The three letters to Timothy and Titus are called the *pastorals,* because they ostensibly carry instructions from Paul to his two pastors, younger associates, concerning their work as pastors or bishops of their congregations. General scholarly opinion, however, holds that the letters are not compositions of Paul, but of a later writer who had adopted parts of an authentic letter and has adapted and applied them to the circumstances of his own day, using the name and authority of the great apostle after his death. They lack the color and fire of authentic letters by Paul, but they share his outlook and much of his theology. Perhaps the proper conclusion is that they are Pauline in character and spirit, but are not literally by Paul himself.

10. ADMINISTRATION BY THE BISHOPS AND DEACONS

The early chruch required the appointment of officials charged with the management and administration of the common property of its members for the benefit of the community (Acts 6:1–6)). They were called *diakonoi*, "servants" and their qualifications are laid down in 1 Timothy 3:8. The *episkopoi*, "overseers" or bishops, were appointed in larger communities (Acts 20:17, 28). There were several of them at Philippi and at Ephesus. This organization developed gradually over the years, but all were expected to qualify by holiness of character.

11. PHILEMON: WHAT WERE THE PRIMITIVE AND DOMESTIC CHAPELS LIKE?

The chapel in the house of Philemon is reminiscent of those used in the early Jewish-Christian communities. The modest worship centers were located generally in the interiors of private houses. They were grouped round a courtyard in the prevailing Mediterranean style, and enclosed on all sides. A third century A.D. Jewsh-Christian chapel of this type was uncovered at *Dura-Europos* on the Euphrates. It was indistinguishable from the houses around it (see diagram) and consisted of a chapel with walls covered by wall-paintings (preserved in Damascus), a big room for the love-meal (agapé) of the community, and an assembly hall, with a seat for the bishop.

Diagram of the domestic church of Dura-Europos (described in the text)

B. CATHOLIC OR GENERAL EPISTLES

The seven final letters of the New Testament, James, 1 and 2 Peter, 1, 2 and 3 John, and Jude, are more general in character than the epistles attributed to Paul and are generally assigned to the late first century A.D.

1. THE OVERALL POLITICAL BACKGROUND

Post-apostolic Christianity (following the days of Peter and Paul) had moved eastward and northward into Asia Minor and Greece, and the congregations were cocentrated in that area. At the same time, Jewish nationalism focussed attention on the land and its political liberation, thus drawing Jewish interest and effort back to Palestine. Both church and synagogue had to adjust their thinking in the light of changing conditions and the different pressures. Jewish-Christians, especially, had to make agonizing decisions about their identity: as they saw the Jewish community move in one direction and the Christian in another, they had to decide to which one they belonged, whereas earlier they could participate in both successfully, and be Jews and Christians at once. Now with the Jewish community closing ranks in the face of the great enemy, Rome, there wasn't room for divergent groups like Christians, and with Christianity becoming increasingly gentile in makeup, the Jewish-Chrstians felt more and more isolated.

During this period,· the relations of the primitive church to Judaism on the one hand, and to the Roman authorities on the other, had remained serious problems. They become even more acute toward the end of the century; the religious and social tensions of this period are reflected in the Epistles of James, Second Peter, and Jude. These writings react against the current surge of Jewish nationalism, and they condemn contemporary revolutionary tendencies. They prescribe instead a policy of submission to the established authorities, not because they approve of them, but because they have been ordained by God, and any change must be instituted by God. Besides, the time is short, and there is no need to engage in seditious or revolutionary activities. God will overwhelm the kingdoms of the world and replace them with his own realm. In the meantime Christians must be obedient and suffer patiently whatever befalls them, as true disciples of Jesus. The iniquities of this world are to be rectified by God and his Messiah, not by violence or "zeal" as the revolutionary spirit was called. There is a strong family resemblance to the political quietism of the original Hassideans of the second century B.C., as reflected in the book of Daniel. The success of the Maccabees had changed quietism to activism on the part of most Jews, but the Essenes, for example, remained faithful to the older ideals. Early Christians followed the same pattern guided by Jesus and his disciples.

It will be remembered that the closest analogy between the new faith and piety taught by Jesus is not to be found in the orthodox tradition, whether in the Temple cult or in theological discussions of the rabbis. It stems rather from the apocalyptic-pietistic movement which in the third and second centuries B.C. found expression in the book of Daniel and in apocalyptic intertestamental writings and attitudes (described in Parts XI, XV and XVI). These were represented in the days of Jesus by fervently messianic congregations, including the movement of John the Baptizer.

2. CONTEMPORARY SOCIAL AND RELIGIOUS CONSIDERATIONS

The current opposition among the early Christians to the *status quo* can be traced to a variety of causes and found a variety of expressions:

a. Fundamentally, many felt that the eschatological consummation or "end of the age" did not happen (Paul, who heralded it, had discussed it in his early writings, 1 and 2 Thessalonians). "Eschatological impatience led to social disorder. Dissatisfied believers materialized eschatology, hoping to have final triumph and joy of the faithful realized in empirical forms on earth." The poorer classes wanted the new church, the Jewish-Christian communal group, to improve their status. The groups seemed to be linked with popular fraternities, and hopes of another and better life were understood by many in a materialistic way, here and now.

b. Jewish influence on the Jewish-Christian community was always an important factor. The Jewish presence affected early Christians both positively and negatively for two reasons: (1) The Jewish-Christian movement was invigorated and enriched by new recruits; (2) Judaism was still a religion officially recognized by Rome. This privilege was not accorded by law to Gentile Christianity which might also be persecuted, as it was, under the severe Roman legislation against fraternities. Hence Jewish-Christians could find shelter under the roof of the synagogue where they would not be persecuted. Jews were allowed to affirm "atheism: in the sense of non-commitment to the pagan deities, if they paid the annual tax required by the emperor, but Christians were not. Thus, Flavius Clement and his wife, Domitilla, both relatives of the emperor, were accused of atheism according to the historians, Suetonius and Dio; Domitilla's catacomb in Rome shows that she was a Christian convert.

The existence of nationalistic anti-Roman movements in this period, inspired by the Palestinian situation and waves of zealotry in the Diaspora, is only too evident from extra-canonical apocalypses such as *Baruch* and *IV Ezra* (so named after historic figures mentioned in the Old Testament).

c. Finally, many contemporary Romans had succumbed to the spell of Stoic and Cynic philosophy with their ideals of freedom and equality.

All these factors were operative among circles in the Roman establishment where strong opposition to Domitian was felt, particularly in the senatorial party. In fact, fraternities and societies, including the Christians, were encouraged by influential Romans. It is true that such corporate propaganda called *ambitus* was condemned officially, but flourished nevertheless. As the conflict between state and opposition grew, the poor Christian community was apparently compromised by its implied connection with the opposition; it could thus be led into unchristian arrogance and consequent persecution. It was the duty of leading Christian personalities such as the

319

authors of the Epistles dealt with in our study, to remind their followers of the fact that genuine wisdom is humble, not impatient.

In sum, the General Epistles contain many expressions which bring to mind the Dead Sea Scrolls, as well as the apocalyptic pietism of books like Daniel and the extra-canonical works like it. Furthermore, while differing from the Pauline epistles in other respects, they agree with Paul in condemning political actions on the part of Christians.

3. CONTRAST BETWEEN THE EPISTLES AND REVELATION

There is a difference in attitude toward the constituted authorities, but neither the General Epistles nor Revelation (see Part XX) advocate violent resistance even in the face of extreme provocation or persecution. While the writers of the General Epistles express neutrality or moderate support for the Roman regime (as does Paul), the author of Revelation spares no language in condemning the Roman empire for its blasphemy in usurping the place of God, and in forcing the faithful to accord divine honors to the emperor, violating both conscience and truth. Yet his counsel was submission and in this ordeal, which would not only win for the martyrs an eternal crown of Glory, but would also trigger a divine response at the appointed time, when the new age would be consummated in the unending reign of God and the Lamb (Jesus Christ who had lived, died and was resurrected).

4. THE EPISTLE OF JAMES

The Epistle of James is addressed to the Christian constituency at large, including both Jewish and Gentile components. It is in the form of an allocution from the head of the church to its members and leaders, emphasizing basic Christian virtues, and the prime importance of patient endurance (e.g. 1:21; 5:7–11). The primeval theme of the book may be outlined as follows:

a. Patience in the midst of afflictions which lead to steadfastness and perfection. Wisdom obtained through prayer. Riches are nothing to boast about. Perseverance in tribulations brings blessedness; man's lust is the cause of tribulations. Importance of being a doer of the word. (chapter 1)

b. The impropriety of currying favor with the rich. Worthlessness of a faith not practiced. (chapter 2)

c. Dangers of a poisoned tongue. Humble living. (chapter 3)

d. Combativeness of the recipients. Business ethics. Judgment on the unrighteous rich. (4:1–5:6)

e. Patient waiting for Christ's return: a manual of discipline; singing and praying; the healing of the sick. The salvation of apostates. (5:7–20).

While the Epistle in its present form and language is to be dated in the sub-apostolic period, it contains many primitive elements which take us back to the earliest period of the church. Some of the sayings are similar to the teachings of Jesus recorded in the Synoptic Gospels, and usually assigned to the Q source. The sayings in James derive from the same oral tradition and in a form that reflects the Semitic original. At the same time, the organization of the community addressed is distinguished by the authority of a committee of the elders, an institution inherited from later Second Temple times, when the elders governed the synagogues. This arrangement conformed also with the organizational chart and operational procedures in the first Jewish-Christian congregations of Jerusalem and Antioch.

5. THE EPISTLES OF PETER

a. *The First Epistle*

The epistle known as First Peter is a message to Christians in northern, central and western Asia Minor, admonishing them to be meek, patient and ready to endure suffering in time of tribulation. On the basis of the data provided it is not possible to pinpoint the occasion or the immediate circumstances; scholars have proposed dates of composition anywhere from the 60's to the 90's of the first century. Although the epistle is attributed to the apostle Peter as the principal author, the actual writer or amanuensis is said to be Silvanus, an early disciple and companion of Paul.

It is supposed that Peter provided the substance of the epistle, but that the precise language and form, as well as the theological nuances were supplied by the secretary. Other scholars hold that it is a "Pauline" composition throughout, perhaps composed by Silvanus, but mistakenly associated with Peter. It is characterized by a shift away from the Jewish-Christian position, and toward gentile Christian views. It has been suggested further that the epistle was intended to be read to new Christians at baptismal and confirmation services. In this respect, First Peter is comparable to the Epistle to the Ephesians, which also appears to have been intended as greeting and admonition to recently baptized Christians.

First Peter calls attention to the incalculable value of the extraordinary gift which they have received through the gospel:

(1) This emphasizes the responsiblity of those baptized for the grace received (1:1–4:6) with admonitions to avoid malice and show loyalty to the authorities; maxims for daily living; fearlessness, evangelical open-mindedness, and readiness to suffer.

(2) The love and steadfastness of the whole congregation (4:7–5:14) in hospitality, cooperation, perseverance in persecution; devotion of the elders to the flock, trust in God, steadfastness, and a wish for peace.

Epistle of Peter 5:12–12
(Papyrus Bodmer; 2nd–3rd
c. A.D.)

b. *The Second Epistle of Peter*

The second epistle attributed to Peter was written by a follower in the name of the Prince of Apostles. In it, the apostle warns Christians to be steady and to avoid corruption in the face of persecution (perhaps under Domitian, ca. A.D. 95); it is addressed to the same churches in Asia Minor which are referred to in the First Epistle, but the Second Epistle is widely regarded as the latest book in the New Testament, and clearly belongs to the post-apostolic age.

Its purpose is to admonish the communities to be steadfast and to warn them against deceivers. Of these two themes, Chapters 1 and 3 discuss the first, and chapter 2 deals with the second. An interesting passage in 1:19 compares prophecy to a "lamp shining in a dark place until the day dawns," a reference to a type of lantern suspended by chains from a handle.

The theme of deception in the second chapter, i.e. of seducers exploiting the Christians, deserves attention. It would appear that senators and other leading aristocrats opposed to the power-hungry emperor, Domitian, used church leaders to gain political adherents among the Christians. This involved political and social propaganda, along with financial remuneration and specious promises of preferment to the naive and unwary Christians. These movements and organizations were vigorously combated by the authorities who, at the same time, persecuted Christians as participants in subversion. To what extent Christians made common cause with the political forces aligned against the emperor we do not know, but the author of the epistle opposes such an unholy alliance. Bad as the emperor may be, Christians are called upon to submit, to obey, and to set an example to all others of perseverance under trials and tribulations, in imitation of the Lord Jesus. Only in this way will the church be seen as true and faithful and be exonerated from false charges. The Gospel must not be perverted or misused for the sake of political propaganda, no matter how great the provocation, or the possible rewards of direct action.

6. THE EPISTLE OF JUDE

This short epistle contains warnings by a Palestinian Jewish-Christian against deceivers and exhortations to preserve faith, love and hope. The author of the Epistle is identified as Jude, the brother of James. It would be natural to recognize in James the head of the Jerusalem church, and the brother of Jesus. Even if this were the intention of the writer, it is not stated explicitly, and in any case may be doubted. It is generally believed that the work dates around the end of the first century A.D., and is addressed to Jewish-Christians. There is a literary relationship between Jude and chapter 2 of Second Peter, but the question of dependence is unresolved. Both may have borrowed from the same original source.

A most instructive element in Jude is the citation of Enoch 1:9. The book of Enoch was not regarded by either Jewish or Christian councils as canonical, yet Jude clearly treats it as inspired scripture. In the pietist schools Enoch the patriarch, the "seventh from Adam," was considered one of the special friends of God, and an authentic prophet. The author of Jude therefore does not hesitate to cite the extra-canonical text of 1 Enoch 1:9 in support of his warnings, since he regards the quotation in question as an ancient prophecy of the destruction of the "teacher of heresy" as in Second Peter.

7. THE EPISTLES OF JOHN

a. *First Epistle General*

The theme of both the first and second Epistles of John is an affirmation of the doctrine of the identity of God and Christ. If one asks what God is as a circular ltter addressed to Jewish-Christians, since its message is worked out in familiar Old Testament terms. Its contents centers around the traditional ritual of the Temple, notably the Day of Atonement, comparing its sacrifice of the propitiatory goat to that of Christ who had offered himself in the heavenly sanctuary. The Jewish-Christians who were concerned about such priestly and cultic matters needed instruction in the sacrificial role of Jesus, which was different from the usual picture of a royal victorious messiah. Another important emphasis is the transition from the old covenant to a new one, an idea which was emphasized at Qumran. This leads to the climax of the book: the finality of Jesus and his message of salvation.

1. CONTENTS

The Epistle emphasizes the superiority of Jesus over all other beings. In 1:12, his superiority over the prophets is affirmed. After that Jesus is placed higher than the angels (1:3–2:18). Jesus, says Hebrews, deserved greater honor than Moses (3:3). Since he was a member of the tribe of Judah, the Epistle does not explicitly mention his descent from David, but he could not be regarded as a priest in the ordinary sense (because

they were of the tribe of Levi); but he was a special high priest after the order of Melchizedek, the ancient model of the high-priesthood, which was superior to that of Aaron (see: King David). He became himself the sacrifice for the sins of the world (chs. 5–7 and thus mediated a new and exalted covenant which was just an imperfect forerunner of the new one (8–10:18). Sacrifices ceased in any case after the destruction of the Temple in A.D. 70. Jesus' sacrifice of his own blood has redeemed men from their sins and made Jewish sacrifices of goats and bulls superfluous. Christ offered his body as a sacrifice and he himself carried his own blood into the heavenly sanctuary (9:12) thereby reconciling God's chosen to him.

The new relationship of the true believer rests on faith (10:12), a matter of belief beyond sight, as in the Johannine gospel. Blessed are those who believe even though they have not seen. The remainder of the Epistle encourages the faithful to endure suffering patiently, illustrating the teaching by examples drawn from biblical and non-biblical tradition, such as the legendary death of the prophet Isaiah related to the extra-canonical *Ascension of Isaiah,* a Jewish-Christian midrash. Isaiah was supposedly put to death by the paganizing king Manasseh of Judah (Ascension 10:19–11:37). They are exhorted to live in brotherly love, disdaining immorality or covetousness, loyal to their "leader" (Ch. 13).

PART XX

A. EPISTLE TO THE HEBREWS

A number of extra-canonical writings are attributed to the Jewish-Christian community which date from sub-Apostolic times during the late first and early second centuries A.D. The only writings of this type which were included in the New Testament are the Epistle to the Hebrews and Revelation, which express the thought of new Christians belonging to the Jewish milieu.

We do not know who wrote Hebrews. Its doctrine, style, and time rule out Paul. It was apparently written in the latter part of the first century A.D. to encourage Jewish-Christians who were enduring bitter persecution and suffering, perhaps at the time of Domitian. Efforts to ascertain the specific community to which the Epistle was addressed have been advanced by the discovery of a third century Greek papyrus. It speaks of the Jewish manner of paraphrasing the Old Testament, as a sort of *midrash* (or interpretative commentary on the text) which was also the practice of the Covenanters of Qumran. The Epistle may be understood

Greek papyrus of the Epistle to the Hebrews (3rd c. A.D.)

with John's reiteration of the commandment to love one's brother (2:7–17). In 2:18–19, the author resumes the discussion, elaborating the threat of the "antichrist," the antithesis to the Messiah who appears in various forms in contemporary apocalyptic literature. John bases his refutation of the Gnostics on the argument that to deny Jesus is to deny God. Section 2:26–29 is a recapitulation of the warning against the false teachers who deny this truth.

Chapter 3:1–12 takes up the moral argument. Knowing that Christian salvation is an accepted fact to his audience, the author of John uses the mystical argument that since Christians are God's children, and are destined to be transformed wholly into his likeness, they can be sure that they will see God. Christians who have been "born of God" cannot sin. The seal of the transformation is in the Spirit which is the means and the reward of obedience to God's commandments (3:13–14).

Chapter 4 opens with a paragraph (verses 1–6) on true and false inspiration. The apostolic church believed that prophecy had been revived and that their brethren could be inspired by the Spirit to declare hidden truths. Nevertheless, all inspiration and all spirits do not necessarily come from God. They had found that there was also a spirit of perversity (that of antichrist) abroad in the world, and the author of John explains how to distinguish between true and false spirits (4:6).

Johannine teaching no longer refers to a second coming of Christ. "He who has the son has life..." proclaims John 5:12, but that life is something to be lived in the present world. It is not postponed to a "future life" and another world. The believer has received the "eternal life'" of Christ, has already triumphed over death and lives in the messianic age.

2 John can be described as a miniature edition (13 verses only) of 1 John, for every phrase in it occurs in the larger work as well and the theme is the same: Christian love as the true road to salvation and the need to guard against deceivers and false teachers.

d. *3 John and Diotrephes*

Unlike 1 and 2 John which deal with doctrinal questions, 3 John is a rebuke to a church leader, Diotrephes, for his insubordination, not his theology. By A.D. 110, the "elders" were no longer the rulers of the church, but had now become the advisers of the bishop who enjoyed a preeminent and all-powerful position. Diotrephes, as bishop, claimed exclusive jurisdiction over the church in Ephesus whereas John, "the Elder," exercised a traditional authority within the larger district. The title which John uses of himself, "the Elder," seems to have been used at first and for a long time in the sense of one of the original Apostolic witnesses. He had authority over the church to which he was writing, although at the time the original pattern of itinerant missionaries was coming to an end, to be replaced by a system of settled local ministries. The writer of 2 John wanted missionaries excluded for fear of their subversive teaching. 3 John calls for them to be reeived and helped. The letter's condemnation was presumably connected with his rejection of these missionaries.

like, then the answer can be found in Jesus. The first Epistle of John is close to the Fourth Gospel in style, vocabulary and thought, and many scholars assume that the author is the same. Some, however, postulate a disciple of the Evangelist or a member of the "Johannine" school.

b. *The Debate with Gnosticism and its Mysteries*

The epistle is aimed especially against the deviation from orthodox church doctrine known as *Gnosticism*. The term covers a variety of belief-systems, and serves as a catch-all for many different groups, but an essential common ingredient is the possession by an elite of special, secret knowledge (i.e. *Gnosis*). The promise held out by different groups to new adherents was to provide this Gnosis, which could only be secured by initiation into certain rites and the practice of an equally secret discipline. Depending upon the hidden teaching of a leader, Gnostics might be ascetic puritans, or unrestrained libertines. Some of the second century Gnostics were able speculative thinkers. There is a proto-Gnostic element in Judaism and in Christianity, especially in eschatologically and apocalyptically centered groups. For them the pivotal factor was the secret or mystery of the last days: not only the timetable of divine action, but the sequence of events and the identity of the principal participants. Knowledge of the secret was reserved to the faithful few and in certain cases unobtainable, i.e., not even the Son knows the hour when the end comes according to the Gospels. Paul also makes much of the special knowledge of salvation that belongs to the Christian. But none of this is Gnosticism in the developed sense of second century Gnostic groups which combined *dualism* (the doctrine of two gods — one good, one evil) *docetism* (that spirit and flesh cannot be combined, and that Jesus only appeared to be a man). To the author of 1 John, Gnosticism is the great threat to the life and faith of the church, and he combats it by restating the Gospel in the language of ethical and metaphysical opposites, often used by Gnostics, but to deny their tenets.

The Gnostics denied the earthly existence of Jesus and, consequently, refused to accept the church's doctrine of Incarnation, i.e. that God had appeared in the flesh in the person of Jesus Christ. For his answer to this contention, the apostle turned back to the earliest phases of Jewish-Christianity and reminded his readers of the apostolic witness to Christ and, furthermore, of Christ's historical existence and his human roots in the Jewish community. He emphasizes the reality of Jesus as the Messiah-Christ and admonishes his readers to live in the "fellowship of love."

c. *Contents of 1 John*

The central theme is stated in the first verses of the epistle (1:1–4) which emphasize the writer's personal experience of fellowship with God through his son, Jesus Christ. The development of this theme centers around three main concepts: the "fellowship" between God and Christians within the religious community; "sin" which separates man from God (1:5–10) and "obedience to God's commandments" which is the only sure way of drawing closer to God. This appears in a number of verses (2:1–6, etc.) and is linked   323

2. AFFINITY WITH THE DEAD SEA SCROLLS

Y. Yadin believes that the Epistle was addressed more specifically to descendants of sectarian Jews related to the community of Qumran, after A.D. 70. A fundamental change must be presumed, however, since the Mosaic *torah* remained the foundation of the Qumran community for its faith and practice, along with their codified rules of Discipline, whereas for the community addressed in Hebrews, Jesus as Messiah — regarded as more glorious even than Moses — had already come. The Qumranites expected not only a kingly messiah or the House of David, but also a priestly messiah from the line of Aaron; but these hopes were never fulfilled and nothing is known of their fate. Hebrews, on the contrary, opens with the emphatic affirmation that the revelation which God had given in the past, was only partial and has now been superseded by the full truth "spoken unto us by his Son."

In Hebrews we find a theological rationale for the termination of bloody sacrifices, stipulated in the Law. Jesus' self-sacrifice is the full, final and perfect offering which makes all further sacrifice futile and unnecessary. Here we have a deliberate break with the traditional Judaism of the Second-Temple period. But the Jewish community itself had to adjust to the termination of sacrifices when the Temple was destroyed by the Romans in A.D. 70. They did not try to maintain or revise such sacrifices but substituted prayers and good work, basing the decision on the words of the prophets who criticized severely the empty worship of the First Temple, with its multitude of animals and its rivers of oil. Thus Judaism and Christianity came essentially to the same conclusion about the proper mode of worship, but by different routes. In the end, Judaism retained, nevertheless, its vision of the Messiah to come, in contrast to Christianity with its crucified and resurrected Messiah.

3. ARCHAEOLOGICAL CONNECTIONS

We are indebted to Hebrews for one significant statement about the site of the crucifixion: "...so Jesus also suffered outside the gate..." (13:12). As to the garden where the tomb was, it stood in the immediate vicinity of the gibbet. Taken together with the testimony of the Gospels about the actual burial of Jesus, there seems to be a reliable basis for the traditional site of the Holy Sepulchre according to those upholding it. Weighty archaeological questions remain, however, as discussed earlier (Part XVII: Site of the Crucifixion), and a solution will depend upon further research and possible new discoveries.

a. Heavenly Court

Unlike Paul, Hebrews describes the saving effect of the death of Jesus in terms, not so much of resurrection (as Paul does), as of his ascension as high priest into the innermost sanctuary of the heavenly temple where he performs his act of intercession, and enters at the right hand of God.

Selected anchor symbols common to tombs in Palestine, or in the Jewish-Christian Priscilla catacombs in Rome. They were regarded as the sign of hope (Heb 6:19–20)

Opposite page: Symbols such as the plow, the ladder, the candelabrum, the water spurting from the arms of the monogram cross, seen on early Christian Roman epitaphs, resemble those found on ossuaries and walls of funerary buildings in Jerusalem. They are attributed to Jewish-Christian teachings. Such are the anchor and fish and signs from a Roman catacomb (epitaph of Licinia Amiata) and miscellaneous signs on Roman catacombs

This image is inherited from Old Testament eschatological traditions, among them Ezekiel's vision of the heavenly throne-chariots in Ch. 1.

There is also a background in ancient mythological pictures, brought to light by archaeological discovery, in which the high god is represented in his heavenly palace surrounded and supported by lesser dieties (cf. Job 1–2). The Ugaritic mythological texts give us vivid glimpses of the meetings of the gods. They were the members of the ancient pantheon who are transposed, in later monotheistic theology, into "angels" or servants of God. Yahweh, as king of the gods holds court in the vision of the prophet Micaiah ben Imlah in 1 Kings 22:19–23, surrounded by his divine entourage of counselors and servants, who station themselves in attendance upon the king. An echo is heard in Proverbs 22:29:

> "Do you see a man skilful in his work?
> he will stand before kings; he will not
> stand before obscure men."

Above all, the quality of glory in heaven signifies *luminosity*. In this connection, it is interesting to recall the early Jewish-Christian belief about the divine appearance at Bethlehem. For them, the Bethlehem grotto became a symbol of passage from darkness to light, when a great star shone out in the heavens.

b. *A Representation of the Tabernacle*

Hebrews conceives of Jesus as the minister of the true tabernacle (8:2), as opposed to the man-made Tabernacle which accompanied the Israelites in the desert. One of the earliest representations of the latter is found in the frieze of the synagogue at Capernaum. Here, as in the synagogue frescoes of Dura-Europos, we have a sanctuary mounted on wheels, suitable for transporting sacred objects from one place to another, until it finally comes to rest in the Temple at Jerusalem.

The frieze from the synagogue of Capenaum represents the Tabernacle during its wanderings in the desert, namely a shrine mounted on wheels. It corresponds to Roman carriages shaped like sanctuaries which served to transport images of the gods from one place to another

B. REVELATION (THE APOCALYPSE)

1. Purpose

The book of Revelation, like other apocalyptic Jewish-Christian writings, is optimistic and courageous in tone. The occasion is a crisis in the life of the church and the purpose is to deal with the apparent failure of the cause of God on earth. Confidence in the future is expressed by a forecast of the triumphal coming of Christ, the establishment of the rule of God in the world, and the final Day of Judgment. The general outline conforms to Daniel in the Old Testment, the little apocalypses in the New Testament, and extra-canonical intertestamental writing, referred to earlier. Its contents, therefore, mix the terrestrial and the cosmic, the historical with the transcendental, the timely with the timeless, and it is often difficult to distinguish one from the other. Furthermore, the narrative is heavily disguised in symbolism of many kinds, deliberately made incomprehensible to all but insiders. It describes the impending downfall of the contemporary social and political structure, expressing the fervent conviction that the destruction of Roman power, which the author regarded as utterly corrupt, was at hand. The empire is depicted in its death throes, torn by internal dissensions, threatened by enemies without, the participants in the gory drama being presented as either the objects or the agents of divine wrath. In the end mankind will face a final judgment divided between the wicked who are to perish and the elect, who will be saved. Apart from the numerous, often obscure allusions to contemporary politics and the struggle between these trying to hold to power, and those seeking it, the internal and external pressure on the Empire, there are signs and symbols pertaining to the basic convictions and ardent hopes of the faithful, which contain and communicate the essential Gospel for those who suffered greatly for their faith. Some of these symbols, in graphic form have also been found and preserved in the region of the Seven Churches of the Apocalypse in Asia Minor where Professors Bagatti and Testa discovered inscriptions, signs and objects representing the five fundamental elements of the Jewish-Christian system of symbols in association with each other.

The book was written to a persecuted Jewish-Christian community outside of Palestine, most likely after the death of Nero in A.D. 68. The famous number of the beast 666 which is mentioned (13:18) is the numerical equivalent of the Hebrew letters in the words Nero Caesar. Each Hebrew letter has a numerical value and in accordance with the system known as *gematria,* the number is used to designate the person or event intended, so that the secret message will be understood only by the initiated (cf. Part XVIII: The Jewish Christians and their symbols). But Nero's persecution was confined to Rome and many scholars are of the opinion that the book in its present form comes from a later date, while incorporating earlier material. Irenaeus (ca. A.D. 180) dates the book during the reign of Domitian, ca. A.D. 95, who was a cruel and capricious enemy of the Christians and persecuted them throughout the empire.

The Seven Churches of the Apoclypse in Asia Minor are symbolized by seven golden candlelabra. Representations appear frequently on coins, reliefs of synagogues and Jewish catacombs

The author of Revelation was a man named John (1:1–9; 22:8) traditionally thought to be the Apostle, one of the Twelve, who is also credited with composing the Fourth Gospel. Since John was a very common name, and since the book reports only that he lived on the island of Patmos in the Aegean Sea, a place of banishment, there is no way to specify his identity. The Greek of Revelation is quite unusual, bearing unmistakable signs of Semitic thought and imagery, and justifying the conclusion that the author was a Jewish-Christian steeped in the Hebrew-Aramaic tradition of the Old Testament and intertestamental literature. The book was a product of the tumultuous years surrounding the death of Nero, the disruption of the Empire, i.e. the year of the four emperors A.D. 69, the climax of the Jewish war and the fall of Jerusalem, and the persecution of Christians. Whether it was written entirely in that period (ca. A.D. 69) or was later edited and revised in the light of a more extensive persecution under Domitian, are matters to be considered.

2. CONTENTS

In the first chapter of Revelation, God is symbolically described as the *alpha* A and *omega* Ω, the first and last letters of the Greek alphabet, implying the first and last things, as all the secrets of the universe can be expressed by these signs and all else between them.

After the Introduction (1:1–3) the Seer sends (greetings (1:4–3:22) to the seven principal Christian churches of Asia Minor: Ephesus, Smyrna, Sardis, Pergamon, Philadelphia, Laodicea, Thyatira. They are described as "priests to their God", a figure used by Levitic sectaries. Their symbols were the seven stars, seven angels, and seven candelabra. These communities, which had existed since Hellenistic times, and their synagogues maintained their Jewish identity while some of them separated in time from the parent synagogue. The seven original synagogues bore the seven-branched candelabrum (*menôra*) of the Temple, the recognized symbol of Judaism from Herodian times, as well as other symbols since discovered in the excavations of Sardis (see Part XVIII). Numerous inscriptions in Smyrna attest to the importance and wealth of the synagogue into the third century A.D. In Revelation, however, the menôra is treated as the biblical symbol of divine light (cf. Zech 4).

Beyond that, these cities possessed splendid palaces, statuary, friezes, temples and other great public buildings, reflecting their great wealth. All these elements are alluded to in the allegorical visions of Revelation.

The Prologue in Heaven (4:1–5:14) clearly dependent on Ezekiel and more ancient myths, is followed by the allegorical vision of the seven seals (6:1–8:1) which can only be opened by the Lamb of God whose blood has redeemed mankind; whereupon he opens the seals and out come the four horsemen who symbolize violence and bloodshed. Then comes the vision of the Seven Trumpets which herald renewed destruction upon earth. The climactic disaster is the fall of Jerusalem, which is predicted. The transition from defeat and suffering to victory and joy is described in terms of the labor pains of a woman in childbirth, a necessary condition of the coming of the Messianic age (8:2–11:19).

The story of the heavenly woman and the child she bears (12) symbolizes the appearance of the messianic community which is barely saved from destruction by divine intervention, and in turn will be triumphant and usher the new age.

The vision of the beasts (13–14) underscores the persecution of the faithful (possibly in Nero's time) but is matched by the vision of the faithful in a heavenly choir. Renewed eschatological symbols appear with the Seven Bowls (15–16), the vision of Rome, the "great harlot", the visions of Gog and Magog (cf. Ezekiel — "Gog of the land of Magog") and that of the Heavenly Jerusalem come down on earth (17:18–22:12).

3. SOME IMAGES OF REVELATION AND THEIR MATERIAL BACKGROUND

The reference to the writing upon the pillars of a temple (3:12) can be illustrated by archaeological evidence from many ancient sites in Palestine, Palmyra and Asia Minor. Inscriptions on Galilean synagogues often record the part donated by benefactors. A column in the synagogue of Capernaum bears such a dedication in Greek ("Herod, the son of Makimos, and his descendants"), and another in Aramaic.

The figure of the scroll with the seven seals in 5:1; 6:1–8:5, which had to be broken one by one, is derived from the careful manner by which the ancients protected the contents of written documents from unauthorized eyes. Kings, bankers, merchants, and owners of estates used single or multiple sealings to safeguard their signatures with the name of the witness recorded beside each. The implication is that the divine judgment against the world, written on the pages of the book with the seals, was to remain a secret until the appointed time and then the seals would be broken by the authorized personnel in the presence of witnesses.

"and its rider had a balance in his hand" (Rev 6:5–6) The normal balance used for weighing consisted of a bar and tongue and the suspended pair of scales. The balance here is symbolical in terms of measure or weight

a. Accursed Rome

While this book expressed a very critical attitude toward the Roman empire, its government and social categories, nevertheless it differs markedly from the political rebellion of the contemporary Jewish *Zealots*. The roots of Jewish and Christian opposition to Rome were the same, namely Roman interference with the free exercise of religious conscience, and the right and duty to worship the one true God. The pretensions of the Roman emperors were blasphemous and had to be resisted at all costs. The difference between Jew and Christian lay in the nature of that resistance, and in the objective to be attained. While the Jewish community itself was divided on the subject, and generally speaking the Diaspora remained loyal to Rome, while the Palestinians revolted, the Christians in and out of Palestine were quiescent and suffered without forcible resistance. The Zealots aimed at establishing an independent state; Christians would be content with religious autonomy, leaving to God and his anointed the larger ques-

A bronze incense shovel of the type found in excavations in Israel (2nd and 3rd c. A.D.). Their use is described in the text

tion of the destruction of the empire and the establishment of the divine realm.

b. *The Four Horses of the Apocalypse* (Chs 6–8:5)

They symbolize the following: first, the rider of the white horse represents the Parthan cavalryman who could humble Rome; second, the rider on a red horse symbolizes the civil war which ravaged the Roman empire in A.D. 68/69, when the Romans would "kill one another" with the *spath*, the great cavalry sword; third, the rider of the black horse stands for famine which would result from the disruption of the economy as a result of the disturbance and fourth, the last horseman symbolizes death, the summation of the vision.

The golden censer described in ch. 8 was either the closed type, which was swung at the end of a chain and has been adopted by the church, or the open type, which is more ancient and consisted of a small flat shovel on which glowing coals were heaped; the incense was either held in the hand or kept piled up in receptacles attached to upper corners of the shovel from which it was taken between the fingers and thrown upon the coals.

The sign of the sixth angel pouring his bowls on the Euphrates (16:12) is a clear allusion to the Parthan (late Persian) kings of the East across the river. The prophecy was not fulfilled until much later: e.g. in A.D. 260 when emperor Valerian was defeated after a Persian invasion.

c. *The Day of Judgment*

Armageddon (16:16) as is known, is the symbolic place of the last battle of the kings of this earth. The Greek form of Har-Megiddo (Mount Megiddo), it is one of the main strategic sites of Palestine in biblical times. It was in that area that the Israelites achieved a notable and decisive victory over the Canaanites (ca. 1125 B.C.) and which is celebrated in the Song of Deborah (Jud 5). It is where King Josiah was defeated and killed by Pharaoh Necho in the 7th c. B.C. and near Lejjun where Emperor Hadrian established the camp of his Sixth Legion in the 2nd c. A.D. A Roman altar, marked Legio VI Ferrata was found there.

The appellation of Babylon the Great and the woman on the seven mountains (17:3–8) is a thinly disguised allusion to Rome, the great enemy of God and the seven kings of the Empire culminating in Nero or perhaps Domitian. It was customary to personify great cities of the ancient Greco-Roman world by female deities, such as the majestic Venus of Pompeii riding a chariot drawn by elephants, or the figure of Minerva leaning on a shield. These hieratic figures are reminiscent of the vision of "Babylon the Great'. The fall of Babylon-Rome is linked to the failure of shipments of wheat from the granaries of the East, without which neither city nor empire could survive (18:17). The pulping of the grapes in Roman wine presses is a figure of bloodshed (19:15) and symbolizes the fate of those who oppose the will of God.

The overthrow of wicked Rome will be the signal for the inauguration of the thousand year reign of Christ. At the same time, the evil dragon will be chained and locked up in the bottomless pit. The imaginary lock can be exemplified by artifacts of the Judeo-Roman type found in Palestine (20:1).

d. *Jewish-Christian Symbols of Dura-Europos*

Then the *Heavenly Jerusalem* (21:12) will come down and take the place of the desecrated city; the concept is common to the latter days of the Second Temple, as known from Rabbinical sources, the mystic *Yerushalayim shel Ma'ala* and, of course, the symbols of Jewish-Christianity. Such a vision is depicted is the frescoes of the synagogue of *Dura Europos* on the Euphrates; they depict the Temple, generally patterned after Herod's monumental structure, with additional walls, gates and decorations to enhance the splendor of the Heavenly City.

The synagogue of Dura-Europos, or at least its first building phases dates apparently to the early part of the third century A.D. It was a small prayer house, apparently Jewish-Christian in character, hidden among private dwellings, with paintings of biblical scenes. During the second phase (first half of the third century) the building included a large court with three colonnades and a spacious prayer hall with a niche for the Ark on the southern wall facing Jerusalem. The reconstructed building stands today in the museum of Damascus, with its valuable representations of biblical and allegorical scenes, many of them explained by short biblical quotations in Greek. The paintings show foreign affinities with either Alexandrian or late Persian art, but are of particular interest to us for the symbolism expressed in early Jewish and Christian art. The most interesting representations are the facade of the Jerusalem Temple. Other items of interest are two Hebrew fragments of the second half of the second century A.D. which appear to be liturgical blessings after meals. J. L. Teicher maintans that they were eucharistic prayers (consecrated elements of the Lord's supper) related to those of the Didache (10:3–4).

The existence of such fragments indicates that Hebrew was used as a liturgical language in the Jewish-Christian church during the first centuries. This finding is corroborated first by the fact that the Hebrew text of the book of Exodus was read in the church at Sardis and secondly by the fact, already mentioned, that Hebrew was used in early Jewish-Christian symbols discovered at the Jewish-Christian cemetery at Dominus Flevit.

At the beginning of the Christian movement, the Church was made up exclusively of Jews and converts to Judaism. Shortly thereafter, Gentiles were admitted to memebership without being required to become Jews as well. In time, as the missionary enterprise spread the Gospel throughout the Empire, the Gentile Church became numerically more powerful and ultimately prevailed. The Jewish-Christian church, cut off from the main stream of Judaism, and increasingly isolated from the dominant Gentile church, gradually lost ground and finally disappeared, unmourned and unremembered, surviving only in the remains uncovered by archaeological excavation.

The most significant monument to early Jewish-Christianity that we have is the New Testament itself. It was composed almost entirely by Jewish Christians (even if Luke was born a Gentile as is often supposed, he almost certainly was a convert to Judaism as well as Christianity). While it became the Scripture of the Gentile Curch, it faithfully reflects and records the origins of the Christian movement completely within the framework of first and second century Judaism: Jesus the founder and John the forerunner, who deliberately restricted the mission to the house of Israel. All the key events in the kerygma occurred in the same framework, and were fixed in the tradition by the Jewish-Christian community: Incarnation, Ministry, Passion, Crucifixion, and Resurrection, the gift of the Spirit and the world-wide mission of the Church. In composing the New Testament, the Jewish-Christian community doubtless wrote its own epitaph, but thereby provided the charter of life and success for its inheritor the Gentile Church.

GENERAL INDEX

R

Rabbis, 237; Rabbinism,
  Christian, 283
Rameses I, 13–14; R. II, 35, 59;
  Rameses and Pithom (cities)
  36; Rameses III, 84–85
Reed Sea, 39–40
Rehoboam, 115–118
Resheph (Job), 211–212
Resurrection, 1, 265, 271, 297
Revelation, book and
  apocalypse, 329–334; symbols
  331–333
Ritual, 54; Temple, 197
Roads, 256–257
Roman empire and
  Christianity, 296 (see Gen.
  Epist.); 331
Romans, book, 315–316
Ruth, book, 206

S

Sabbath, 226
Sacrifice 45–46, 51;
  of children, 52, 170
Sadducees, 245 f.; 265–266;
  268, 294
Sages, Proverbs, 214
Samaria, 25, 101–102;
  119–122, 151
Samaritans, 227 (Nehemiah);
  288
Samson, 69, 76
Samuel, 47; books 83–98
Sanctuary, 41, 42, 56, 80, 93;
  116–117; 125–126;
  see Temple
Sanhedrin, 294
Saul, 94. Saul, see Paul
Shechem, 14, 19, 30, 32, 66,
  72, 77
Schism of the kingdom,
  115–116
Scrolls, see D.S.S.
Sea Peoples (Philistines),
  28, 40, 63, 84–88
Seals, 31, 94; royal seal
  impressions, 132 f.
Seleucids, 231, 236, 239
Sennacherib, 129, 155–156, 174
Septuagint transl. 20, 220
Sermon on the Mount, 282–283
Servant (Suffering) Songs,
  Isaiah 160, 164; 303 (N.T.)
Seth, 13, 21, 58
Setting-in-life, 17, 54; 254, 267
  (N.T.); Psalms, 200 f.
Settlement in Canaan, 35,
  76–77
Shalmaneser III 122–123
Shekels, 148, 226, 235;
Ships, 109–110
Shosu, Shutu, 15, 34, 58–59;
  Sheth, 189
Sidonians, 80, 110
Simeon, 19, 30, 32, 73
Snake; serpent, 44, 66, 199
Social changes, 14, 141–146;
  180–181; 221–230;
  cf. Material changes

Solomon, 21–22, 53; 86; 104;
  and Song of Songs, 204;
  and Proverbs, 215;
  Ecclesiastes, 219; Solomon's
  Porch, see Hanuyot
Song of the Sea, 39, 47
  (Miriam); of the Well, 57;
  of Moses, 64; of Deborah, 75;
  of Solomon 204–205, 211;
  see Poetry
Source-critical method, 4
Stele, 13, 14, 21; cf. Inscriptions
Sumer, Sumerians, 5; sources,
  traditions, 7, 9, 11, 12,
  17–18, 211
Symbols 181 (mimetic);
  archaic 189 f.; visions,
  194–195; 238
Synagogues, 295–296;
  Capernaum, 280; Mount
  Zion 294; Church-synagogue,
  294; Post apostolic s. 310
Synoptic Gospels, 276–278;
  sources, similarities and
  divergences 276–278;
  apocalypse, 278

T

Tabernacle (Sinai) 41, 45;
  Feast of Tabernacles 290–291
Temple, 36, 45; First,
  104–106; Ezekiel's ideal,
  183; Second T. and ritual,
  197; 269–270; Temple
  forts, 14
Ten Commandments, 47–48,
  52
Teraphim, 23, 52
Thessalonians, book, 311–313
Timnah sanctuary, 10–11;
  copper-mining, 10–11
Timothy, book, 317
Titus, book, 317
Tobiads, 227–228; 240 f.
Transjordan, 74, 220–221,
  227–228
Tombs, 131–132; Siloam
  epitaph, 154; Bnei Hezir T.,
  251; T. in Kidron valley,
  251; Jewish T., 274; T. of
  Adam, 281; Christian T.
  281; Dominus Flevit
  Jewish-Christian cemetery,
  333; Garden Tomb 273 f.
Tophet, 52, 170
Torah 2, 159; see Pentateuch
Trade, 109–110
Tower of Babel, 9–10;
Trade, 109–110
Tribal Federation
  (amphiction y), 93–94
Tyre, 182–183; Tyrian ships,
  111–112, 182
Tyropoeon vale, street, 187,
  256

U

Unconquered Canaan
  (Judges), 79
Ugarit, 9, 24, 138, 150;

Ug. texts and sources,
  211–212; in Psalms, 198;
  City of U., 198
United Kingdom (monarchy),
  21–22; 101–103
Universalism (prophets), 141
Upper City, Jerusalem, 187,
  225 (see Mišneh,
  Makhteš); 247, 248 f.
Uzziah, 121, 127; 149

V

Via Dolorosa, 271;
  see Praetorium and Way
  of the Cross
Visions; see Prophets, 194–195;
  331 f.

W

Walls of Jerusalem;
  see Hezekiah, 224 f; 247
Wanderings; wilderness, 54;
  Way of the Arabah, 61;
  King's Highway, 59, 61
Water systems, 107–108; 130;
  see Hydraulic systems
Way of the Cross, 271–272;
  see Via Dolorosa
Way, movement of, 296
Wealth, 229–230
Wisdom literature, 207–208;
  213; Egyptian and Mesopo-
  tamian Precepts of sages,
  214–217; in Job 209–213
Worship, in Psalms, 197–203
Writing, 90–91; pictographs,
  90–91 and alphabet;
  Writing on the wall,
  234–235; Writing and
  Canon of the Bible, 237

X

Xystos, 242, 250;
  see Gymnasium

Y

Yahweh (Sinai), 41;
  Yahwist source, 3–4
Yehud (YHWD) seal,
  Nehemiah's time, 224

Z

Zadok (House of) 36, 242;
  245–246; 260; Zadokite
  Document (DSS), 260
Zeal (revolutionary spirit,
  Paul) 318; Zealots, 265,
  268) 331
Zebulun, 32, 75
Zechariah, book, 194–195;
  222; 290
Zedekiah, 167, 172, 176
Zephaniah, book, 187
Zerubbabel, 193–194; 222
Ziggurat, 10 (Tower of Babel;
  Babylon)
Zion, 97–99
Zoan (Tanis) 13–14, 21, 34
Zophar (Job), 209–213

INDEX OF BIBLICAL REFERENCES

INTERTESTAMENTAL PERIOD

NEW TESTAMENT

ACKNOWLEDGEMENTS

The publisher and editors are deeply indebted to Professor Benjamin Mazar's books, articles and views, and to the other scholars quoted in this book for their valuable insights and interpretations.

The editors are grateful to D. R. Burton (Program on Studies in Religion, the University of Michigan) for his comprehensive editing and restyling; to Ruth Elon for the graphic layout and design, and to Hassia Ben Harari for her valuable help.

A List of Illustrations with Acknowledgements

By courtesy of the Israel Department of Antiquities and Museums (5, 13, 18, 23, 51(2), 53, 61, 70, 74, 76, 86, 88, 89, 90, 94, 99, 111, 115, 117(6), 118, 120, 127, 130, 133, 134, 147, 151, 152, 161, 164(2), 168, 174, 177, 200, 204, 210, 226, 233, 314, 329).

By courtesy of the Archaeological Institute, University of Tel Aviv (14, 26, 27(3), 31 (Photo-Credit Abraham Hai), 81, 82, 117, 142, 144, 145, 166, 171.

By courtesy of the Archaeological Excavations in Jerusalem; Temple Mount (108, 127, 128, 130, 132, 176, 200, 201, 224, 226, 247, 249, 251, 256(3), 257, 270, 272, 273).

Beno Rothenberg (10, 35, 42(3), 43(2), 44(2), 56, 213)

Ben Gurion University, Beersheba (87)

Ruth Amiran (Philistines, 69, 83, 85)

Raphael Gibeon (9)

Government Press Office, Photographic Dept. (23, 86, 107 (3), 108, 161, 169, 187, 222, 227, 228, 242, 248, 251, 255, 259)

Department of Museums, Cyprus (23, 25, 52, 147)

University of Chicago (45, 69, 70, 73, 230); University of Pennsylvania (180); Bildarchiv Photo Marburg (113, 152); Giraudon, Paris (125, 135, 153); Archives Photographiques, Paris (48, 50, 105, 148, 189, 199, 213); Professor A. J. Calloway (71); State Museum, Berlin (59); Anderson, Roma (240); Musée de l'Homme, Paris (43, 193).

British Museum (4, 6, 9, 108, 110, 112, 123(2), 134, 153(2), 155(2), 178, 182, 195, 220, 331); Schweich Lectures, London (272).

Bureau of Tourism, Ankara (299, 300)

Studium Biblicum Franciscanum (268, 269, 279, 280, 289, 305, 309)

Shrine of the Book (261)

Photo Credits: Garo Nalbandian (14, 77, 78, 96, 97, 130, 241, 250, 254)

The other illustrations in the book are derived from G. Cornfeld's photographic archive.